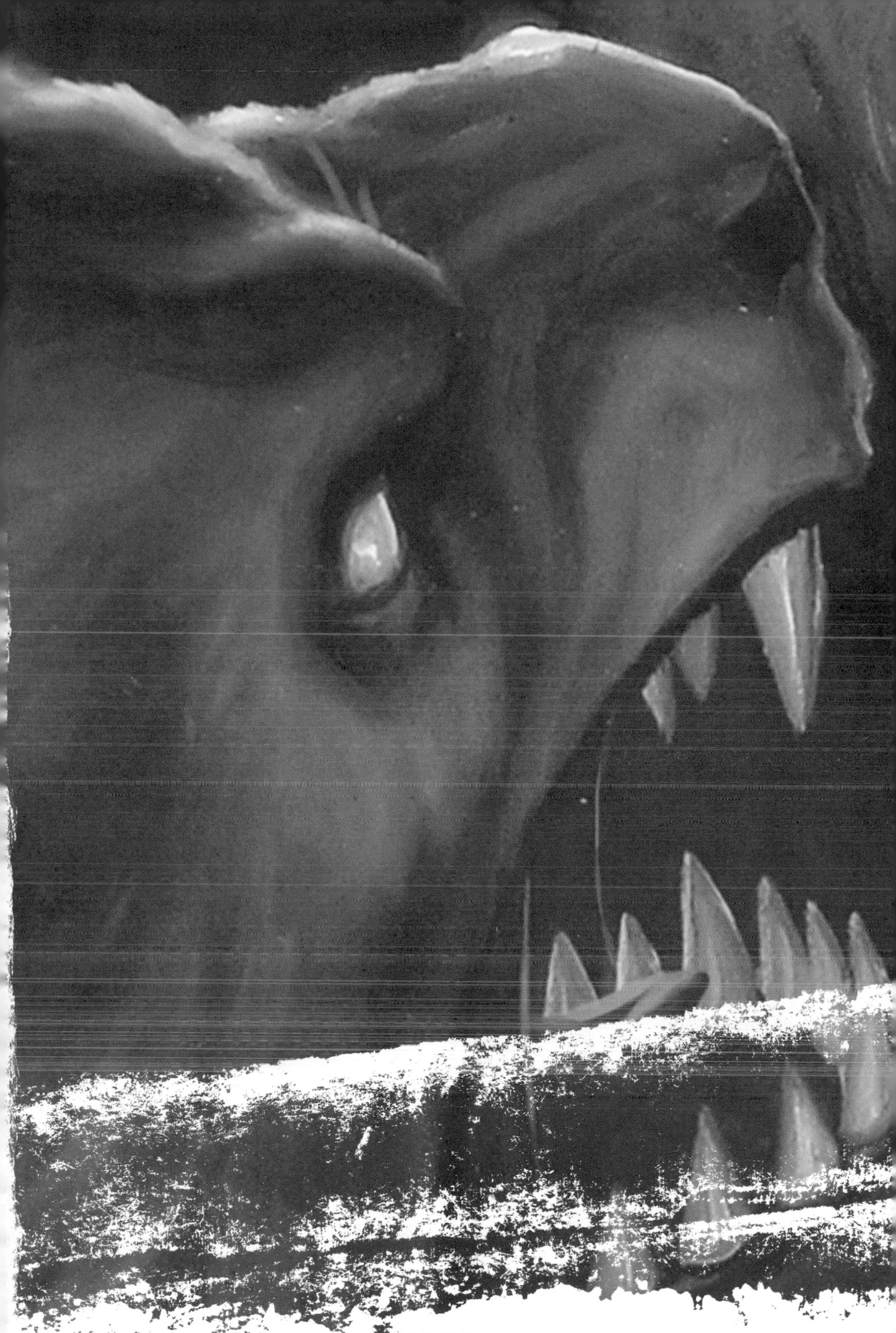

VERTIGO

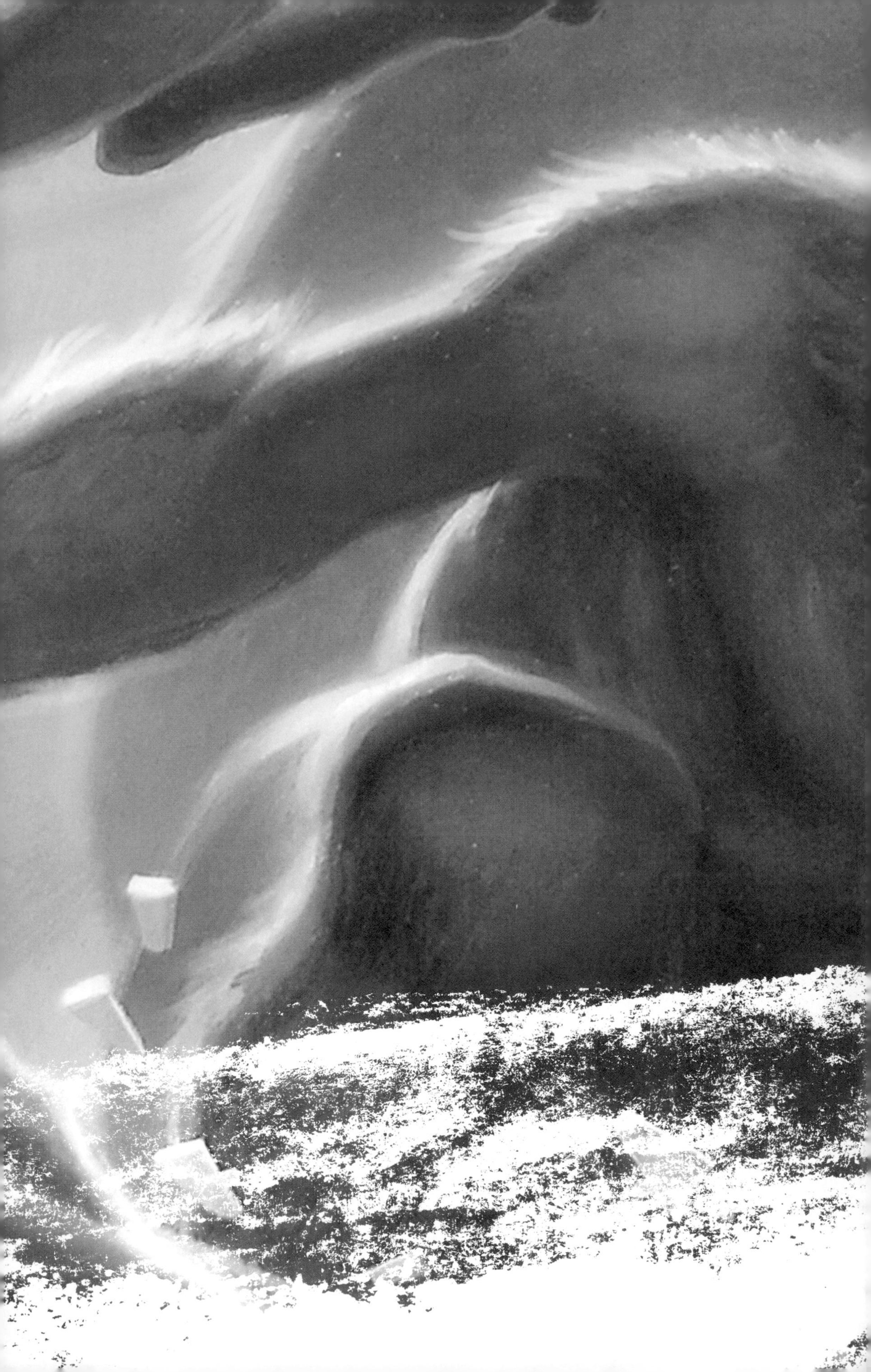

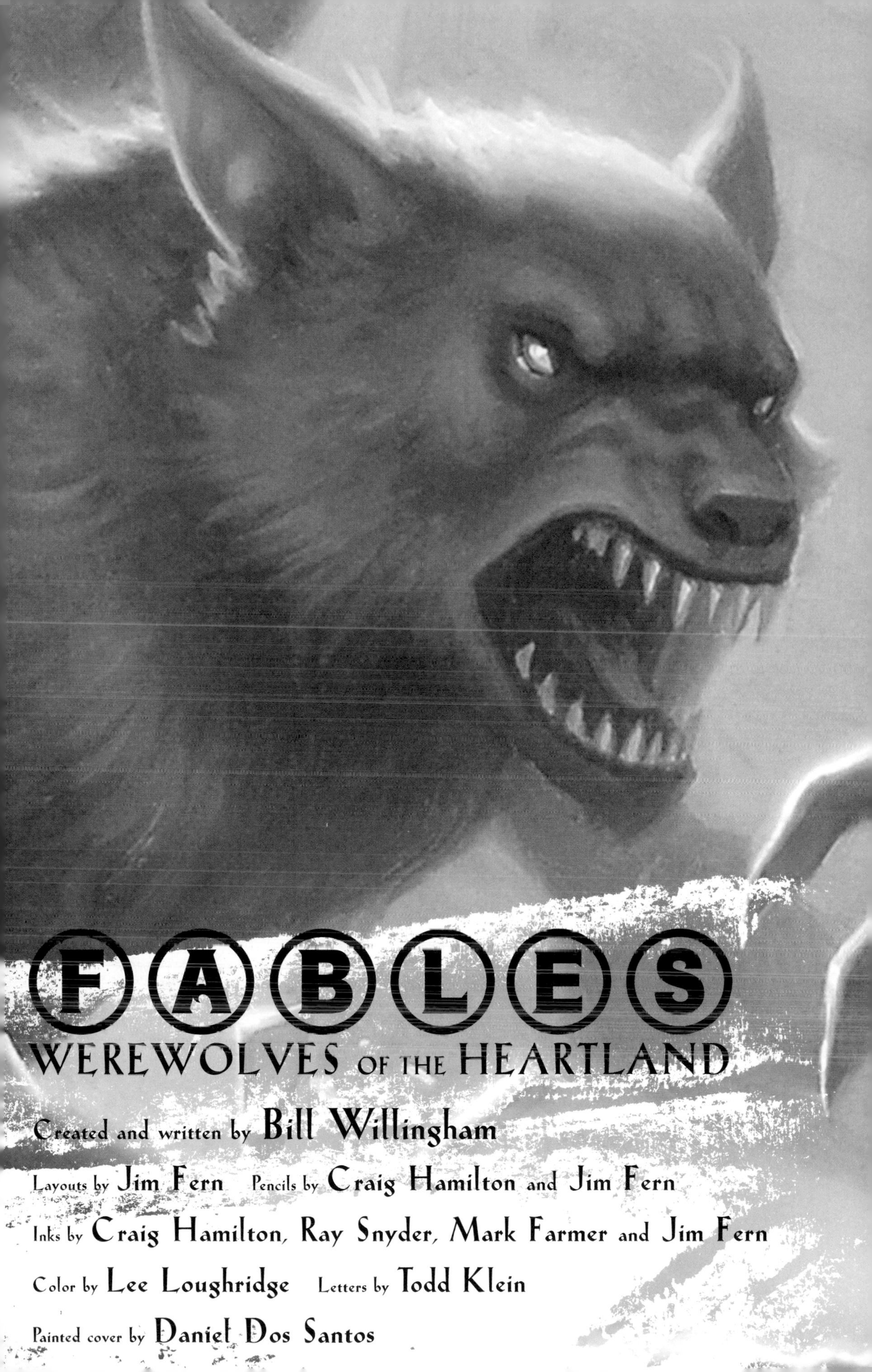

FABLES

WEREWOLVES OF THE HEARTLAND

Created and written by **Bill Willingham**

Layouts by **Jim Fern** Pencils by **Craig Hamilton** and **Jim Fern**

Inks by **Craig Hamilton, Ray Snyder, Mark Farmer** and **Jim Fern**

Color by **Lee Loughridge** Letters by **Todd Klein**

Painted cover by **Daniel Dos Santos**

This book is lovingly dedicated to
the actual residents of Story City, Iowa
(as opposed to the entirely fictional versions portrayed here).

Sorry for the mess.

Shelly Bond Editor **Gregory Lockard** Assistant Editor
Robbin Brosterman Design Director – Books **Louis Prandi** Publication Design

Karen Berger Senior VP – Executive Editor, Vertigo **Bob Harras** VP – Editor-in-Chief

Diane Nelson President **Dan DiDio** and **Jim Lee** Co-Publishers **Geoff Johns** Chief Creative Officer
John Rood Executive VP – Sales, Marketing and Business Development **Amy Genkins** Senior VP – Business and Legal Affairs
Nairi Gardiner Senior VP – Finance **Jeff Boison** VP – Publishing Operations **Mark Chiarello** VP – Art Direction and Design
John Cunningham VP – Marketing **Terri Cunningham** VP – Talent Relations and Services **Alison Gill** Senior VP – Manufacturing and Operations
Hank Kanalz Senior VP – Digital **Jay Kogan** VP – Business and Legal Affairs, Publishing **Jack Mahan** VP – Business Affairs, Talent
Nick Napolitano VP – Manufacturing Administration **Sue Pohja** VP – Book Sales **Courtney Simmons** Senior VP – Publicity **Bob Wayne** Senior VP – Sales

FABLES: WEREWOLVES OF THE HEARTLAND
Published by DC Comics. Copyright © 2012 Bill
Willingham and DC Comics. All Rights Reserved. All
characters, their distinctive likenesses and related ele-
ments featured in this publication are trademarks of
Bill Willingham. Vertigo is a trademark of DC Comics.
The stories, characters and incidents featured in this
publication are entirely fictional. DC Comics does not
read or accept unsolicited submissions of ideas, sto-
ries or artwork. DC Comics. 1700 Broadway, New
York, NY 10019. A Warner Bros. Entertainment
Company. ISBN: 978-1-4012-2479-0.

Library of Congress Cataloging-in-Publication Data

Willingham, Bill.
    Fables : werewolves of the heartland / Bill Willingham, Jim Fern, Craig Hamilton,
Ray Snyder, Mark Farmer.
      p. cm.
    ISBN 978-1-4012-2479-0 (alk. paper)
    1. Graphic novels. I. Fern, Jim. II. Hamilton, Craig, 1964- III. Farmer, Mark. IV.
Title. V. Title: Werewolves of the heartland.
    PN6727.W52F45 2012
    741.5'973–dc23
                                    2012030367

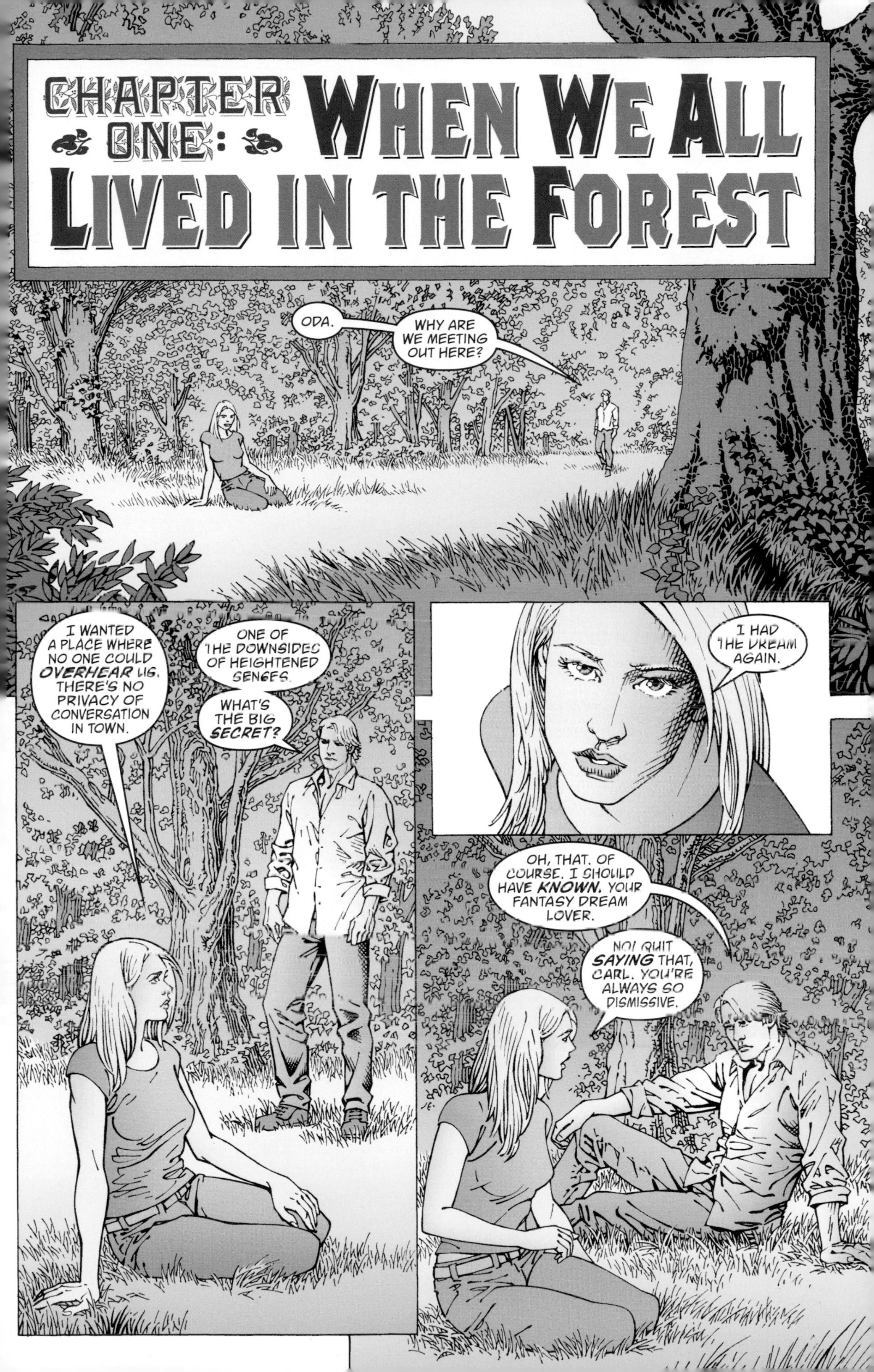
CHAPTER ONE: WHEN WE ALL LIVED IN THE FOREST
ODA.
WHY ARE WE MEETING OUT HERE?
I WANTED A PLACE WHERE NO ONE COULD OVERHEAR US. THERE'S NO PRIVACY OF CONVERSATION IN TOWN.
ONE OF THE DOWNSIDES OF HEIGHTENED SENSES.
WHAT'S THE BIG SECRET?
I HAD THE DREAM AGAIN.
OH, THAT. OF COURSE. I SHOULD HAVE KNOWN. YOUR FANTASY DREAM LOVER.
NO! QUIT SAYING THAT, CARL. YOU'RE ALWAYS SO DISMISSIVE.

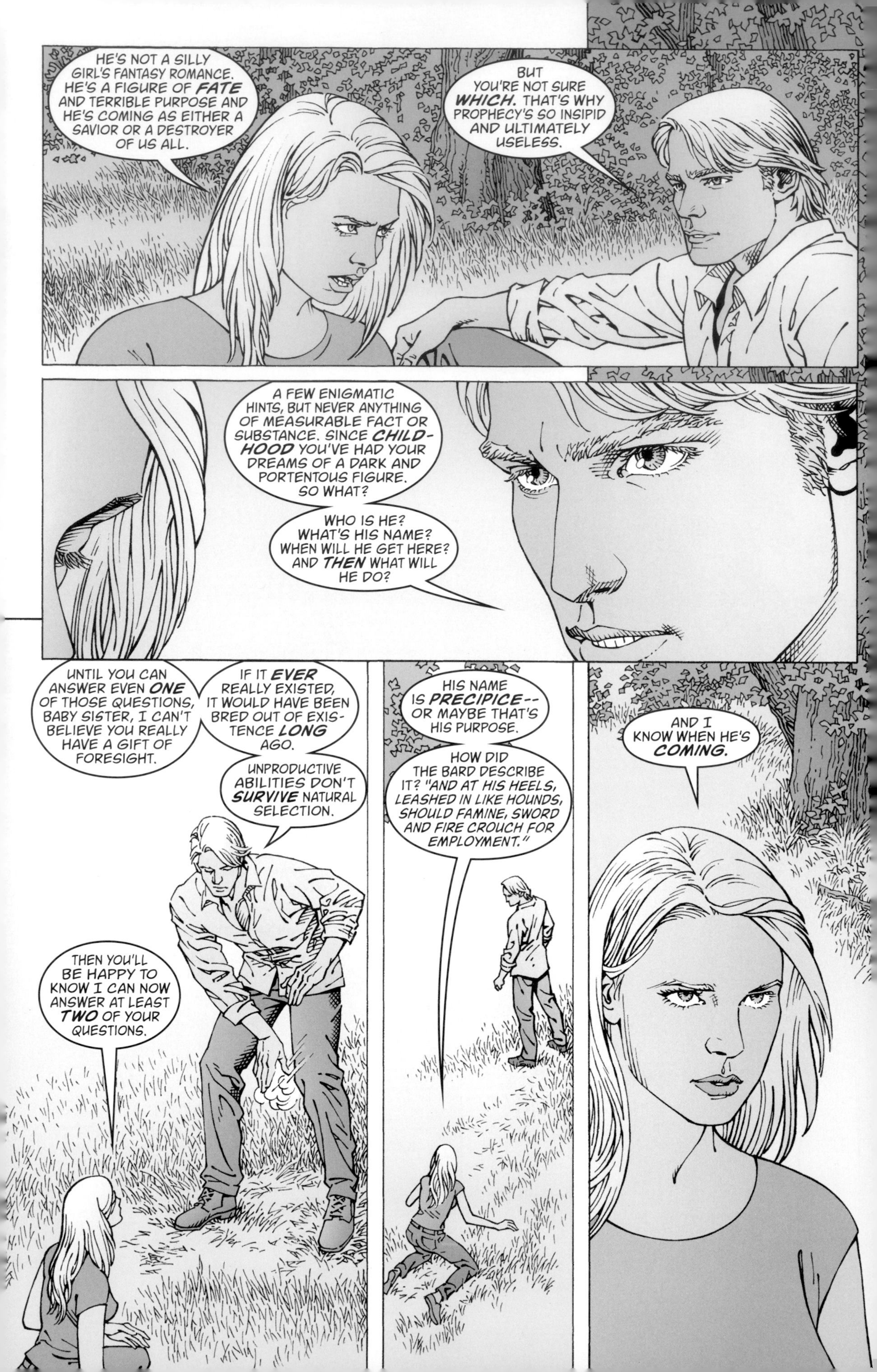
HE'S NOT A SILLY GIRL'S FANTASY ROMANCE. HE'S A FIGURE OF FATE AND TERRIBLE PURPOSE AND HE'S COMING AS EITHER A SAVIOR OR A DESTROYER OF US ALL.
BUT YOU'RE NOT SURE WHICH. THAT'S WHY PROPHECY'S SO INSIPID AND ULTIMATELY USELESS.
A FEW ENIGMATIC HINTS, BUT NEVER ANYTHING OF MEASURABLE FACT OR SUBSTANCE. SINCE CHILD-HOOD YOU'VE HAD YOUR DREAMS OF A DARK AND PORTENTOUS FIGURE. SO WHAT?
WHO IS HE? WHAT'S HIS NAME? WHEN WILL HE GET HERE? AND THEN WHAT WILL HE DO?
UNTIL YOU CAN ANSWER EVEN ONE OF THOSE QUESTIONS, BABY SISTER, I CAN'T BELIEVE YOU REALLY HAVE A GIFT OF FORESIGHT.
IF IT EVER REALLY EXISTED, IT WOULD HAVE BEEN BRED OUT OF EXIS-TENCE LONG AGO.
UNPRODUCTIVE ABILITIES DON'T SURVIVE NATURAL SELECTION.
THEN YOU'LL BE HAPPY TO KNOW I CAN NOW ANSWER AT LEAST TWO OF YOUR QUESTIONS.
HIS NAME IS PRECIPICE-- OR MAYBE THAT'S HIS PURPOSE.
HOW DID THE BARD DESCRIBE IT? "AND AT HIS HEELS, LEASHED IN LIKE HOUNDS, SHOULD FAMINE, SWORD AND FIRE CROUCH FOR EMPLOYMENT."
AND I KNOW WHEN HE'S COMING.

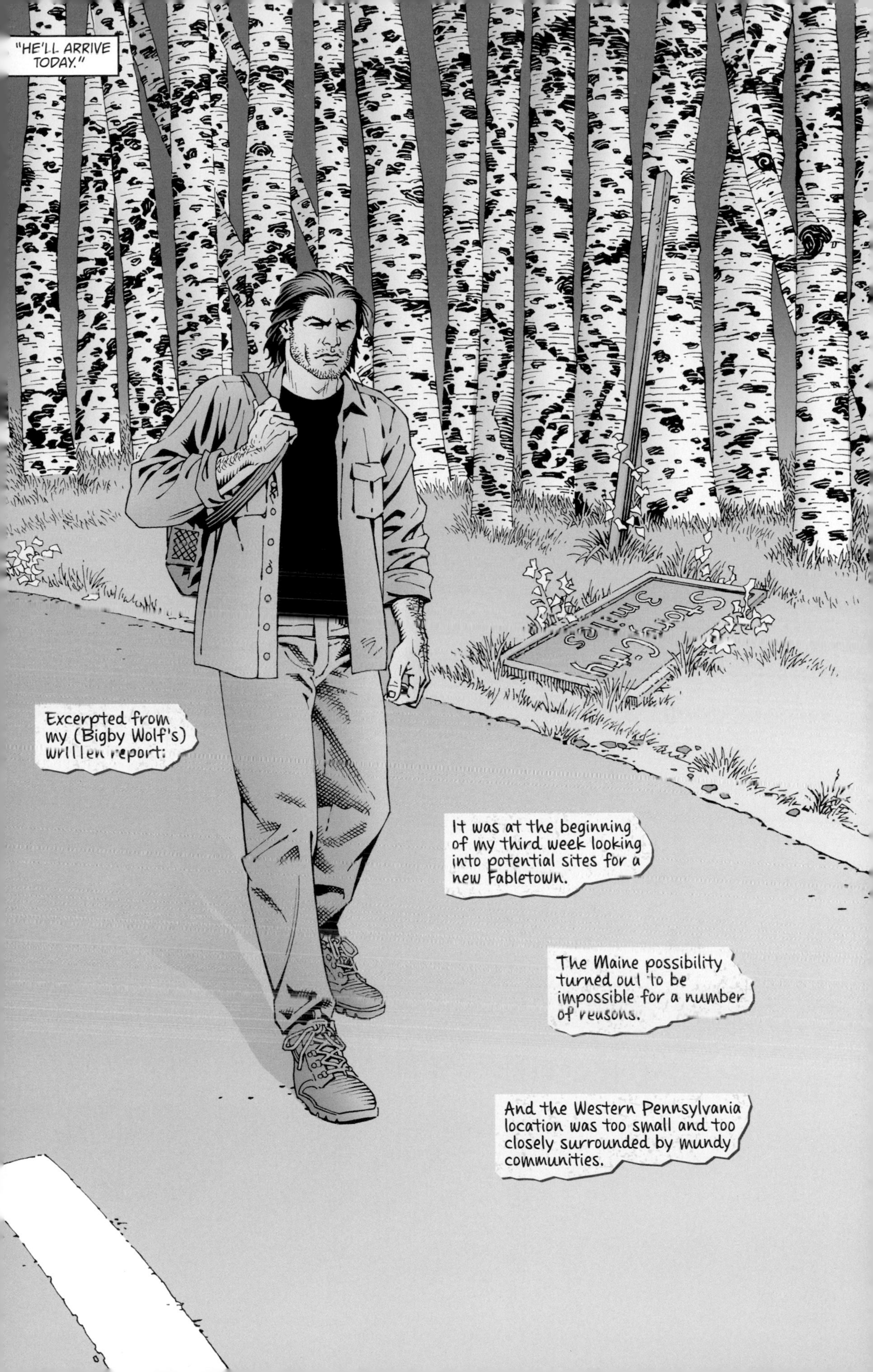
"HE'LL ARRIVE TODAY."
Story City
3 miles
Excerpted from my (Bigby Wolf's) written report:
It was at the beginning of my third week looking into potential sites for a new Fabletown.
The Maine possibility turned out to be impossible for a number of reasons.
And the Western Pennsylvania location was too small and too closely surrounded by mundy communities.

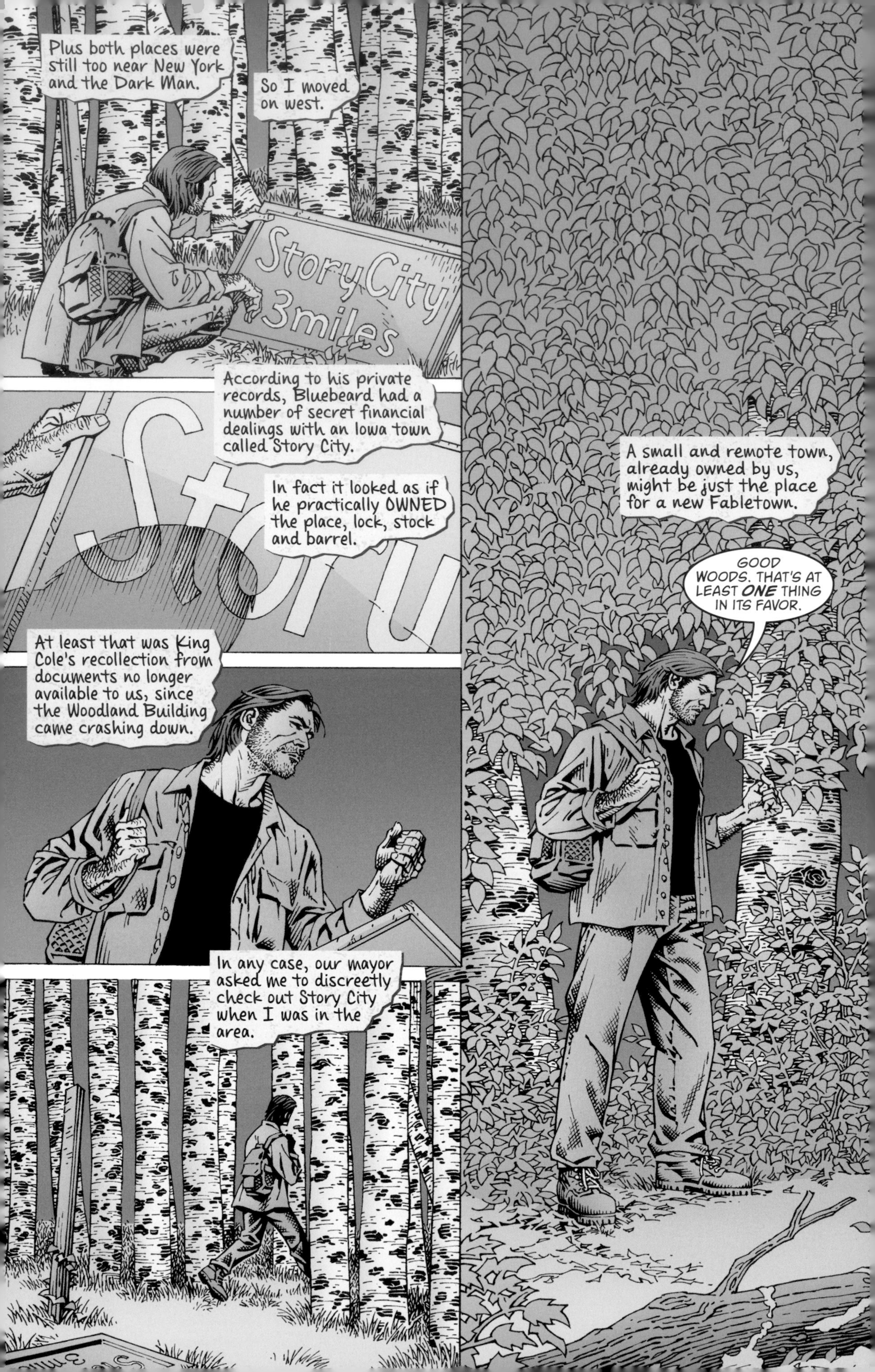
Plus both places were still too near New York and the Dark Man.
So I moved on west.
Story City 3miles
According to his private records, Bluebeard had a number of secret financial dealings with an Iowa town called Story City.
In fact it looked as if he practically OWNED the place, lock, stock and barrel.
At least that was King Cole's recollection from documents no longer available to us, since the Woodland Building came crashing down.
In any case, our mayor asked me to discreetly check out Story City when I was in the area.
A small and remote town, already owned by us, might be just the place for a new Fabletown.
GOOD WOODS. THAT'S AT LEAST ONE THING IN ITS FAVOR.

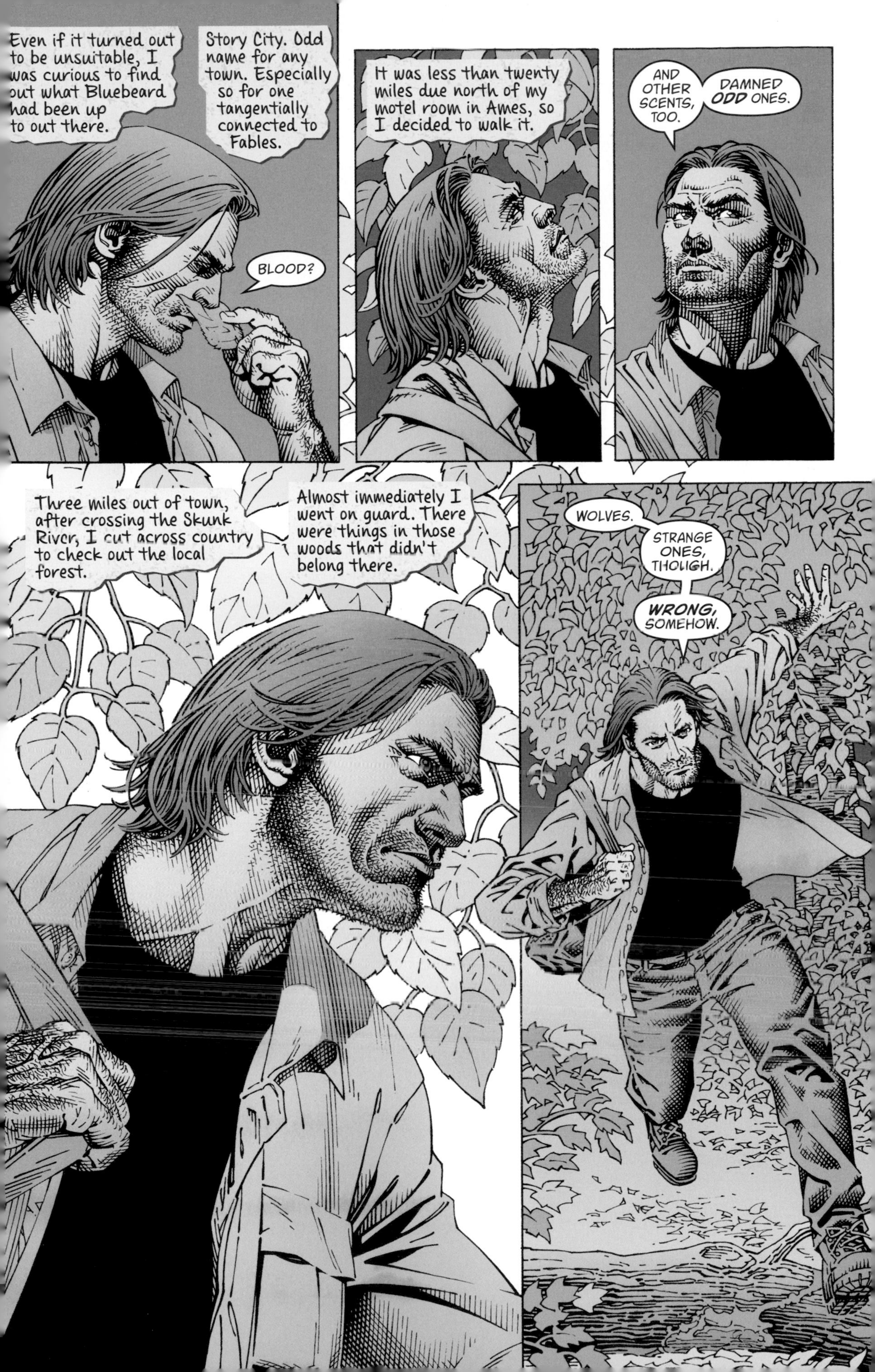
Even if it turned out to be unsuitable, I was curious to find out what Bluebeard had been up to out there.
Story City. Odd name for any town. Especially so for one tangentially connected to Fables.
BLOOD?
It was less than twenty miles due north of my motel room in Ames, so I decided to walk it.
AND OTHER SCENTS, TOO.
DAMNED ODD ONES.
Three miles out of town, after crossing the Skunk River, I cut across country to check out the local forest.
Almost immediately I went on guard. There were things in those woods that didn't belong there.
WOLVES.
STRANGE ONES, THOUGH.
WRONG, SOMEHOW.

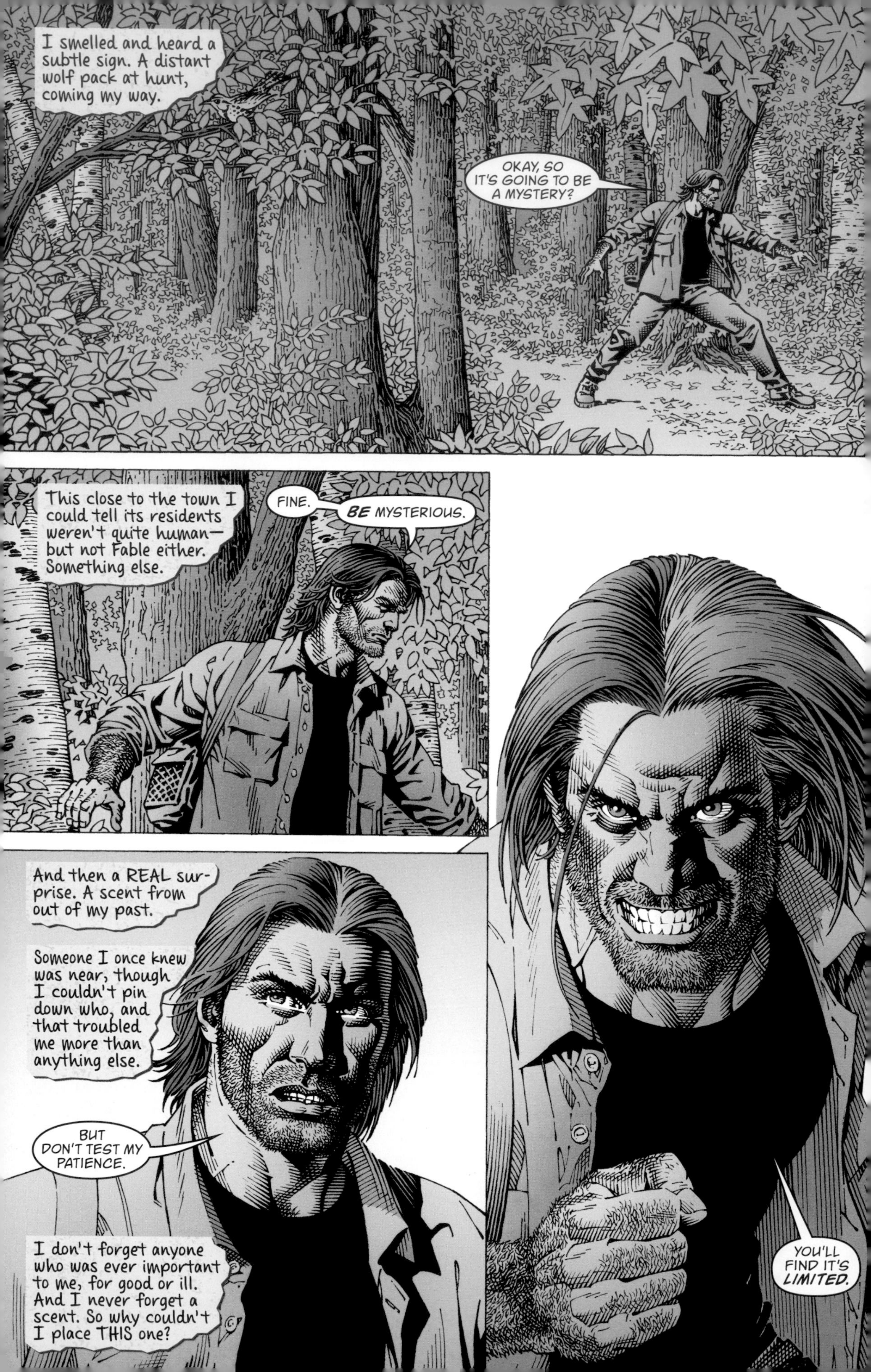

I smelled and heard a subtle sign. A distant wolf pack at hunt, coming my way.
OKAY, SO IT'S GOING TO BE A MYSTERY?
This close to the town I could tell its residents weren't quite human— but not Fable either. Something else.
FINE.
BE MYSTERIOUS.
And then a REAL surprise. A scent from out of my past.
Someone I once knew was near, though I couldn't pin down who, and that troubled me more than anything else.
BUT DON'T TEST MY PATIENCE.
I don't forget anyone who was ever important to me, for good or ill. And I never forget a scent. So why couldn't I place THIS one?
YOU'LL FIND IT'S LIMITED.

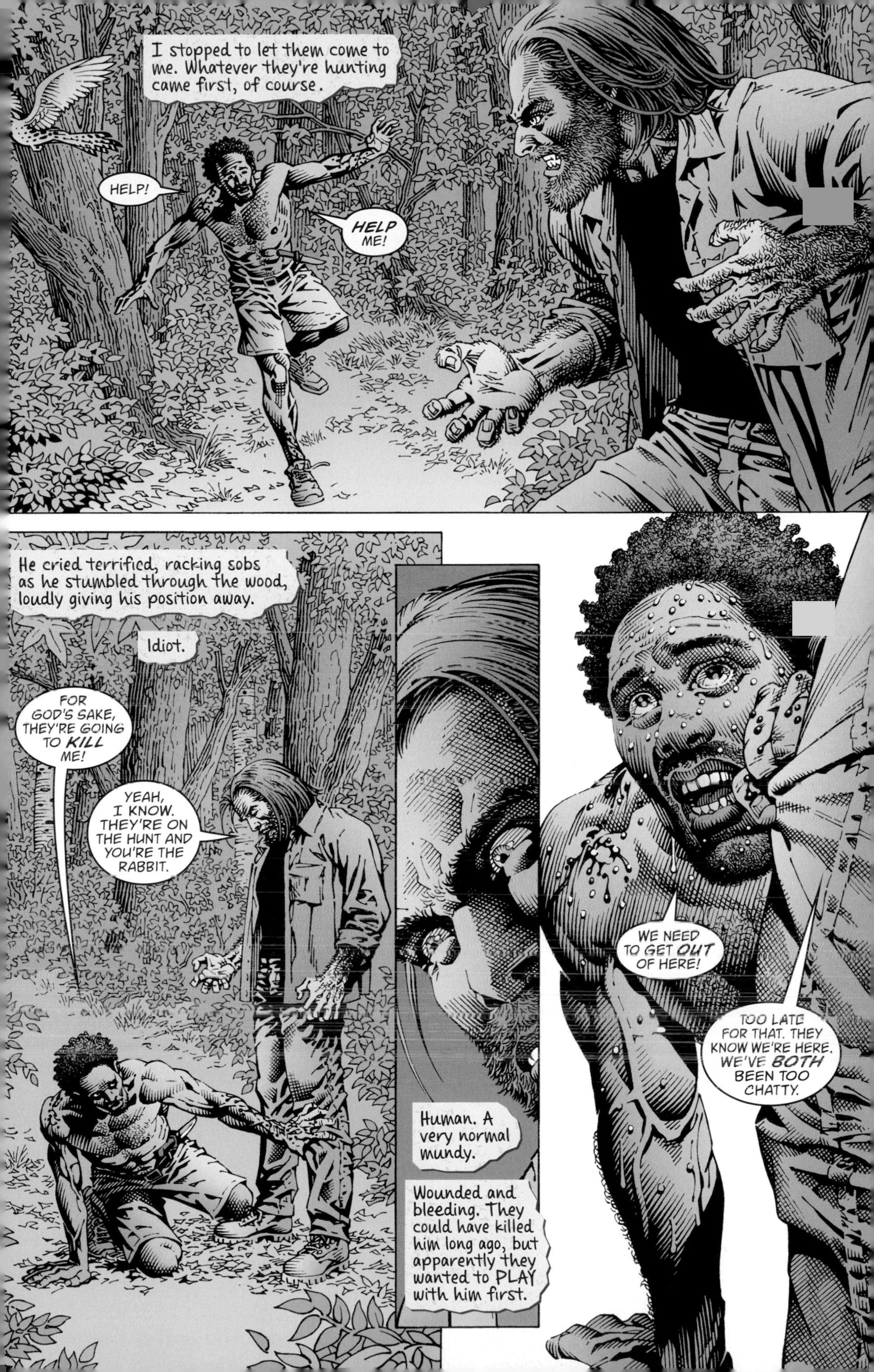
I stopped to let them come to me. Whatever they're hunting came first, of course.
HELP!
HELP ME!
He cried terrified, racking sobs as he stumbled through the wood, loudly giving his position away.
Idiot.
FOR GOD'S SAKE, THEY'RE GOING TO KILL ME!
YEAH, I KNOW. THEY'RE ON THE HUNT AND YOU'RE THE RABBIT.
Human. A very normal mundy.
Wounded and bleeding. They could have killed him long ago, but apparently they wanted to PLAY with him first.
WE NEED TO GET OUT OF HERE!
TOO LATE FOR THAT. THEY KNOW WE'RE HERE. WE'VE BOTH BEEN TOO CHATTY.

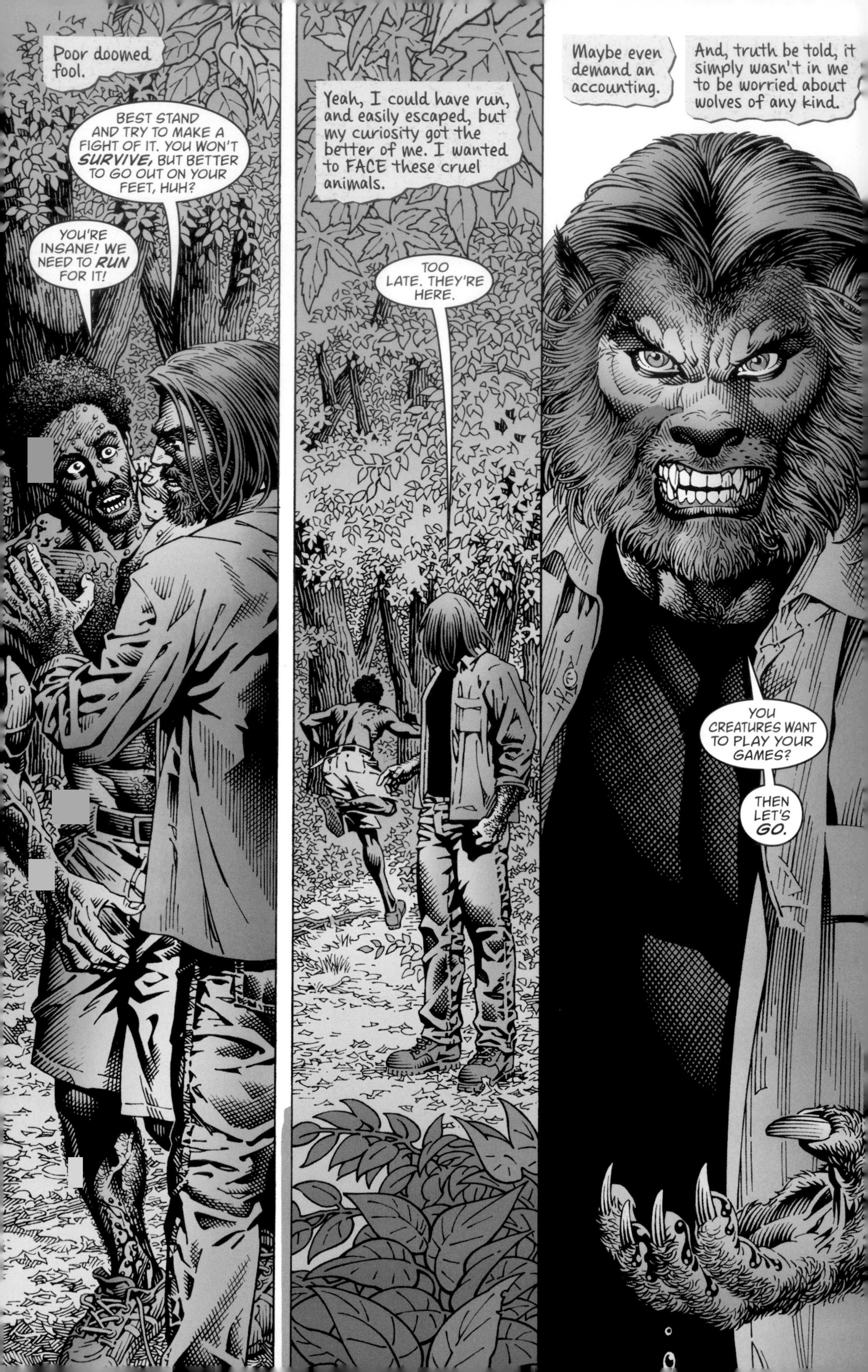

Poor doomed fool.
BEST STAND AND TRY TO MAKE A FIGHT OF IT. YOU WON'T ***SURVIVE,*** BUT BETTER TO GO OUT ON YOUR FEET, HUH?
YOU'RE INSANE! WE NEED TO ***RUN*** FOR IT!
Yeah, I could have run, and easily escaped, but my curiosity got the better of me. I wanted to FACE these cruel animals.
TOO LATE. THEY'RE HERE.
Maybe even demand an accounting.
And, truth be told, it simply wasn't in me to be worried about wolves of any kind.
YOU CREATURES WANT TO PLAY YOUR GAMES?
THEN LET'S ***GO.***

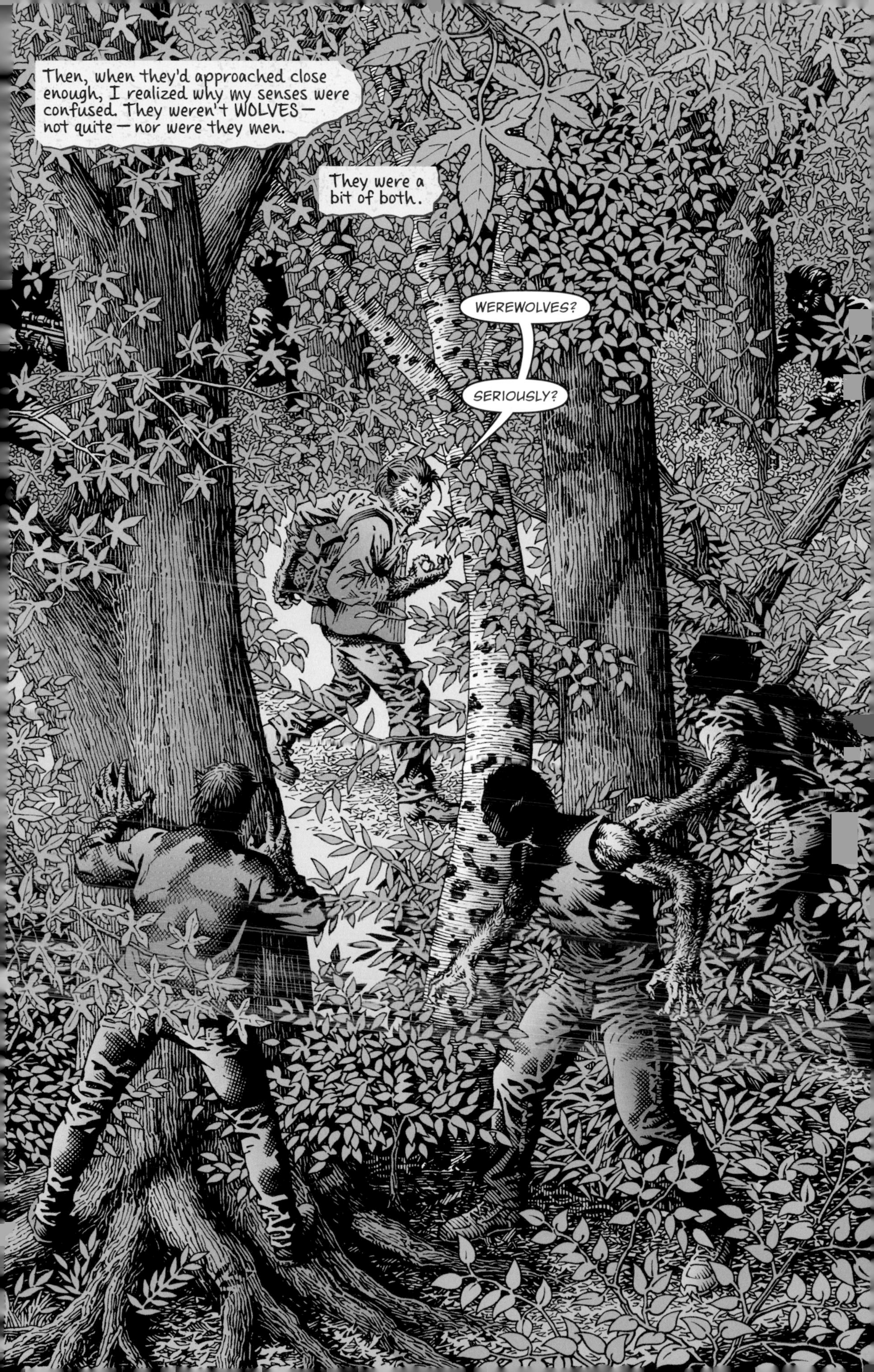
Then, when they'd approached close enough, I realized why my senses were confused. They weren't WOLVES — not quite — nor were they men.
They were a bit of both.
WEREWOLVES?
SERIOUSLY?

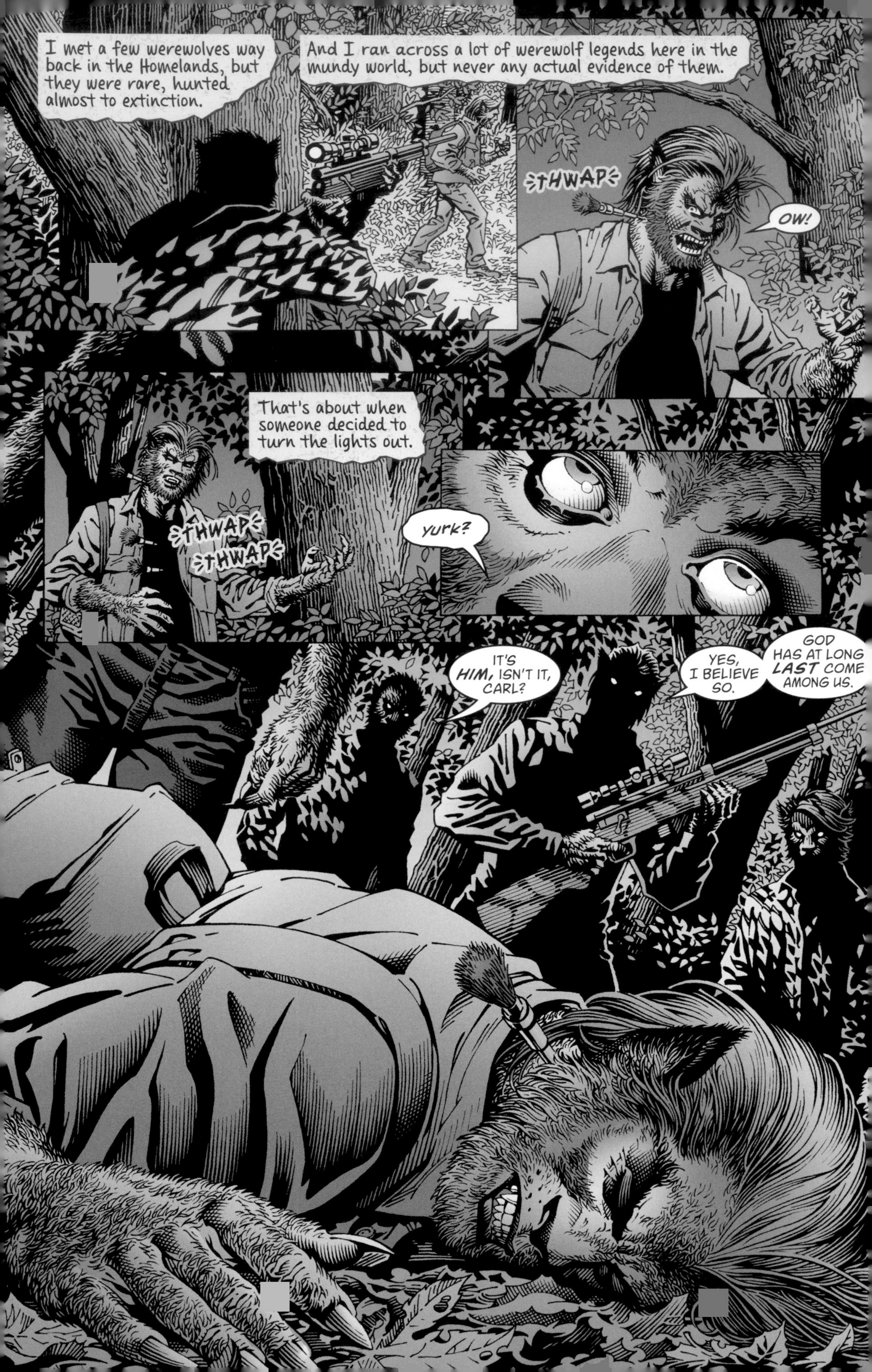
I met a few werewolves way back in the Homelands, but they were rare, hunted almost to extinction.
And I ran across a lot of werewolf legends here in the mundy world, but never any actual evidence of them.
THWAP
OW!
That's about when someone decided to turn the lights out.
THWAP
THWAP
yurk?
IT'S HIM, ISN'T IT, CARL?
YES, I BELIEVE SO.
GOD HAS AT LONG LAST COME AMONG US.

CHAPTER TWO:
WOLVES AT WAR

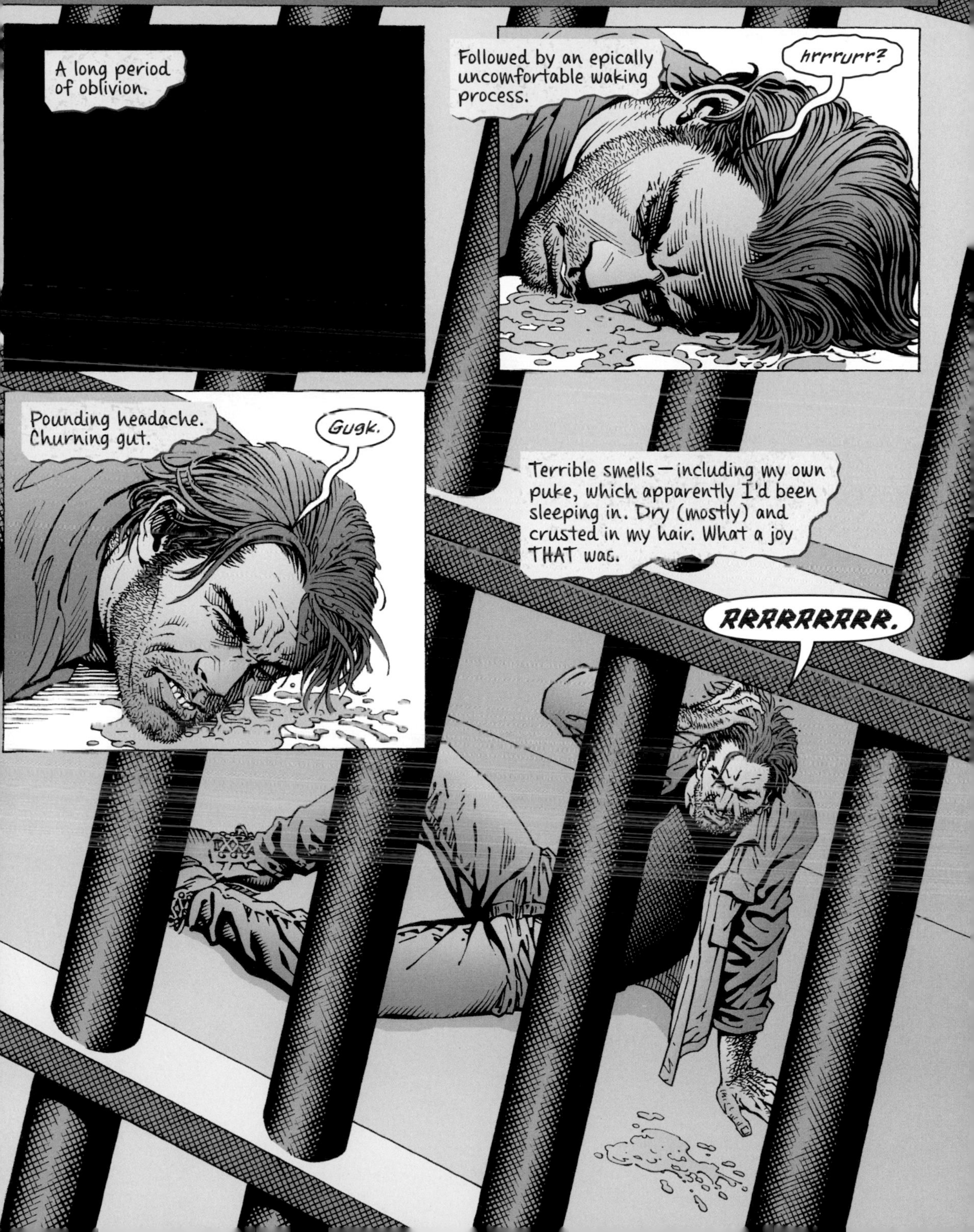
A long period of oblivion.
Followed by an epically uncomfortable waking process.
hrrrurr?
Pounding headache. Churning gut.
Gugk.
Terrible smells—including my own puke, which apparently I'd been sleeping in. Dry (mostly) and crusted in my hair. What a joy THAT was.
RRRRRRRRR.

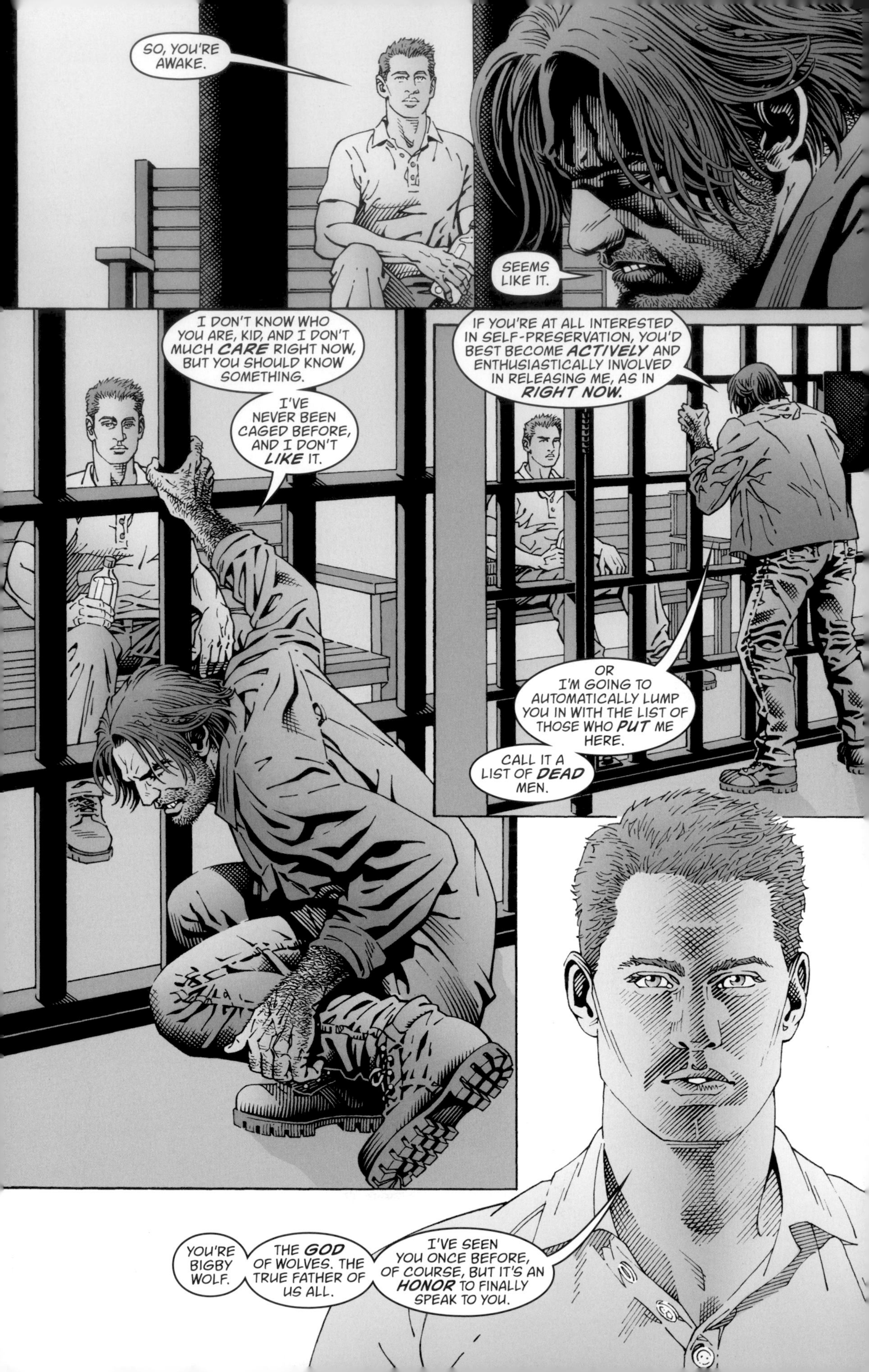
SO, YOU'RE AWAKE.
SEEMS LIKE IT.
I DON'T KNOW WHO YOU ARE, KID, AND I DON'T MUCH CARE RIGHT NOW, BUT YOU SHOULD KNOW SOMETHING.
I'VE NEVER BEEN CAGED BEFORE, AND I DON'T LIKE IT.
IF YOU'RE AT ALL INTERESTED IN SELF-PRESERVATION, YOU'D BEST BECOME ACTIVELY AND ENTHUSIASTICALLY INVOLVED IN RELEASING ME, AS IN RIGHT NOW.
OR I'M GOING TO AUTOMATICALLY LUMP YOU IN WITH THE LIST OF THOSE WHO PUT ME HERE.
CALL IT A LIST OF DEAD MEN.
YOU'RE BIGBY WOLF.
THE GOD OF WOLVES. THE TRUE FATHER OF US ALL.
I'VE SEEN YOU ONCE BEFORE, OF COURSE, BUT IT'S AN HONOR TO FINALLY SPEAK TO YOU.

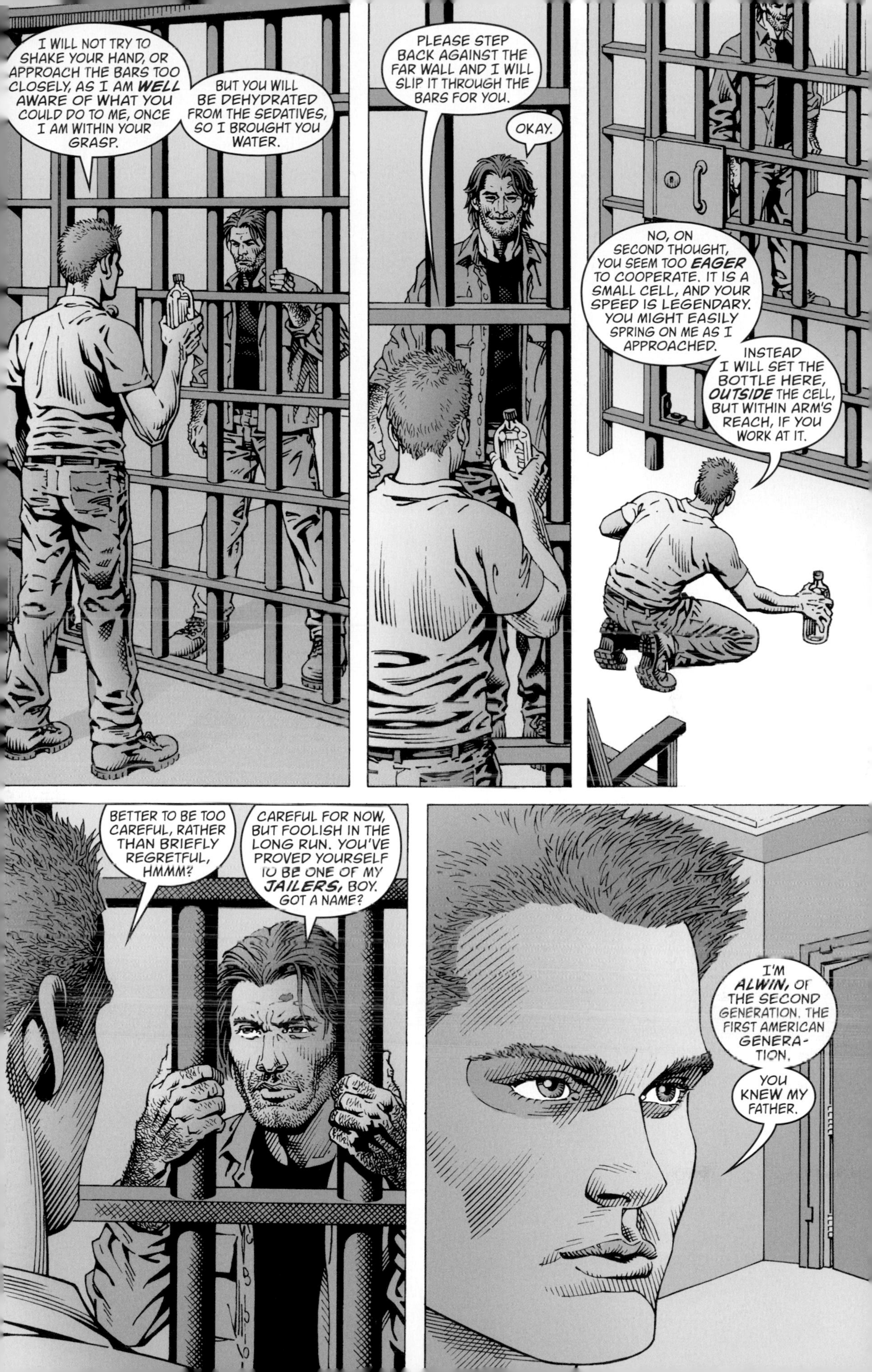
I WILL NOT TRY TO SHAKE YOUR HAND, OR APPROACH THE BARS TOO CLOSELY, AS I AM WELL AWARE OF WHAT YOU COULD DO TO ME, ONCE I AM WITHIN YOUR GRASP.
BUT YOU WILL BE DEHYDRATED FROM THE SEDATIVES, SO I BROUGHT YOU WATER.
PLEASE STEP BACK AGAINST THE FAR WALL AND I WILL SLIP IT THROUGH THE BARS FOR YOU.
OKAY.
NO, ON SECOND THOUGHT, YOU SEEM TOO EAGER TO COOPERATE. IT IS A SMALL CELL, AND YOUR SPEED IS LEGENDARY. YOU MIGHT EASILY SPRING ON ME AS I APPROACHED.
INSTEAD I WILL SET THE BOTTLE HERE, OUTSIDE THE CELL, BUT WITHIN ARM'S REACH, IF YOU WORK AT IT.
BETTER TO BE TOO CAREFUL, RATHER THAN BRIEFLY REGRETFUL, HMMM?
CAREFUL FOR NOW, BUT FOOLISH IN THE LONG RUN. YOU'VE PROVED YOURSELF TO BE ONE OF MY JAILERS, BOY. GOT A NAME?
I'M ALWIN, OF THE SECOND GENERATION. THE FIRST AMERICAN GENERATION.
YOU KNEW MY FATHER.

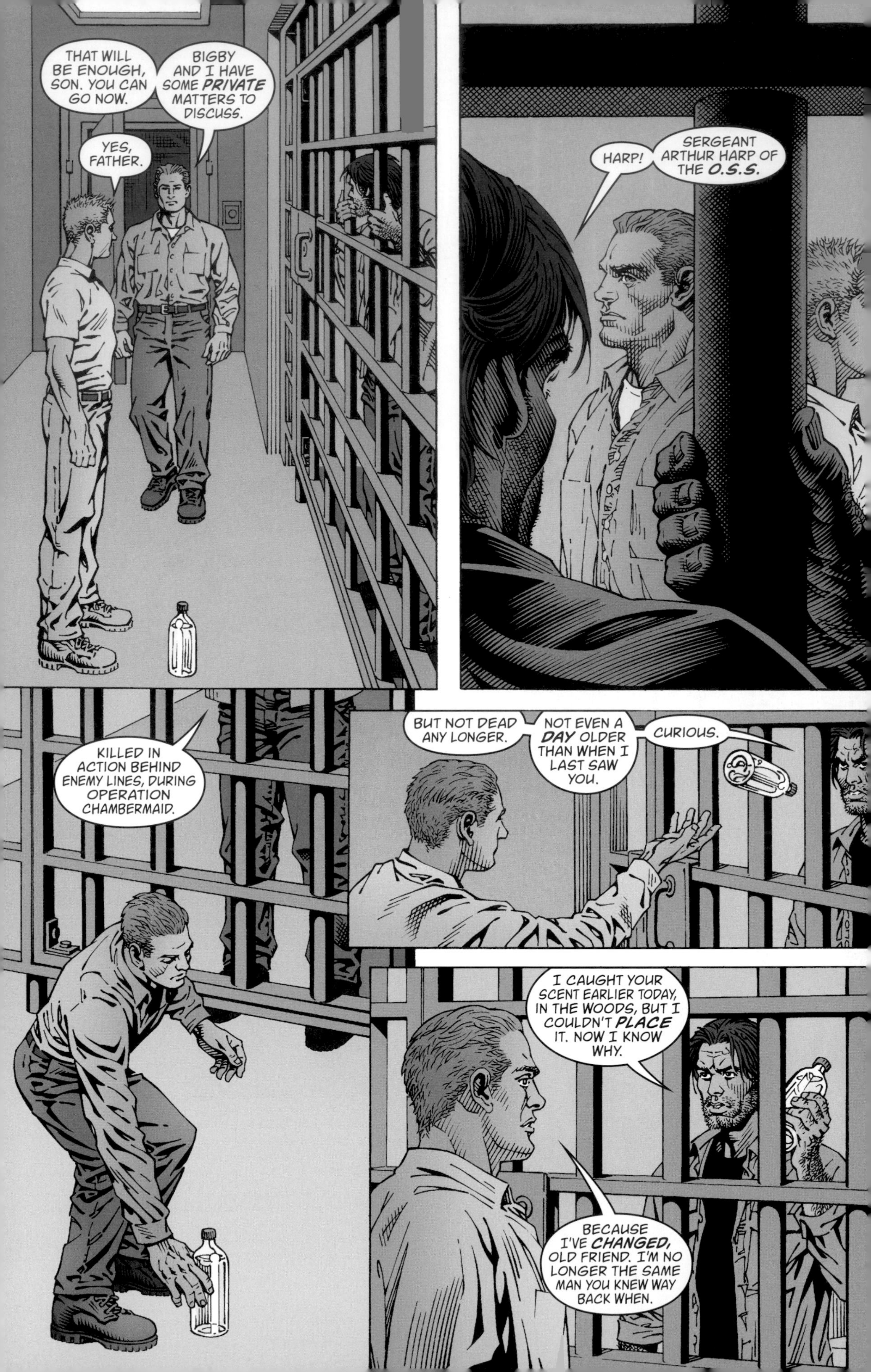
THAT WILL BE ENOUGH, SON. YOU CAN GO NOW.
BIGBY AND I HAVE SOME PRIVATE MATTERS TO DISCUSS.
YES, FATHER.
HARP!
SERGEANT ARTHUR HARP OF THE O.S.S.
KILLED IN ACTION BEHIND ENEMY LINES, DURING OPERATION CHAMBERMAID.
BUT NOT DEAD ANY LONGER.
NOT EVEN A DAY OLDER THAN WHEN I LAST SAW YOU.
CURIOUS.
I CAUGHT YOUR SCENT EARLIER TODAY, IN THE WOODS, BUT I COULDN'T PLACE IT. NOW I KNOW WHY.
BECAUSE I'VE CHANGED, OLD FRIEND. I'M NO LONGER THE SAME MAN YOU KNEW WAY BACK WHEN.

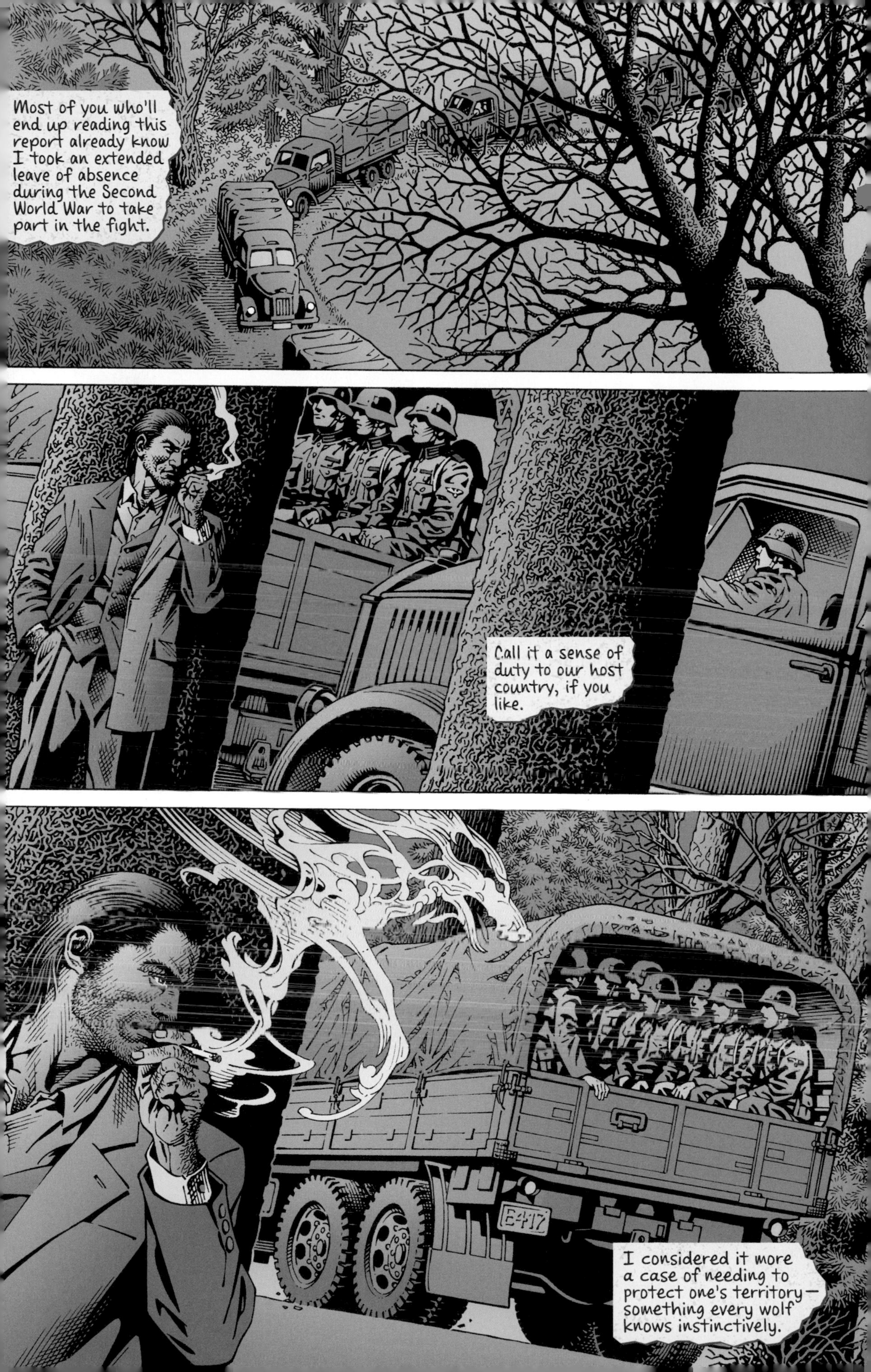
Most of you who'll end up reading this report already know I took an extended leave of absence during the Second World War to take part in the fight.
Call it a sense of duty to our host country, if you like.
E-417
I considered it more a case of needing to protect one's territory— something every wolf knows instinctively.

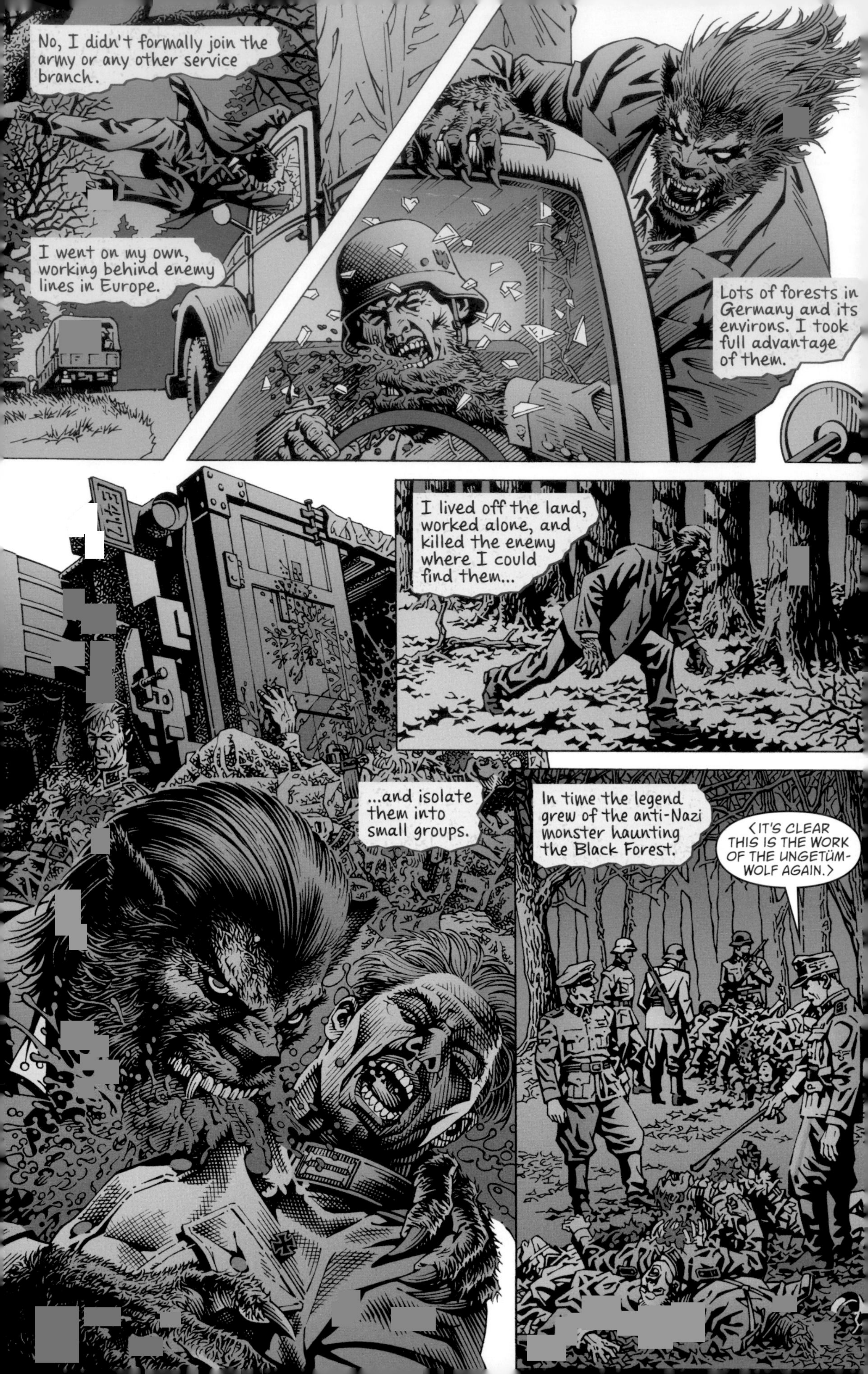
No, I didn't formally join the army or any other service branch.
I went on my own, working behind enemy lines in Europe.
Lots of forests in Germany and its environs. I took full advantage of them.
I lived off the land, worked alone, and killed the enemy where I could find them...
...and isolate them into small groups.
In time the legend grew of the anti-Nazi monster haunting the Black Forest.
<IT'S CLEAR THIS IS THE WORK OF THE UNGETÜM-WOLF AGAIN.>

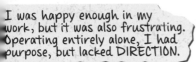

I was happy enough in my work, but it was also frustrating. Operating entirely alone, I had purpose, but lacked DIRECTION.

‹BUT WHY WIPE OUT A SIMPLE GUARD PLATOON ON TRAINING MANEUVERS, WHEN A STRATEGIC *SIGNALS* COMPANY WAS BILLETED ONLY THREE MILES AWAY?›

I had no way of singling out the relatively insignificant from the more important, from the truly VITAL targets.

‹WHO CAN SAY? LEARN TO COUNT YOUR BLESSINGS, OBERSHARFÜHRER.›

Sowing fear and horror behind enemy lines was helpful enough, but how much better could my one-man war be if I had access to even the most BASIC war-time intelligence?

January 20, 1942.

The Wannsee Estate in the suburbs of Berlin.

‹SPREAD OUT!›

‹FIND HIM! *ALIVE* IF POSSIBLE!›

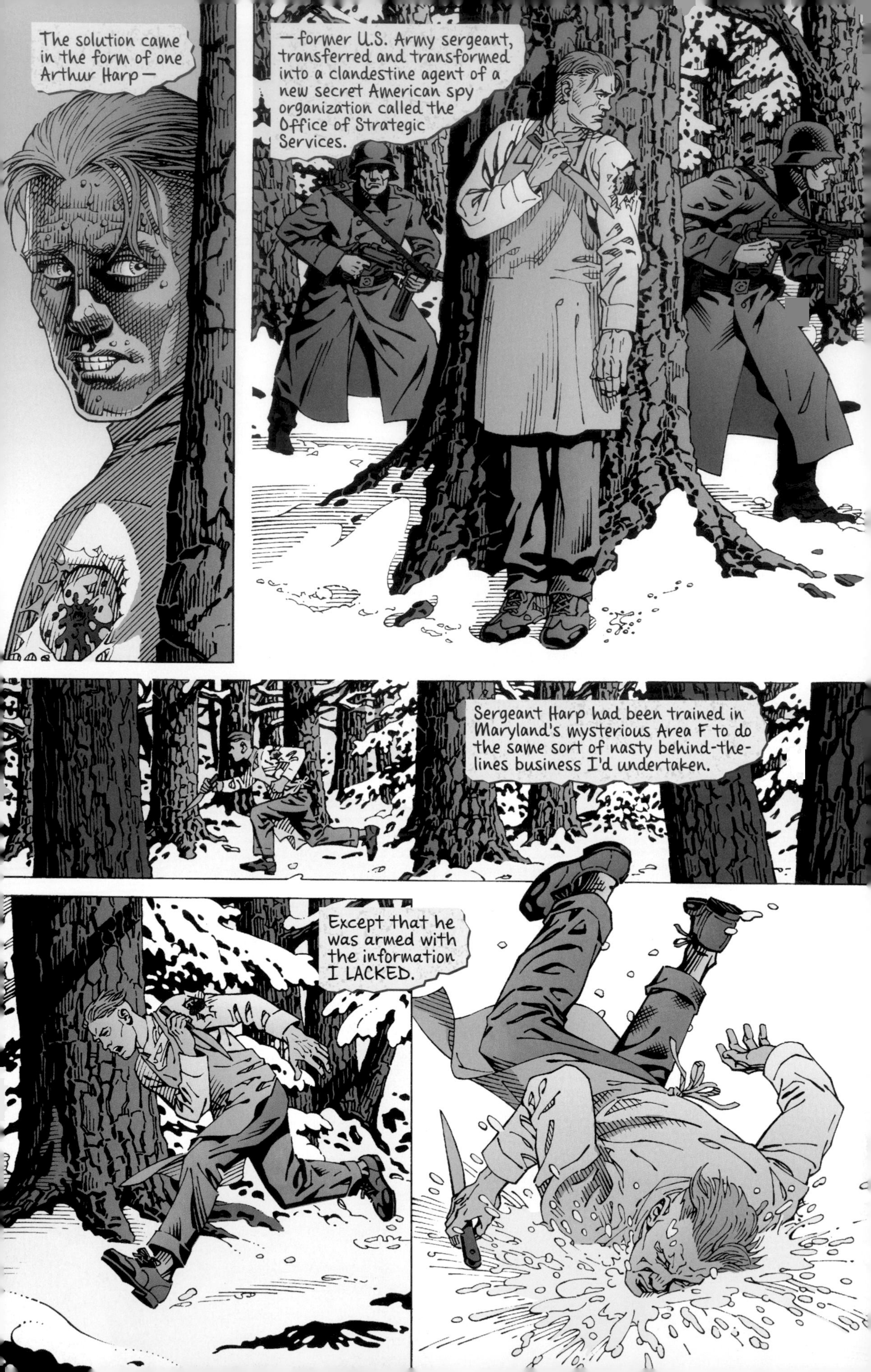
The solution came in the form of one Arthur Harp—
—former U.S. Army sergeant, transferred and transformed into a clandestine agent of a new secret American spy organization called the Office of Strategic Services.
Sergeant Harp had been trained in Maryland's mysterious Area F to do the same sort of nasty behind-the-lines business I'd undertaken.
Except that he was armed with the information I LACKED.

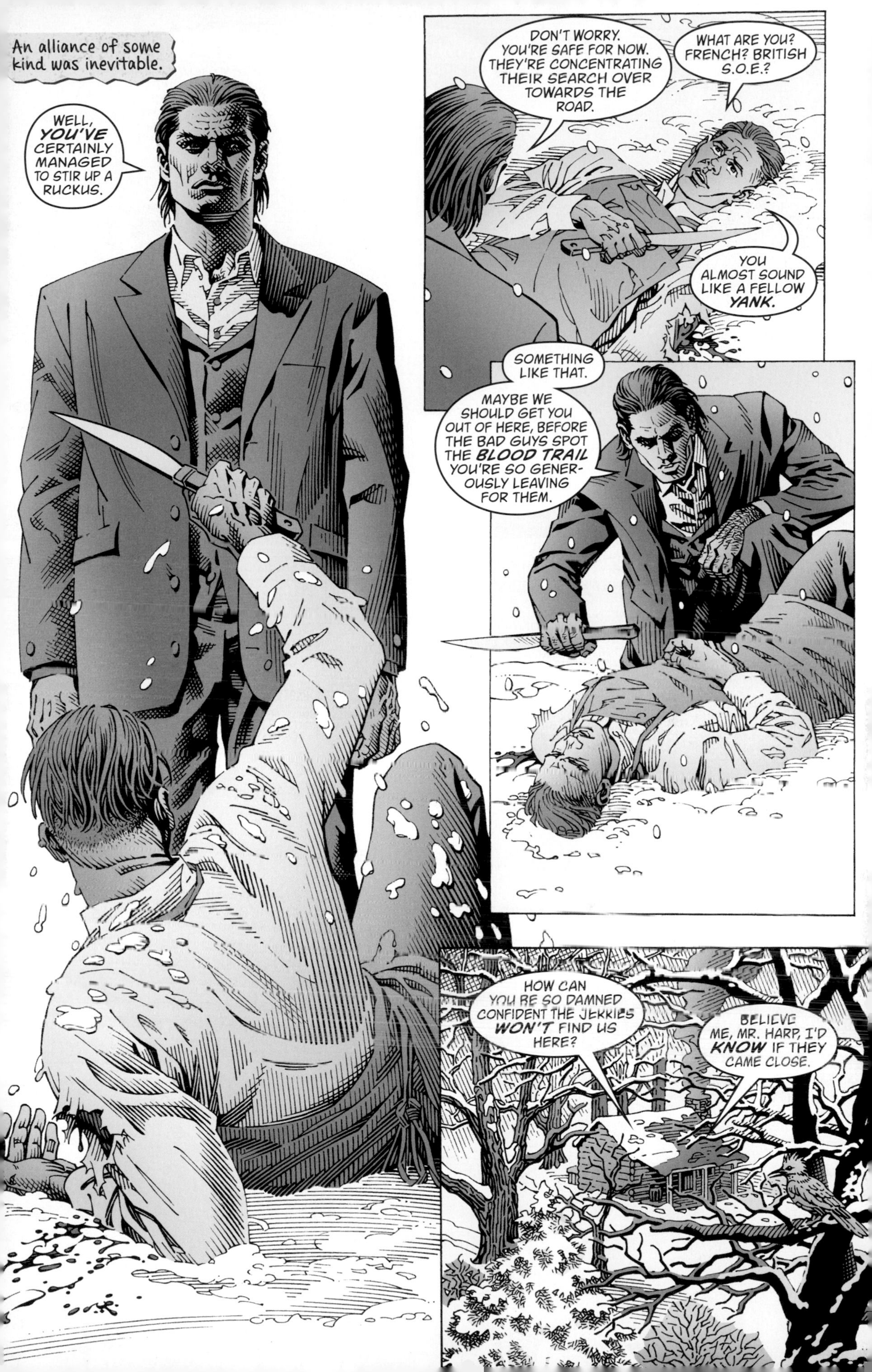
An alliance of some kind was inevitable.
WELL, YOU'VE CERTAINLY MANAGED TO STIR UP A RUCKUS.
DON'T WORRY. YOU'RE SAFE FOR NOW. THEY'RE CONCENTRATING THEIR SEARCH OVER TOWARDS THE ROAD.
WHAT ARE YOU? FRENCH? BRITISH S.O.E.?
YOU ALMOST SOUND LIKE A FELLOW YANK.
SOMETHING LIKE THAT.
MAYBE WE SHOULD GET YOU OUT OF HERE, BEFORE THE BAD GUYS SPOT THE BLOOD TRAIL YOU'RE SO GENEROUSLY LEAVING FOR THEM.
HOW CAN YOU BE SO DAMNED CONFIDENT THE JERRIES WON'T FIND US HERE?
BELIEVE ME, MR. HARP, I'D KNOW IF THEY CAME CLOSE.

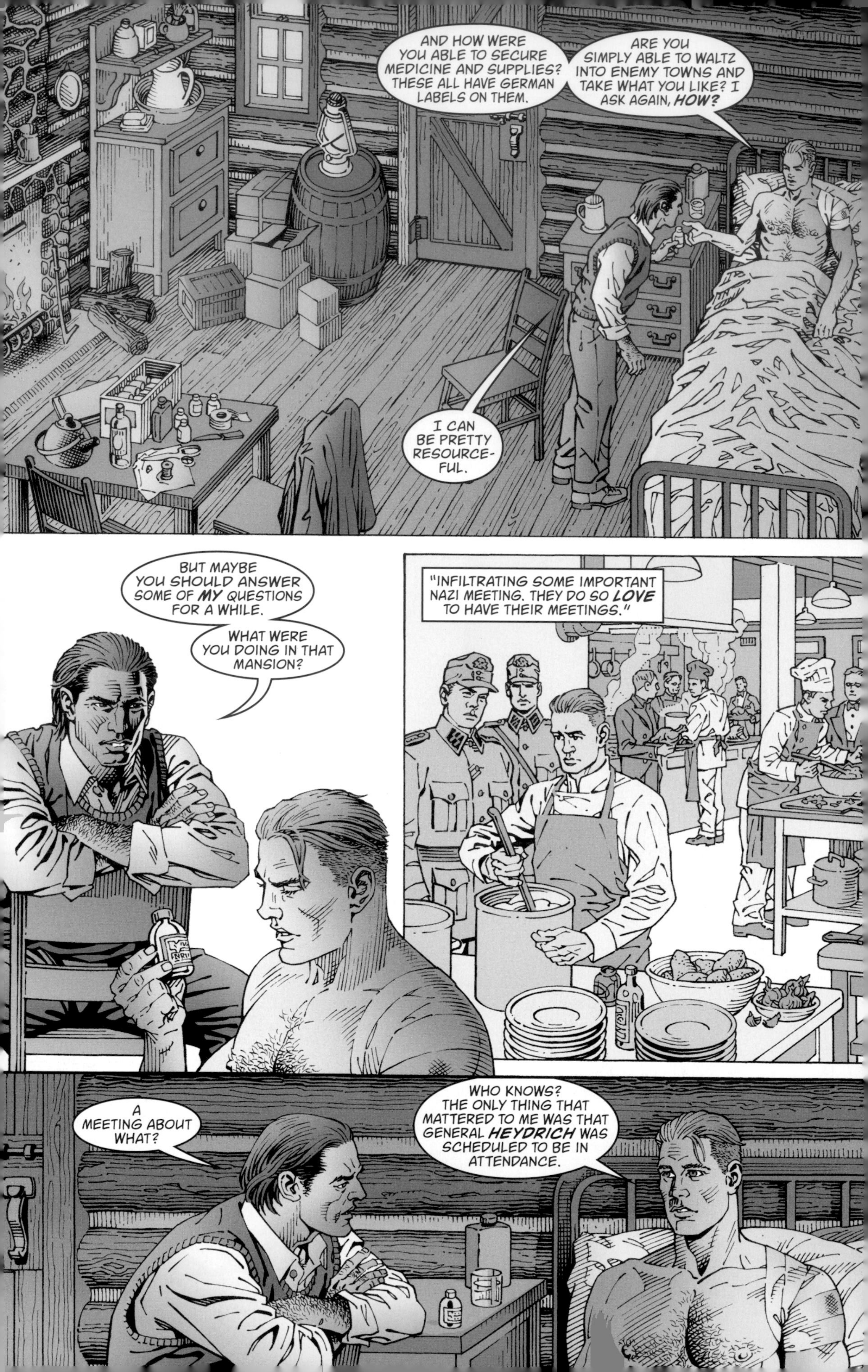
AND HOW WERE YOU ABLE TO SECURE MEDICINE AND SUPPLIES? THESE ALL HAVE GERMAN LABELS ON THEM.
ARE YOU SIMPLY ABLE TO WALTZ INTO ENEMY TOWNS AND TAKE WHAT YOU LIKE? I ASK AGAIN, *HOW?*
I CAN BE PRETTY RESOURCE-FUL.
BUT MAYBE YOU SHOULD ANSWER SOME OF *MY* QUESTIONS FOR A WHILE.
WHAT WERE YOU DOING IN THAT MANSION?
"INFILTRATING SOME IMPORTANT NAZI MEETING. THEY DO SO *LOVE* TO HAVE THEIR MEETINGS."
A MEETING ABOUT WHAT?
WHO KNOWS? THE ONLY THING THAT MATTERED TO ME WAS THAT GENERAL *HEYDRICH* WAS SCHEDULED TO BE IN ATTENDANCE.

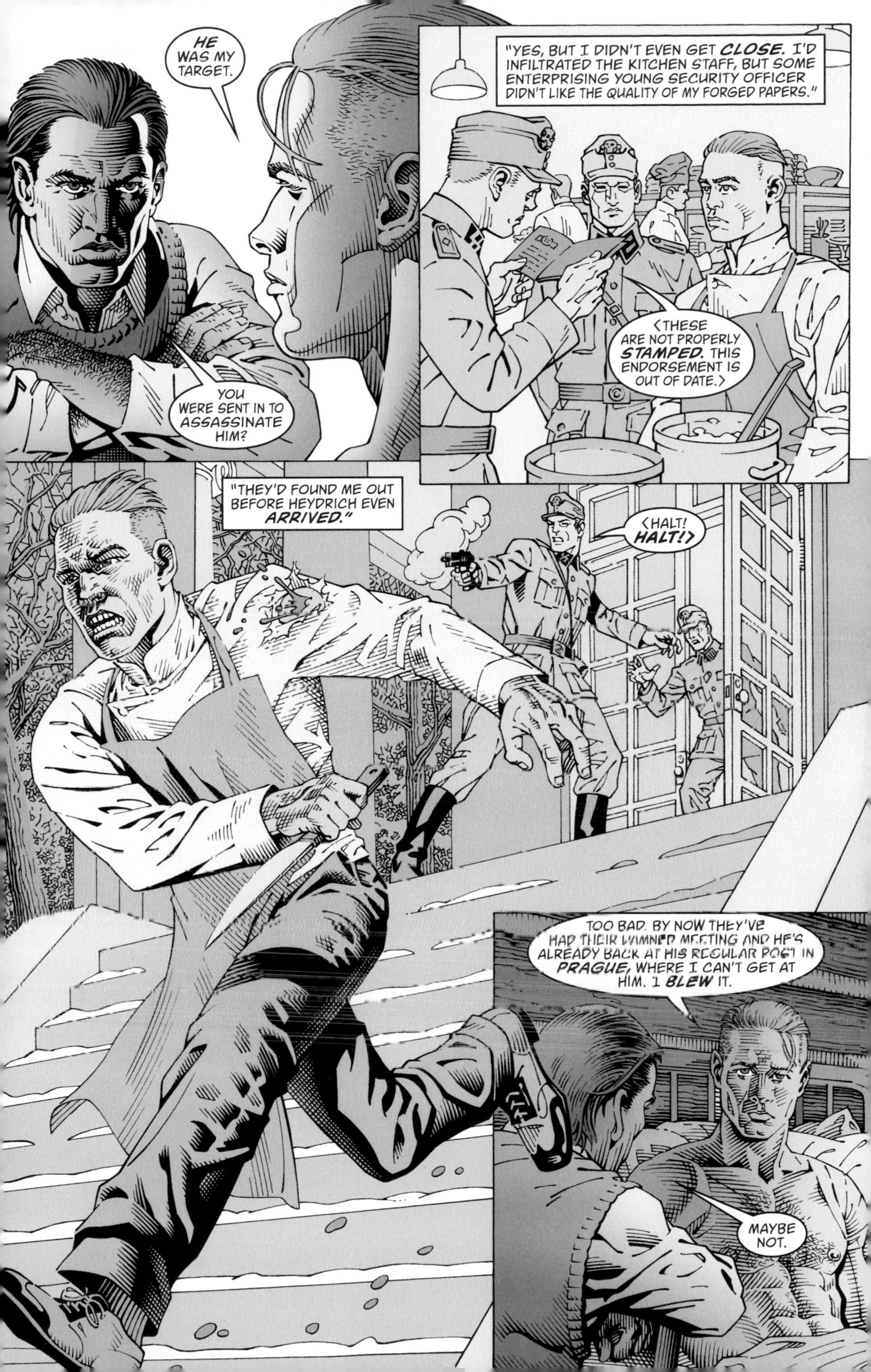
HE WAS MY TARGET.
YOU WERE SENT IN TO ASSASSINATE HIM?
"YES, BUT I DIDN'T EVEN GET CLOSE. I'D INFILTRATED THE KITCHEN STAFF, BUT SOME ENTERPRISING YOUNG SECURITY OFFICER DIDN'T LIKE THE QUALITY OF MY FORGED PAPERS."
<THESE ARE NOT PROPERLY STAMPED. THIS ENDORSEMENT IS OUT OF DATE.>
"THEY'D FOUND ME OUT BEFORE HEYDRICH EVEN ARRIVED."
<HALT! HALT!>
TOO BAD. BY NOW THEY'VE HAD THEIR DINNER MEETING AND HE'S ALREADY BACK AT HIS REGULAR POST IN PRAGUE, WHERE I CAN'T GET AT HIM. I BLEW IT.
MAYBE NOT.

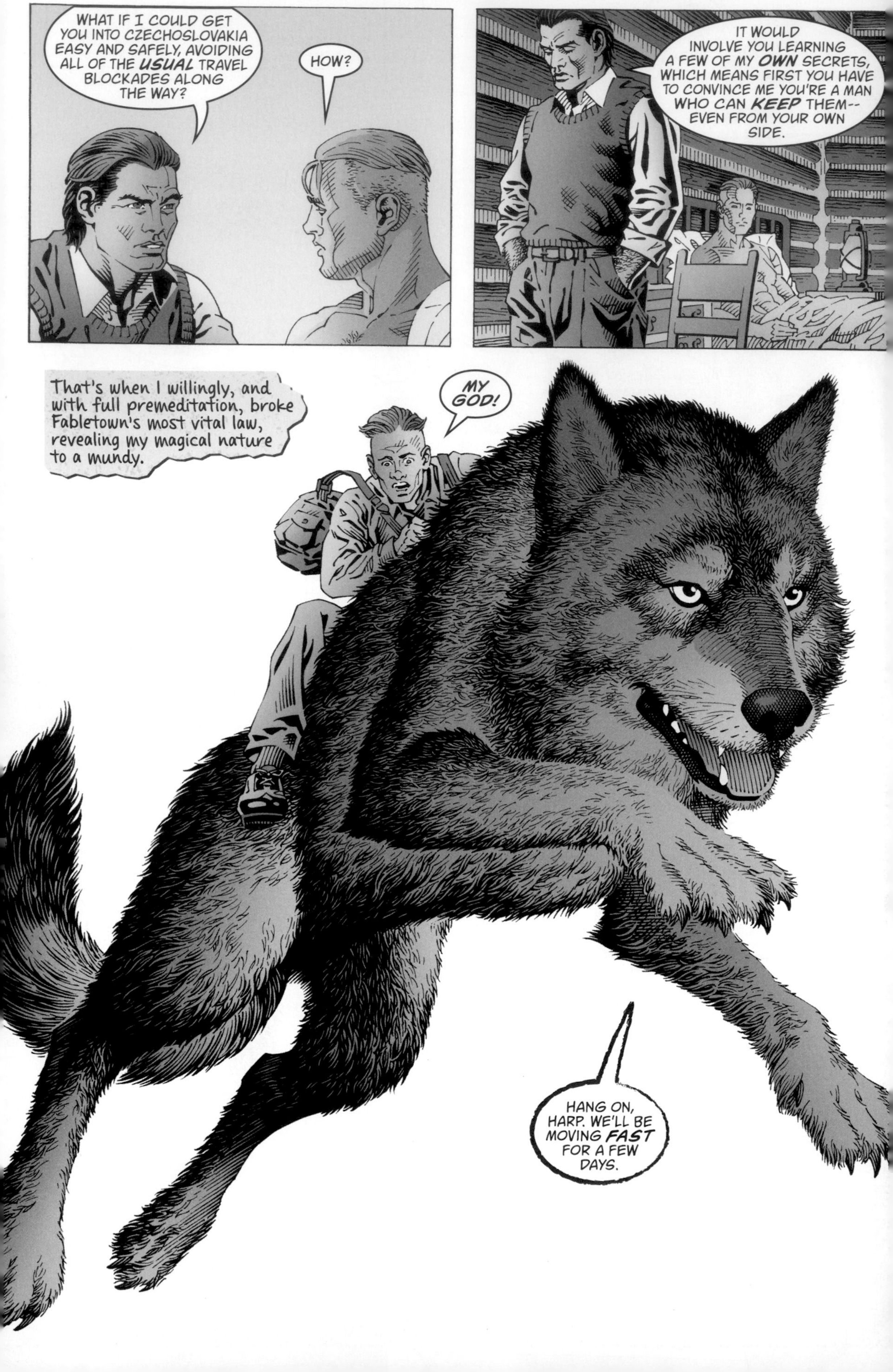
WHAT IF I COULD GET YOU INTO CZECHOSLOVAKIA EASY AND SAFELY, AVOIDING ALL OF THE USUAL TRAVEL BLOCKADES ALONG THE WAY?
HOW?
IT WOULD INVOLVE YOU LEARNING A FEW OF MY OWN SECRETS, WHICH MEANS FIRST YOU HAVE TO CONVINCE ME YOU'RE A MAN WHO CAN KEEP THEM-- EVEN FROM YOUR OWN SIDE.
That's when I willingly, and with full premeditation, broke Fabletown's most vital law, revealing my magical nature to a mundy.
MY GOD!
HANG ON, HARP. WE'LL BE MOVING FAST FOR A FEW DAYS.

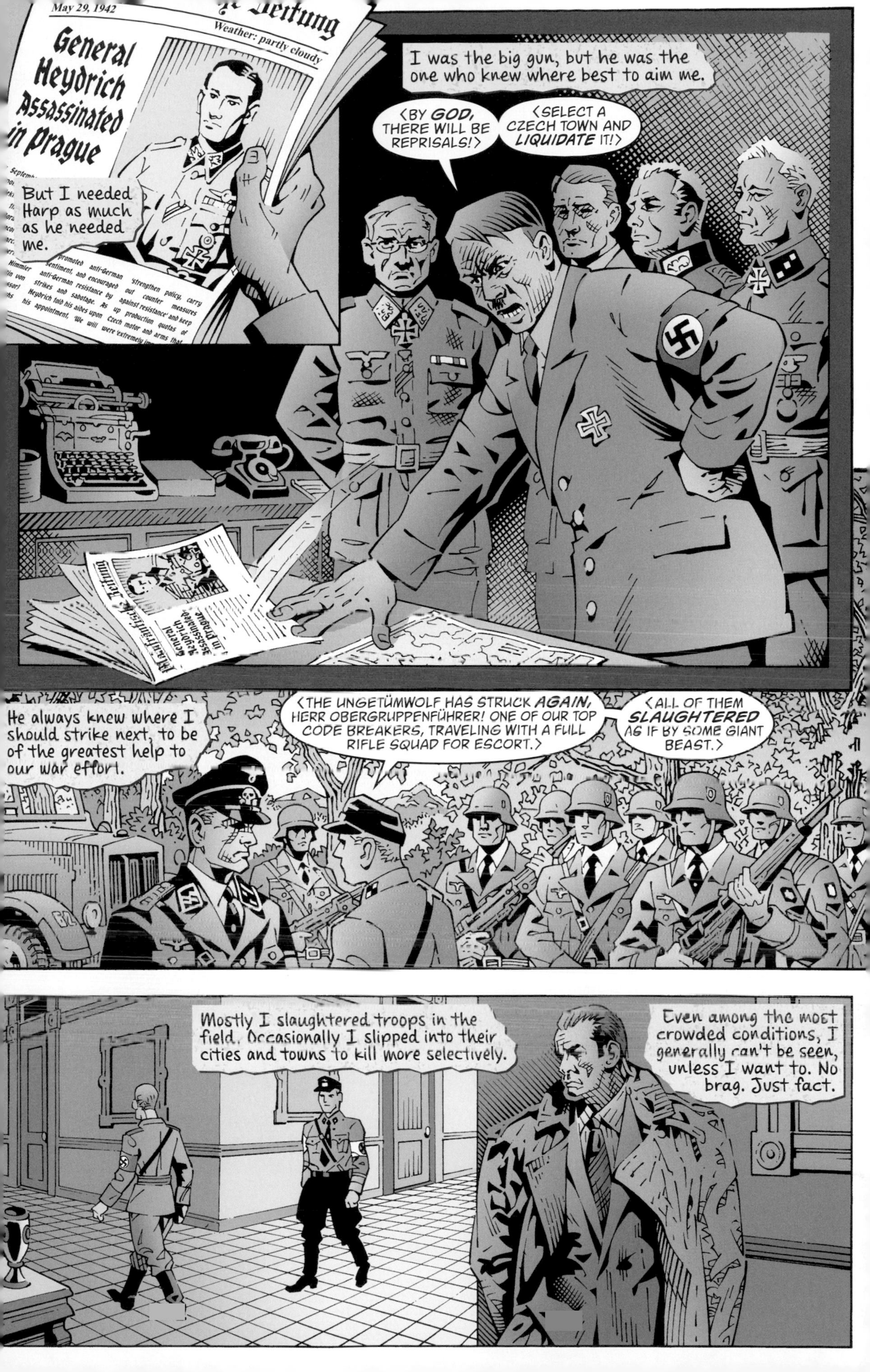
May 29, 1942
Zeitung
Weather: partly cloudy
General Heydrich Assassinated in Prague
I was the big gun, but he was the one who knew where best to aim me.
But I needed Harp as much as he needed me.
<BY GOD, THERE WILL BE REPRISALS!>
<SELECT A CZECH TOWN AND LIQUIDATE IT!>
He always knew where I should strike next, to be of the greatest help to our war effort.
<THE UNGETÜMWOLF HAS STRUCK AGAIN, HERR OBERGRUPPENFÜHRER! ONE OF OUR TOP CODE BREAKERS, TRAVELING WITH A FULL RIFLE SQUAD FOR ESCORT.>
<ALL OF THEM SLAUGHTERED AS IF BY SOME GIANT BEAST.>
Mostly I slaughtered troops in the field. Occasionally I slipped into their cities and towns to kill more selectively.
Even among the most crowded conditions, I generally can't be seen, unless I want to. No brag. Just fact.

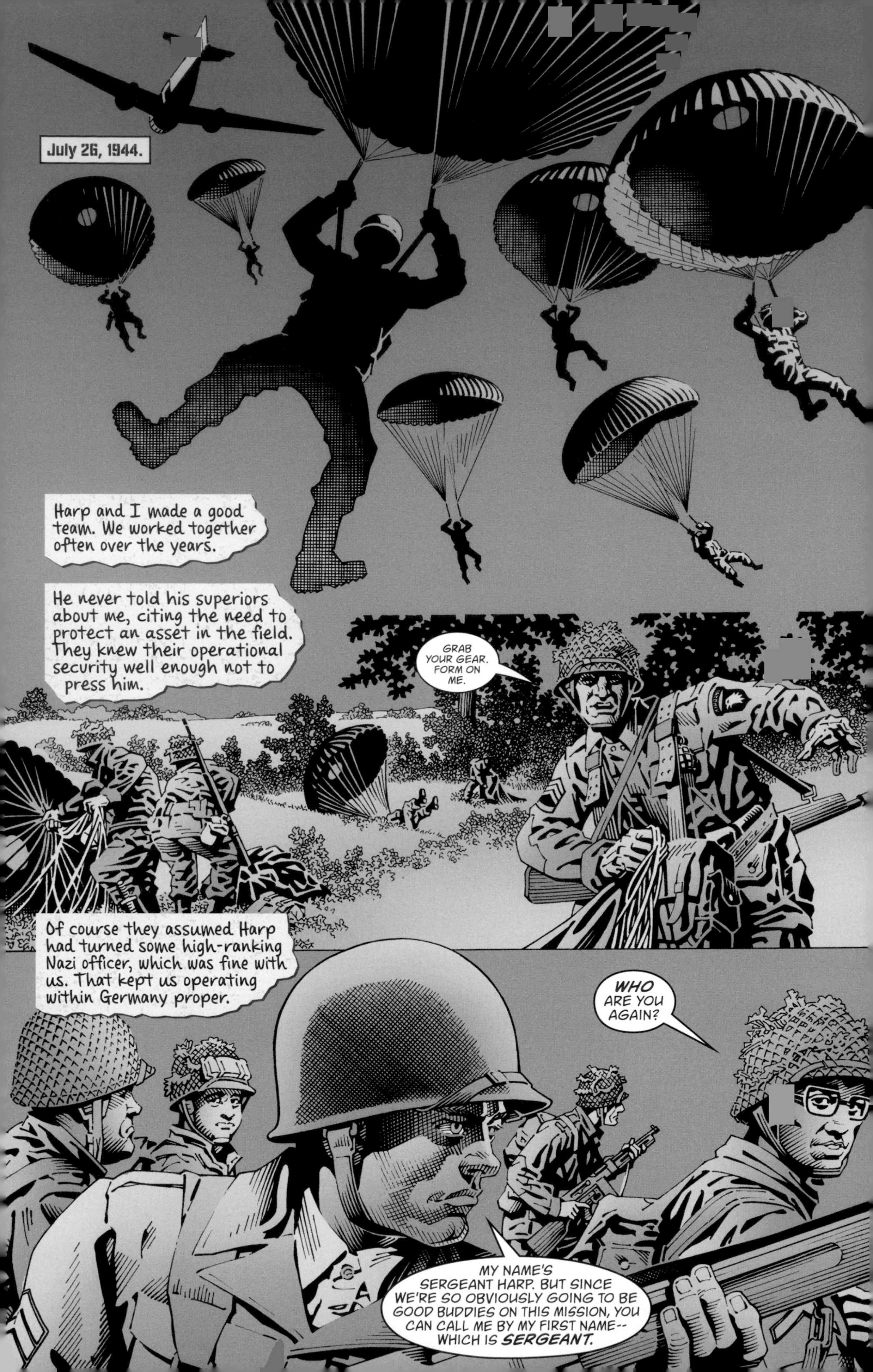
July 26, 1944.
Harp and I made a good team. We worked together often over the years.
He never told his superiors about me, citing the need to protect an asset in the field. They knew their operational security well enough not to press him.
GRAB YOUR GEAR. FORM ON ME.
Of course they assumed Harp had turned some high-ranking Nazi officer, which was fine with us. That kept us operating within Germany proper.
WHO ARE YOU AGAIN?
MY NAME'S SERGEANT HARP. BUT SINCE WE'RE SO OBVIOUSLY GOING TO BE GOOD BUDDIES ON THIS MISSION, YOU CAN CALL ME BY MY FIRST NAME-- WHICH IS SERGEANT.

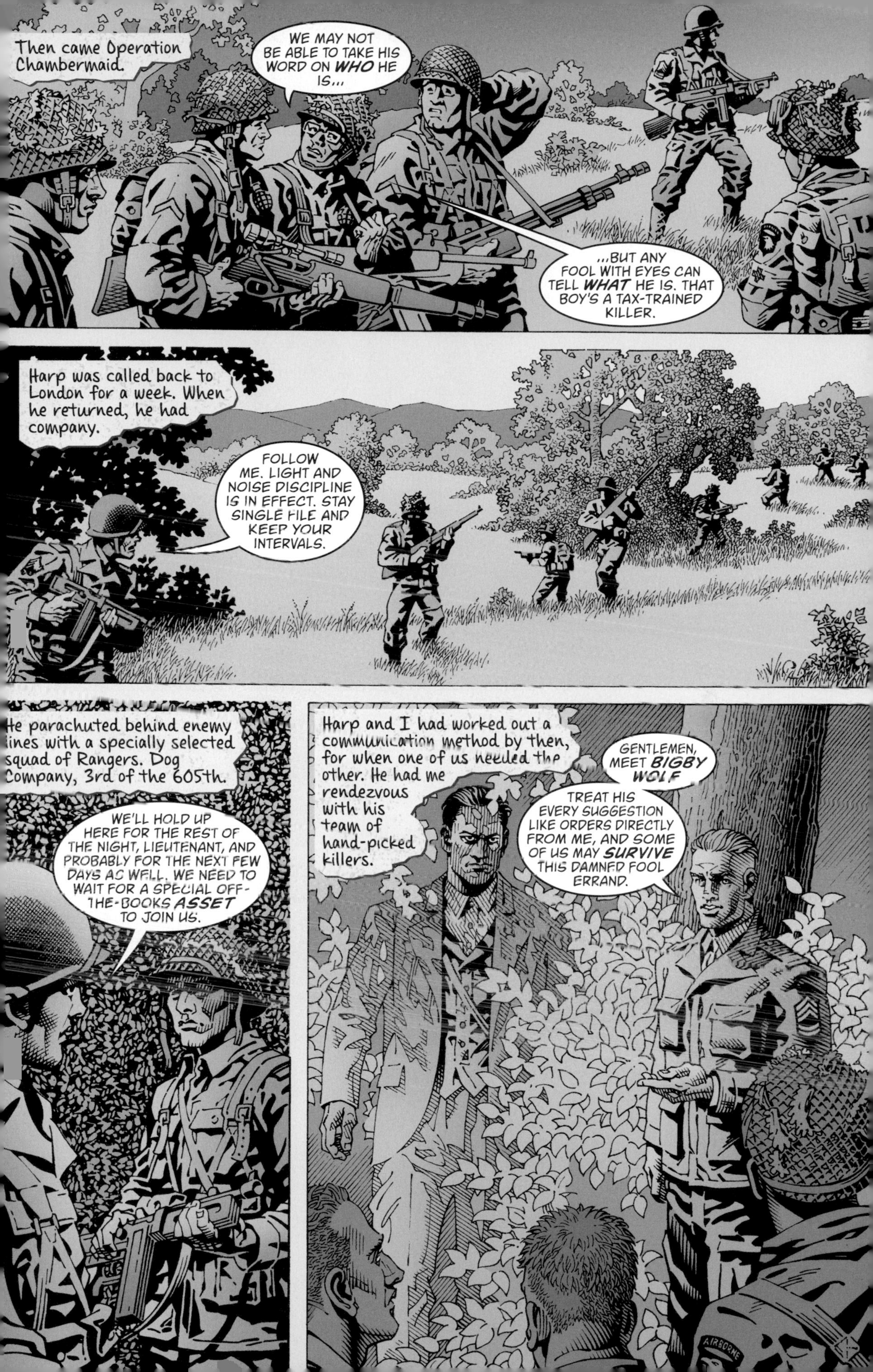
Then came Operation Chambermaid.
WE MAY NOT BE ABLE TO TAKE HIS WORD ON WHO HE IS...
...BUT ANY FOOL WITH EYES CAN TELL WHAT HE IS. THAT BOY'S A TAX-TRAINED KILLER.
Harp was called back to London for a week. When he returned, he had company.
FOLLOW ME. LIGHT AND NOISE DISCIPLINE IS IN EFFECT. STAY SINGLE FILE AND KEEP YOUR INTERVALS.
He parachuted behind enemy lines with a specially selected squad of Rangers. Dog Company, 3rd of the 605th.
WE'LL HOLD UP HERE FOR THE REST OF THE NIGHT, LIEUTENANT, AND PROBABLY FOR THE NEXT FEW DAYS AS WELL. WE NEED TO WAIT FOR A SPECIAL OFF-THE-BOOKS ASSET TO JOIN US.
Harp and I had worked out a communication method by then, for when one of us needed the other. He had me rendezvous with his team of hand-picked killers.
GENTLEMEN, MEET BIGBY WOLF.
TREAT HIS EVERY SUGGESTION LIKE ORDERS DIRECTLY FROM ME, AND SOME OF US MAY SURVIVE THIS DAMNED FOOL ERRAND.
AIRBORNE

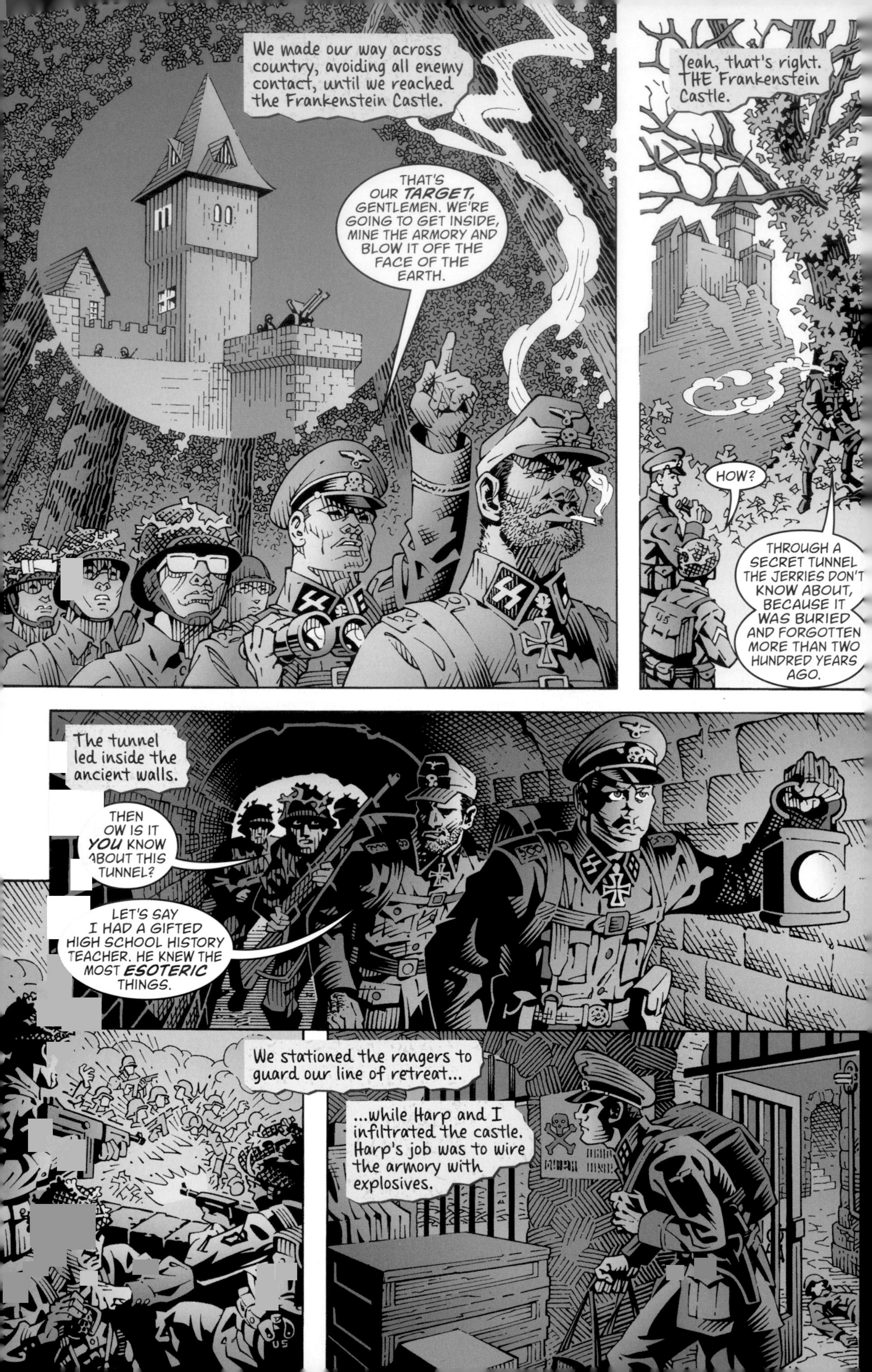
We made our way across country, avoiding all enemy contact, until we reached the Frankenstein Castle.
THAT'S OUR *TARGET,* GENTLEMEN. WE'RE GOING TO GET INSIDE, MINE THE ARMORY AND BLOW IT OFF THE FACE OF THE EARTH.
Yeah, that's right. THE Frankenstein Castle.
HOW?
THROUGH A SECRET TUNNEL THE JERRIES DON'T KNOW ABOUT, BECAUSE IT WAS BURIED AND FORGOTTEN MORE THAN TWO HUNDRED YEARS AGO.
The tunnel led inside the ancient walls.
THEN OW IS IT *YOU* KNOW ABOUT THIS TUNNEL?
LET'S SAY I HAD A GIFTED HIGH SCHOOL HISTORY TEACHER. HE KNEW THE MOST *ESOTERIC* THINGS.
We stationed the rangers to guard our line of retreat...
...while Harp and I infiltrated the castle. Harp's job was to wire the armory with explosives.

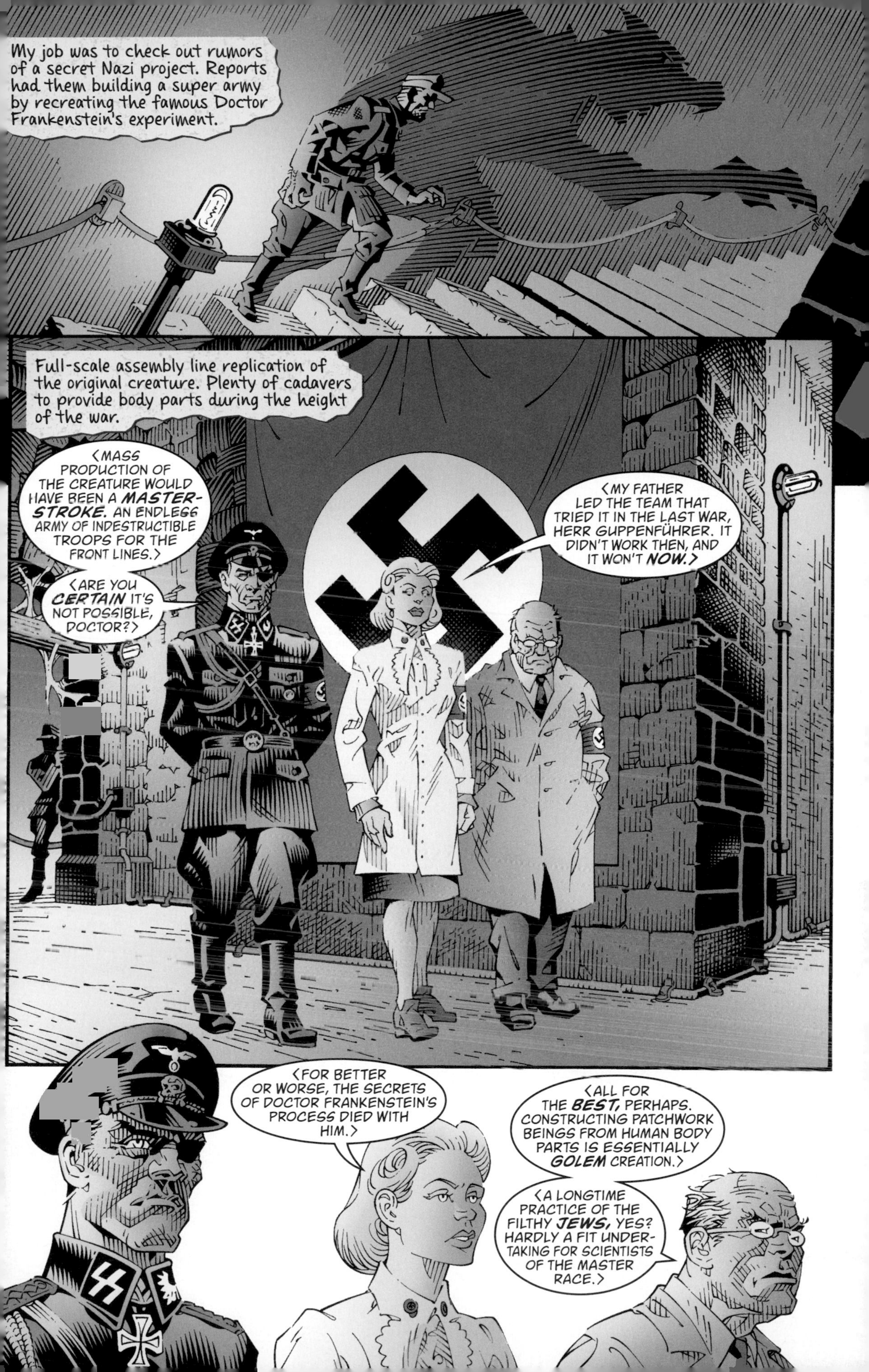
My job was to check out rumors of a secret Nazi project. Reports had them building a super army by recreating the famous Doctor Frankenstein's experiment.
Full-scale assembly line replication of the original creature. Plenty of cadavers to provide body parts during the height of the war.
<MASS PRODUCTION OF THE CREATURE WOULD HAVE BEEN A MASTERSTROKE. AN ENDLESS ARMY OF INDESTRUCTIBLE TROOPS FOR THE FRONT LINES.>
<MY FATHER LED THE TEAM THAT TRIED IT IN THE LAST WAR, HERR GUPPENFÜHRER. IT DIDN'T WORK THEN, AND IT WON'T NOW.>
<ARE YOU CERTAIN IT'S NOT POSSIBLE, DOCTOR?>
<FOR BETTER OR WORSE, THE SECRETS OF DOCTOR FRANKENSTEIN'S PROCESS DIED WITH HIM.>
<ALL FOR THE BEST, PERHAPS. CONSTRUCTING PATCHWORK BEINGS FROM HUMAN BODY PARTS IS ESSENTIALLY GOLEM CREATION.>
<A LONGTIME PRACTICE OF THE FILTHY JEWS, YES? HARDLY A FIT UNDERTAKING FOR SCIENTISTS OF THE MASTER RACE.>

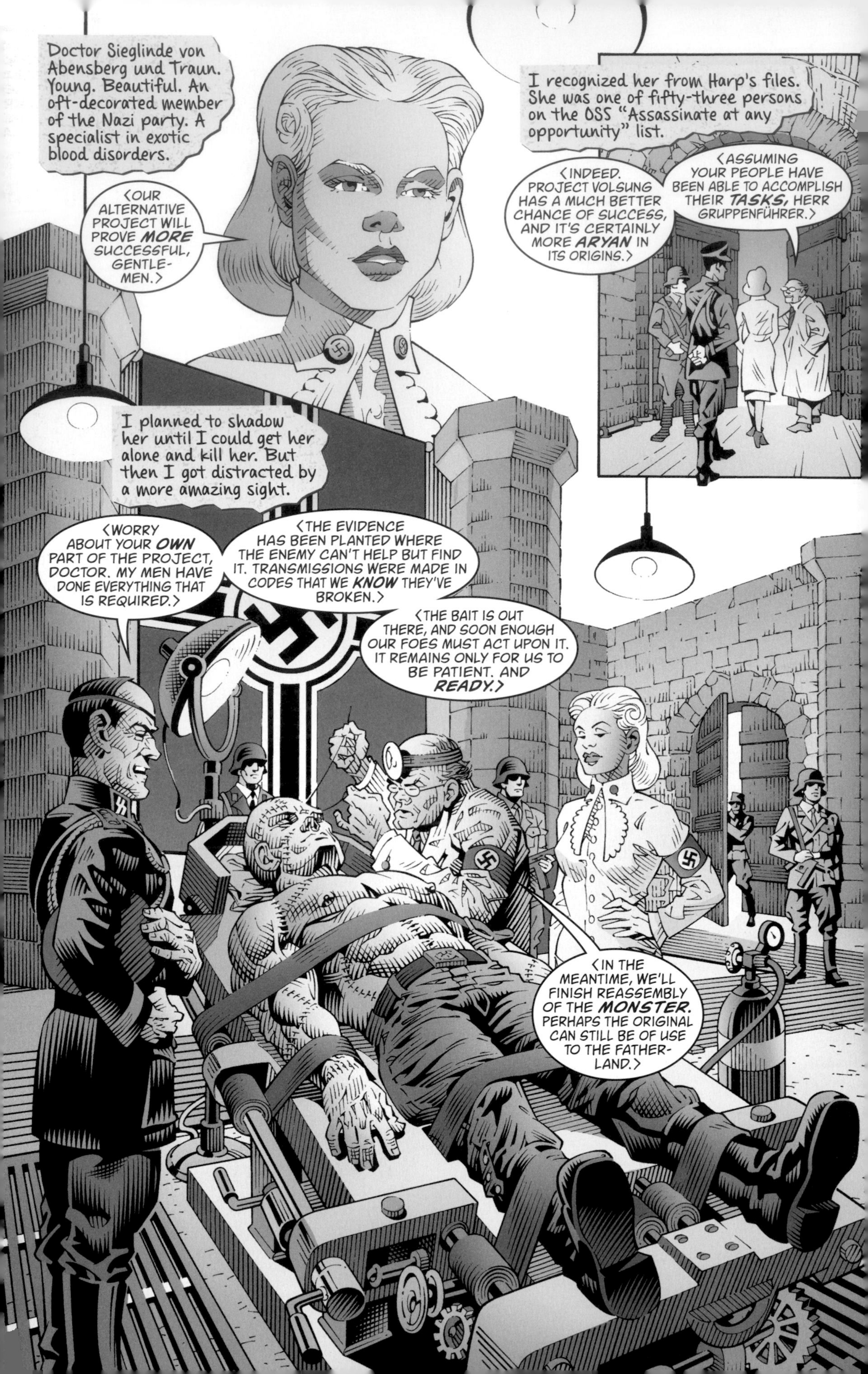
Doctor Sieglinde von Abensberg und Traun. Young. Beautiful. An oft-decorated member of the Nazi party. A specialist in exotic blood disorders.
<OUR ALTERNATIVE PROJECT WILL PROVE MORE SUCCESSFUL, GENTLE-MEN.>
I recognized her from Harp's files. She was one of fifty-three persons on the OSS "Assassinate at any opportunity" list.
<INDEED. PROJECT VOLSUNG HAS A MUCH BETTER CHANCE OF SUCCESS, AND IT'S CERTAINLY MORE ARYAN IN ITS ORIGINS.>
<ASSUMING YOUR PEOPLE HAVE BEEN ABLE TO ACCOMPLISH THEIR TASKS, HERR GRUPPENFÜHRER.>
I planned to shadow her until I could get her alone and kill her. But then I got distracted by a more amazing sight.
<WORRY ABOUT YOUR OWN PART OF THE PROJECT, DOCTOR. MY MEN HAVE DONE EVERYTHING THAT IS REQUIRED.>
<THE EVIDENCE HAS BEEN PLANTED WHERE THE ENEMY CAN'T HELP BUT FIND IT. TRANSMISSIONS WERE MADE IN CODES THAT WE KNOW THEY'VE BROKEN.>
<THE BAIT IS OUT THERE, AND SOON ENOUGH OUR FOES MUST ACT UPON IT. IT REMAINS ONLY FOR US TO BE PATIENT. AND READY.>
<IN THE MEANTIME, WE'LL FINISH REASSEMBLY OF THE MONSTER. PERHAPS THE ORIGINAL CAN STILL BE OF USE TO THE FATHER-LAND.>

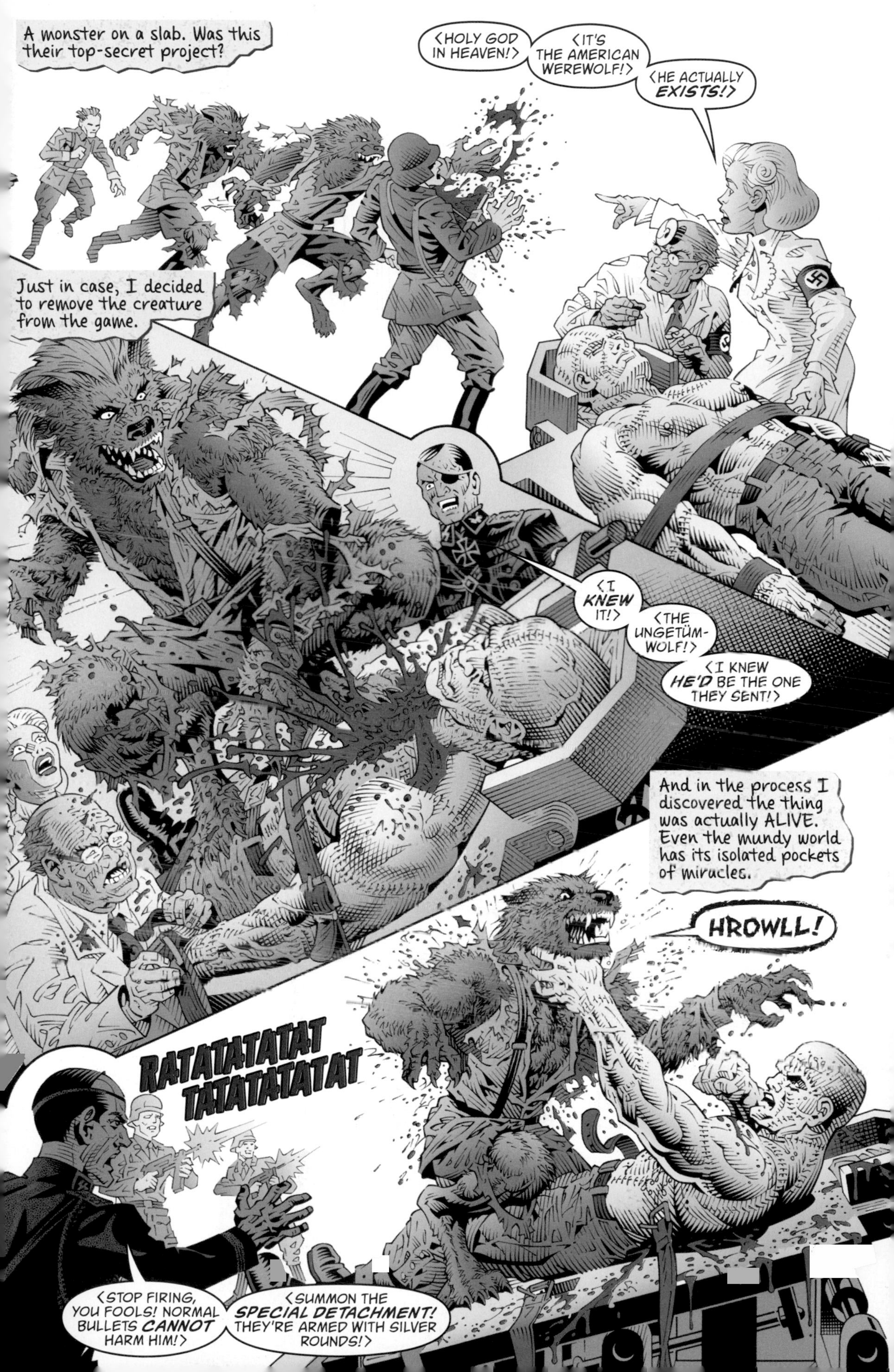
A monster on a slab. Was this their top-secret project?
‹HOLY GOD IN HEAVEN!›
‹IT'S THE AMERICAN WEREWOLF!›
‹HE ACTUALLY EXISTS!›
Just in case, I decided to remove the creature from the game.
‹I KNEW IT!›
‹THE UNGETÜM-WOLF!›
‹I KNEW HE'D BE THE ONE THEY SENT!›
And in the process I discovered the thing was actually ALIVE. Even the mundy world has its isolated pockets of miracles.
HROWLL!
RATATATATAT TATATATATAT
‹STOP FIRING, YOU FOOLS! NORMAL BULLETS CANNOT HARM HIM!›
‹SUMMON THE SPECIAL DETACHMENT! THEY'RE ARMED WITH SILVER ROUNDS!›

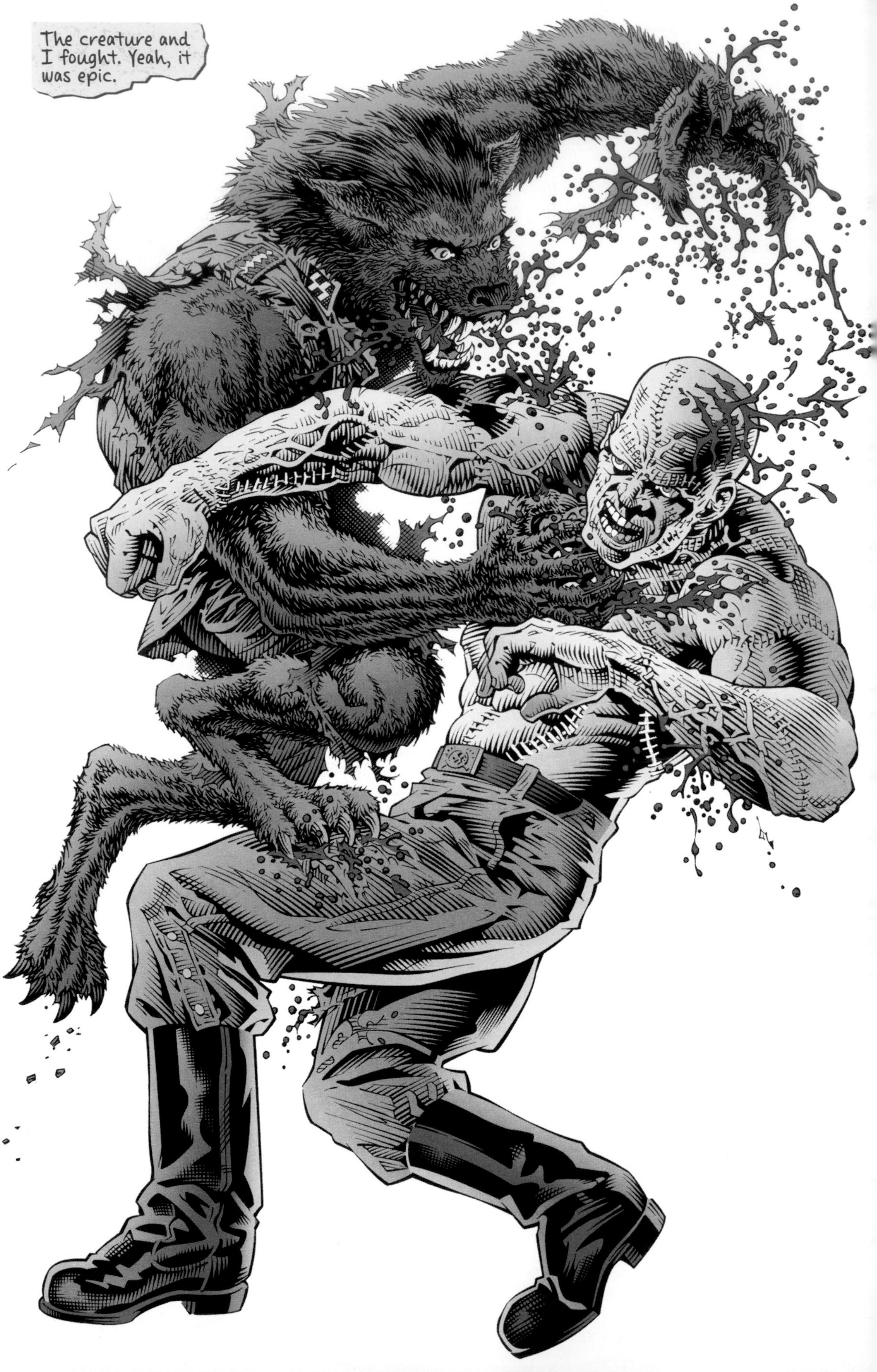
The creature and I fought. Yeah, it was epic.

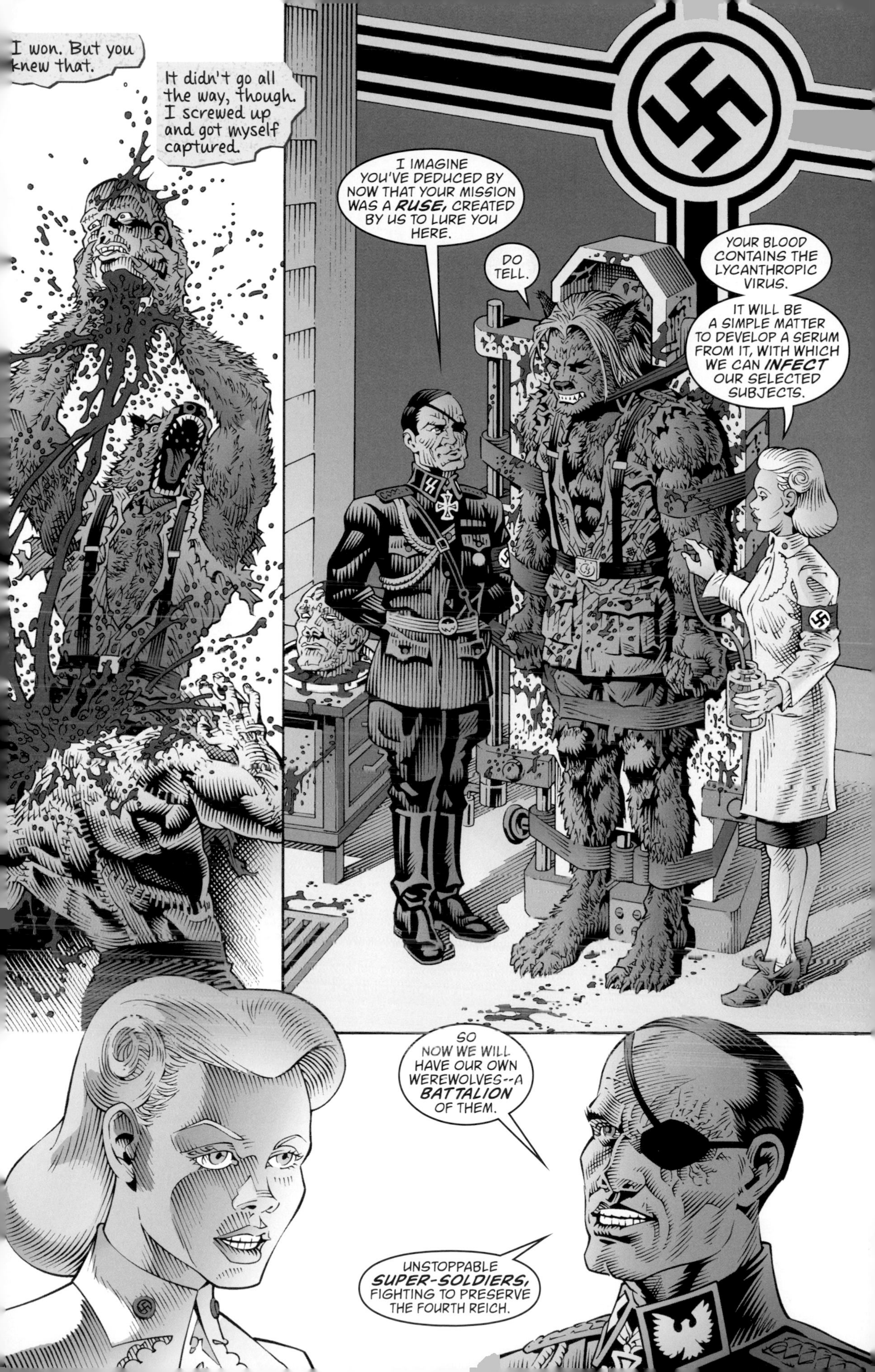
I won. But you knew that.
It didn't go all the way, though. I screwed up and got myself captured.
I IMAGINE YOU'VE DEDUCED BY NOW THAT YOUR MISSION WAS A RUSE, CREATED BY US TO LURE YOU HERE.
DO TELL.
YOUR BLOOD CONTAINS THE LYCANTHROPIC VIRUS.
IT WILL BE A SIMPLE MATTER TO DEVELOP A SERUM FROM IT, WITH WHICH WE CAN INFECT OUR SELECTED SUBJECTS.
SO NOW WE WILL HAVE OUR OWN WEREWOLVES--A BATTALION OF THEM.
UNSTOPPABLE SUPER-SOLDIERS, FIGHTING TO PRESERVE THE FOURTH REICH.

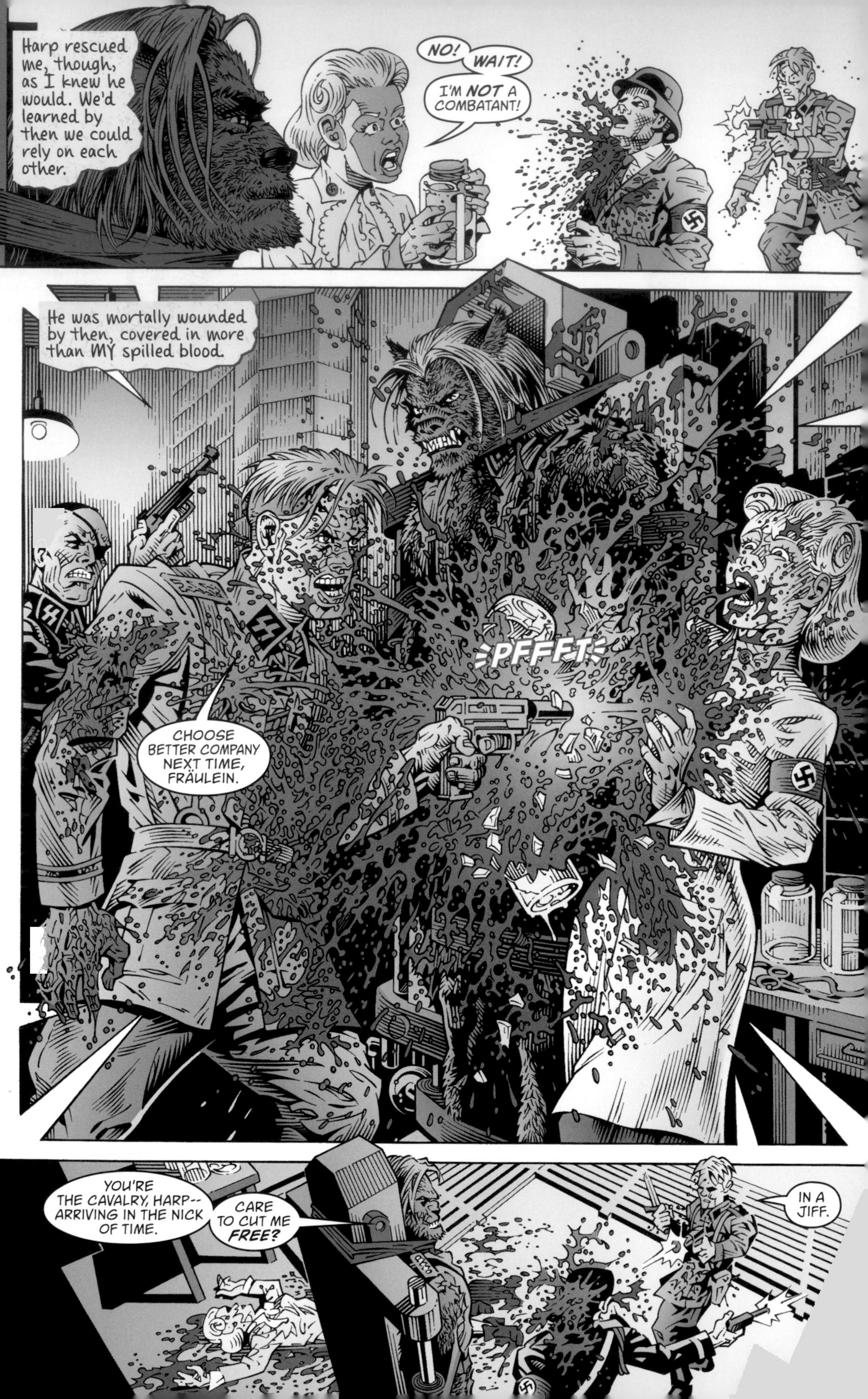
Harp rescued me, though, as I knew he would. We'd learned by then we could rely on each other.
NO!
WAIT!
I'M NOT A COMBATANT!
He was mortally wounded by then, covered in more than MY spilled blood.
PFFFT
CHOOSE BETTER COMPANY NEXT TIME, FRÄULEIN.
YOU'RE THE CAVALRY, HARP-- ARRIVING IN THE NICK OF TIME.
CARE TO CUT ME FREE?
IN A JIFF.

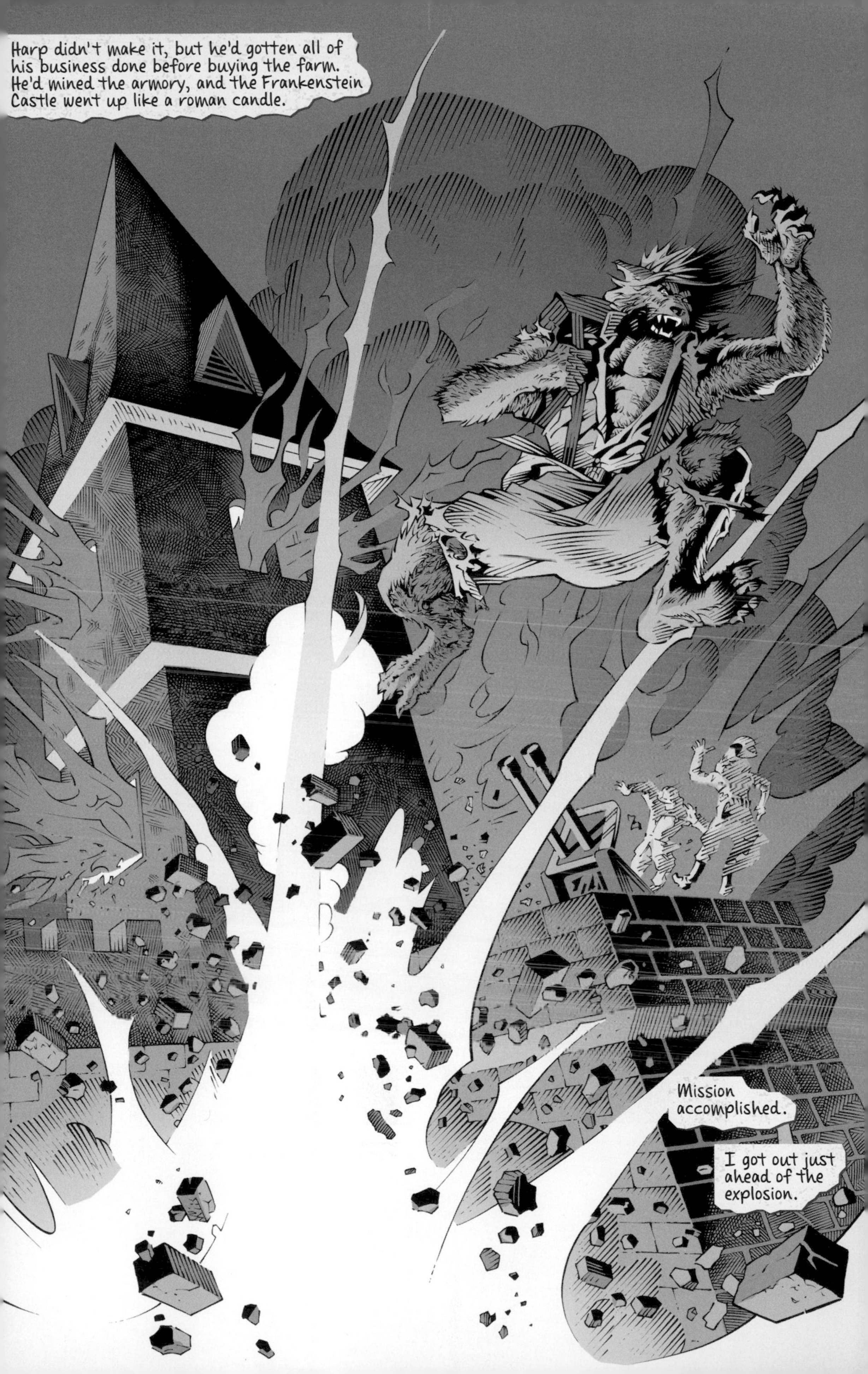
Harp didn't make it, but he'd gotten all of his business done before buying the farm. He'd mined the armory, and the Frankenstein Castle went up like a roman candle.
Mission accomplished.
I got out just ahead of the explosion.

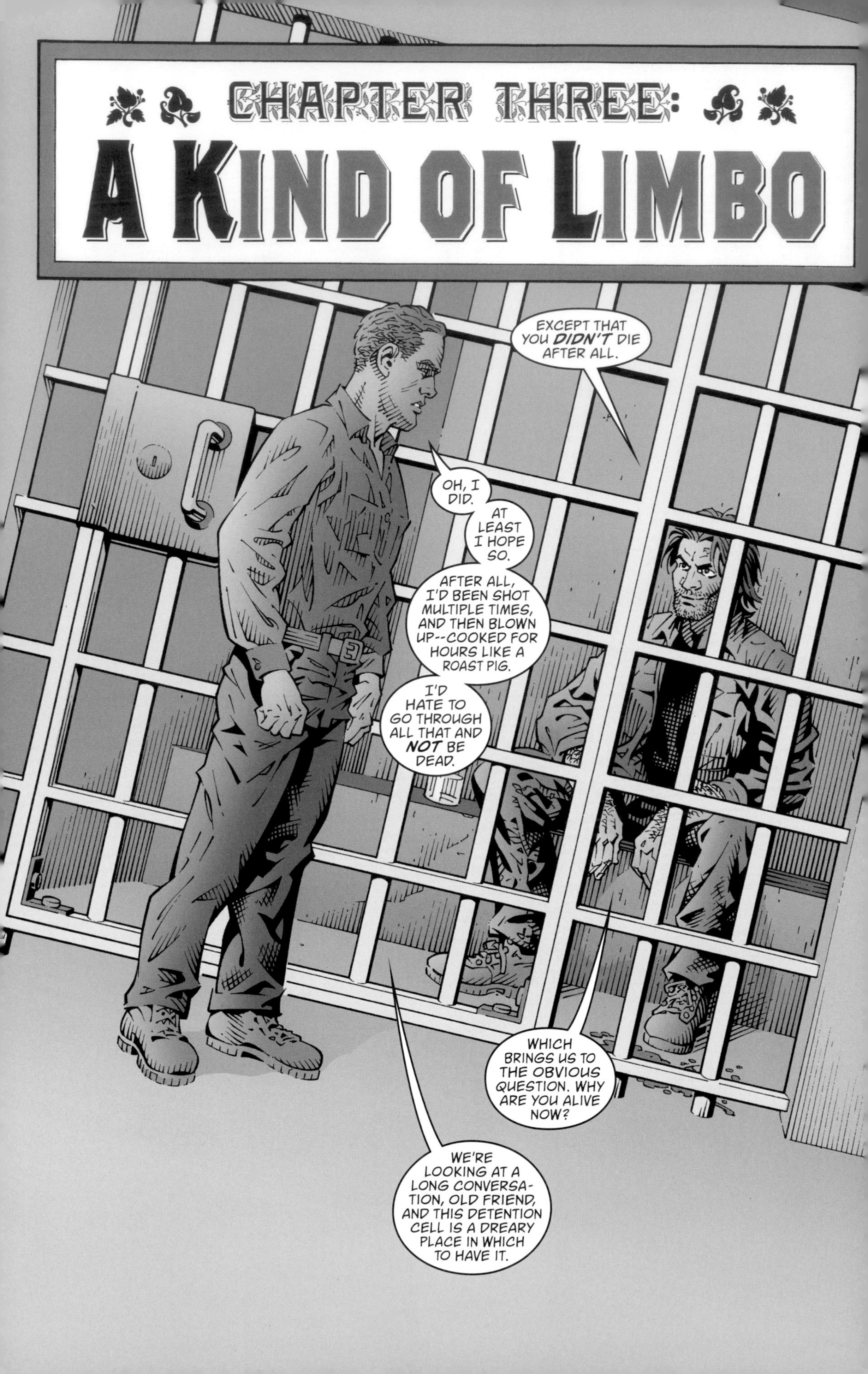
CHAPTER THREE:
A KIND OF LIMBO
EXCEPT THAT YOU DIDN'T DIE AFTER ALL.
OH, I DID.
AT LEAST I HOPE SO.
AFTER ALL, I'D BEEN SHOT MULTIPLE TIMES, AND THEN BLOWN UP--COOKED FOR HOURS LIKE A ROAST PIG.
I'D HATE TO GO THROUGH ALL THAT AND NOT BE DEAD.
WHICH BRINGS US TO THE OBVIOUS QUESTION. WHY ARE YOU ALIVE NOW?
WE'RE LOOKING AT A LONG CONVERSATION, OLD FRIEND, AND THIS DETENTION CELL IS A DREARY PLACE IN WHICH TO HAVE IT.

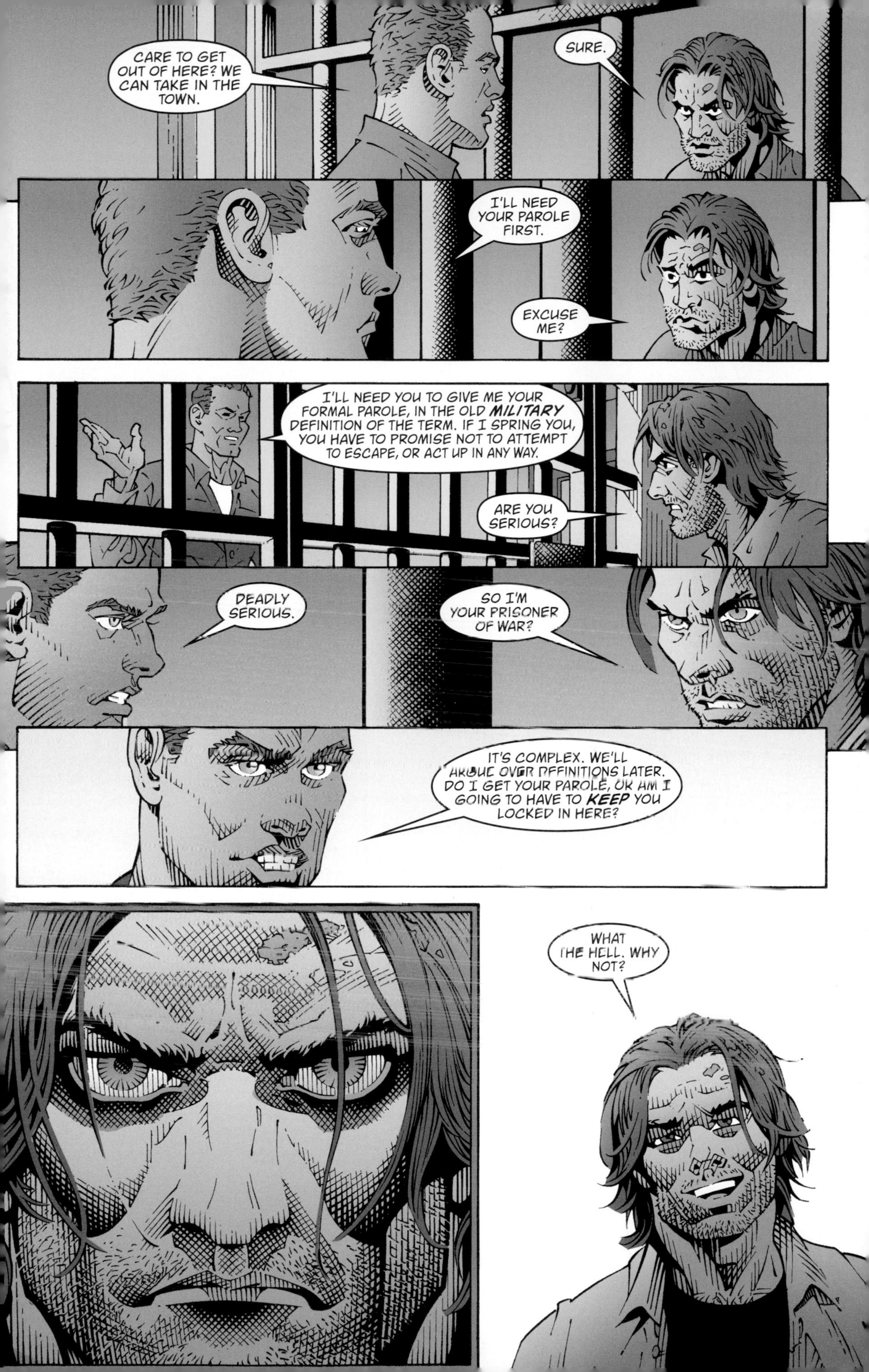
CARE TO GET OUT OF HERE? WE CAN TAKE IN THE TOWN.
SURE.
I'LL NEED YOUR PAROLE FIRST.
EXCUSE ME?
I'LL NEED YOU TO GIVE ME YOUR FORMAL PAROLE, IN THE OLD MILITARY DEFINITION OF THE TERM. IF I SPRING YOU, YOU HAVE TO PROMISE NOT TO ATTEMPT TO ESCAPE, OR ACT UP IN ANY WAY.
ARE YOU SERIOUS?
DEADLY SERIOUS.
SO I'M YOUR PRISONER OF WAR?
IT'S COMPLEX. WE'LL ARGUE OVER DEFINITIONS LATER. DO I GET YOUR PAROLE, OR AM I GOING TO HAVE TO KEEP YOU LOCKED IN HERE?
WHAT THE HELL. WHY NOT?

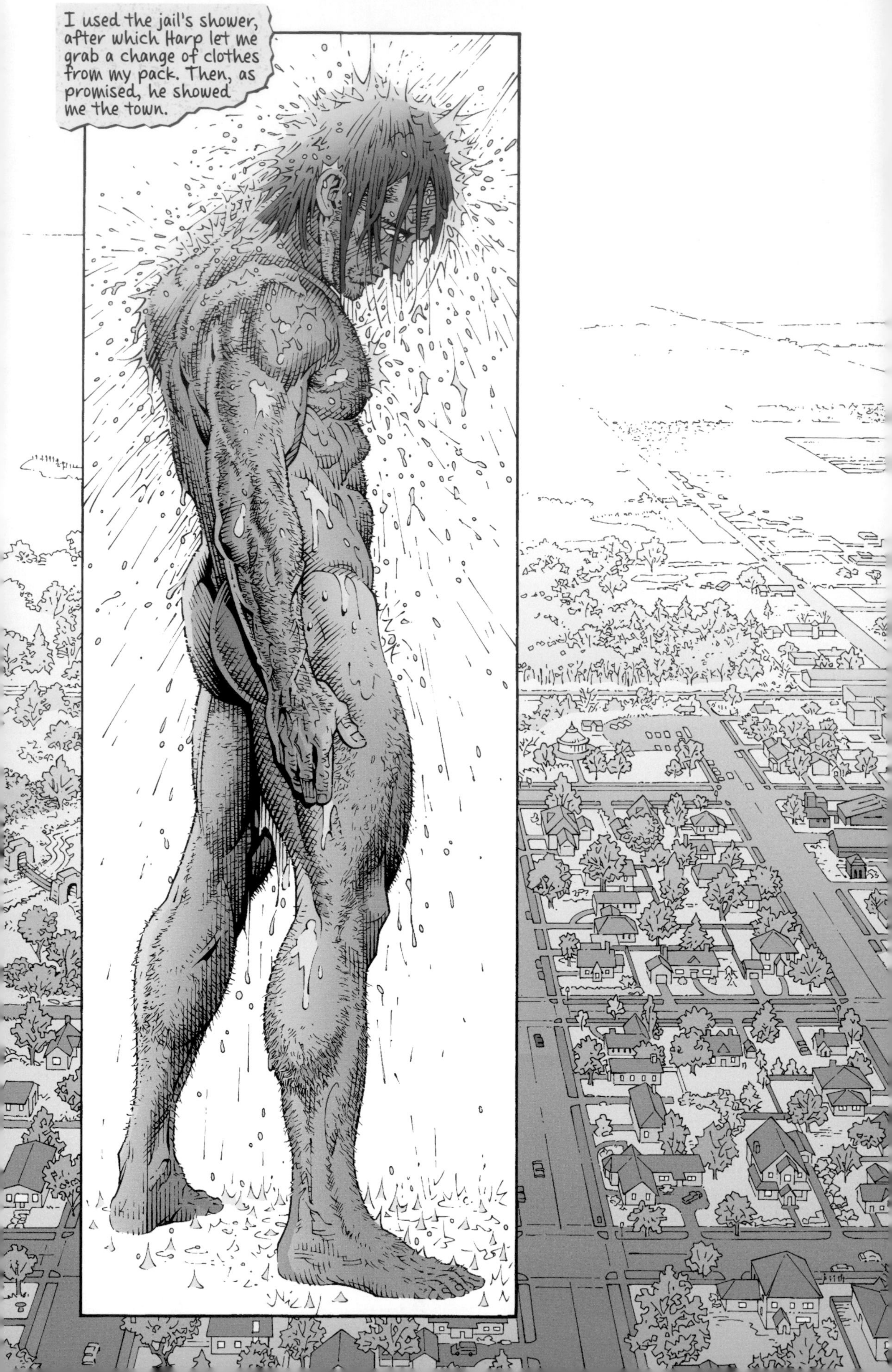
I used the jail's shower, after which Harp let me grab a change of clothes from my pack. Then, as promised, he showed me the town.

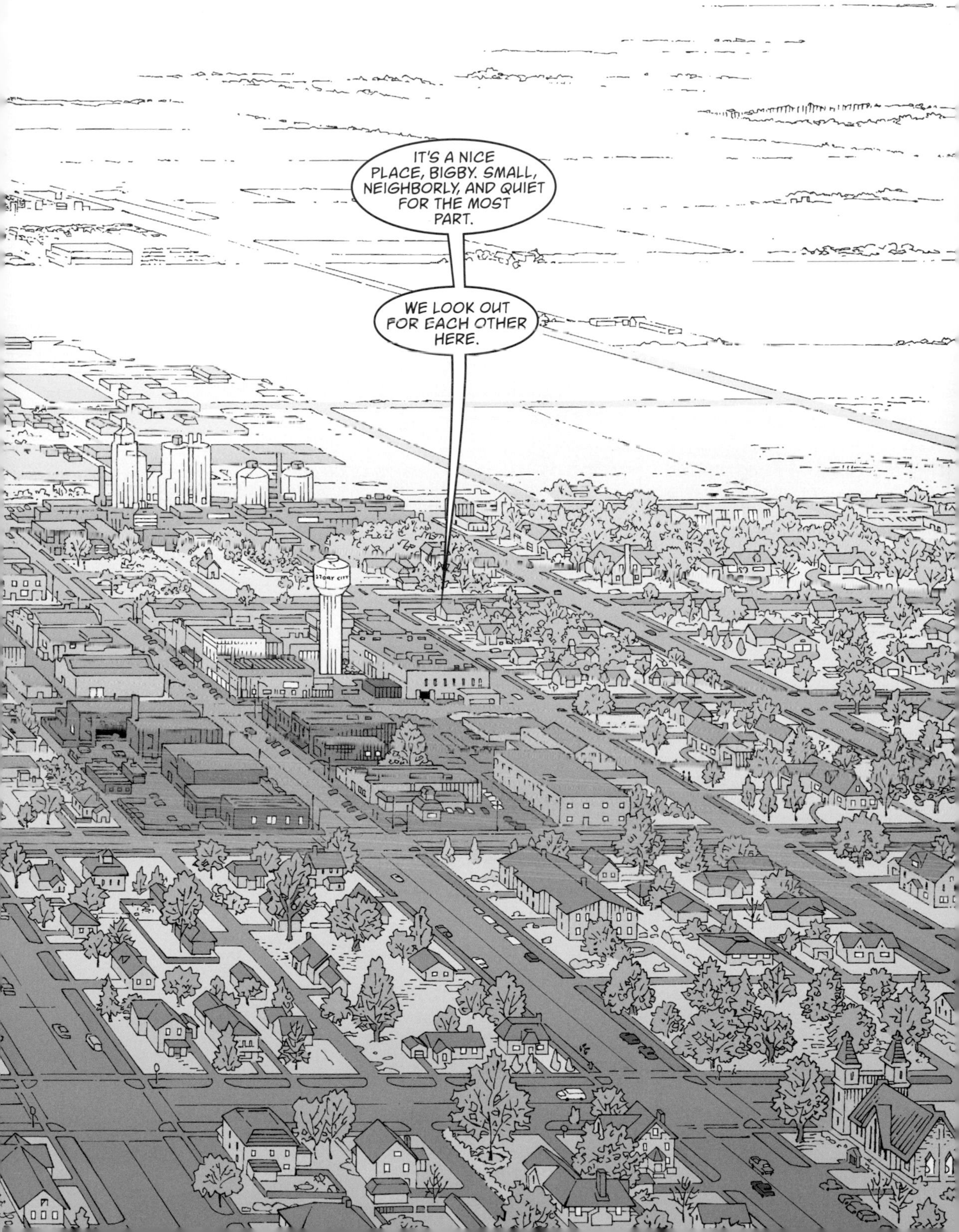
IT'S A NICE PLACE, BIGBY. SMALL, NEIGHBORLY, AND QUIET FOR THE MOST PART.
WE LOOK OUT FOR EACH OTHER HERE.
STORY CITY

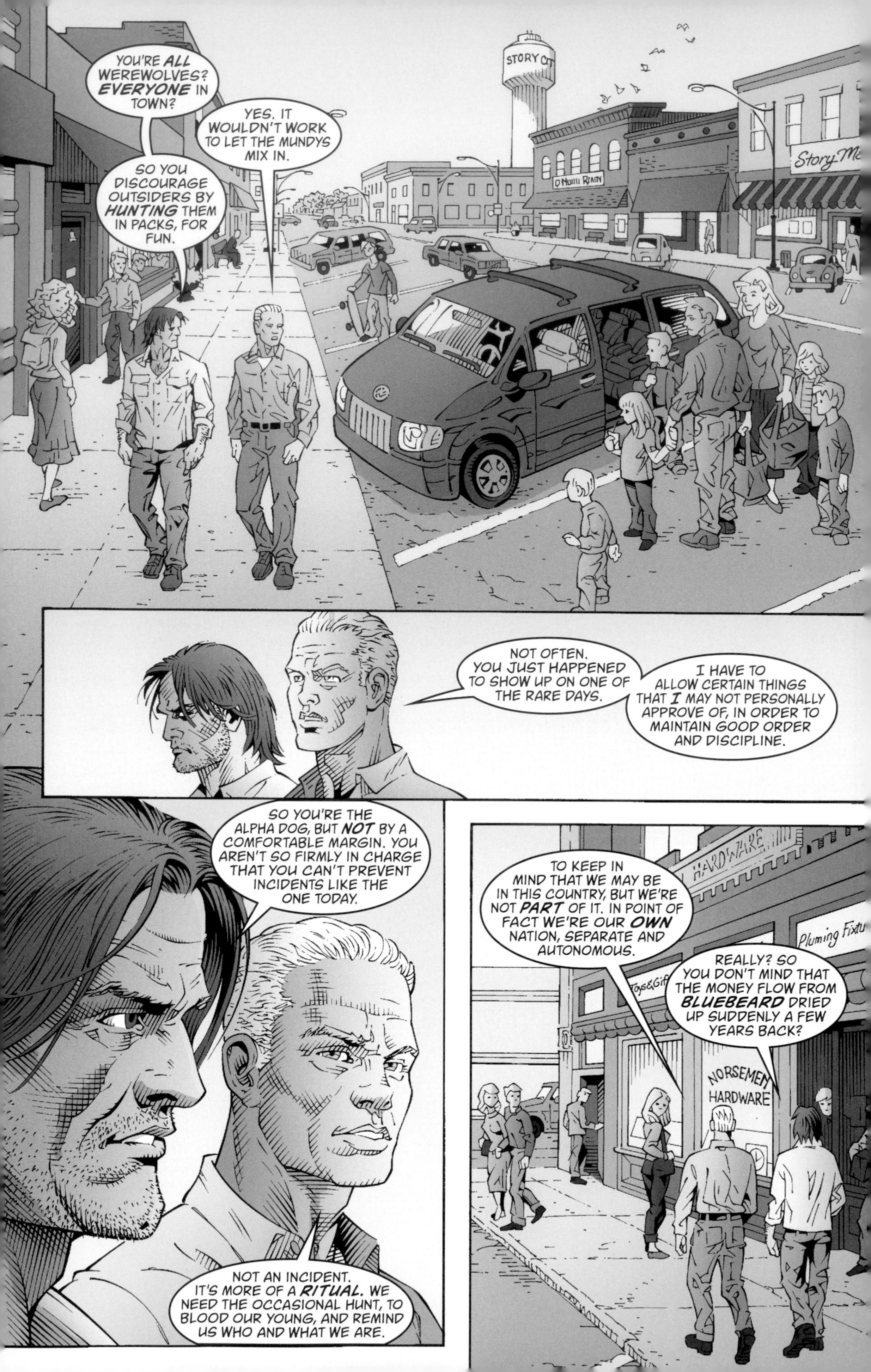
STORY CITY
YOU'RE ALL WEREWOLVES? EVERYONE IN TOWN?
YES. IT WOULDN'T WORK TO LET THE MUNDYS MIX IN.
SO YOU DISCOURAGE OUTSIDERS BY HUNTING THEM IN PACKS, FOR FUN.
NOT OFTEN. YOU JUST HAPPENED TO SHOW UP ON ONE OF THE RARE DAYS.
I HAVE TO ALLOW CERTAIN THINGS THAT I MAY NOT PERSONALLY APPROVE OF, IN ORDER TO MAINTAIN GOOD ORDER AND DISCIPLINE.
SO YOU'RE THE ALPHA DOG, BUT NOT BY A COMFORTABLE MARGIN. YOU AREN'T SO FIRMLY IN CHARGE THAT YOU CAN'T PREVENT INCIDENTS LIKE THE ONE TODAY.
NOT AN INCIDENT. IT'S MORE OF A RITUAL. WE NEED THE OCCASIONAL HUNT, TO BLOOD OUR YOUNG, AND REMIND US WHO AND WHAT WE ARE.
HARDWARE
TO KEEP IN MIND THAT WE MAY BE IN THIS COUNTRY, BUT WE'RE NOT PART OF IT. IN POINT OF FACT WE'RE OUR OWN NATION, SEPARATE AND AUTONOMOUS.
REALLY? SO YOU DON'T MIND THAT THE MONEY FLOW FROM BLUEBEARD DRIED UP SUDDENLY A FEW YEARS BACK?
NORSEMEN HARDWARE

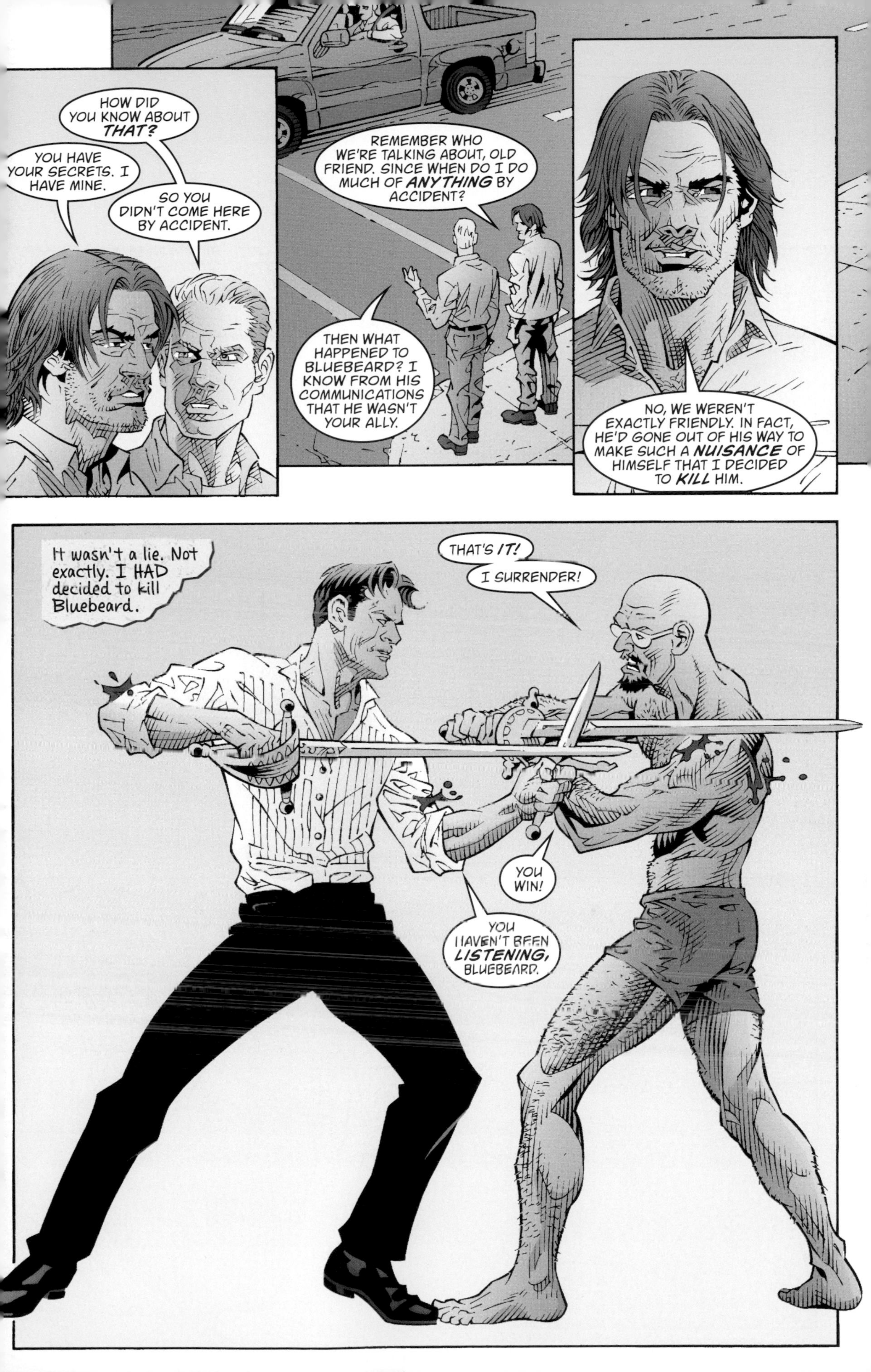
HOW DID YOU KNOW ABOUT THAT?
YOU HAVE YOUR SECRETS. I HAVE MINE.
SO YOU DIDN'T COME HERE BY ACCIDENT.
REMEMBER WHO WE'RE TALKING ABOUT, OLD FRIEND. SINCE WHEN DO I DO MUCH OF ANYTHING BY ACCIDENT?
THEN WHAT HAPPENED TO BLUEBEARD? I KNOW FROM HIS COMMUNICATIONS THAT HE WASN'T YOUR ALLY.
NO, WE WEREN'T EXACTLY FRIENDLY. IN FACT, HE'D GONE OUT OF HIS WAY TO MAKE SUCH A NUISANCE OF HIMSELF THAT I DECIDED TO KILL HIM.
It wasn't a lie. Not exactly. I HAD decided to kill Bluebeard.
THAT'S IT!
I SURRENDER!
YOU WIN!
YOU HAVEN'T BEEN LISTENING, BLUEBEARD.

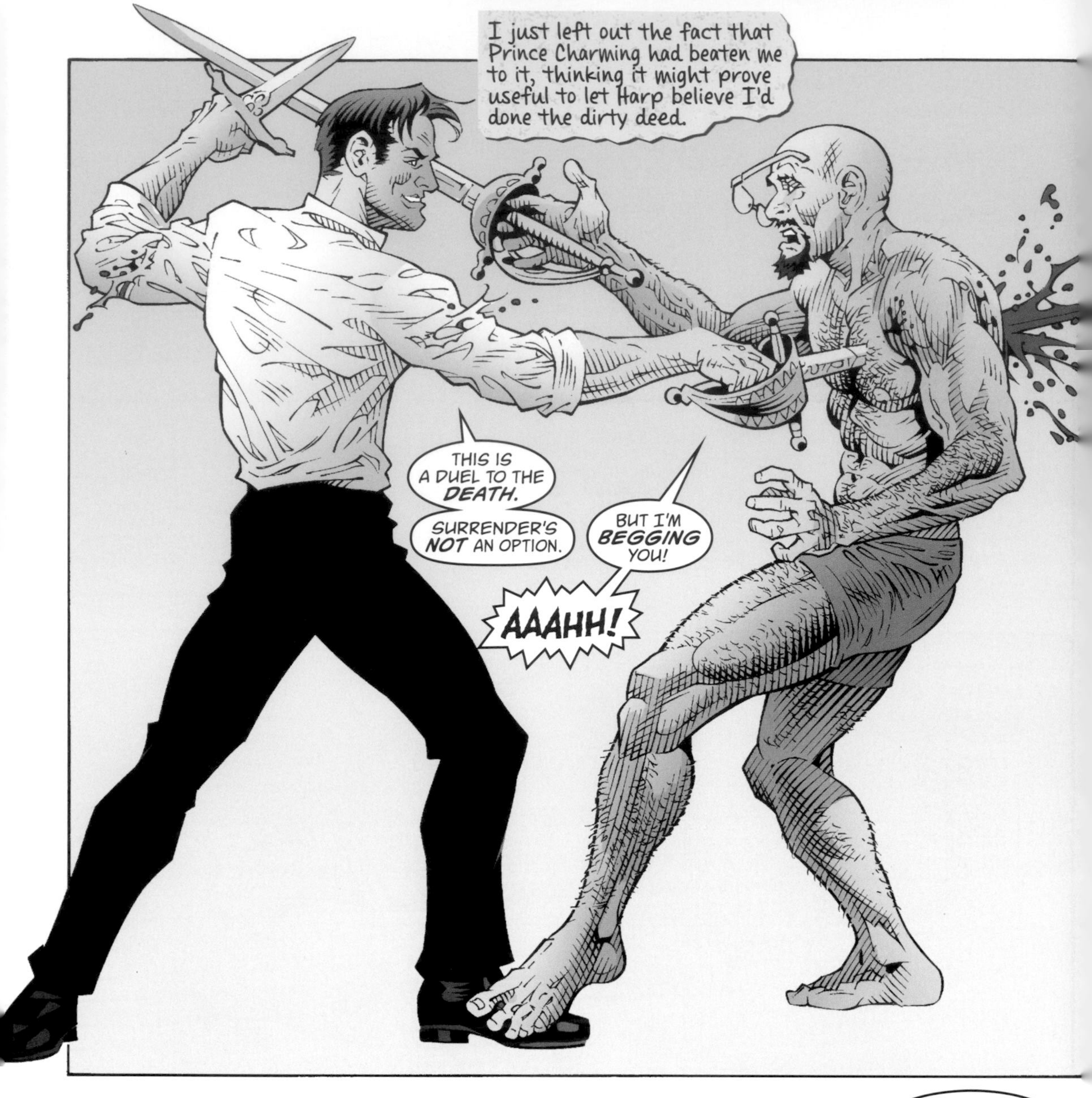
I just left out the fact that Prince Charming had beaten me to it, thinking it might prove useful to let Harp believe I'd done the dirty deed.
THIS IS A DUEL TO THE DEATH.
SURRENDER'S NOT AN OPTION.
BUT I'M BEGGING YOU!
AAAHH!

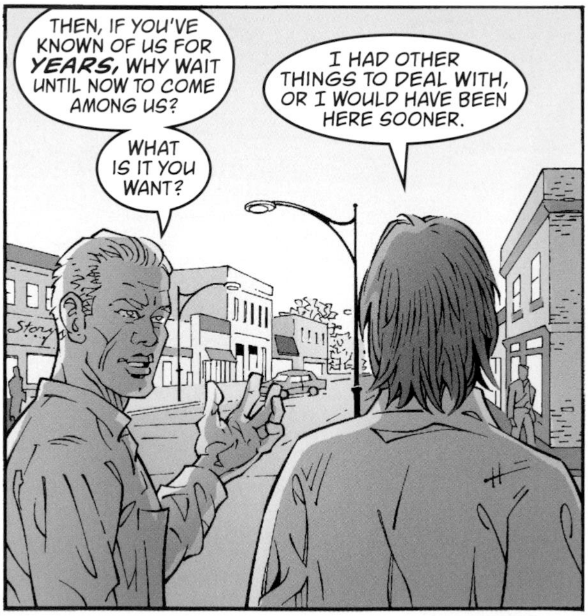
THEN, IF YOU'VE KNOWN OF US FOR YEARS, WHY WAIT UNTIL NOW TO COME AMONG US?
WHAT IS IT YOU WANT?
I HAD OTHER THINGS TO DEAL WITH, OR I WOULD HAVE BEEN HERE SOONER.

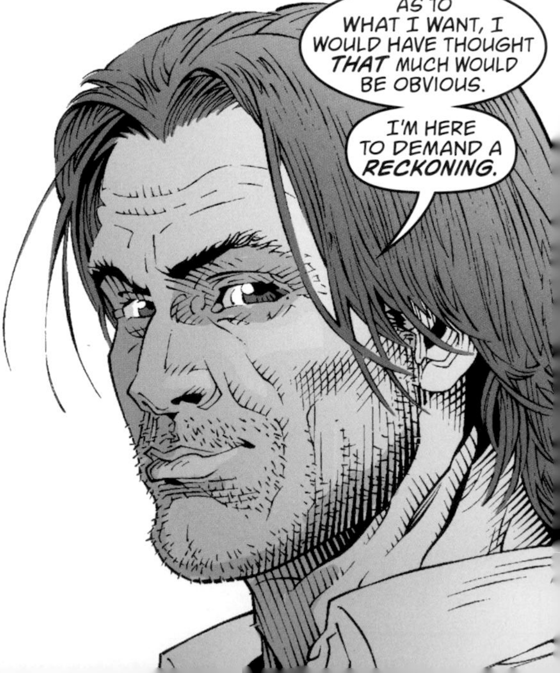
AS TO WHAT I WANT, I WOULD HAVE THOUGHT THAT MUCH WOULD BE OBVIOUS.
I'M HERE TO DEMAND A RECKONING.

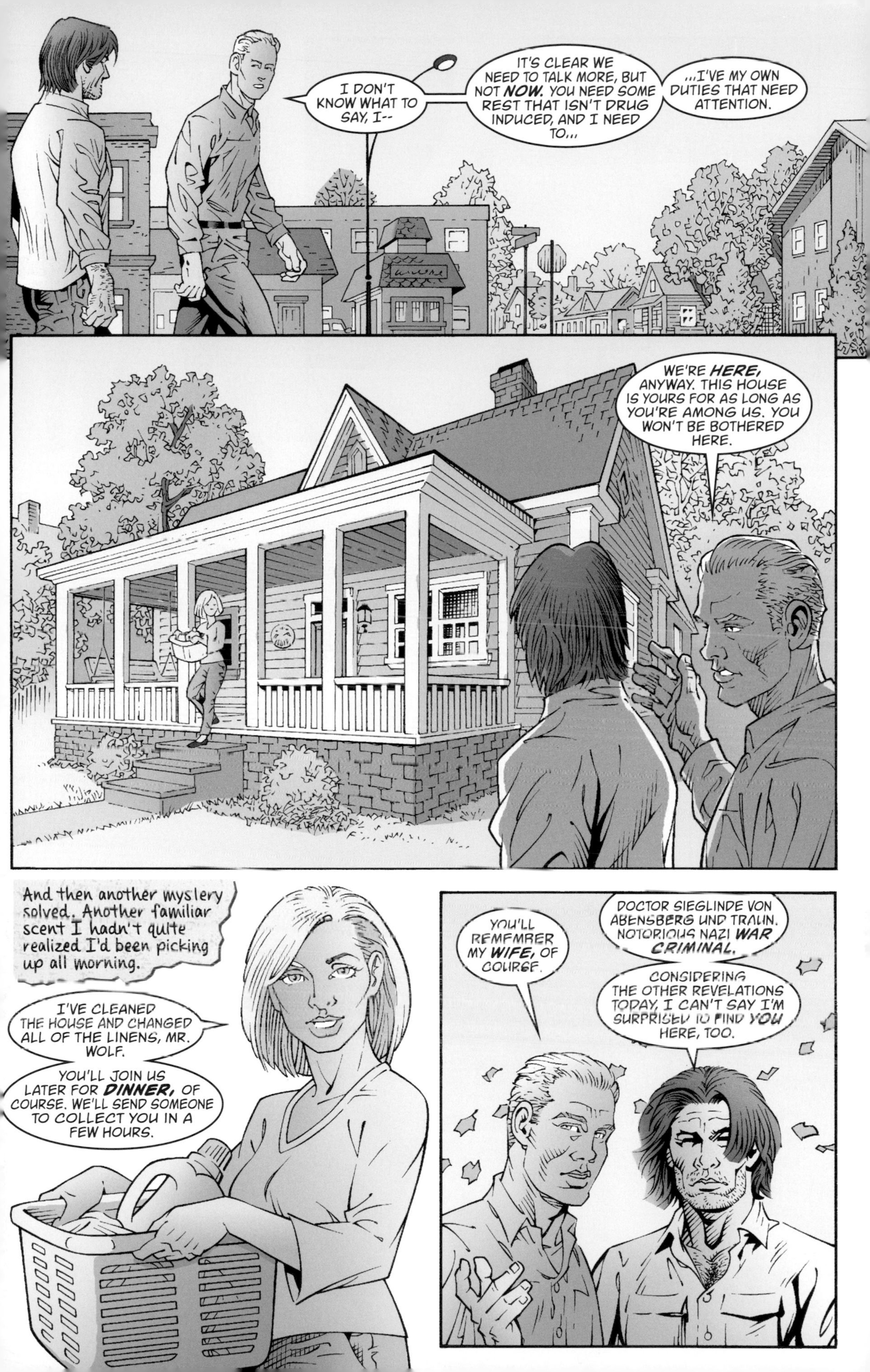
I DON'T KNOW WHAT TO SAY, I--
IT'S CLEAR WE NEED TO TALK MORE, BUT NOT NOW. YOU NEED SOME REST THAT ISN'T DRUG INDUCED, AND I NEED TO...
...I'VE MY OWN DUTIES THAT NEED ATTENTION.
WE'RE HERE, ANYWAY. THIS HOUSE IS YOURS FOR AS LONG AS YOU'RE AMONG US. YOU WON'T BE BOTHERED HERE.
And then another mystery solved. Another familiar scent I hadn't quite realized I'd been picking up all morning.
I'VE CLEANED THE HOUSE AND CHANGED ALL OF THE LINENS, MR. WOLF.
YOU'LL JOIN US LATER FOR DINNER, OF COURSE. WE'LL SEND SOMEONE TO COLLECT YOU IN A FEW HOURS.
YOU'LL REMEMBER MY WIFE, OF COURSE.
DOCTOR SIEGLINDE VON ABENSBERG UND TRAUN. NOTORIOUS NAZI WAR CRIMINAL.
CONSIDERING THE OTHER REVELATIONS TODAY, I CAN'T SAY I'M SURPRISED TO FIND YOU HERE, TOO.

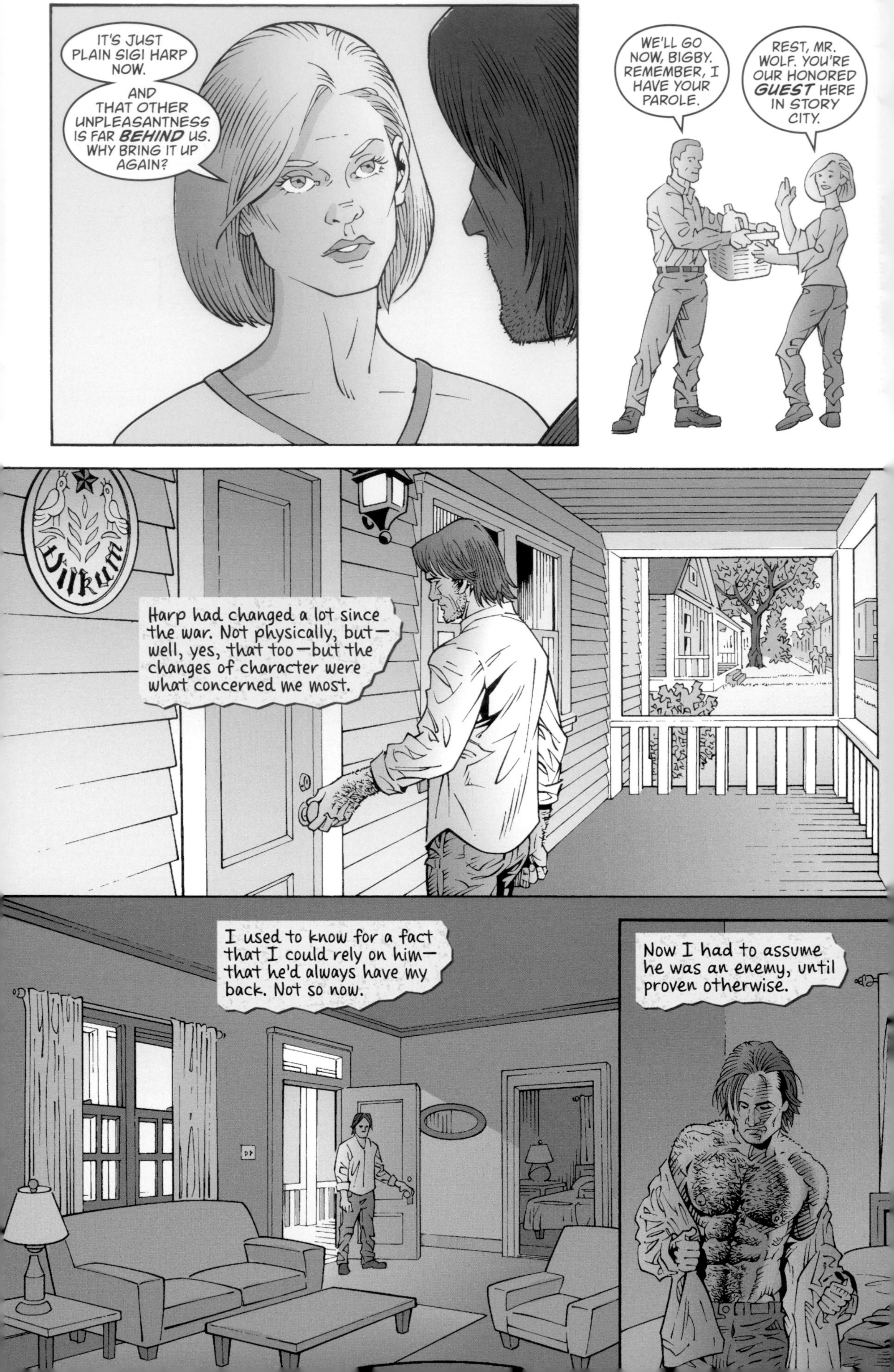
IT'S JUST PLAIN SIGI HARP NOW.
AND THAT OTHER UNPLEASANTNESS IS FAR BEHIND US. WHY BRING IT UP AGAIN?
WE'LL GO NOW, BIGBY. REMEMBER, I HAVE YOUR PAROLE.
REST, MR. WOLF. YOU'RE OUR HONORED GUEST HERE IN STORY CITY.
Vilkum
Harp had changed a lot since the war. Not physically, but—well, yes, that too—but the changes of character were what concerned me most.
I used to know for a fact that I could rely on him—that he'd always have my back. Not so now.
Now I had to assume he was an enemy, until proven otherwise.

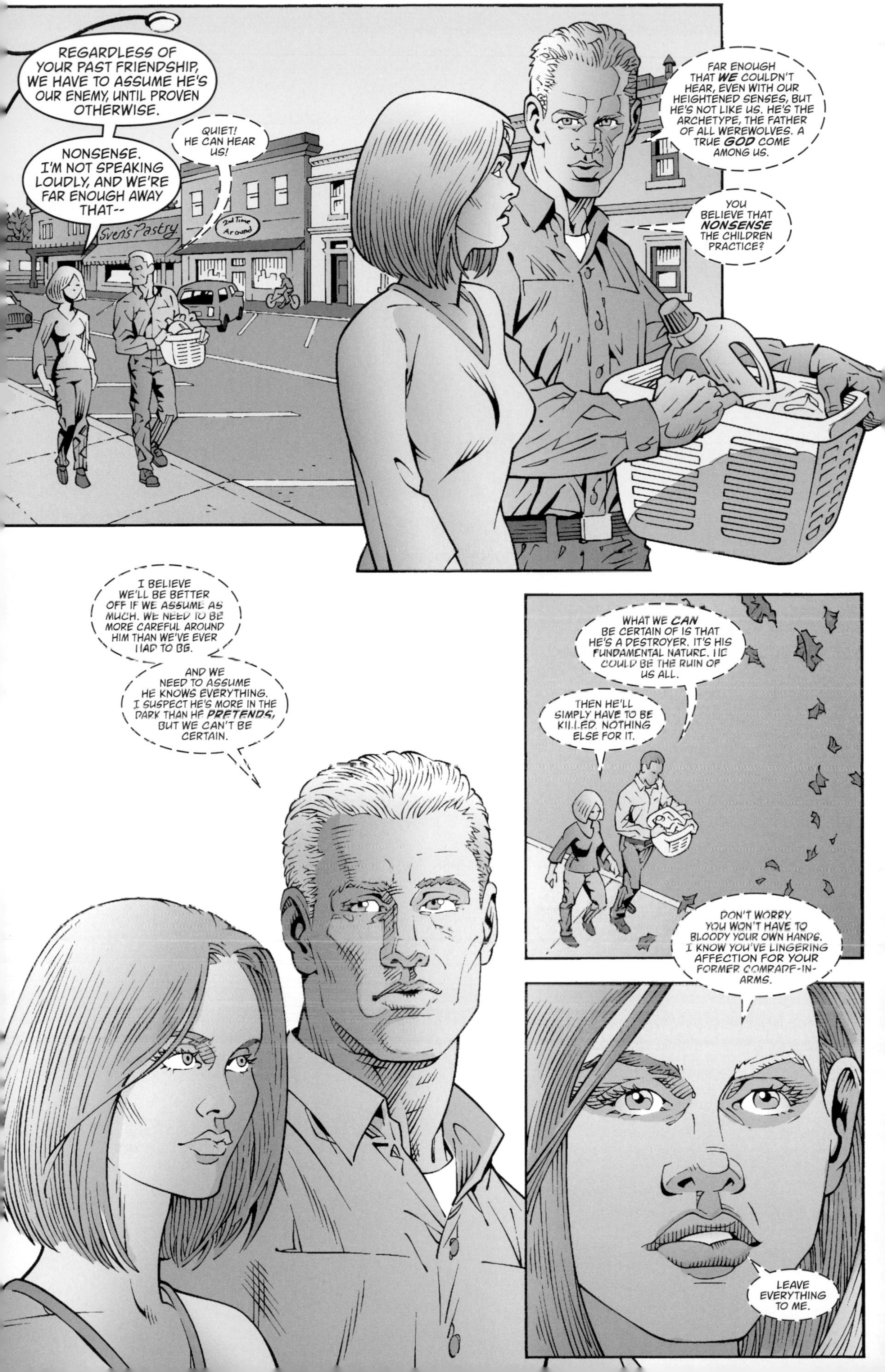
REGARDLESS OF YOUR PAST FRIENDSHIP, WE HAVE TO ASSUME HE'S OUR ENEMY, UNTIL PROVEN OTHERWISE.
NONSENSE. I'M NOT SPEAKING LOUDLY, AND WE'RE FAR ENOUGH AWAY THAT--
QUIET! HE CAN HEAR US!
Sven's Pastry
2nd Time Around
FAR ENOUGH THAT WE COULDN'T HEAR, EVEN WITH OUR HEIGHTENED SENSES, BUT HE'S NOT LIKE US. HE'S THE ARCHETYPE, THE FATHER OF ALL WEREWOLVES. A TRUE GOD COME AMONG US.
YOU BELIEVE THAT NONSENSE THE CHILDREN PRACTICE?
I BELIEVE WE'LL BE BETTER OFF IF WE ASSUME AS MUCH. WE NEED TO BE MORE CAREFUL AROUND HIM THAN WE'VE EVER HAD TO BE.
AND WE NEED TO ASSUME HE KNOWS EVERYTHING. I SUSPECT HE'S MORE IN THE DARK THAN HE PRETENDS, BUT WE CAN'T BE CERTAIN.
WHAT WE CAN BE CERTAIN OF IS THAT HE'S A DESTROYER. IT'S HIS FUNDAMENTAL NATURE. HE COULD BE THE RUIN OF US ALL.
THEN HE'LL SIMPLY HAVE TO BE KILLED. NOTHING ELSE FOR IT.
DON'T WORRY. YOU WON'T HAVE TO BLOODY YOUR OWN HANDS. I KNOW YOU'VE LINGERING AFFECTION FOR YOUR FORMER COMRADE-IN-ARMS.
LEAVE EVERYTHING TO ME.

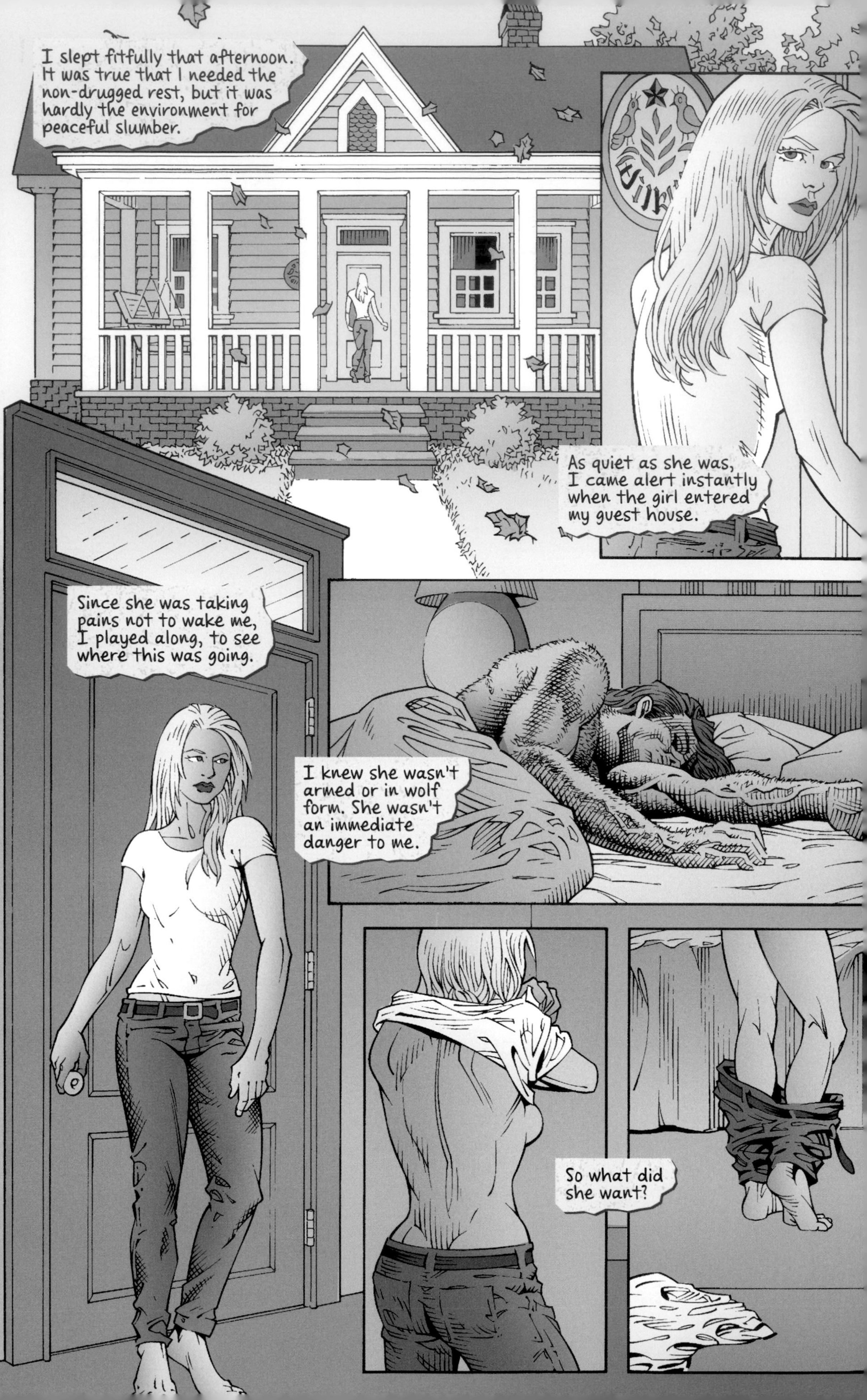
I slept fitfully that afternoon. It was true that I needed the non-drugged rest, but it was hardly the environment for peaceful slumber.
As quiet as she was, I came alert instantly when the girl entered my guest house.
Since she was taking pains not to wake me, I played along, to see where this was going.
I knew she wasn't armed or in wolf form. She wasn't an immediate danger to me.
So what did she want?

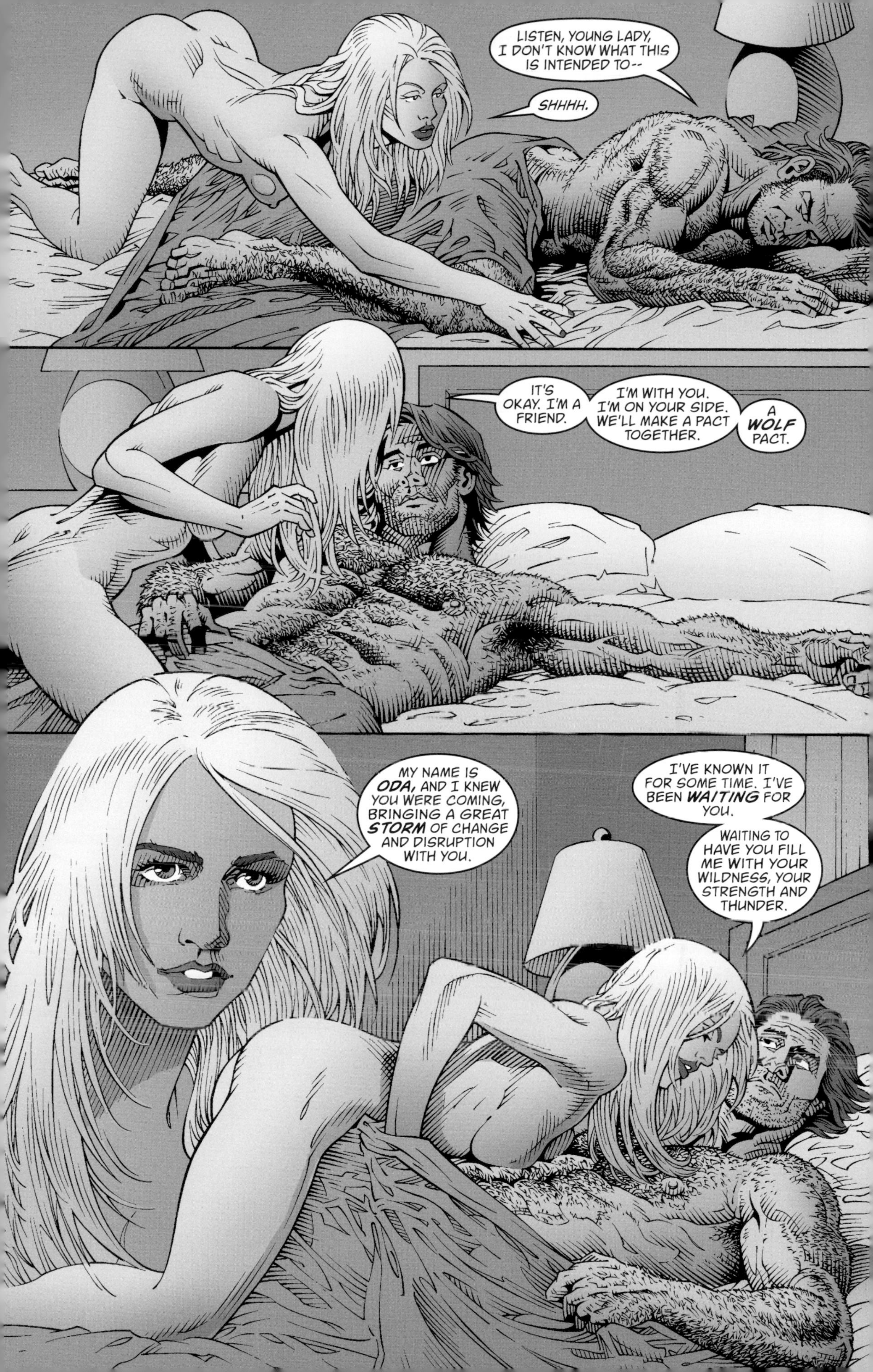
LISTEN, YOUNG LADY, I DON'T KNOW WHAT THIS IS INTENDED TO--
SHHHH.
IT'S OKAY. I'M A FRIEND.
I'M WITH YOU. I'M ON YOUR SIDE. WE'LL MAKE A PACT TOGETHER.
A WOLF PACT.
MY NAME IS ODA, AND I KNEW YOU WERE COMING, BRINGING A GREAT STORM OF CHANGE AND DISRUPTION WITH YOU.
I'VE KNOWN IT FOR SOME TIME. I'VE BEEN WAITING FOR YOU.
WAITING TO HAVE YOU FILL ME WITH YOUR WILDNESS, YOUR STRENGTH AND THUNDER.

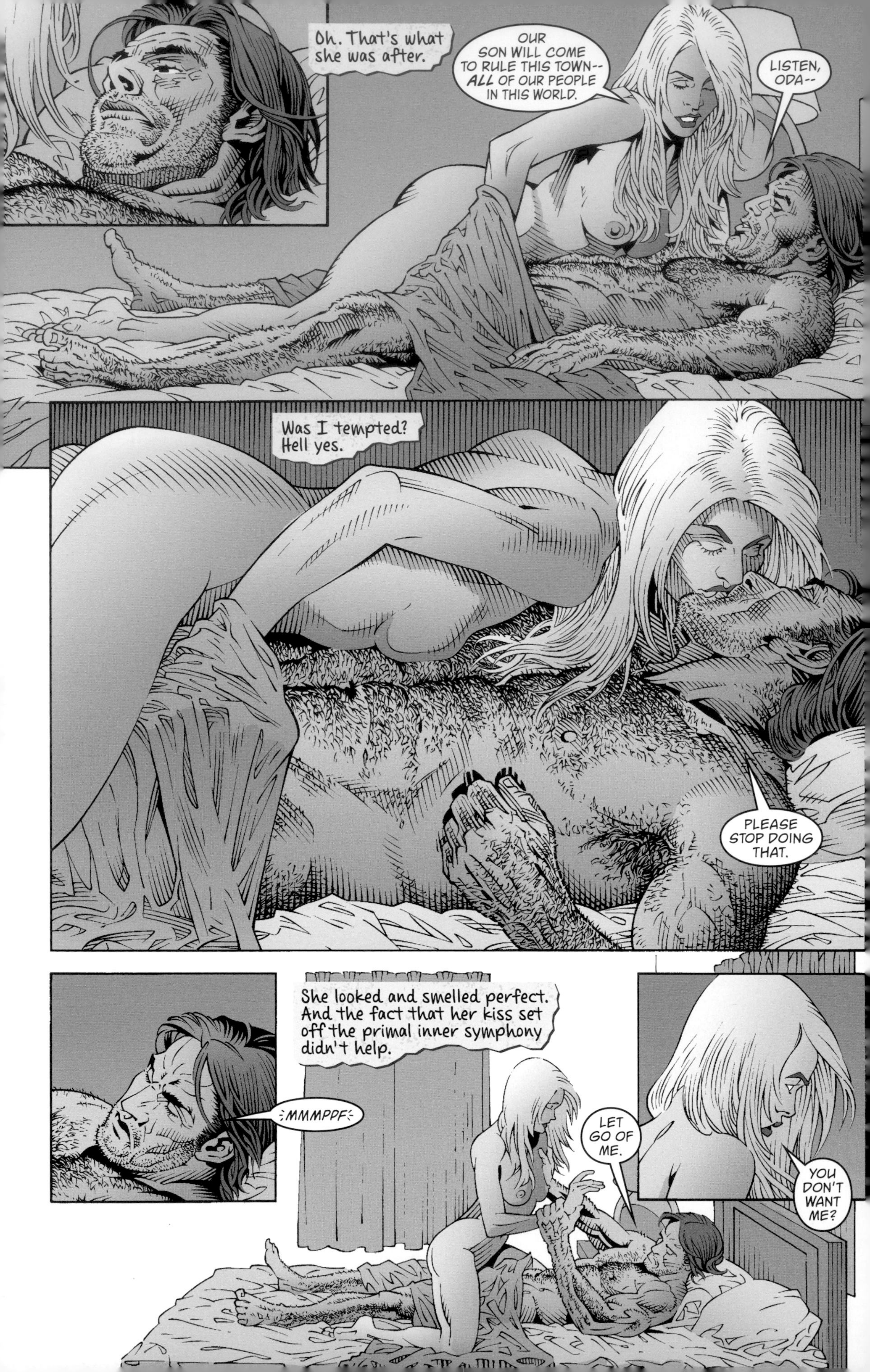
Oh. That's what she was after.
OUR SON WILL COME TO RULE THIS TOWN-- ALL OF OUR PEOPLE IN THIS WORLD.
LISTEN, ODA--
Was I tempted? Hell yes.
PLEASE STOP DOING THAT.
She looked and smelled perfect. And the fact that her kiss set off the primal inner symphony didn't help.
MMMPPF
LET GO OF ME.
YOU DON'T WANT ME?

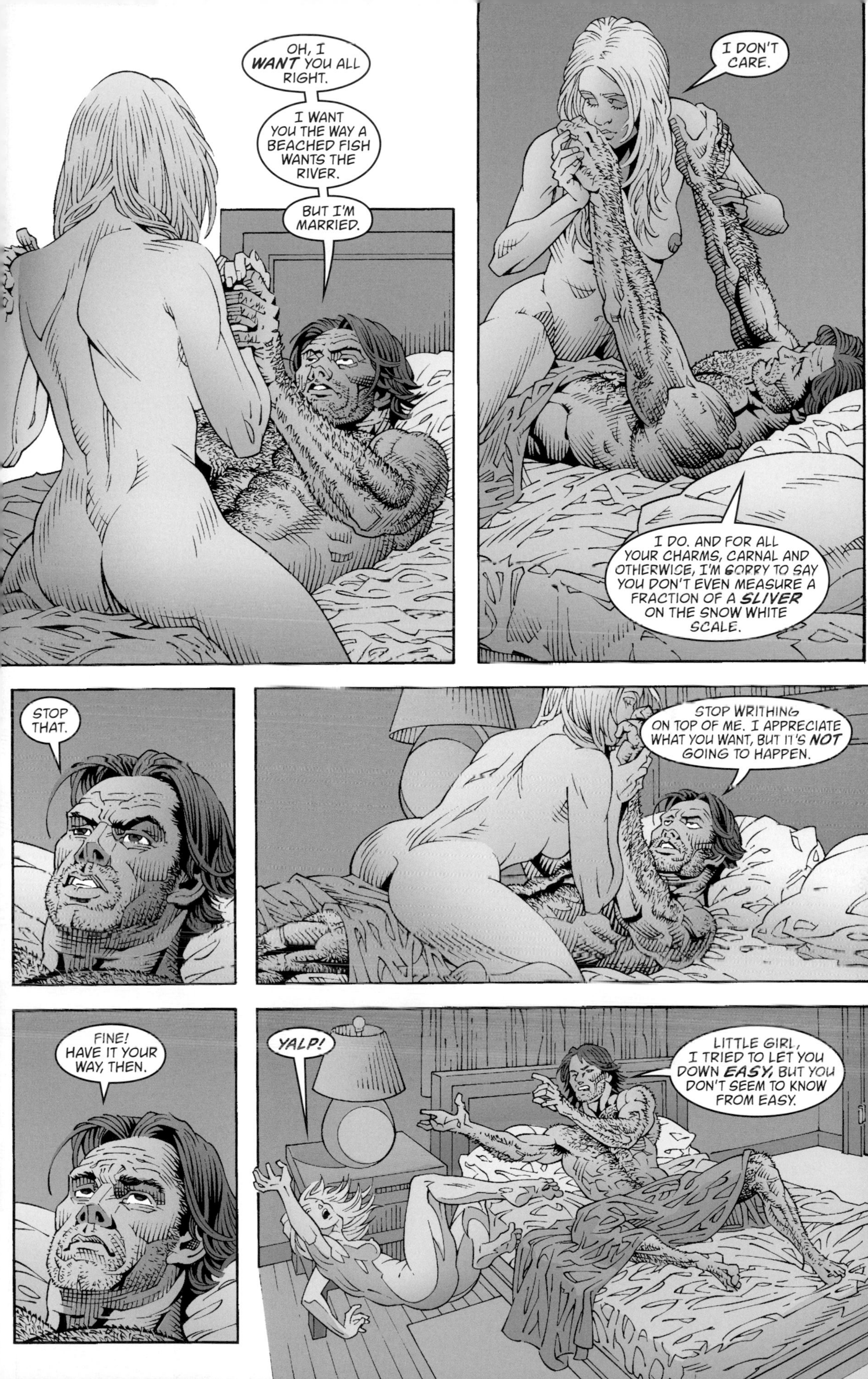
OH, I *WANT* YOU ALL RIGHT.
I WANT YOU THE WAY A BEACHED FISH WANTS THE RIVER.
BUT I'M MARRIED.
I DON'T CARE.
I DO. AND FOR ALL YOUR CHARMS, CARNAL AND OTHERWISE, I'M SORRY TO SAY YOU DON'T EVEN MEASURE A FRACTION OF A *SLIVER* ON THE SNOW WHITE SCALE.
STOP THAT.
STOP WRITHING ON TOP OF ME. I APPRECIATE WHAT YOU WANT, BUT IT'S *NOT* GOING TO HAPPEN.
FINE! HAVE IT YOUR WAY, THEN.
YALP!
LITTLE GIRL, I TRIED TO LET YOU DOWN *EASY,* BUT YOU DON'T SEEM TO KNOW FROM EASY.

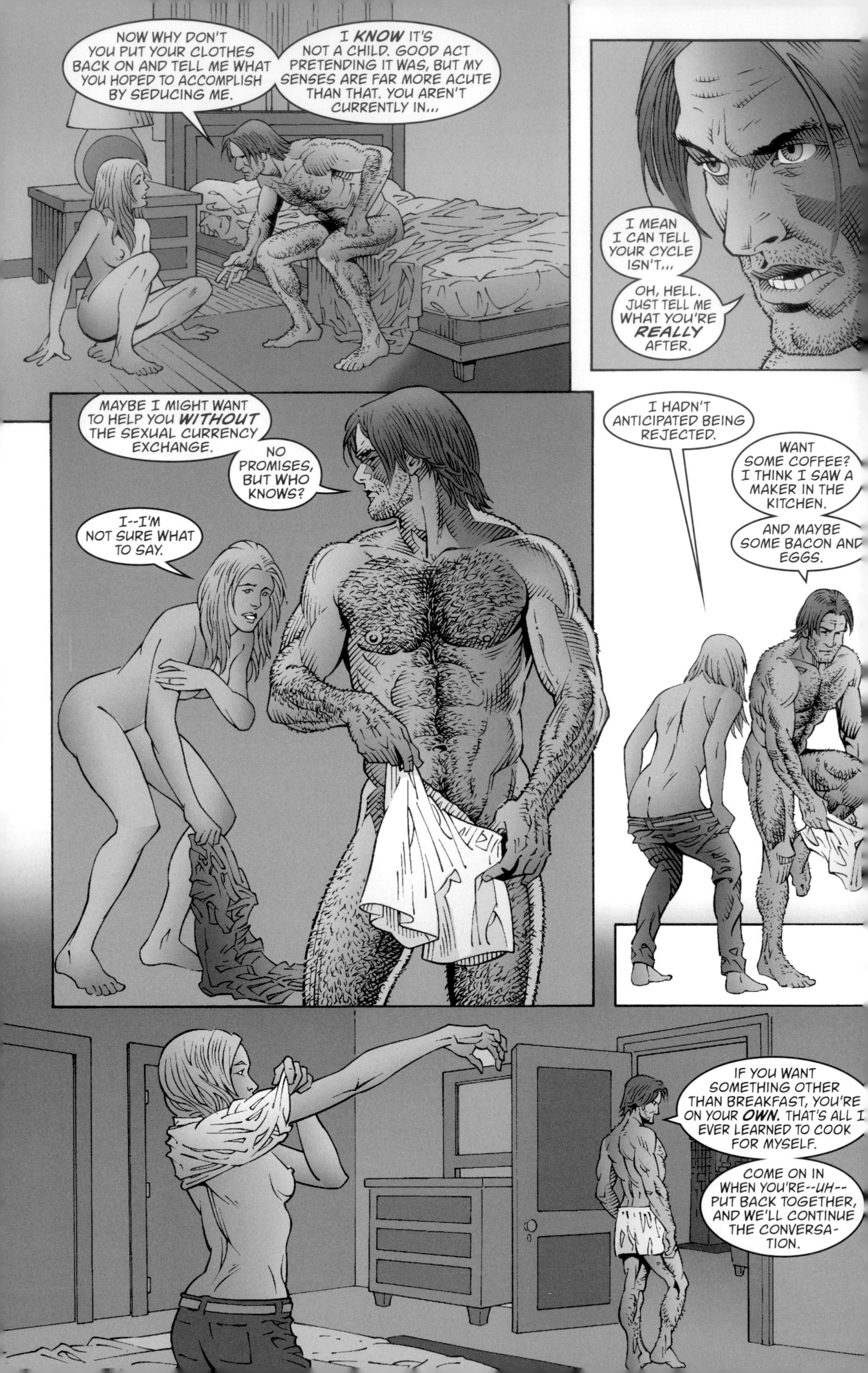
NOW WHY DON'T YOU PUT YOUR CLOTHES BACK ON AND TELL ME WHAT YOU HOPED TO ACCOMPLISH BY SEDUCING ME.
I KNOW IT'S NOT A CHILD. GOOD ACT PRETENDING IT WAS, BUT MY SENSES ARE FAR MORE ACUTE THAN THAT. YOU AREN'T CURRENTLY IN...
I MEAN I CAN TELL YOUR CYCLE ISN'T...
OH, HELL. JUST TELL ME WHAT YOU'RE REALLY AFTER.
MAYBE I MIGHT WANT TO HELP YOU WITHOUT THE SEXUAL CURRENCY EXCHANGE.
NO PROMISES, BUT WHO KNOWS?
I--I'M NOT SURE WHAT TO SAY.
I HADN'T ANTICIPATED BEING REJECTED.
WANT SOME COFFEE? I THINK I SAW A MAKER IN THE KITCHEN.
AND MAYBE SOME BACON AND EGGS.
IF YOU WANT SOMETHING OTHER THAN BREAKFAST, YOU'RE ON YOUR OWN. THAT'S ALL I EVER LEARNED TO COOK FOR MYSELF.
COME ON IN WHEN YOU'RE--UH--PUT BACK TOGETHER, AND WE'LL CONTINUE THE CONVERSA-TION.

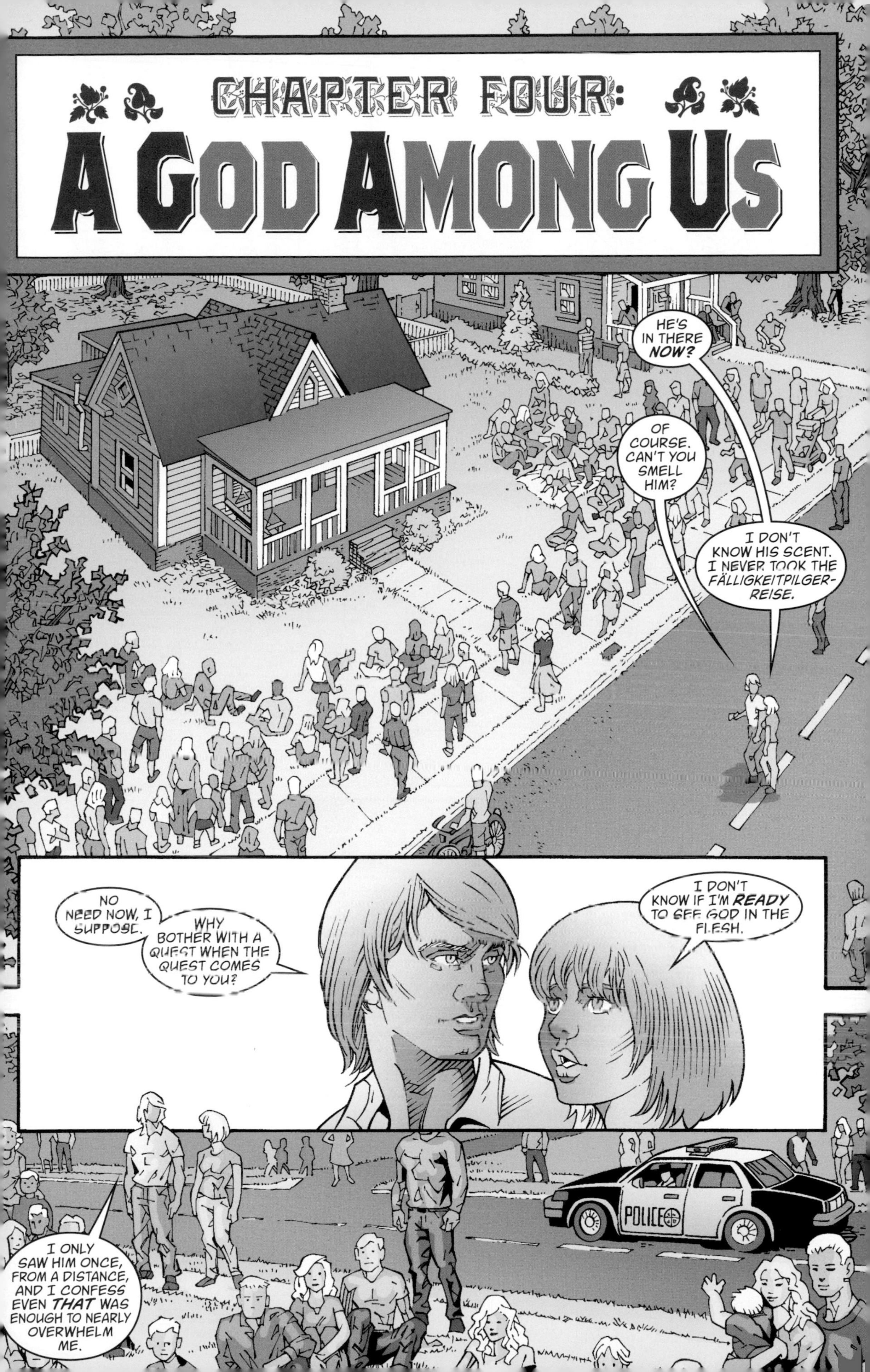
CHAPTER FOUR:
A GOD AMONG US
HE'S IN THERE NOW?
OF COURSE. CAN'T YOU SMELL HIM?
I DON'T KNOW HIS SCENT. I NEVER TOOK THE FÄLLIGKEITPILGER-REISE.
NO NEED NOW, I SUPPOSE.
WHY BOTHER WITH A QUEST WHEN THE QUEST COMES TO YOU?
I DON'T KNOW IF I'M READY TO SEE GOD IN THE FLESH.
I ONLY SAW HIM ONCE, FROM A DISTANCE, AND I CONFESS EVEN THAT WAS ENOUGH TO NEARLY OVERWHELM ME.
POLICE

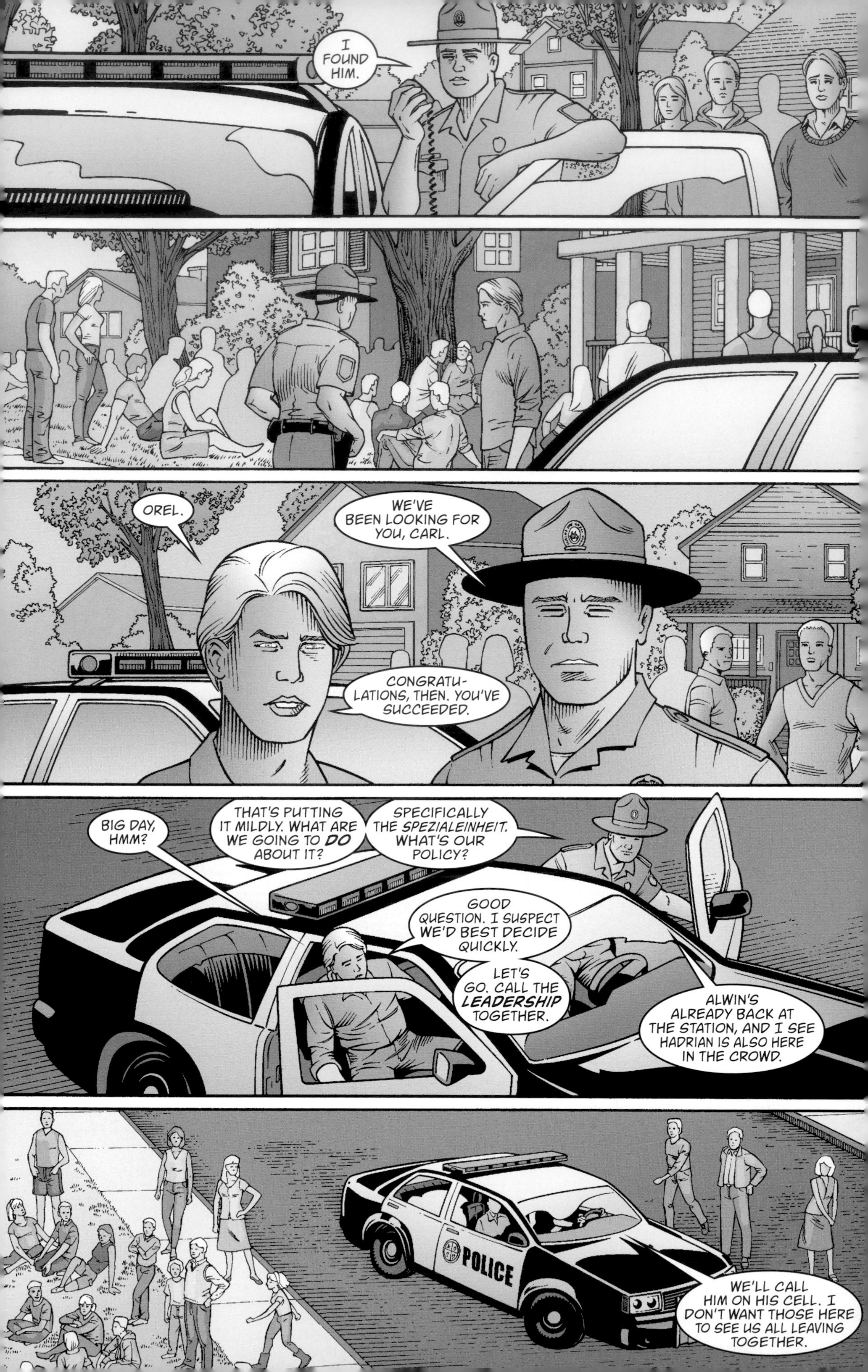
I FOUND HIM.
OREL.
WE'VE BEEN LOOKING FOR YOU, CARL.
CONGRATULATIONS, THEN. YOU'VE SUCCEEDED.
BIG DAY, HMM?
THAT'S PUTTING IT MILDLY. WHAT ARE WE GOING TO DO ABOUT IT?
SPECIFICALLY THE SPEZIALEINHEIT. WHAT'S OUR POLICY?
GOOD QUESTION. I SUSPECT WE'D BEST DECIDE QUICKLY.
LET'S GO. CALL THE LEADERSHIP TOGETHER.
ALWIN'S ALREADY BACK AT THE STATION, AND I SEE HADRIAN IS ALSO HERE IN THE CROWD.
POLICE
WE'LL CALL HIM ON HIS CELL. I DON'T WANT THOSE HERE TO SEE US ALL LEAVING TOGETHER.

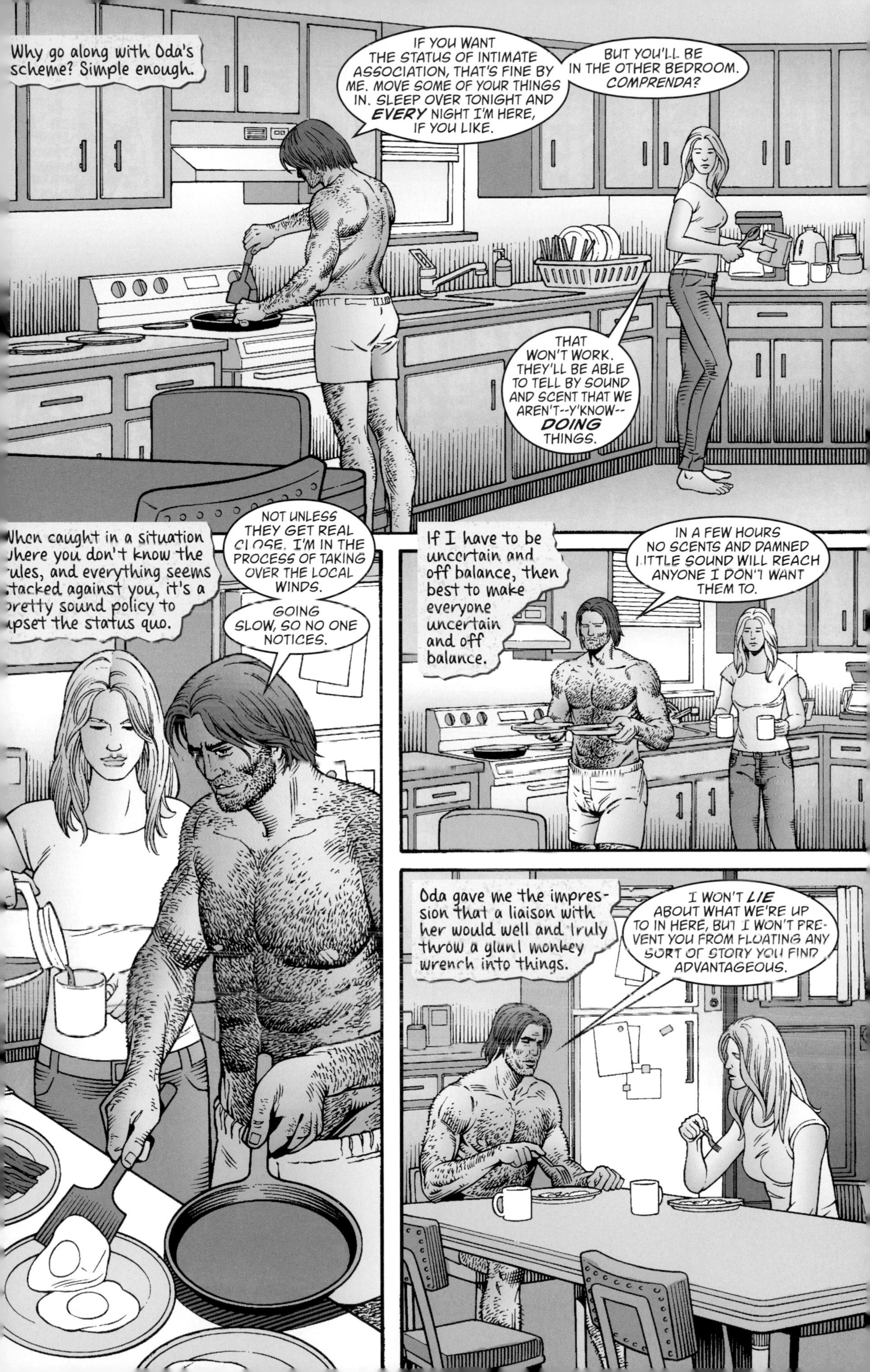

Why go along with Oda's scheme? Simple enough.
IF YOU WANT THE STATUS OF INTIMATE ASSOCIATION, THAT'S FINE BY ME. MOVE SOME OF YOUR THINGS IN. SLEEP OVER TONIGHT AND EVERY NIGHT I'M HERE, IF YOU LIKE.
BUT YOU'LL BE IN THE OTHER BEDROOM. COMPRENDA?
THAT WON'T WORK. THEY'LL BE ABLE TO TELL BY SOUND AND SCENT THAT WE AREN'T--Y'KNOW--DOING THINGS.
When caught in a situation where you don't know the rules, and everything seems stacked against you, it's a pretty sound policy to upset the status quo.
NOT UNLESS THEY GET REAL CLOSE. I'M IN THE PROCESS OF TAKING OVER THE LOCAL WINDS.
GOING SLOW, SO NO ONE NOTICES.
If I have to be uncertain and off balance, then best to make everyone uncertain and off balance.
IN A FEW HOURS NO SCENTS AND DAMNED LITTLE SOUND WILL REACH ANYONE I DON'T WANT THEM TO.
Oda gave me the impression that a liaison with her would well and truly throw a giant monkey wrench into things.
I WON'T LIE ABOUT WHAT WE'RE UP TO IN HERE, BUT I WON'T PREVENT YOU FROM FLOATING ANY SORT OF STORY YOU FIND ADVANTAGEOUS.

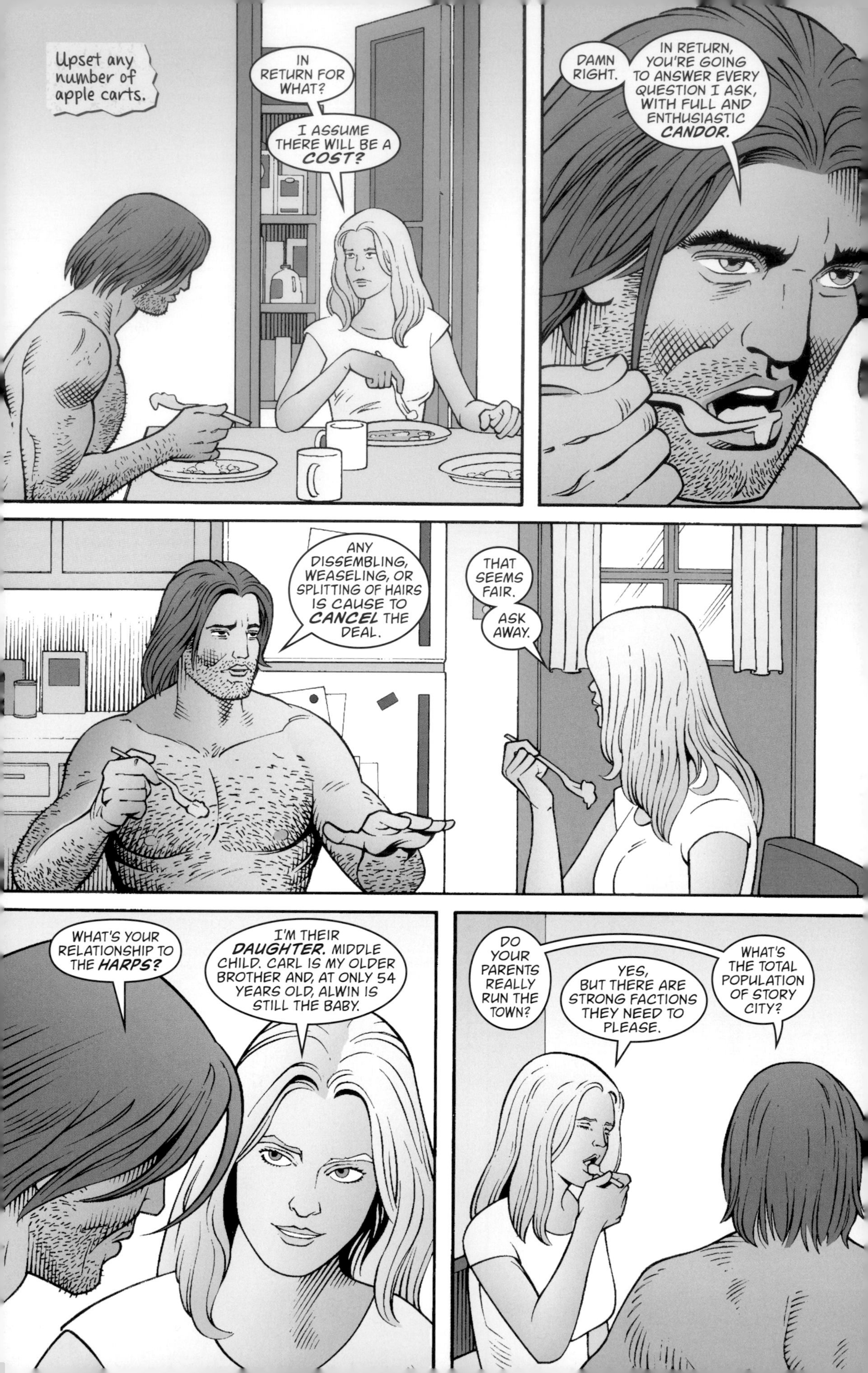
Upset any number of apple carts.
IN RETURN FOR WHAT?
I ASSUME THERE WILL BE A COST?
DAMN RIGHT.
IN RETURN, YOU'RE GOING TO ANSWER EVERY QUESTION I ASK, WITH FULL AND ENTHUSIASTIC CANDOR.
ANY DISSEMBLING, WEASELING, OR SPLITTING OF HAIRS IS CAUSE TO CANCEL THE DEAL.
THAT SEEMS FAIR.
ASK AWAY.
WHAT'S YOUR RELATIONSHIP TO THE HARPS?
I'M THEIR DAUGHTER. MIDDLE CHILD. CARL IS MY OLDER BROTHER AND, AT ONLY 54 YEARS OLD, ALWIN IS STILL THE BABY.
DO YOUR PARENTS REALLY RUN THE TOWN?
YES, BUT THERE ARE STRONG FACTIONS THEY NEED TO PLEASE.
WHAT'S THE TOTAL POPULATION OF STORY CITY?

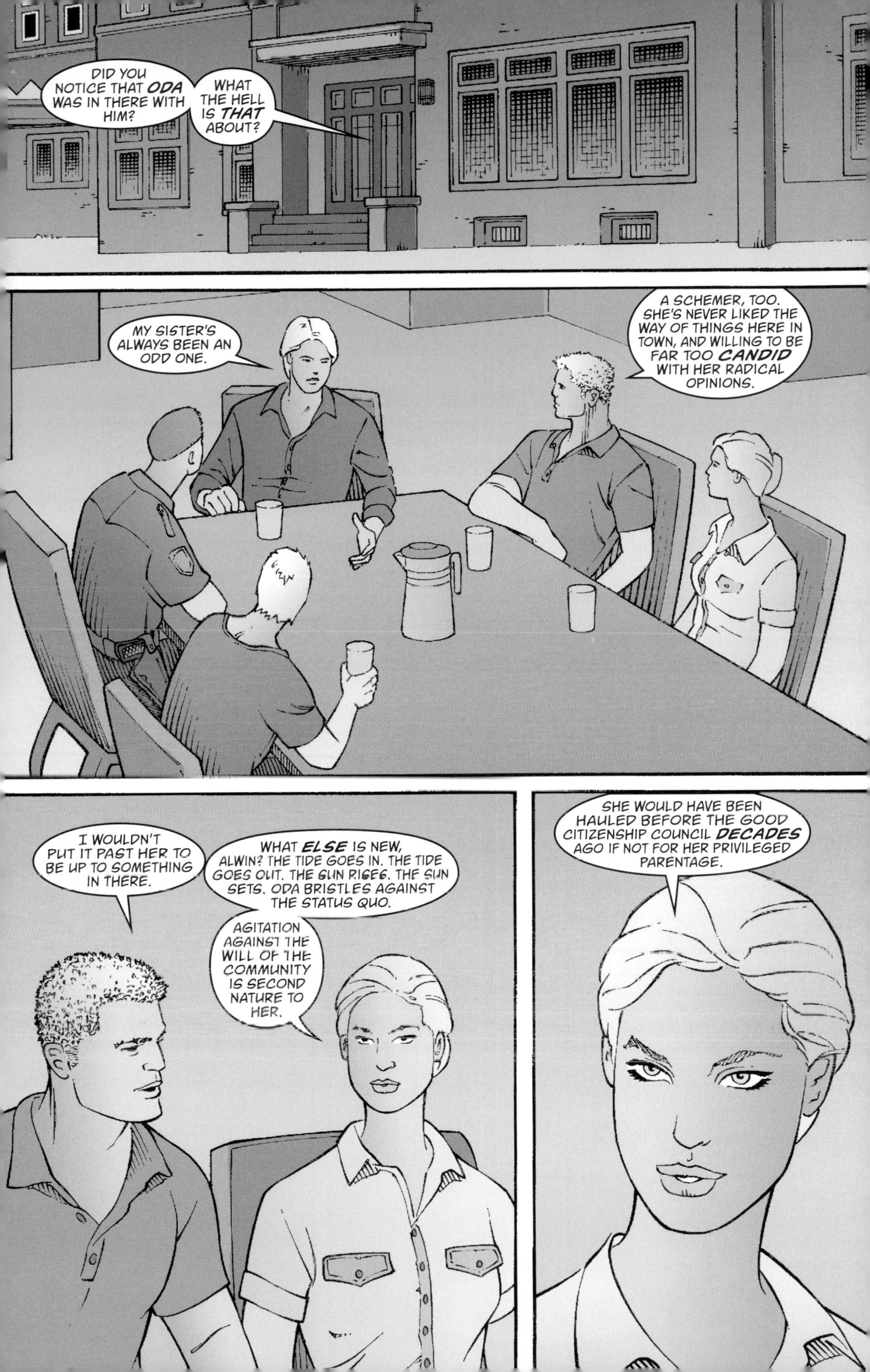
DID YOU NOTICE THAT ODA WAS IN THERE WITH HIM?
WHAT THE HELL IS THAT ABOUT?
MY SISTER'S ALWAYS BEEN AN ODD ONE.
A SCHEMER, TOO. SHE'S NEVER LIKED THE WAY OF THINGS HERE IN TOWN, AND WILLING TO BE FAR TOO CANDID WITH HER RADICAL OPINIONS.
I WOULDN'T PUT IT PAST HER TO BE UP TO SOMETHING IN THERE.
WHAT ELSE IS NEW, ALWIN? THE TIDE GOES IN. THE TIDE GOES OUT. THE SUN RISES. THE SUN SETS. ODA BRISTLES AGAINST THE STATUS QUO.
AGITATION AGAINST THE WILL OF THE COMMUNITY IS SECOND NATURE TO HER.
SHE WOULD HAVE BEEN HAULED BEFORE THE GOOD CITIZENSHIP COUNCIL DECADES AGO IF NOT FOR HER PRIVILEGED PARENTAGE.

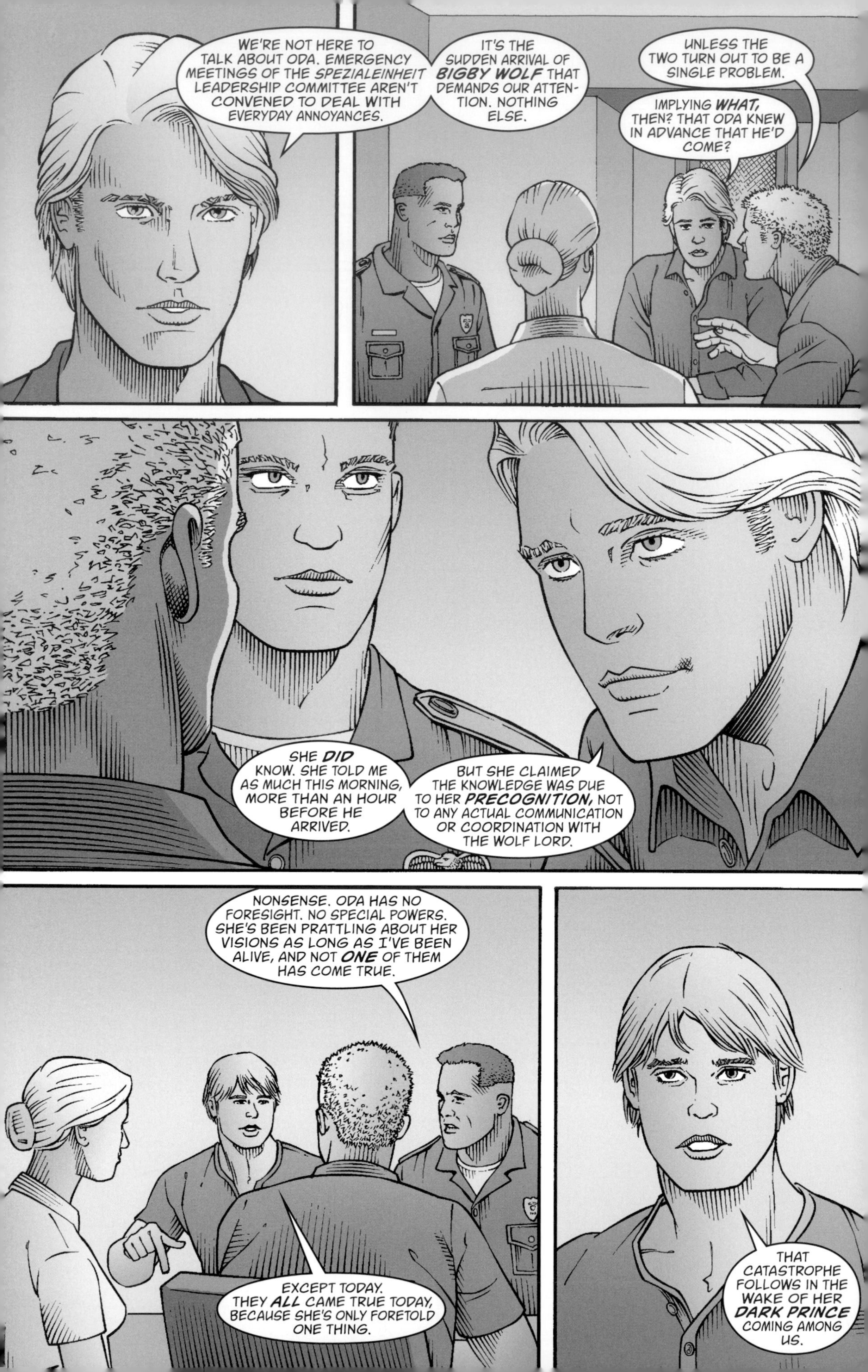
WE'RE NOT HERE TO TALK ABOUT ODA. EMERGENCY MEETINGS OF THE SPEZIALEINHEIT LEADERSHIP COMMITTEE AREN'T CONVENED TO DEAL WITH EVERYDAY ANNOYANCES.
IT'S THE SUDDEN ARRIVAL OF BIGBY WOLF THAT DEMANDS OUR ATTENTION. NOTHING ELSE.
UNLESS THE TWO TURN OUT TO BE A SINGLE PROBLEM.
IMPLYING WHAT, THEN? THAT ODA KNEW IN ADVANCE THAT HE'D COME?
SHE DID KNOW. SHE TOLD ME AS MUCH THIS MORNING, MORE THAN AN HOUR BEFORE HE ARRIVED.
BUT SHE CLAIMED THE KNOWLEDGE WAS DUE TO HER PRECOGNITION, NOT TO ANY ACTUAL COMMUNICATION OR COORDINATION WITH THE WOLF LORD.
NONSENSE. ODA HAS NO FORESIGHT. NO SPECIAL POWERS. SHE'S BEEN PRATTLING ABOUT HER VISIONS AS LONG AS I'VE BEEN ALIVE, AND NOT ONE OF THEM HAS COME TRUE.
EXCEPT TODAY. THEY ALL CAME TRUE TODAY, BECAUSE SHE'S ONLY FORETOLD ONE THING.
THAT CATASTROPHE FOLLOWS IN THE WAKE OF HER DARK PRINCE COMING AMONG US.

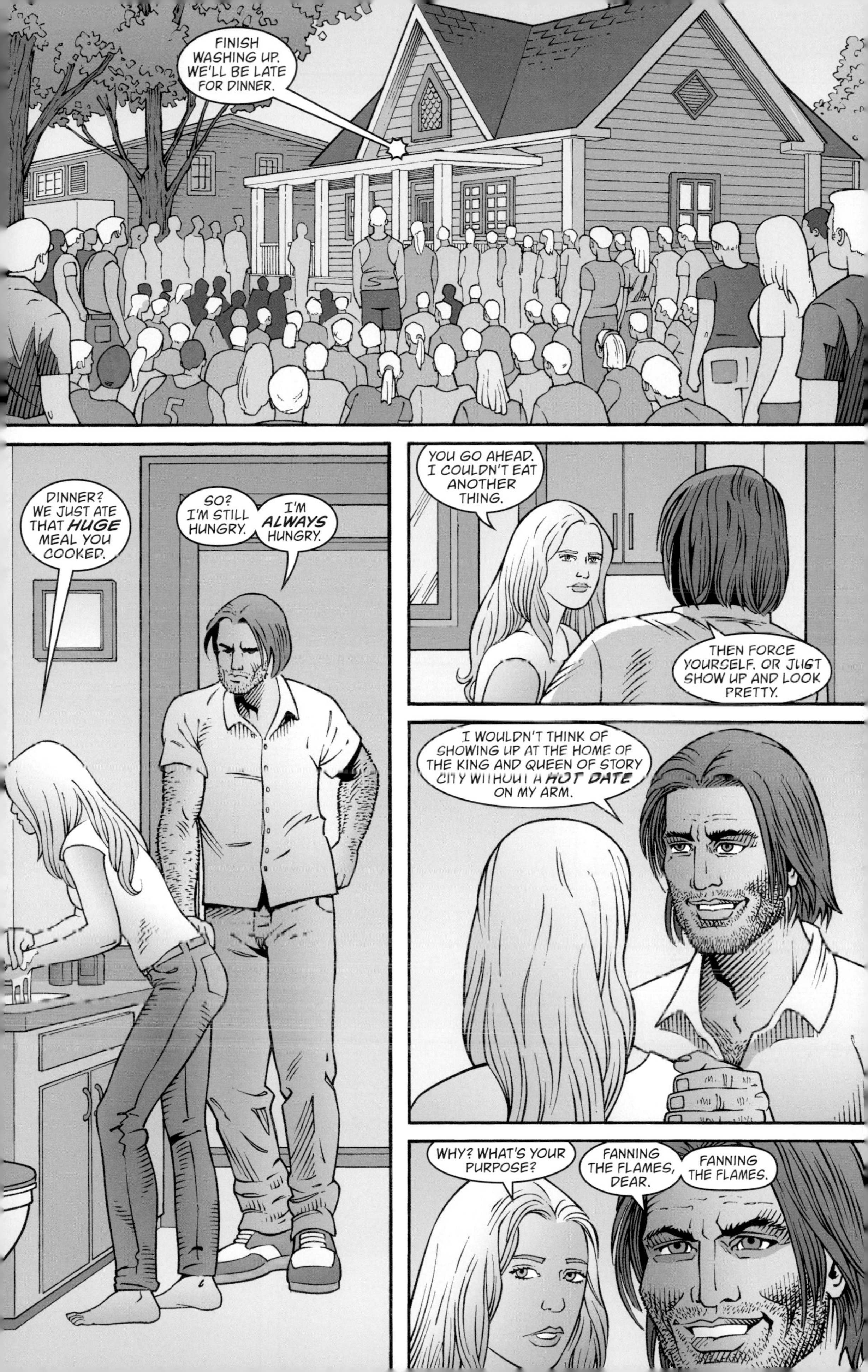
FINISH WASHING UP. WE'LL BE LATE FOR DINNER.
DINNER? WE JUST ATE THAT HUGE MEAL YOU COOKED.
SO? I'M STILL HUNGRY.
I'M ALWAYS HUNGRY.
YOU GO AHEAD. I COULDN'T EAT ANOTHER THING.
THEN FORCE YOURSELF. OR JUST SHOW UP AND LOOK PRETTY.
I WOULDN'T THINK OF SHOWING UP AT THE HOME OF THE KING AND QUEEN OF STORY CITY WITHOUT A HOT DATE ON MY ARM.
WHY? WHAT'S YOUR PURPOSE?
FANNING THE FLAMES, DEAR.
FANNING THE FLAMES.

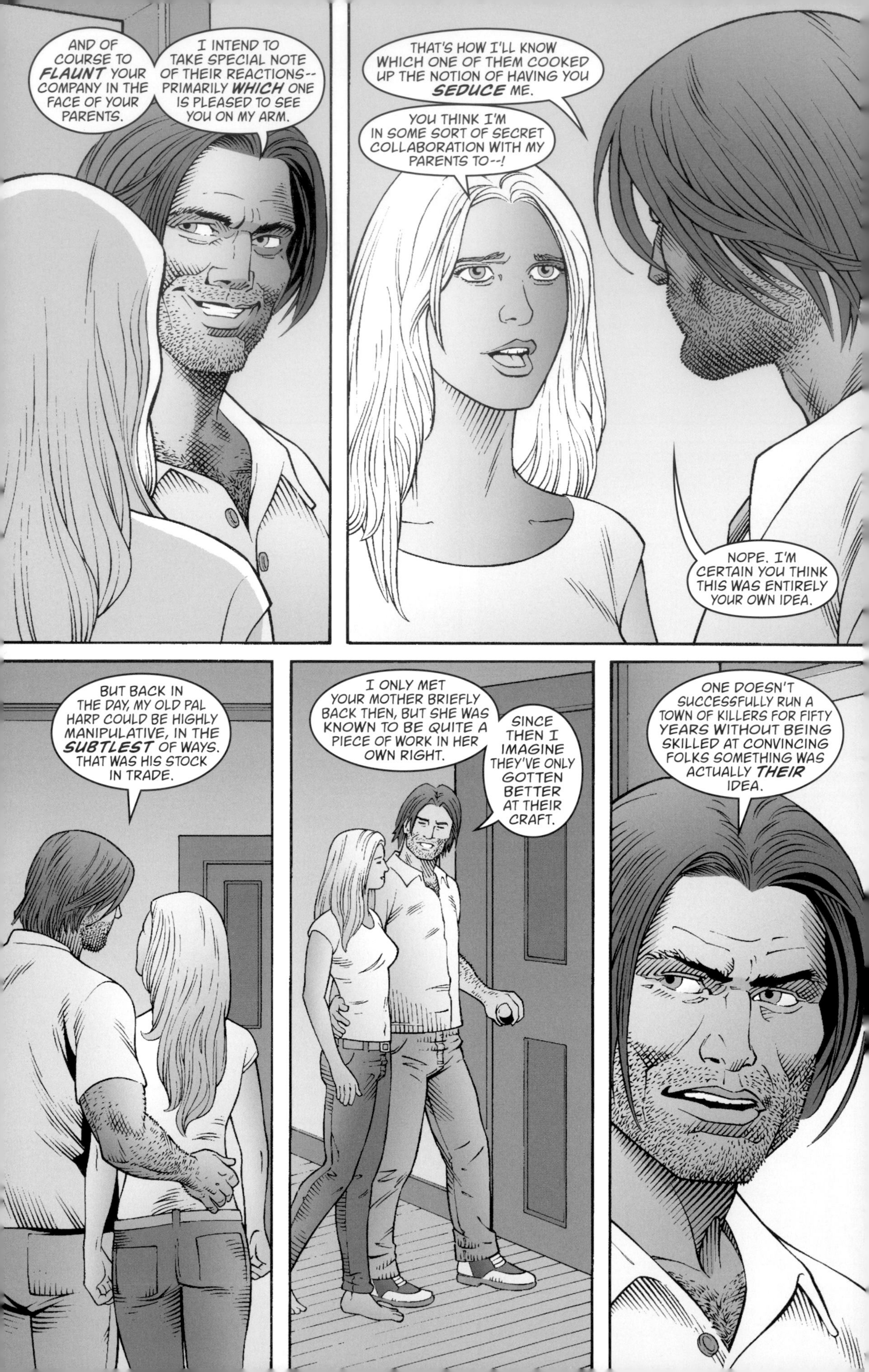
AND OF COURSE TO FLAUNT YOUR COMPANY IN THE FACE OF YOUR PARENTS.
I INTEND TO TAKE SPECIAL NOTE OF THEIR REACTIONS-- PRIMARILY WHICH ONE IS PLEASED TO SEE YOU ON MY ARM.
THAT'S HOW I'LL KNOW WHICH ONE OF THEM COOKED UP THE NOTION OF HAVING YOU SEDUCE ME.
YOU THINK I'M IN SOME SORT OF SECRET COLLABORATION WITH MY PARENTS TO--!
NOPE. I'M CERTAIN YOU THINK THIS WAS ENTIRELY YOUR OWN IDEA.
BUT BACK IN THE DAY, MY OLD PAL HARP COULD BE HIGHLY MANIPULATIVE, IN THE SUBTLEST OF WAYS. THAT WAS HIS STOCK IN TRADE.
I ONLY MET YOUR MOTHER BRIEFLY BACK THEN, BUT SHE WAS KNOWN TO BE QUITE A PIECE OF WORK IN HER OWN RIGHT.
SINCE THEN I IMAGINE THEY'VE ONLY GOTTEN BETTER AT THEIR CRAFT.
ONE DOESN'T SUCCESSFULLY RUN A TOWN OF KILLERS FOR FIFTY YEARS WITHOUT BEING SKILLED AT CONVINCING FOLKS SOMETHING WAS ACTUALLY THEIR IDEA.

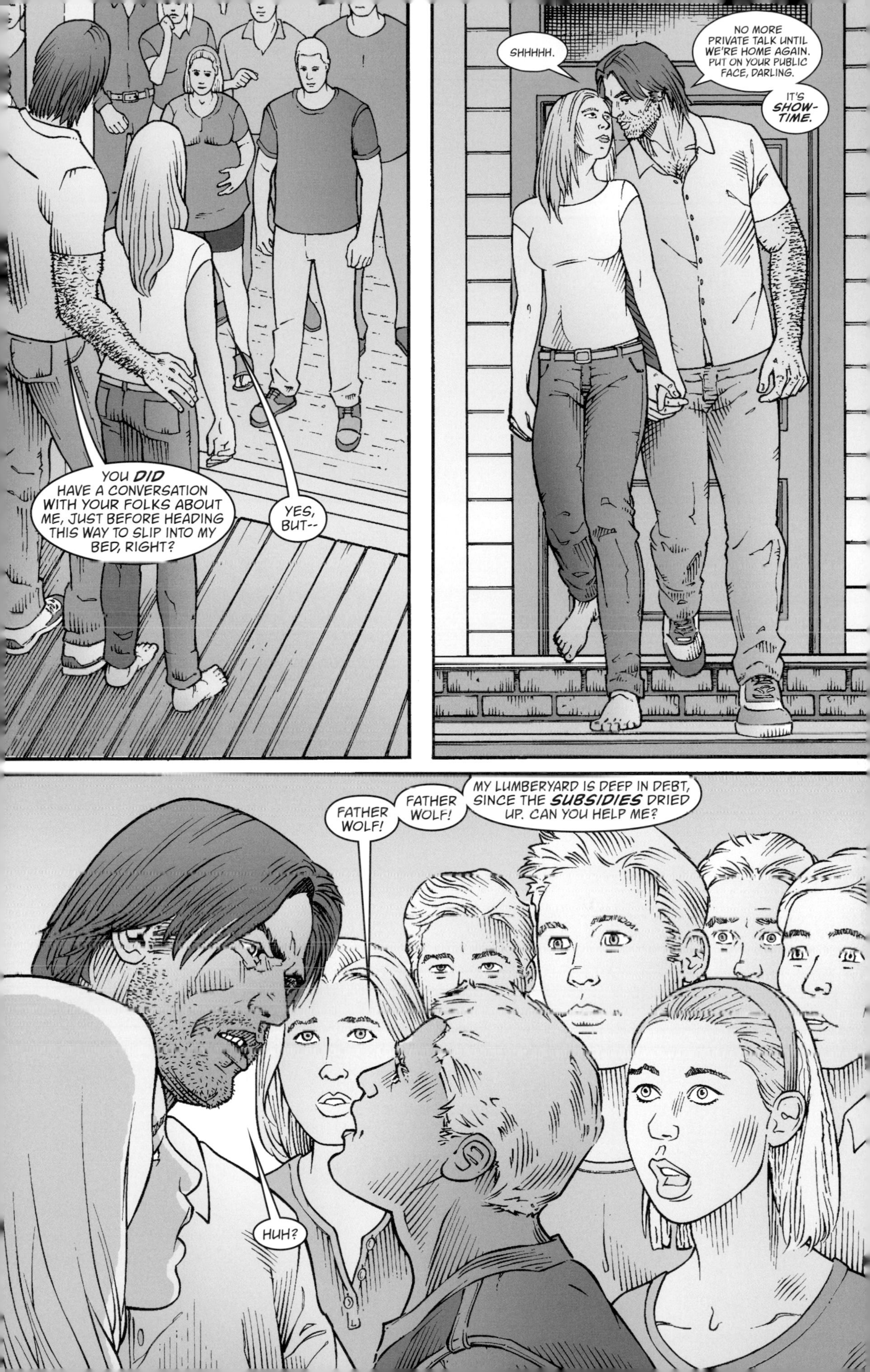
YOU DID HAVE A CONVERSATION WITH YOUR FOLKS ABOUT ME, JUST BEFORE HEADING THIS WAY TO SLIP INTO MY BED, RIGHT?
YES, BUT--
SHHHHH.
NO MORE PRIVATE TALK UNTIL WE'RE HOME AGAIN. PUT ON YOUR PUBLIC FACE, DARLING.
IT'S SHOW-TIME.
FATHER WOLF!
FATHER WOLF!
MY LUMBERYARD IS DEEP IN DEBT, SINCE THE SUBSIDIES DRIED UP. CAN YOU HELP ME?
HUH?

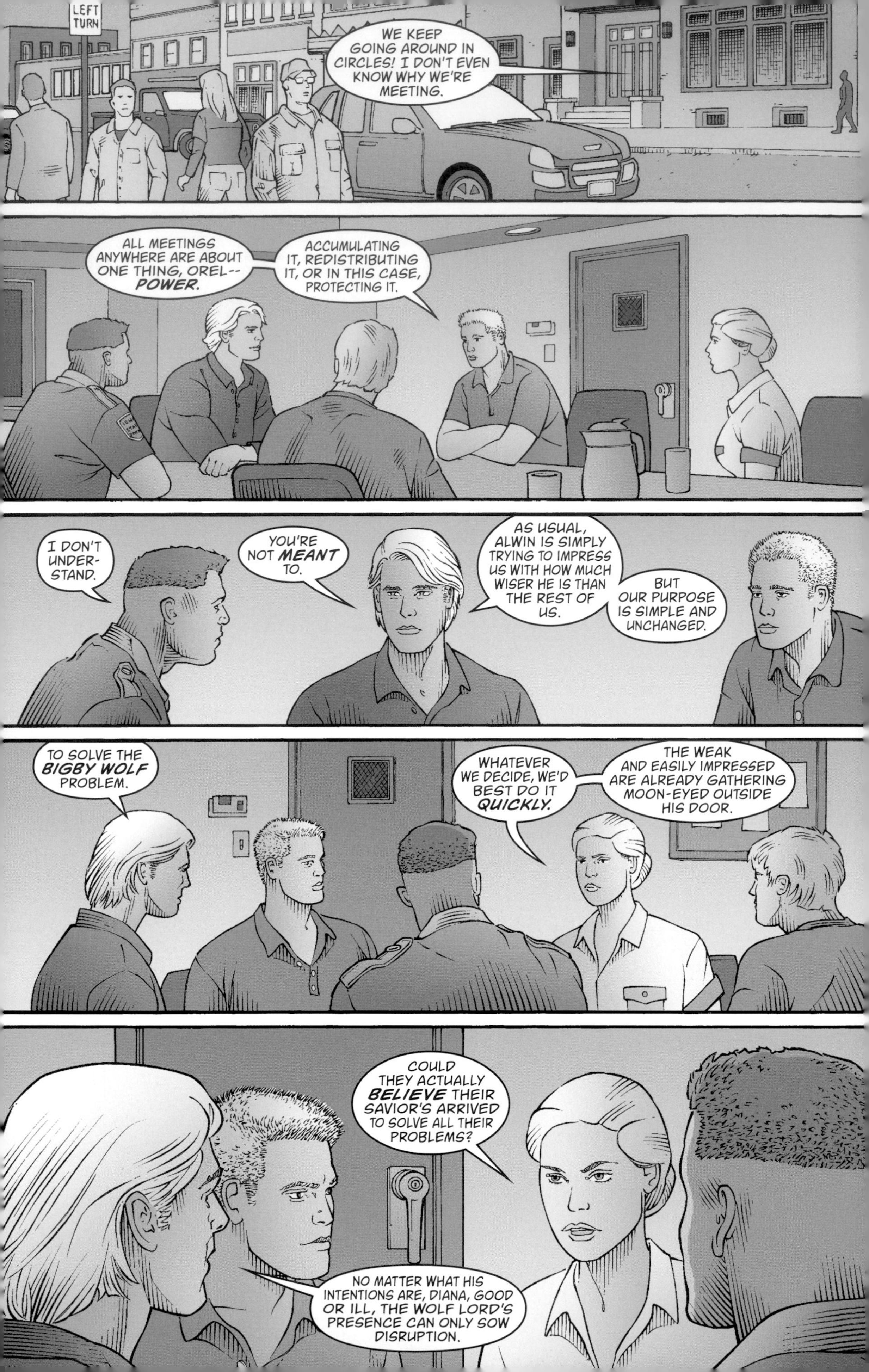
LEFT TURN
WE KEEP GOING AROUND IN CIRCLES! I DON'T EVEN KNOW WHY WE'RE MEETING.
ALL MEETINGS ANYWHERE ARE ABOUT ONE THING, OREL-- **POWER.**
ACCUMULATING IT, REDISTRIBUTING IT, OR IN THIS CASE, PROTECTING IT.
I DON'T UNDER-STAND.
YOU'RE NOT **MEANT** TO.
AS USUAL, ALWIN IS SIMPLY TRYING TO IMPRESS US WITH HOW MUCH WISER HE IS THAN THE REST OF US.
BUT OUR PURPOSE IS SIMPLE AND UNCHANGED.
TO SOLVE THE **BIGBY WOLF** PROBLEM.
WHATEVER WE DECIDE, WE'D BEST DO IT **QUICKLY.**
THE WEAK AND EASILY IMPRESSED ARE ALREADY GATHERING MOON-EYED OUTSIDE HIS DOOR.
COULD THEY ACTUALLY **BELIEVE** THEIR SAVIOR'S ARRIVED TO SOLVE ALL THEIR PROBLEMS?
NO MATTER WHAT HIS INTENTIONS ARE, DIANA, GOOD OR ILL, THE WOLF LORD'S PRESENCE CAN ONLY SOW DISRUPTION.

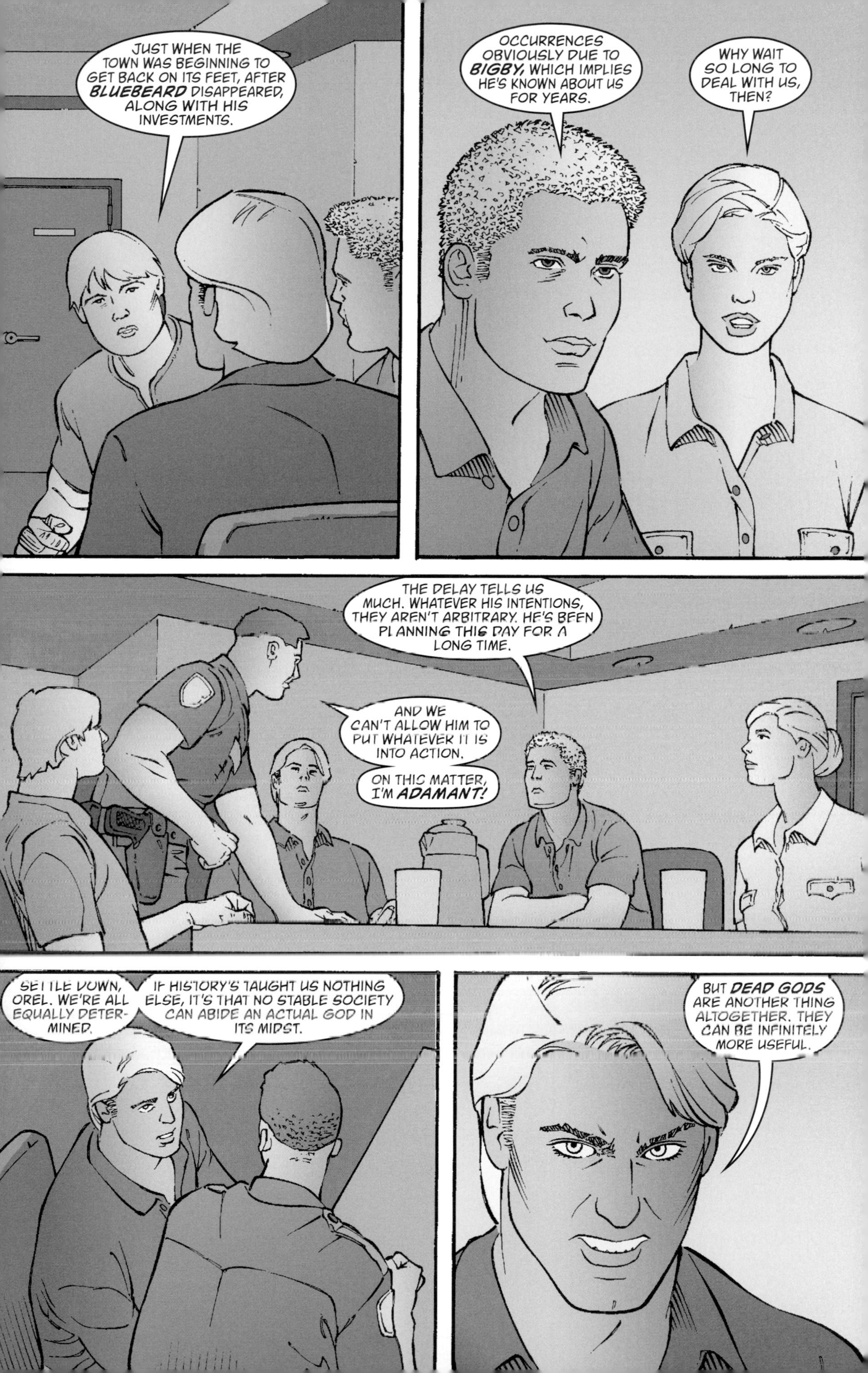
JUST WHEN THE TOWN WAS BEGINNING TO GET BACK ON ITS FEET, AFTER BLUEBEARD DISAPPEARED, ALONG WITH HIS INVESTMENTS.
OCCURRENCES OBVIOUSLY DUE TO BIGBY, WHICH IMPLIES HE'S KNOWN ABOUT US FOR YEARS.
WHY WAIT SO LONG TO DEAL WITH US, THEN?
THE DELAY TELLS US MUCH. WHATEVER HIS INTENTIONS, THEY AREN'T ARBITRARY. HE'S BEEN PLANNING THIS DAY FOR A LONG TIME.
AND WE CAN'T ALLOW HIM TO PUT WHATEVER IT IS INTO ACTION.
ON THIS MATTER, I'M ADAMANT!
SETTLE DOWN, OREL. WE'RE ALL EQUALLY DETERMINED.
IF HISTORY'S TAUGHT US NOTHING ELSE, IT'S THAT NO STABLE SOCIETY CAN ABIDE AN ACTUAL GOD IN ITS MIDST.
BUT DEAD GODS ARE ANOTHER THING ALTOGETHER. THEY CAN BE INFINITELY MORE USEFUL.

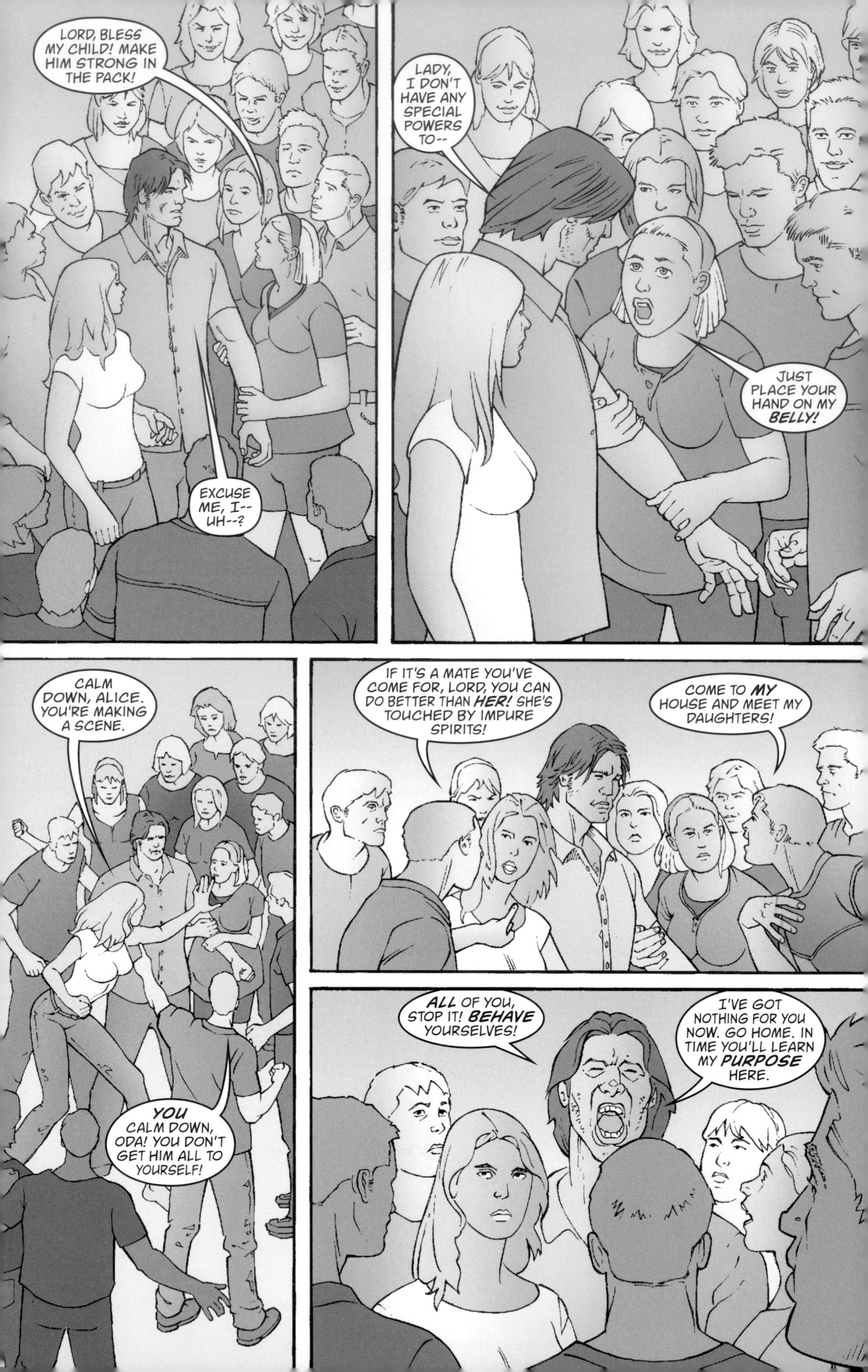
LORD, BLESS MY CHILD! MAKE HIM STRONG IN THE PACK!
EXCUSE ME, I-- UH--?
LADY, I DON'T HAVE ANY SPECIAL POWERS TO--
JUST PLACE YOUR HAND ON MY BELLY!
CALM DOWN, ALICE. YOU'RE MAKING A SCENE.
YOU CALM DOWN, ODA! YOU DON'T GET HIM ALL TO YOURSELF!
IF IT'S A MATE YOU'VE COME FOR, LORD, YOU CAN DO BETTER THAN HER! SHE'S TOUCHED BY IMPURE SPIRITS!
COME TO MY HOUSE AND MEET MY DAUGHTERS!
ALL OF YOU, STOP IT! BEHAVE YOURSELVES!
I'VE GOT NOTHING FOR YOU NOW. GO HOME. IN TIME YOU'LL LEARN MY PURPOSE HERE.

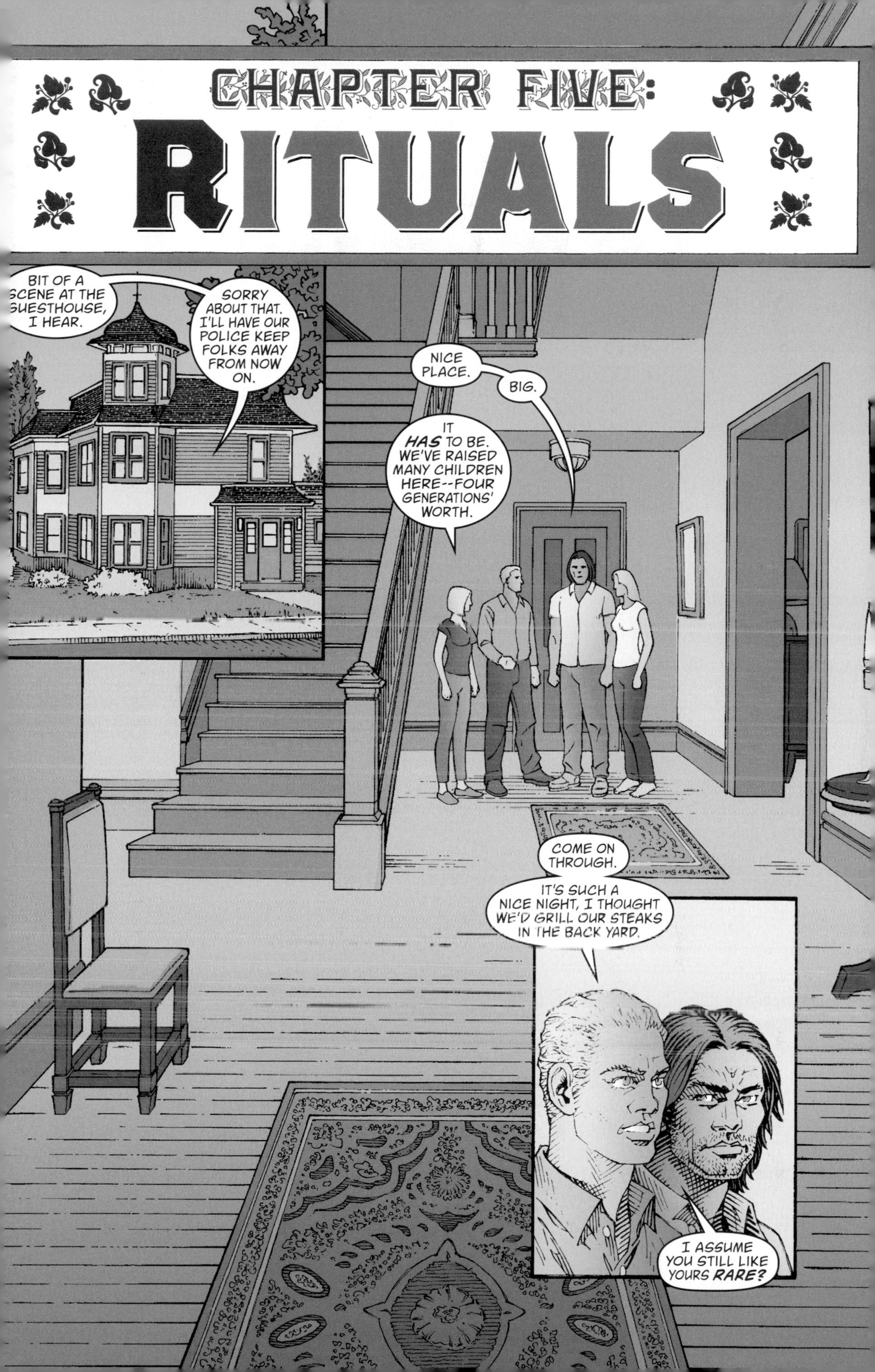
CHAPTER FIVE:
RITUALS
BIT OF A SCENE AT THE GUESTHOUSE, I HEAR.
SORRY ABOUT THAT. I'LL HAVE OUR POLICE KEEP FOLKS AWAY FROM NOW ON.
NICE PLACE.
BIG.
IT HAS TO BE. WE'VE RAISED MANY CHILDREN HERE--FOUR GENERATIONS' WORTH.
COME ON THROUGH.
IT'S SUCH A NICE NIGHT, I THOUGHT WE'D GRILL OUR STEAKS IN THE BACK YARD.
I ASSUME YOU STILL LIKE YOURS RARE?

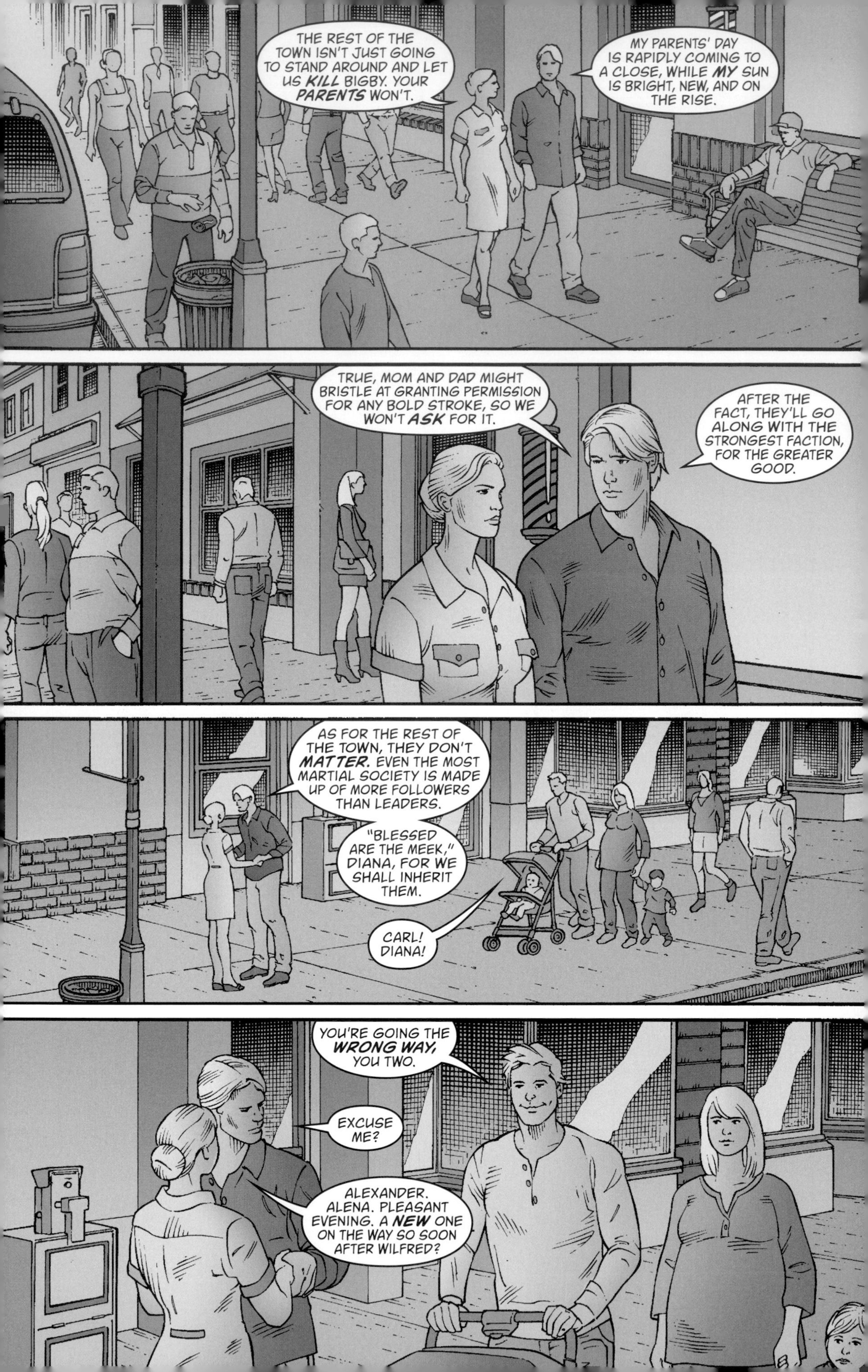
THE REST OF THE TOWN ISN'T JUST GOING TO STAND AROUND AND LET US KILL BIGBY. YOUR PARENTS WON'T.
MY PARENTS' DAY IS RAPIDLY COMING TO A CLOSE, WHILE MY SUN IS BRIGHT, NEW, AND ON THE RISE.
TRUE, MOM AND DAD MIGHT BRISTLE AT GRANTING PERMISSION FOR ANY BOLD STROKE, SO WE WON'T ASK FOR IT.
AFTER THE FACT, THEY'LL GO ALONG WITH THE STRONGEST FACTION, FOR THE GREATER GOOD.
AS FOR THE REST OF THE TOWN, THEY DON'T MATTER. EVEN THE MOST MARTIAL SOCIETY IS MADE UP OF MORE FOLLOWERS THAN LEADERS.
"BLESSED ARE THE MEEK," DIANA, FOR WE SHALL INHERIT THEM.
CARL! DIANA!
YOU'RE GOING THE WRONG WAY, YOU TWO.
EXCUSE ME?
ALEXANDER. ALENA. PLEASANT EVENING. A NEW ONE ON THE WAY SO SOON AFTER WILFRED?

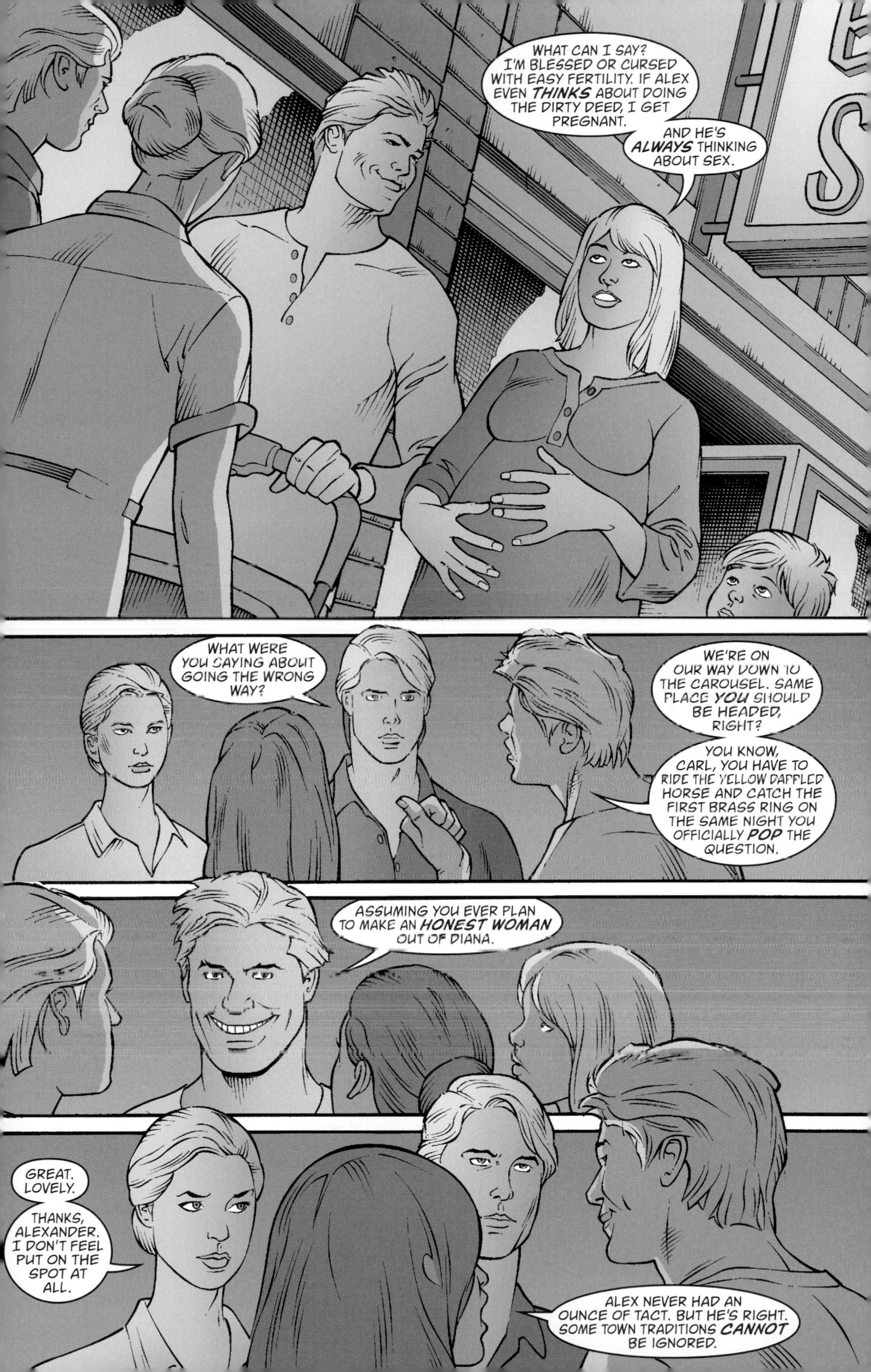
WHAT CAN I SAY? I'M BLESSED OR CURSED WITH EASY FERTILITY. IF ALEX EVEN *THINKS* ABOUT DOING THE DIRTY DEED, I GET PREGNANT.
AND HE'S *ALWAYS* THINKING ABOUT SEX.
WHAT WERE YOU SAYING ABOUT GOING THE WRONG WAY?
WE'RE ON OUR WAY DOWN TO THE CAROUSEL. SAME PLACE *YOU* SHOULD BE HEADED, RIGHT?
YOU KNOW, CARL, YOU HAVE TO RIDE THE YELLOW DAPPLED HORSE AND CATCH THE FIRST BRASS RING ON THE SAME NIGHT YOU OFFICIALLY *POP* THE QUESTION.
ASSUMING YOU EVER PLAN TO MAKE AN *HONEST WOMAN* OUT OF DIANA.
GREAT. LOVELY.
THANKS, ALEXANDER. I DON'T FEEL PUT ON THE SPOT AT ALL.
ALEX NEVER HAD AN OUNCE OF TACT. BUT HE'S RIGHT. SOME TOWN TRADITIONS *CANNOT* BE IGNORED.

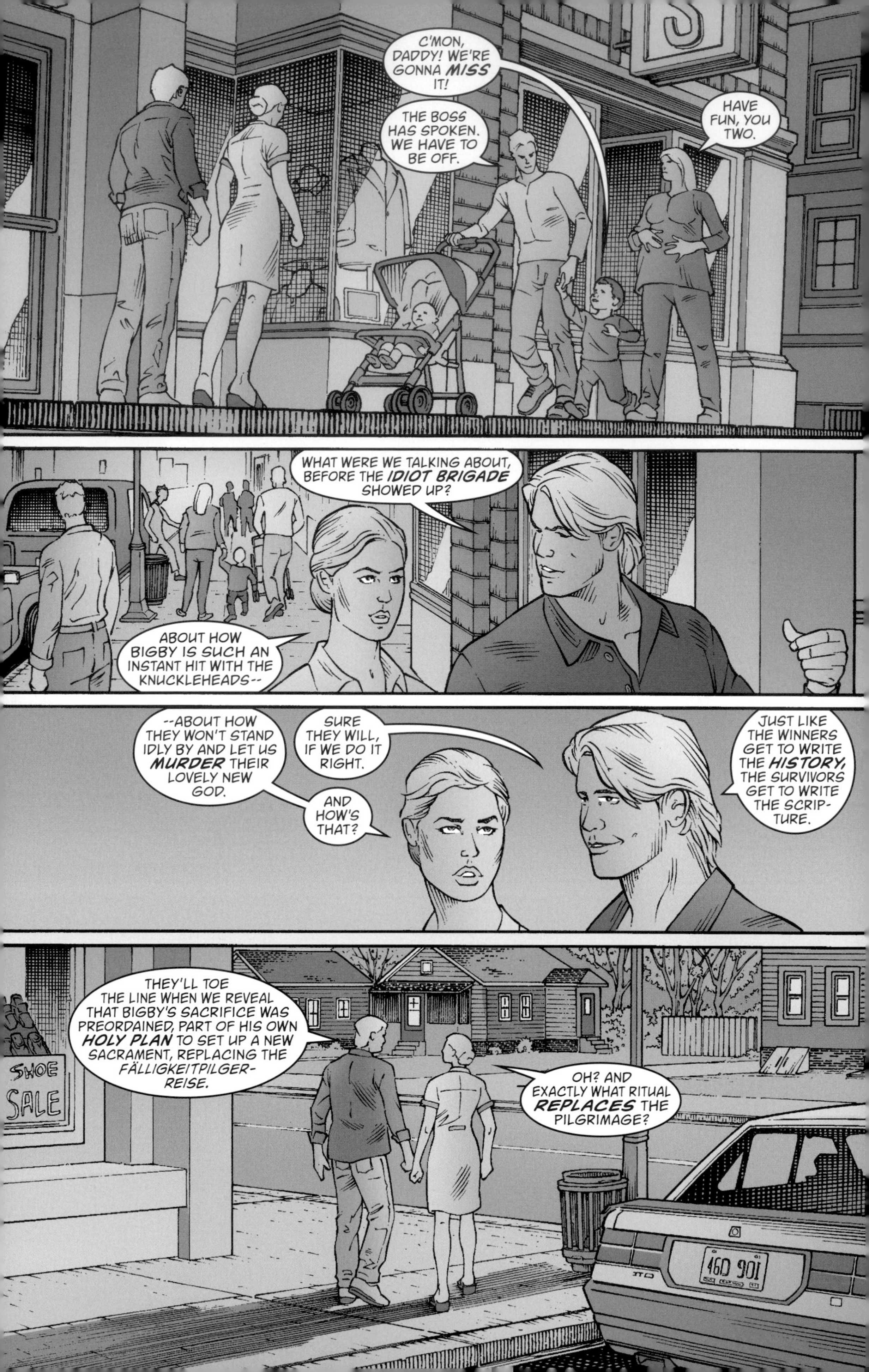

C'MON, DADDY! WE'RE GONNA MISS IT!
THE BOSS HAS SPOKEN. WE HAVE TO BE OFF.
HAVE FUN, YOU TWO.
WHAT WERE WE TALKING ABOUT, BEFORE THE IDIOT BRIGADE SHOWED UP?
ABOUT HOW BIGBY IS SUCH AN INSTANT HIT WITH THE KNUCKLEHEADS--
--ABOUT HOW THEY WON'T STAND IDLY BY AND LET US MURDER THEIR LOVELY NEW GOD.
SURE THEY WILL, IF WE DO IT RIGHT.
AND HOW'S THAT?
JUST LIKE THE WINNERS GET TO WRITE THE HISTORY, THE SURVIVORS GET TO WRITE THE SCRIP-TURE.
THEY'LL TOE THE LINE WHEN WE REVEAL THAT BIGBY'S SACRIFICE WAS PREORDAINED, PART OF HIS OWN HOLY PLAN TO SET UP A NEW SACRAMENT, REPLACING THE FÄLLIGKEITPILGER-REISE.
OH? AND EXACTLY WHAT RITUAL REPLACES THE PILGRIMAGE?
SHOE SALE
46D 901

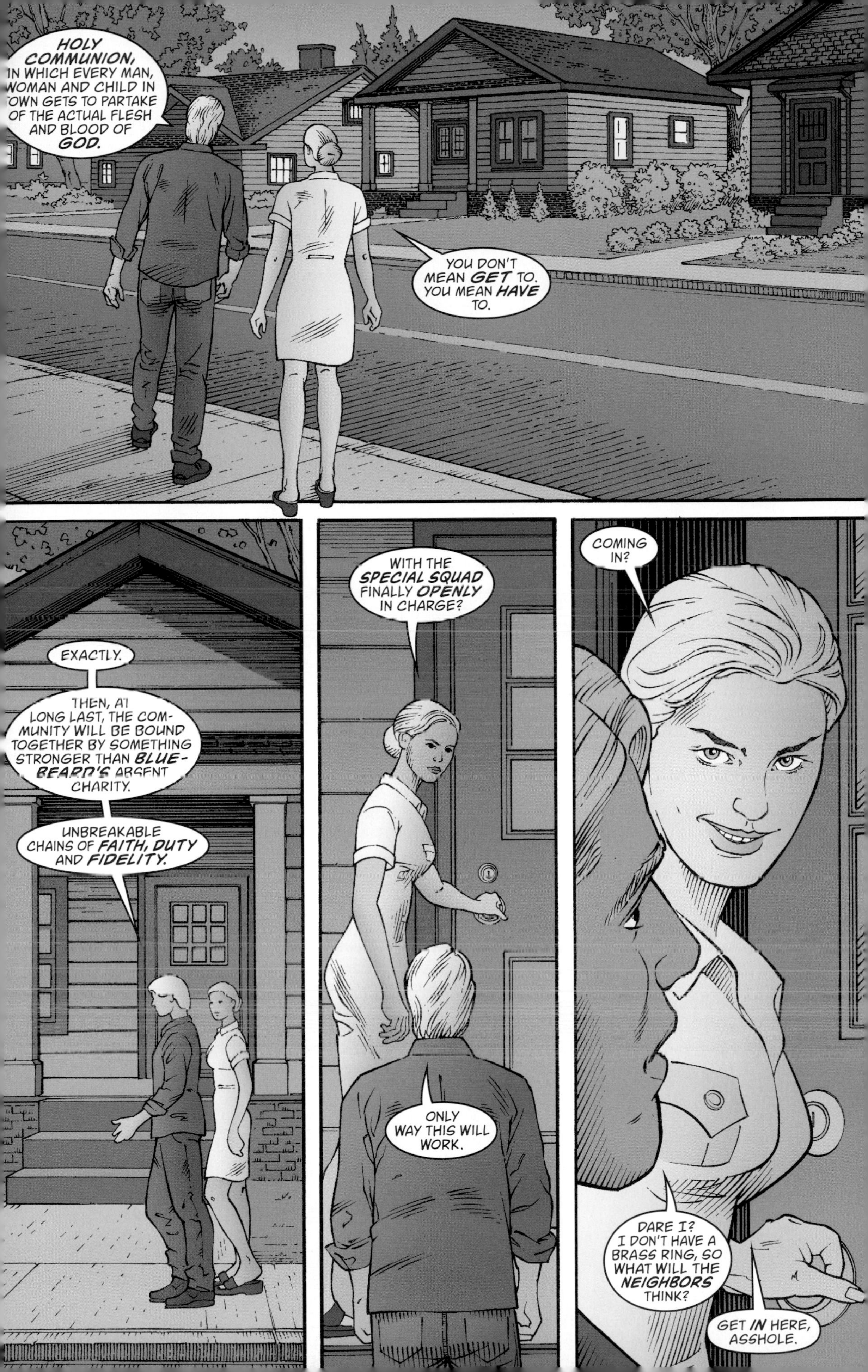
HOLY COMMUNION, IN WHICH EVERY MAN, WOMAN AND CHILD IN TOWN GETS TO PARTAKE OF THE ACTUAL FLESH AND BLOOD OF GOD.
YOU DON'T MEAN GET TO. YOU MEAN HAVE TO.
EXACTLY.
THEN, AT LONG LAST, THE COMMUNITY WILL BE BOUND TOGETHER BY SOMETHING STRONGER THAN BLUEBEARD'S ABSENT CHARITY.
UNBREAKABLE CHAINS OF FAITH, DUTY AND FIDELITY.
WITH THE SPECIAL SQUAD FINALLY OPENLY IN CHARGE?
ONLY WAY THIS WILL WORK.
COMING IN?
DARE I? I DON'T HAVE A BRASS RING, SO WHAT WILL THE NEIGHBORS THINK?
GET IN HERE, ASSHOLE.

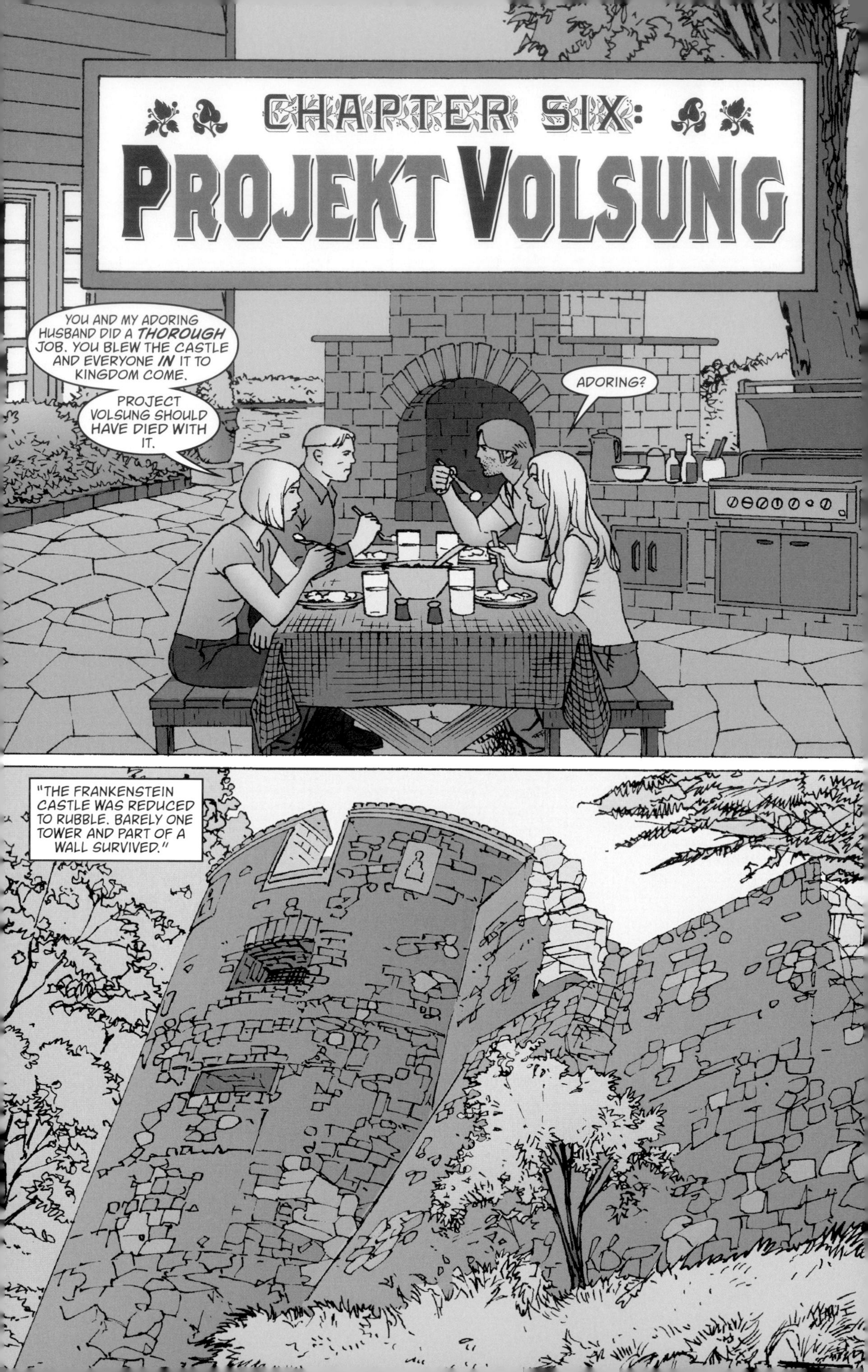
CHAPTER SIX:
PROJEKT VOLSUNG
YOU AND MY ADORING HUSBAND DID A THOROUGH JOB. YOU BLEW THE CASTLE AND EVERYONE IN IT TO KINGDOM COME.
PROJECT VOLSUNG SHOULD HAVE DIED WITH IT.
ADORING?
"THE FRANKENSTEIN CASTLE WAS REDUCED TO RUBBLE. BARELY ONE TOWER AND PART OF A WALL SURVIVED."

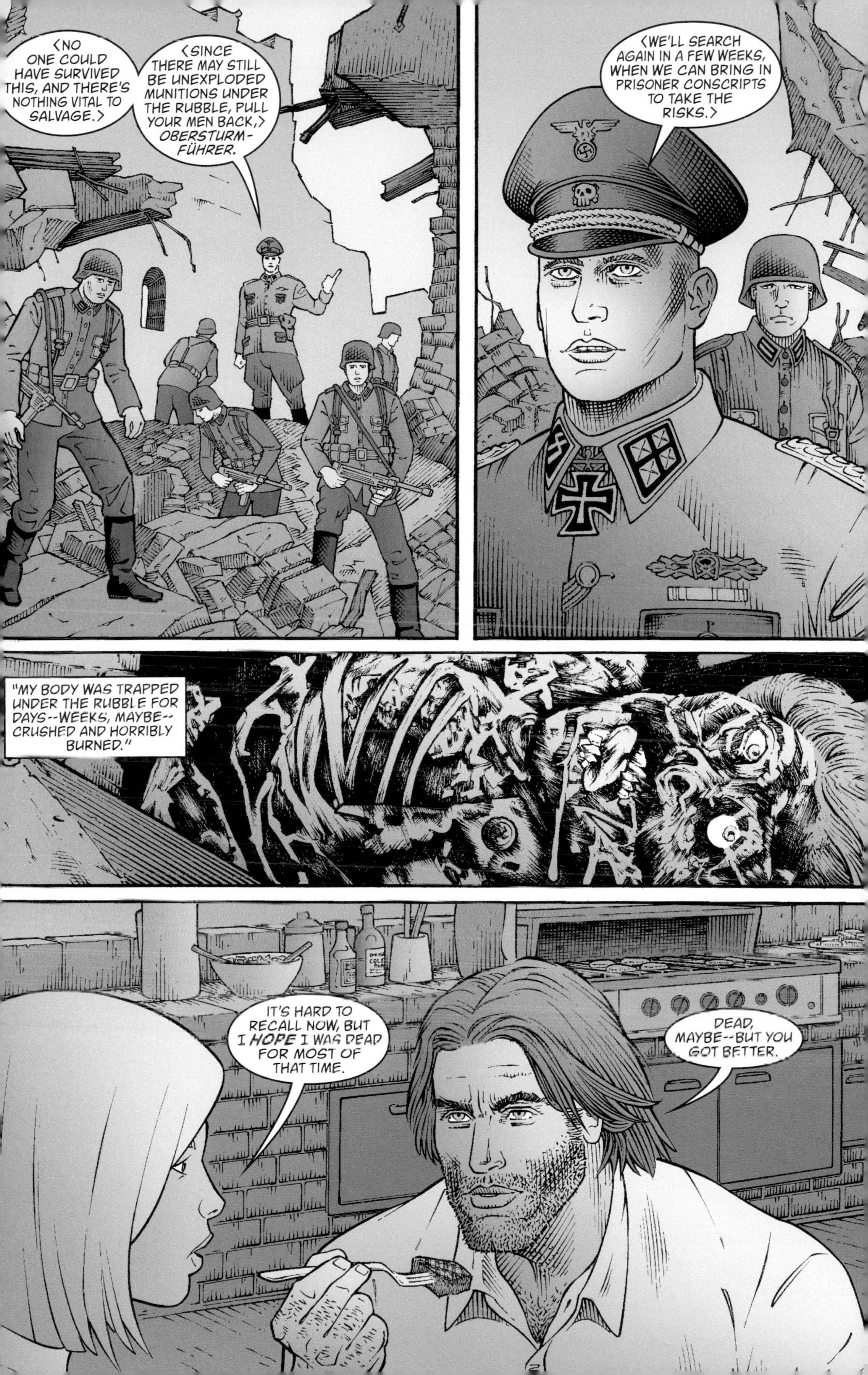

<NO ONE COULD HAVE SURVIVED THIS, AND THERE'S NOTHING VITAL TO SALVAGE.>
<SINCE THERE MAY STILL BE UNEXPLODED MUNITIONS UNDER THE RUBBLE, PULL YOUR MEN BACK,> OBERSTURM-FÜHRER.
<WE'LL SEARCH AGAIN IN A FEW WEEKS, WHEN WE CAN BRING IN PRISONER CONSCRIPTS TO TAKE THE RISKS.>
"MY BODY WAS TRAPPED UNDER THE RUBBLE FOR DAYS--WEEKS, MAYBE--CRUSHED AND HORRIBLY BURNED."
IT'S HARD TO RECALL NOW, BUT I *HOPE* I WAS DEAD FOR MOST OF THAT TIME.
DEAD, MAYBE--BUT YOU GOT BETTER.

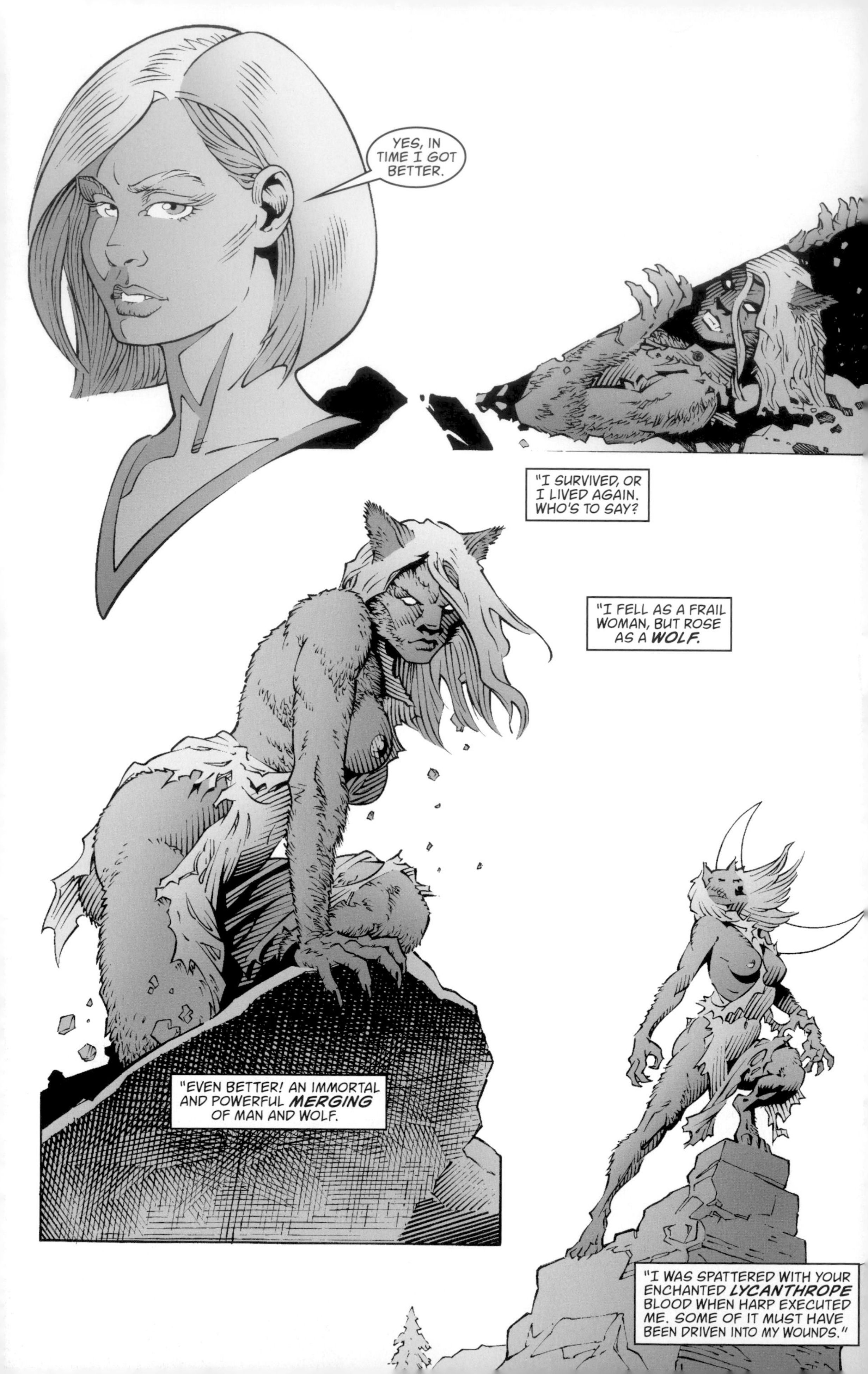
YES, IN TIME I GOT BETTER.
"I SURVIVED, OR I LIVED AGAIN. WHO'S TO SAY?
"I FELL AS A FRAIL WOMAN, BUT ROSE AS A WOLF.
"EVEN BETTER! AN IMMORTAL AND POWERFUL MERGING OF MAN AND WOLF.
"I WAS SPATTERED WITH YOUR ENCHANTED LYCANTHROPE BLOOD WHEN HARP EXECUTED ME. SOME OF IT MUST HAVE BEEN DRIVEN INTO MY WOUNDS."

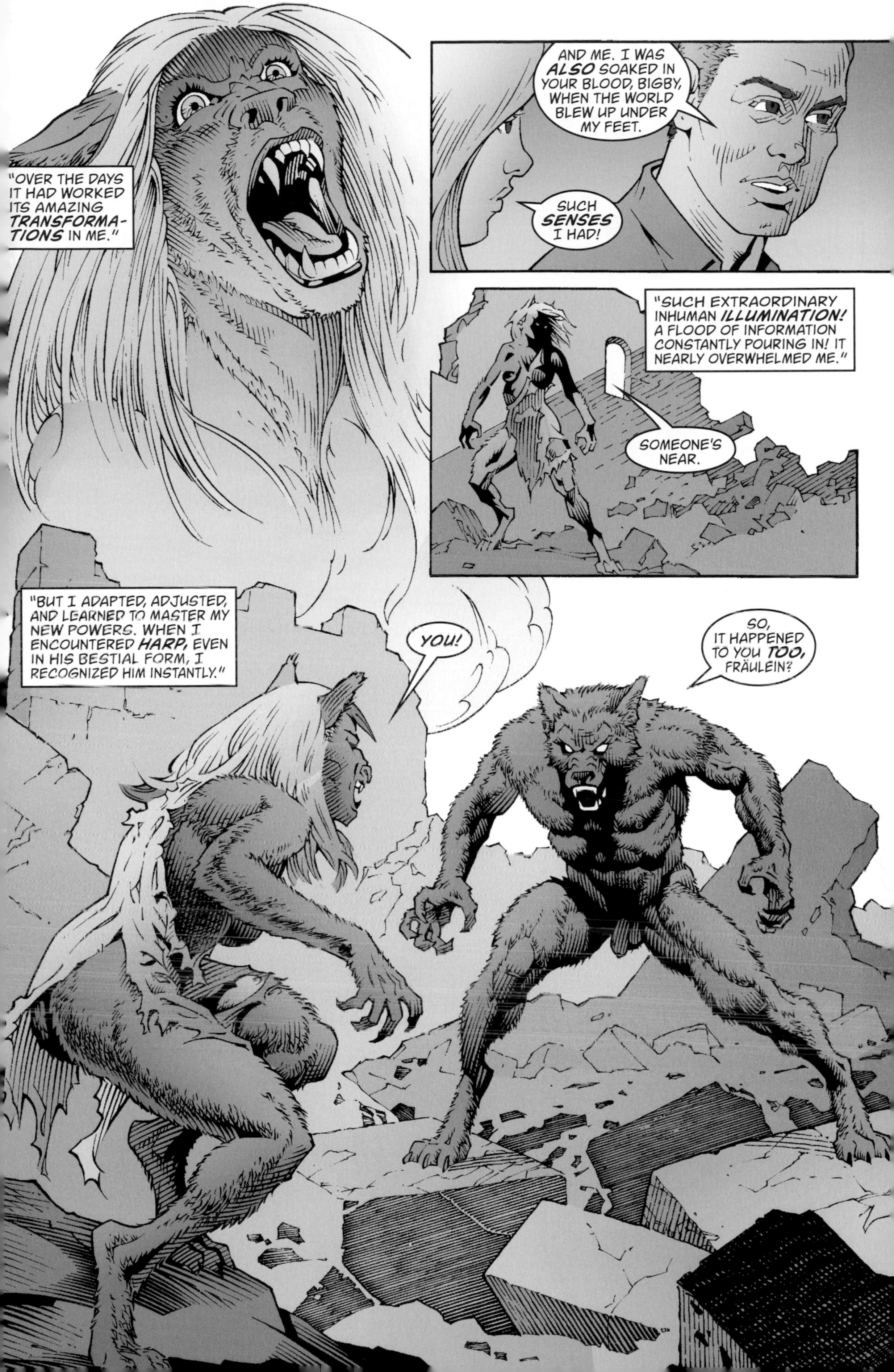
"OVER THE DAYS IT HAD WORKED ITS AMAZING TRANSFORMATIONS IN ME."
AND ME. I WAS ALSO SOAKED IN YOUR BLOOD, BIGBY, WHEN THE WORLD BLEW UP UNDER MY FEET.
SUCH SENSES I HAD!
"SUCH EXTRAORDINARY INHUMAN ILLUMINATION! A FLOOD OF INFORMATION CONSTANTLY POURING IN! IT NEARLY OVERWHELMED ME."
SOMEONE'S NEAR.
"BUT I ADAPTED, ADJUSTED, AND LEARNED TO MASTER MY NEW POWERS. WHEN I ENCOUNTERED HARP, EVEN IN HIS BESTIAL FORM, I RECOGNIZED HIM INSTANTLY."
YOU!
SO, IT HAPPENED TO YOU TOO, FRÄULEIN?

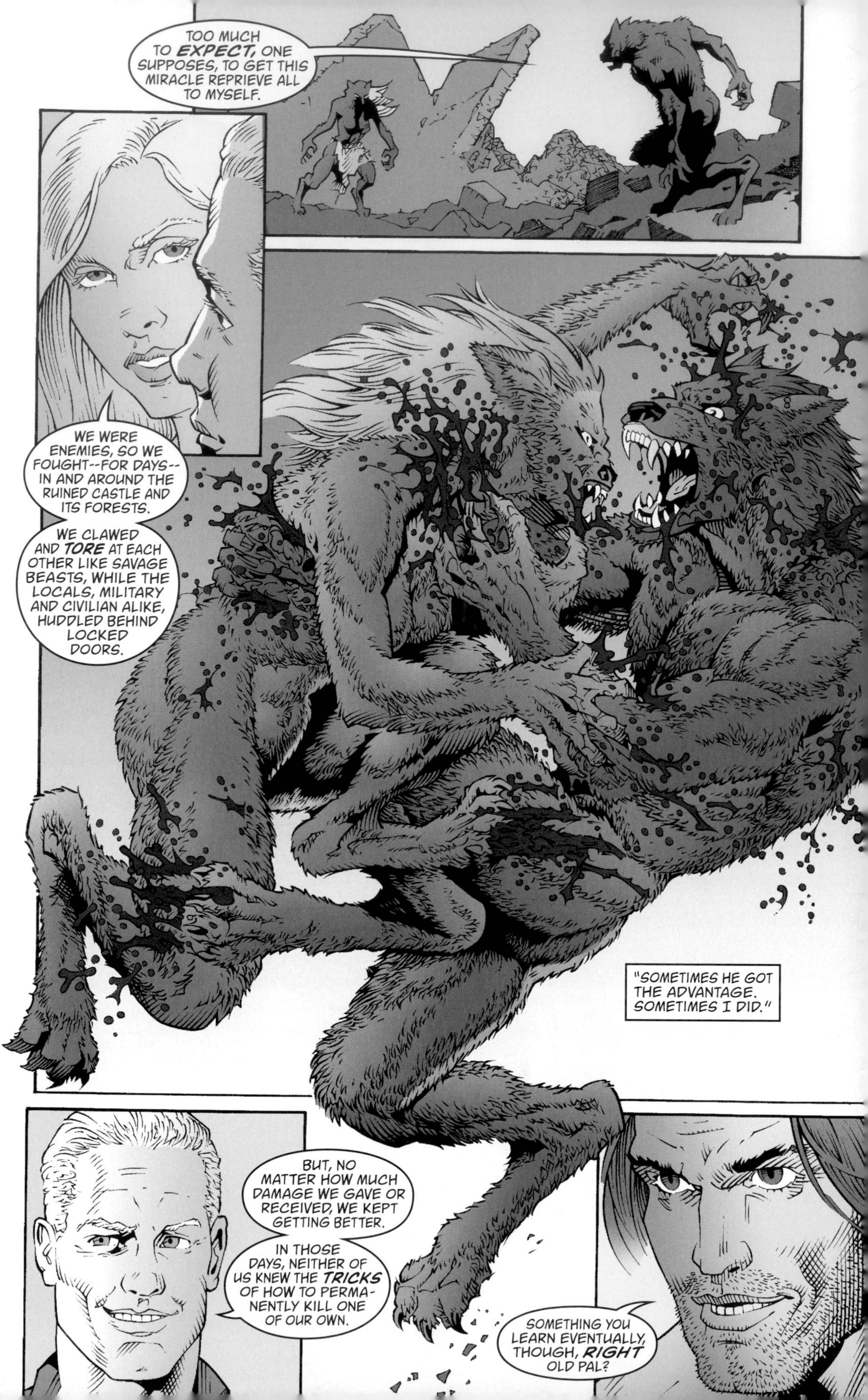

TOO MUCH TO EXPECT, ONE SUPPOSES, TO GET THIS MIRACLE REPRIEVE ALL TO MYSELF.
WE WERE ENEMIES, SO WE FOUGHT--FOR DAYS-- IN AND AROUND THE RUINED CASTLE AND ITS FORESTS.
WE CLAWED AND TORE AT EACH OTHER LIKE SAVAGE BEASTS, WHILE THE LOCALS, MILITARY AND CIVILIAN ALIKE, HUDDLED BEHIND LOCKED DOORS.
"SOMETIMES HE GOT THE ADVANTAGE. SOMETIMES I DID."
BUT, NO MATTER HOW MUCH DAMAGE WE GAVE OR RECEIVED, WE KEPT GETTING BETTER.
IN THOSE DAYS, NEITHER OF US KNEW THE TRICKS OF HOW TO PERMA-NENTLY KILL ONE OF OUR OWN.
SOMETHING YOU LEARN EVENTUALLY, THOUGH, RIGHT OLD PAL?

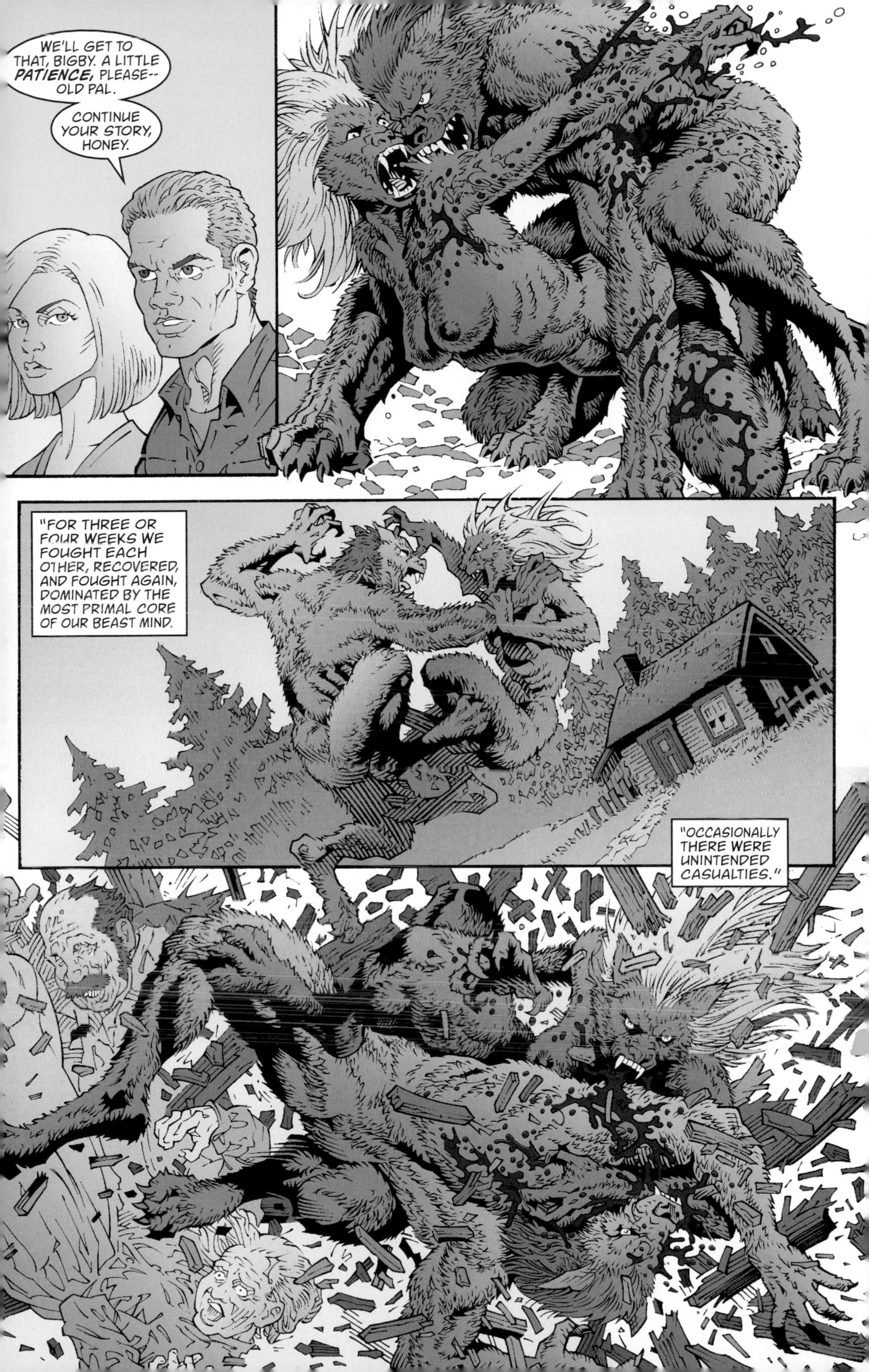
WE'LL GET TO THAT, BIGBY. A LITTLE *PATIENCE,* PLEASE-- OLD PAL.
CONTINUE YOUR STORY, HONEY.
"FOR THREE OR FOUR WEEKS WE FOUGHT EACH OTHER, RECOVERED, AND FOUGHT AGAIN, DOMINATED BY THE MOST PRIMAL CORE OF OUR BEAST MIND.
"OCCASIONALLY THERE WERE UNINTENDED CASUALTIES."

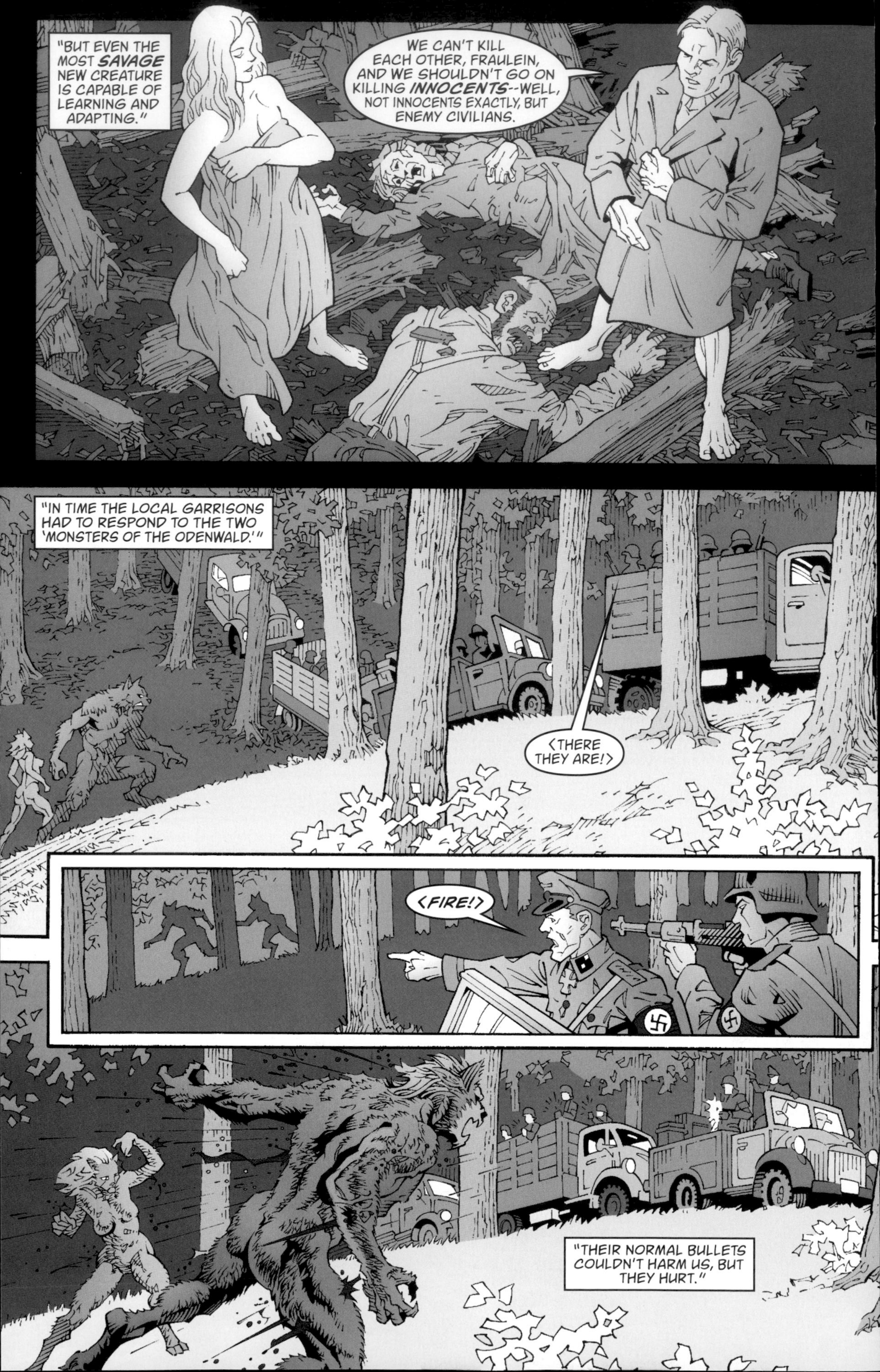
"BUT EVEN THE MOST SAVAGE NEW CREATURE IS CAPABLE OF LEARNING AND ADAPTING."
WE CAN'T KILL EACH OTHER, FRAULEIN, AND WE SHOULDN'T GO ON KILLING INNOCENTS--WELL, NOT INNOCENTS EXACTLY, BUT ENEMY CIVILIANS.
"IN TIME THE LOCAL GARRISONS HAD TO RESPOND TO THE TWO 'MONSTERS OF THE ODENWALD.'"
<THERE THEY ARE!>
<FIRE!>
"THEIR NORMAL BULLETS COULDN'T HARM US, BUT THEY HURT."

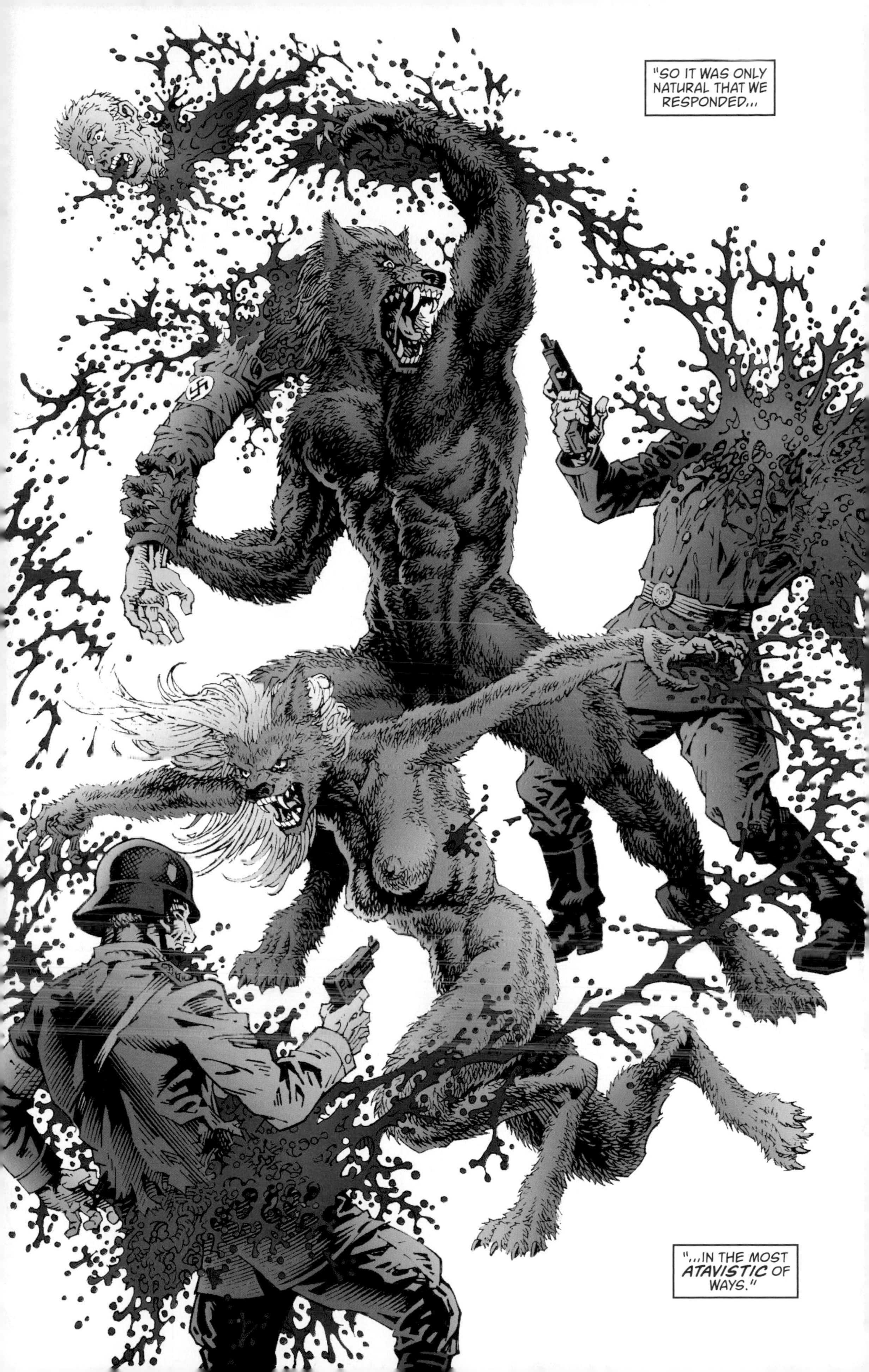
"SO IT WAS ONLY NATURAL THAT WE RESPONDED...
"...IN THE MOST ATAVISTIC OF WAYS."

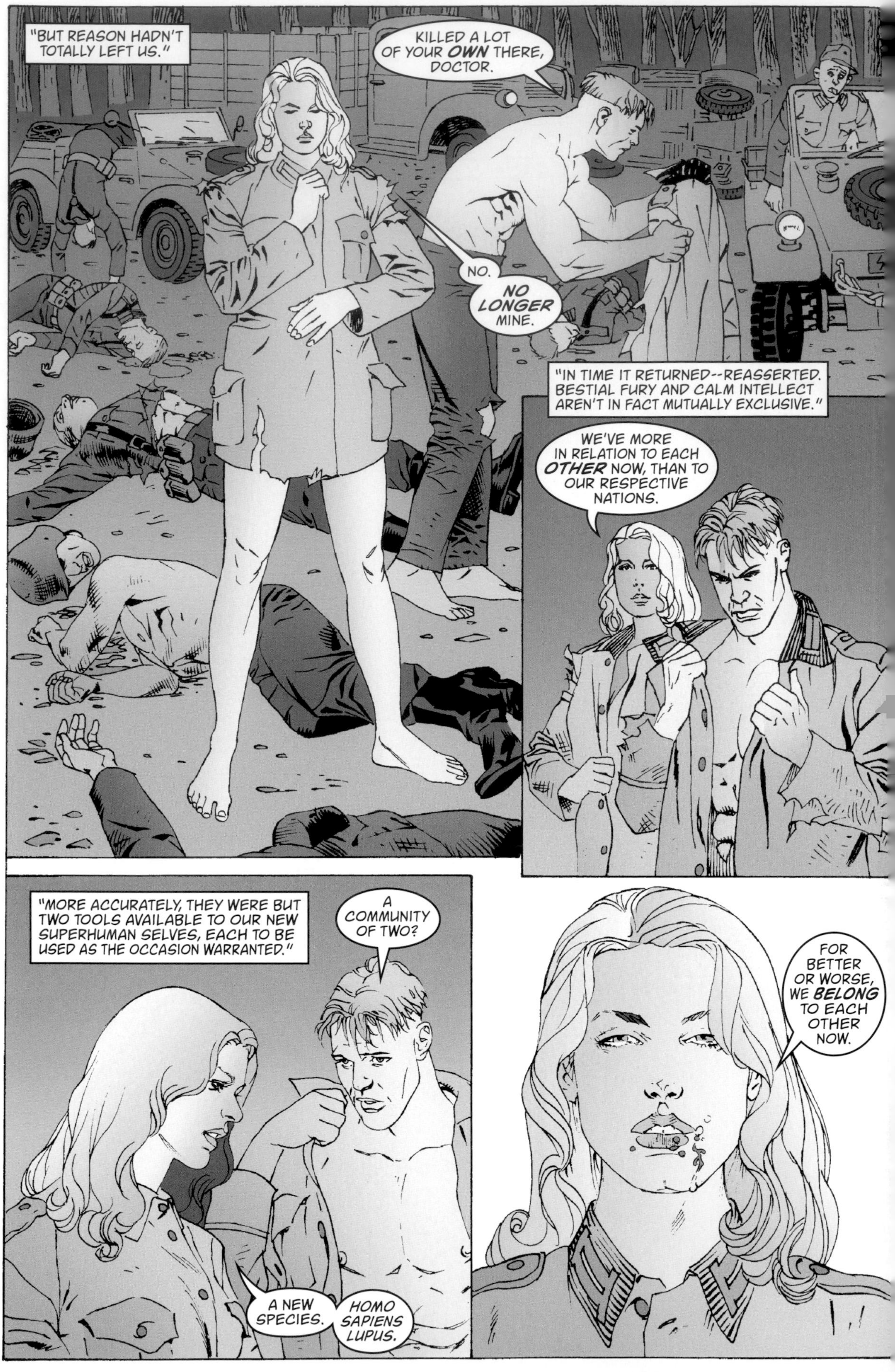
"BUT REASON HADN'T TOTALLY LEFT US."
KILLED A LOT OF YOUR OWN THERE, DOCTOR.
NO. NO LONGER MINE.
"IN TIME IT RETURNED--REASSERTED. BESTIAL FURY AND CALM INTELLECT AREN'T IN FACT MUTUALLY EXCLUSIVE."
WE'VE MORE IN RELATION TO EACH OTHER NOW, THAN TO OUR RESPECTIVE NATIONS.
"MORE ACCURATELY, THEY WERE BUT TWO TOOLS AVAILABLE TO OUR NEW SUPERHUMAN SELVES, EACH TO BE USED AS THE OCCASION WARRANTED."
A COMMUNITY OF TWO?
A NEW SPECIES.
HOMO SAPIENS LUPUS.
FOR BETTER OR WORSE, WE BELONG TO EACH OTHER NOW.

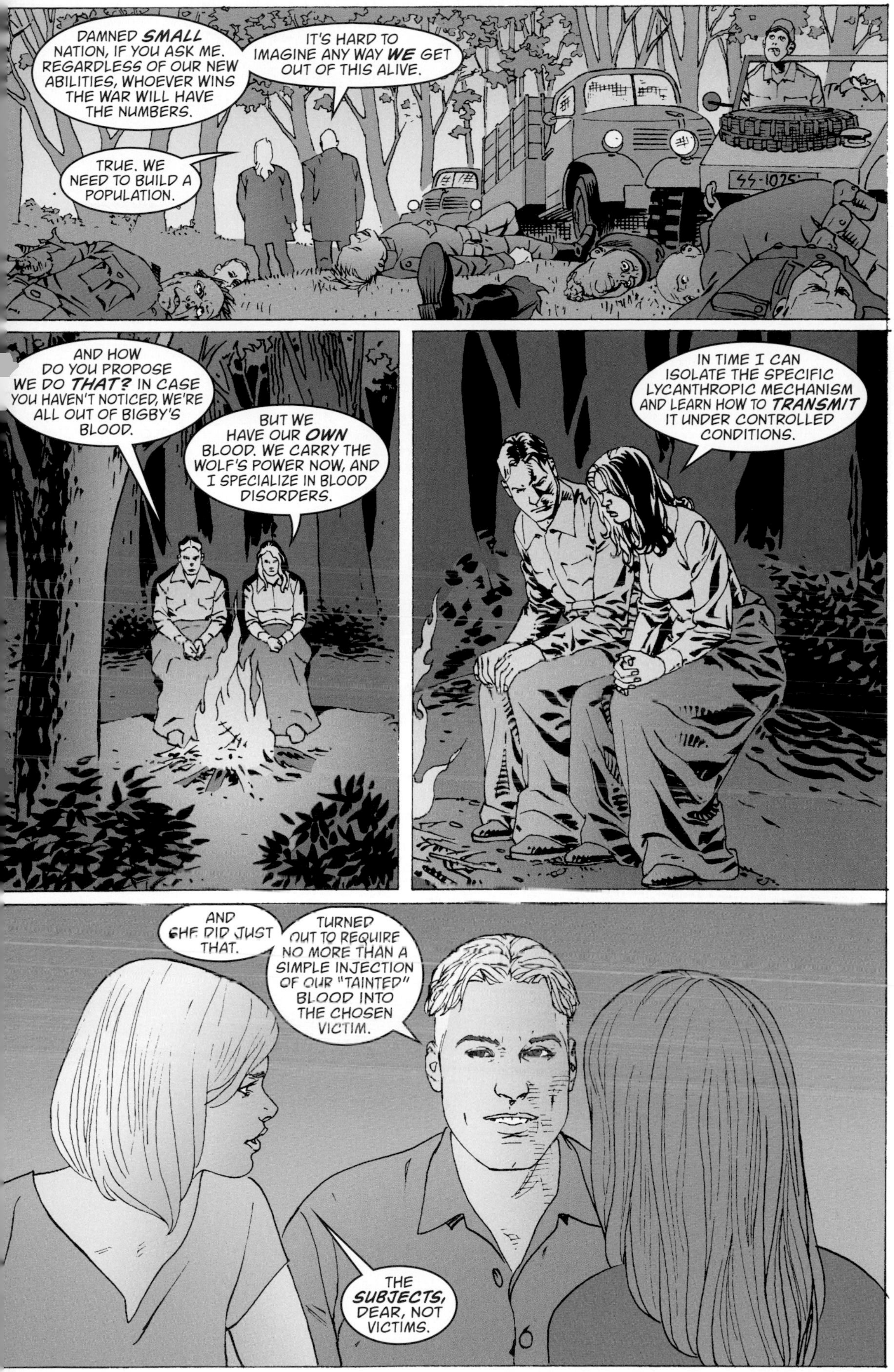
DAMNED SMALL NATION, IF YOU ASK ME. REGARDLESS OF OUR NEW ABILITIES, WHOEVER WINS THE WAR WILL HAVE THE NUMBERS.
IT'S HARD TO IMAGINE ANY WAY WE GET OUT OF THIS ALIVE.
TRUE. WE NEED TO BUILD A POPULATION.
AND HOW DO YOU PROPOSE WE DO THAT? IN CASE YOU HAVEN'T NOTICED, WE'RE ALL OUT OF BIGBY'S BLOOD.
BUT WE HAVE OUR OWN BLOOD. WE CARRY THE WOLF'S POWER NOW, AND I SPECIALIZE IN BLOOD DISORDERS.
IN TIME I CAN ISOLATE THE SPECIFIC LYCANTHROPIC MECHANISM AND LEARN HOW TO TRANSMIT IT UNDER CONTROLLED CONDITIONS.
AND SHE DID JUST THAT.
TURNED OUT TO REQUIRE NO MORE THAN A SIMPLE INJECTION OF OUR "TAINTED" BLOOD INTO THE CHOSEN VICTIM.
THE SUBJECTS, DEAR, NOT VICTIMS.

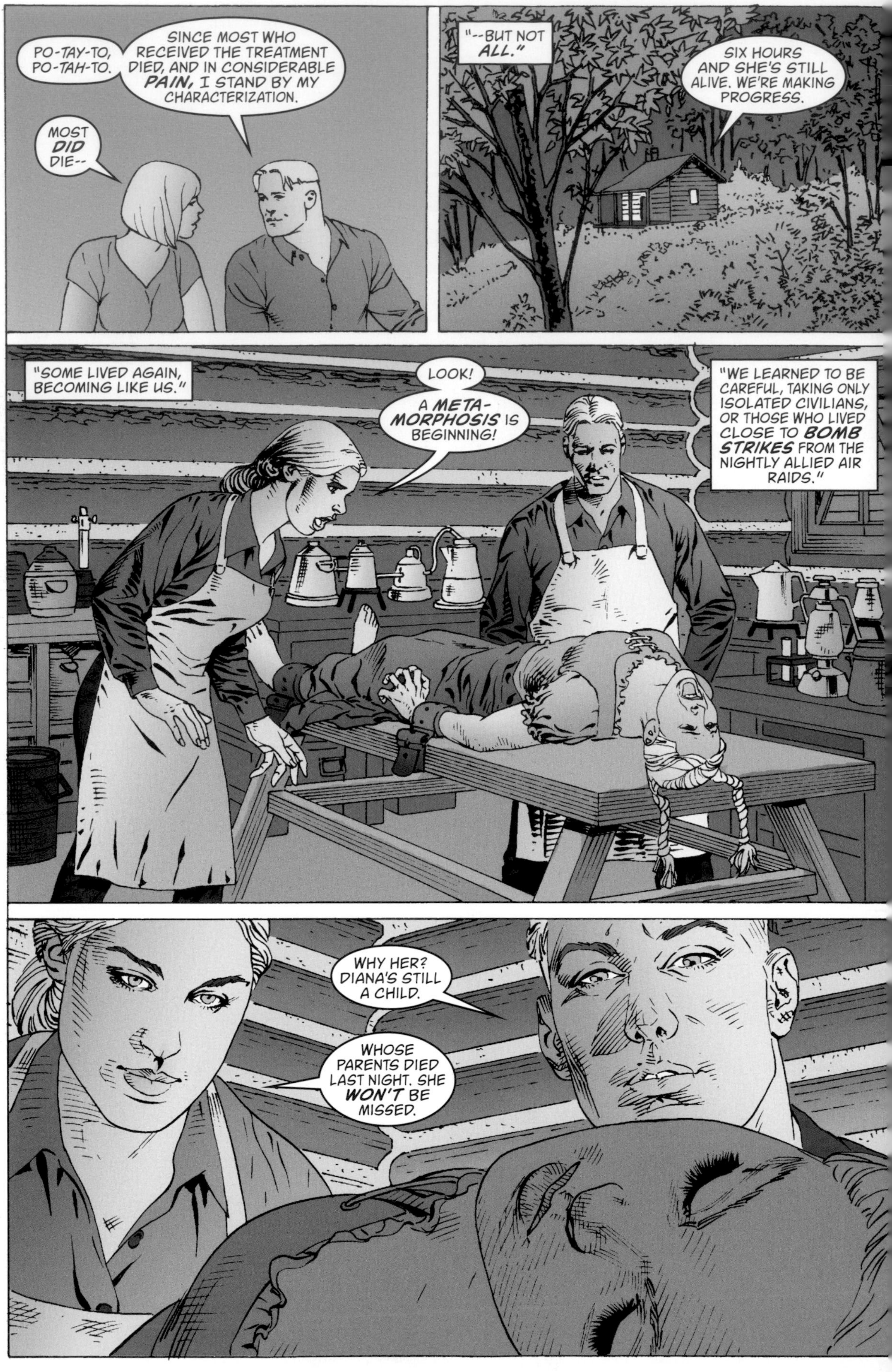
PO-TAY-TO, PO-TAH-TO.
SINCE MOST WHO RECEIVED THE TREATMENT DIED, AND IN CONSIDERABLE PAIN, I STAND BY MY CHARACTERIZATION.
MOST DID DIE--
"--BUT NOT ALL."
SIX HOURS AND SHE'S STILL ALIVE. WE'RE MAKING PROGRESS.
"SOME LIVED AGAIN, BECOMING LIKE US."
LOOK!
A META-MORPHOSIS IS BEGINNING!
"WE LEARNED TO BE CAREFUL, TAKING ONLY ISOLATED CIVILIANS, OR THOSE WHO LIVED CLOSE TO BOMB STRIKES FROM THE NIGHTLY ALLIED AIR RAIDS."
WHY HER? DIANA'S STILL A CHILD.
WHOSE PARENTS DIED LAST NIGHT. SHE WON'T BE MISSED.

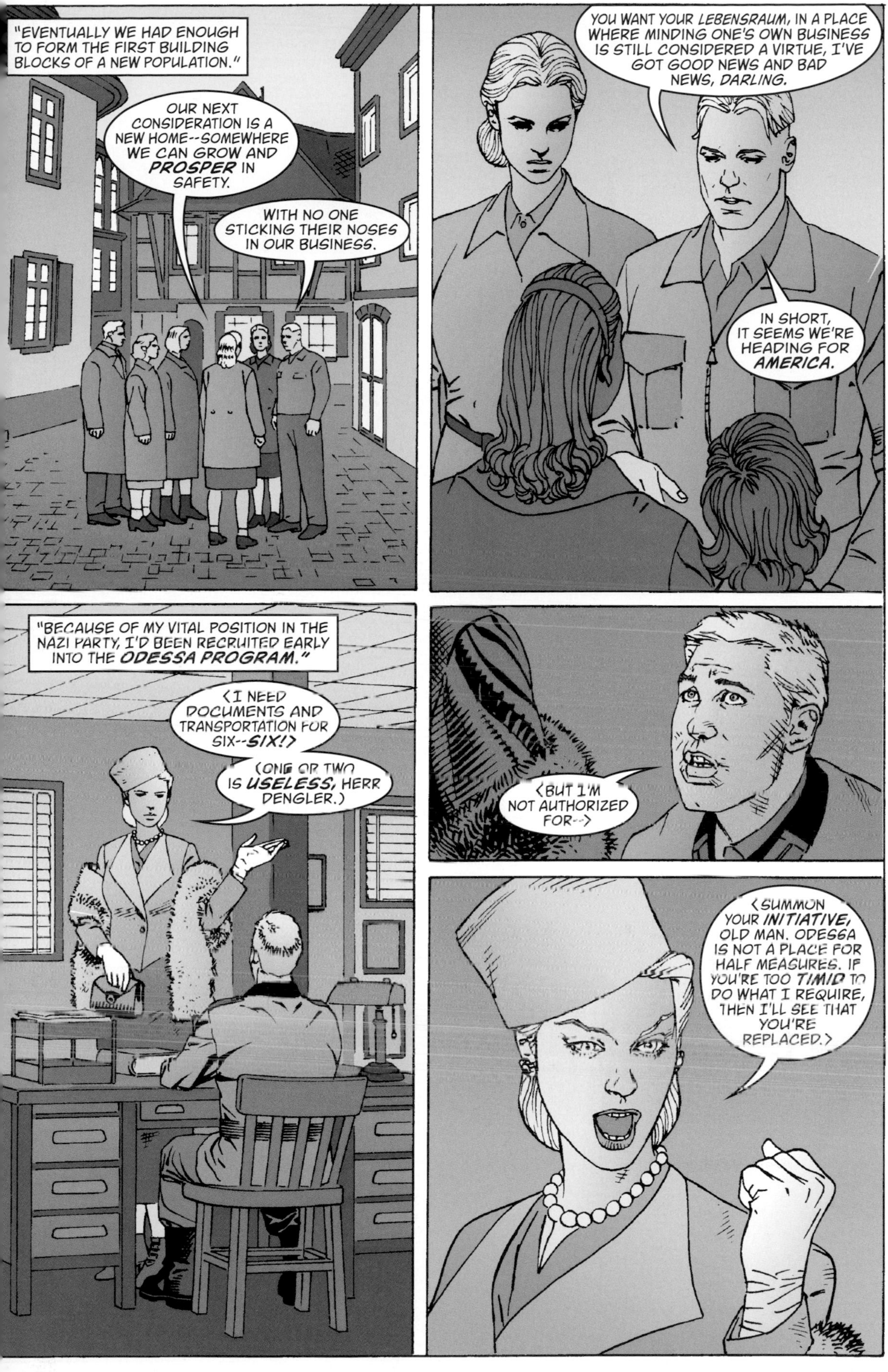
"EVENTUALLY WE HAD ENOUGH TO FORM THE FIRST BUILDING BLOCKS OF A NEW POPULATION."
OUR NEXT CONSIDERATION IS A NEW HOME--SOMEWHERE WE CAN GROW AND PROSPER IN SAFETY.
WITH NO ONE STICKING THEIR NOSES IN OUR BUSINESS.
YOU WANT YOUR LEBENSRAUM, IN A PLACE WHERE MINDING ONE'S OWN BUSINESS IS STILL CONSIDERED A VIRTUE, I'VE GOT GOOD NEWS AND BAD NEWS, DARLING.
IN SHORT, IT SEEMS WE'RE HEADING FOR AMERICA.
"BECAUSE OF MY VITAL POSITION IN THE NAZI PARTY, I'D BEEN RECRUITED EARLY INTO THE ODESSA PROGRAM."
<I NEED DOCUMENTS AND TRANSPORTATION FOR SIX--SIX!>
(ONE OR TWO IS USELESS, HERR DENGLER.)
<BUT I'M NOT AUTHORIZED FOR-->
<SUMMON YOUR INITIATIVE, OLD MAN. ODESSA IS NOT A PLACE FOR HALF MEASURES. IF YOU'RE TOO TIMID TO DO WHAT I REQUIRE, THEN I'LL SEE THAT YOU'RE REPLACED.>

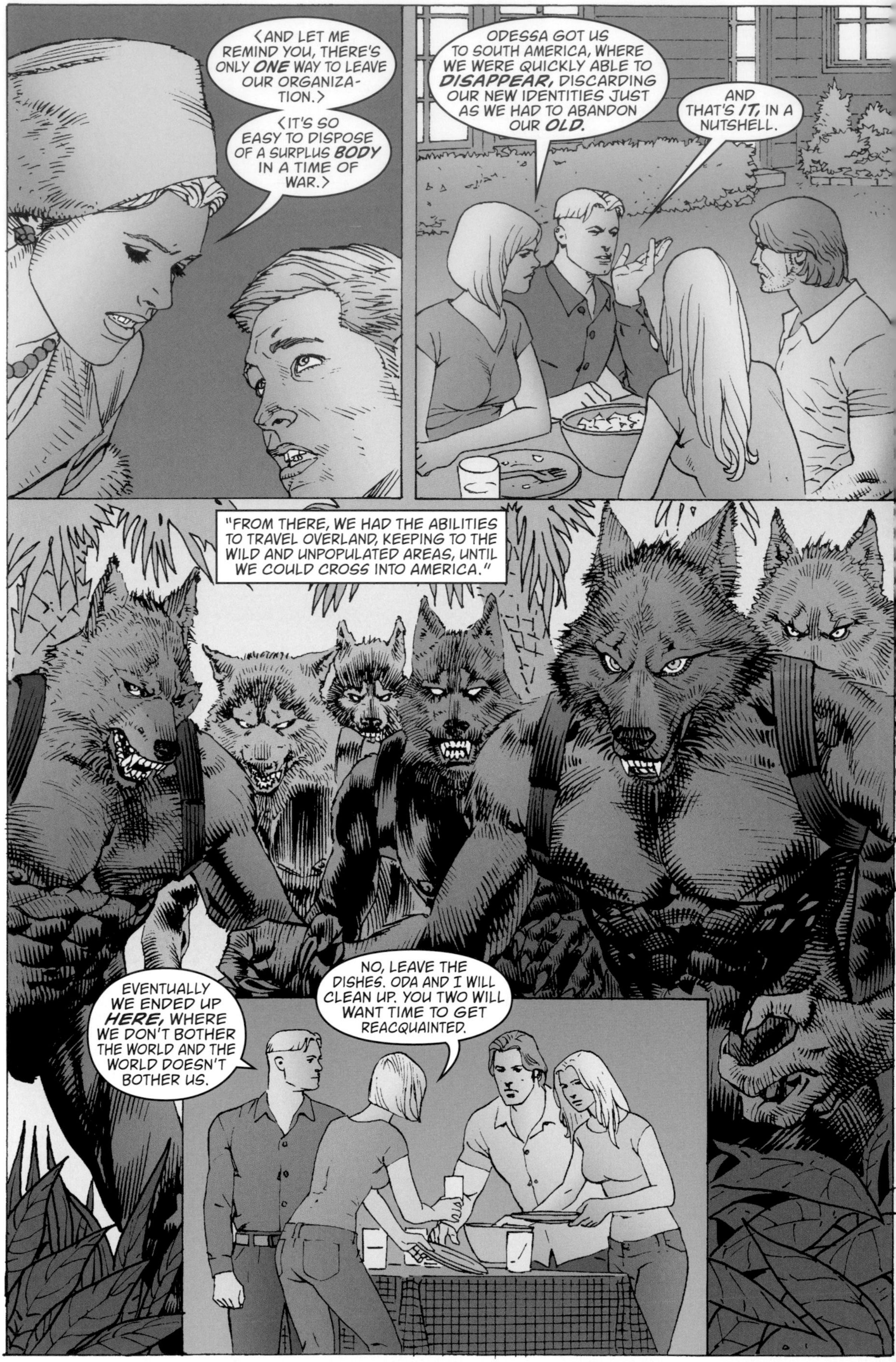
<AND LET ME REMIND YOU, THERE'S ONLY ONE WAY TO LEAVE OUR ORGANIZATION.>
<IT'S SO EASY TO DISPOSE OF A SURPLUS BODY IN A TIME OF WAR.>
ODESSA GOT US TO SOUTH AMERICA, WHERE WE WERE QUICKLY ABLE TO DISAPPEAR, DISCARDING OUR NEW IDENTITIES JUST AS WE HAD TO ABANDON OUR OLD.
AND THAT'S IT, IN A NUTSHELL.
"FROM THERE, WE HAD THE ABILITIES TO TRAVEL OVERLAND, KEEPING TO THE WILD AND UNPOPULATED AREAS, UNTIL WE COULD CROSS INTO AMERICA."
EVENTUALLY WE ENDED UP HERE, WHERE WE DON'T BOTHER THE WORLD AND THE WORLD DOESN'T BOTHER US.
NO, LEAVE THE DISHES. ODA AND I WILL CLEAN UP. YOU TWO WILL WANT TIME TO GET REACQUAINTED.

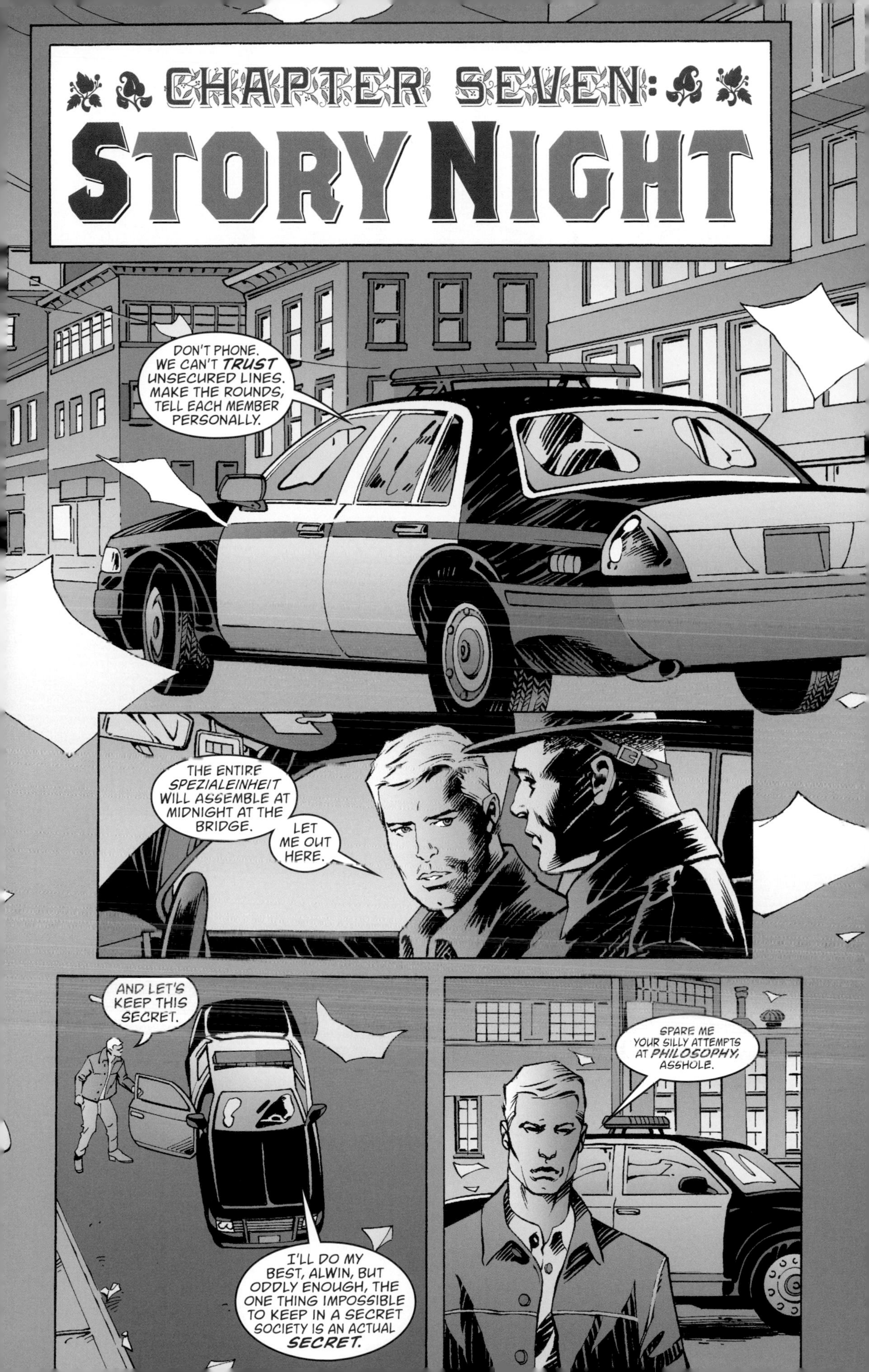
CHAPTER SEVEN:
STORY NIGHT
DON'T PHONE. WE CAN'T TRUST UNSECURED LINES. MAKE THE ROUNDS, TELL EACH MEMBER PERSONALLY.
THE ENTIRE SPEZIALEINHEIT WILL ASSEMBLE AT MIDNIGHT AT THE BRIDGE.
LET ME OUT HERE.
AND LET'S KEEP THIS SECRET.
I'LL DO MY BEST, ALWIN, BUT ODDLY ENOUGH, THE ONE THING IMPOSSIBLE TO KEEP IN A SECRET SOCIETY IS AN ACTUAL SECRET.
SPARE ME YOUR SILLY ATTEMPTS AT PHILOSOPHY, ASSHOLE.

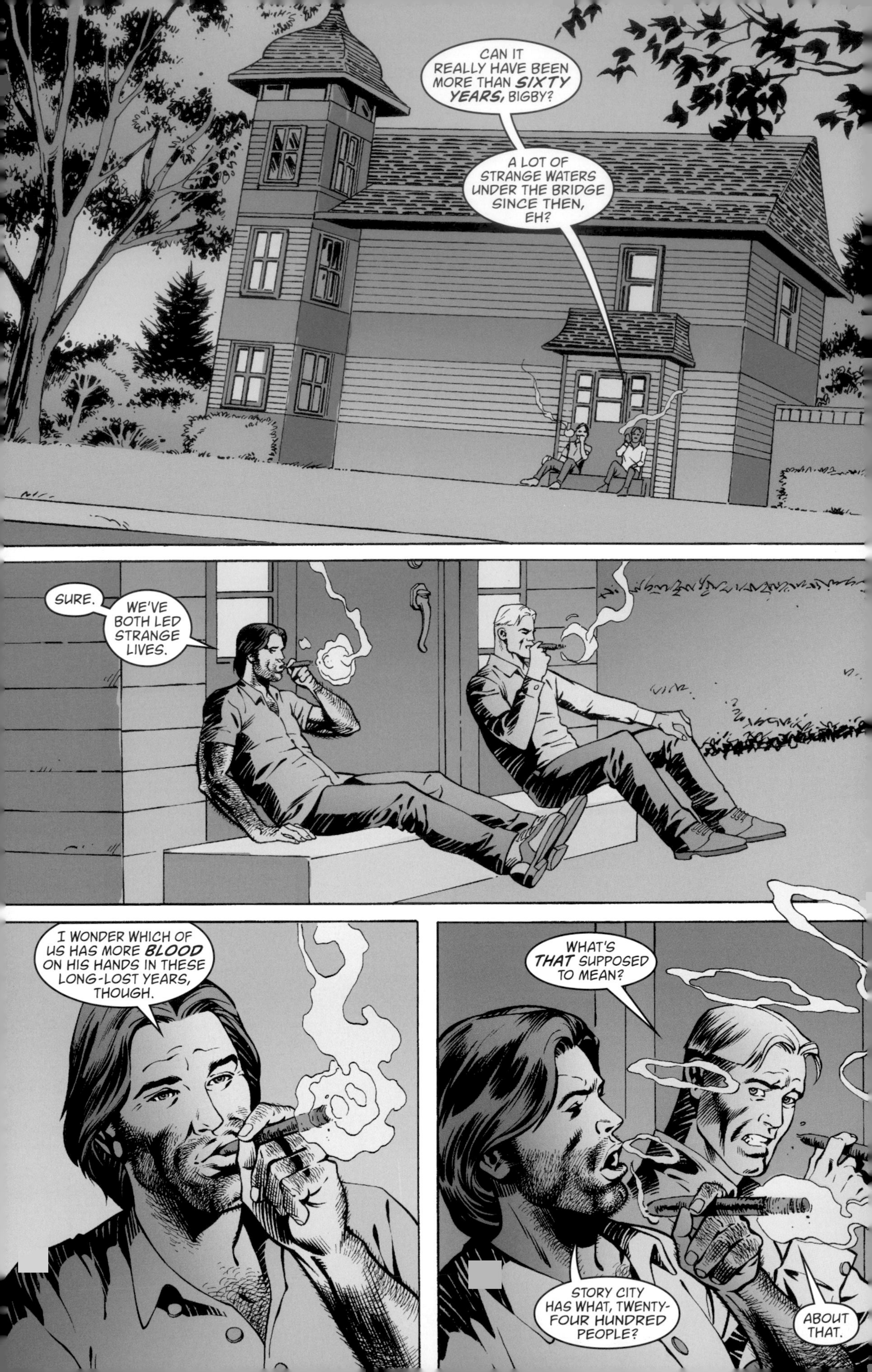
CAN IT REALLY HAVE BEEN MORE THAN SIXTY YEARS, BIGBY?
A LOT OF STRANGE WATERS UNDER THE BRIDGE SINCE THEN, EH?
SURE.
WE'VE BOTH LED STRANGE LIVES.
I WONDER WHICH OF US HAS MORE BLOOD ON HIS HANDS IN THESE LONG-LOST YEARS, THOUGH.
WHAT'S THAT SUPPOSED TO MEAN?
STORY CITY HAS WHAT, TWENTY-FOUR HUNDRED PEOPLE?
ABOUT THAT.

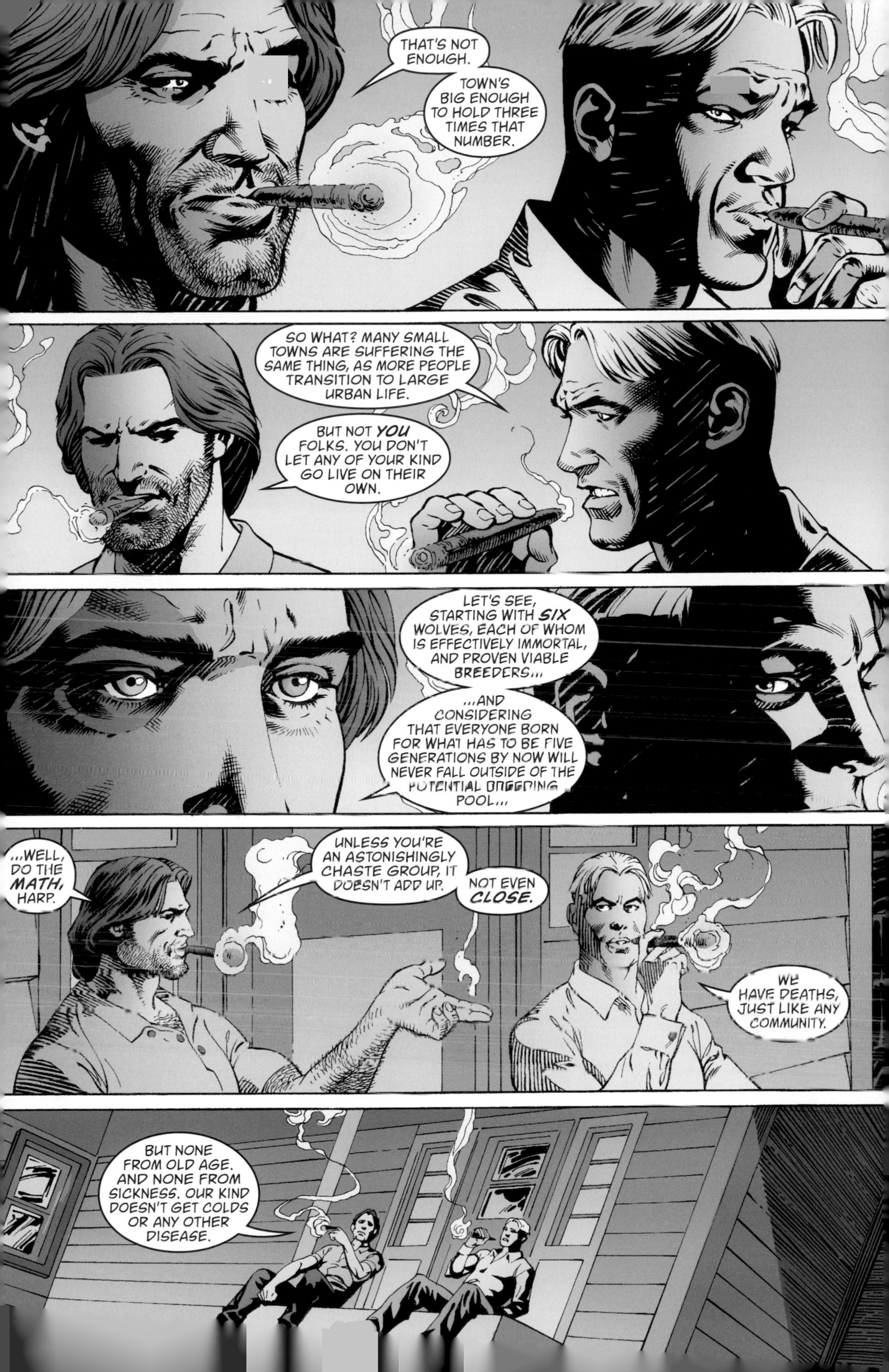
THAT'S NOT ENOUGH.
TOWN'S BIG ENOUGH TO HOLD THREE TIMES THAT NUMBER.
SO WHAT? MANY SMALL TOWNS ARE SUFFERING THE SAME THING, AS MORE PEOPLE TRANSITION TO LARGE URBAN LIFE.
BUT NOT YOU FOLKS. YOU DON'T LET ANY OF YOUR KIND GO LIVE ON THEIR OWN.
LET'S SEE, STARTING WITH SIX WOLVES, EACH OF WHOM IS EFFECTIVELY IMMORTAL, AND PROVEN VIABLE BREEDERS...
...AND CONSIDERING THAT EVERYONE BORN FOR WHAT HAS TO BE FIVE GENERATIONS BY NOW WILL NEVER FALL OUTSIDE OF THE POTENTIAL BREEDING POOL...
...WELL, DO THE MATH, HARP.
UNLESS YOU'RE AN ASTONISHINGLY CHASTE GROUP, IT DOESN'T ADD UP.
NOT EVEN CLOSE.
WE HAVE DEATHS, JUST LIKE ANY COMMUNITY.
BUT NONE FROM OLD AGE. AND NONE FROM SICKNESS. OUR KIND DOESN'T GET COLDS OR ANY OTHER DISEASE.

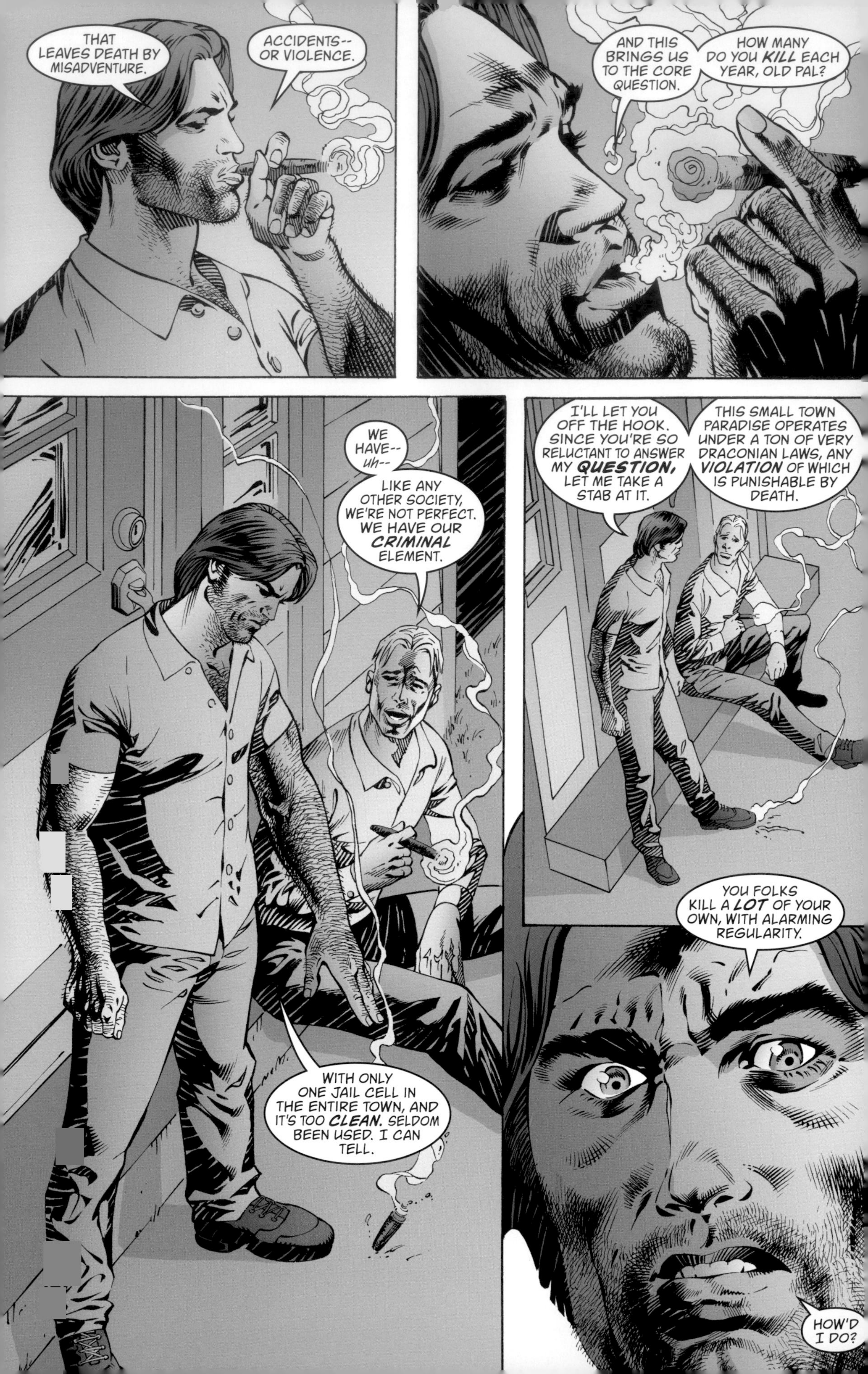
THAT LEAVES DEATH BY MISADVENTURE.
ACCIDENTS-- OR VIOLENCE.
AND THIS BRINGS US TO THE CORE QUESTION.
HOW MANY DO YOU KILL EACH YEAR, OLD PAL?
WE HAVE-- uh--
LIKE ANY OTHER SOCIETY, WE'RE NOT PERFECT. WE HAVE OUR CRIMINAL ELEMENT.
WITH ONLY ONE JAIL CELL IN THE ENTIRE TOWN, AND IT'S TOO CLEAN. SELDOM BEEN USED. I CAN TELL.
I'LL LET YOU OFF THE HOOK. SINCE YOU'RE SO RELUCTANT TO ANSWER MY QUESTION, LET ME TAKE A STAB AT IT.
THIS SMALL TOWN PARADISE OPERATES UNDER A TON OF VERY DRACONIAN LAWS, ANY VIOLATION OF WHICH IS PUNISHABLE BY DEATH.
YOU FOLKS KILL A LOT OF YOUR OWN, WITH ALARMING REGULARITY.
HOW'D I DO?

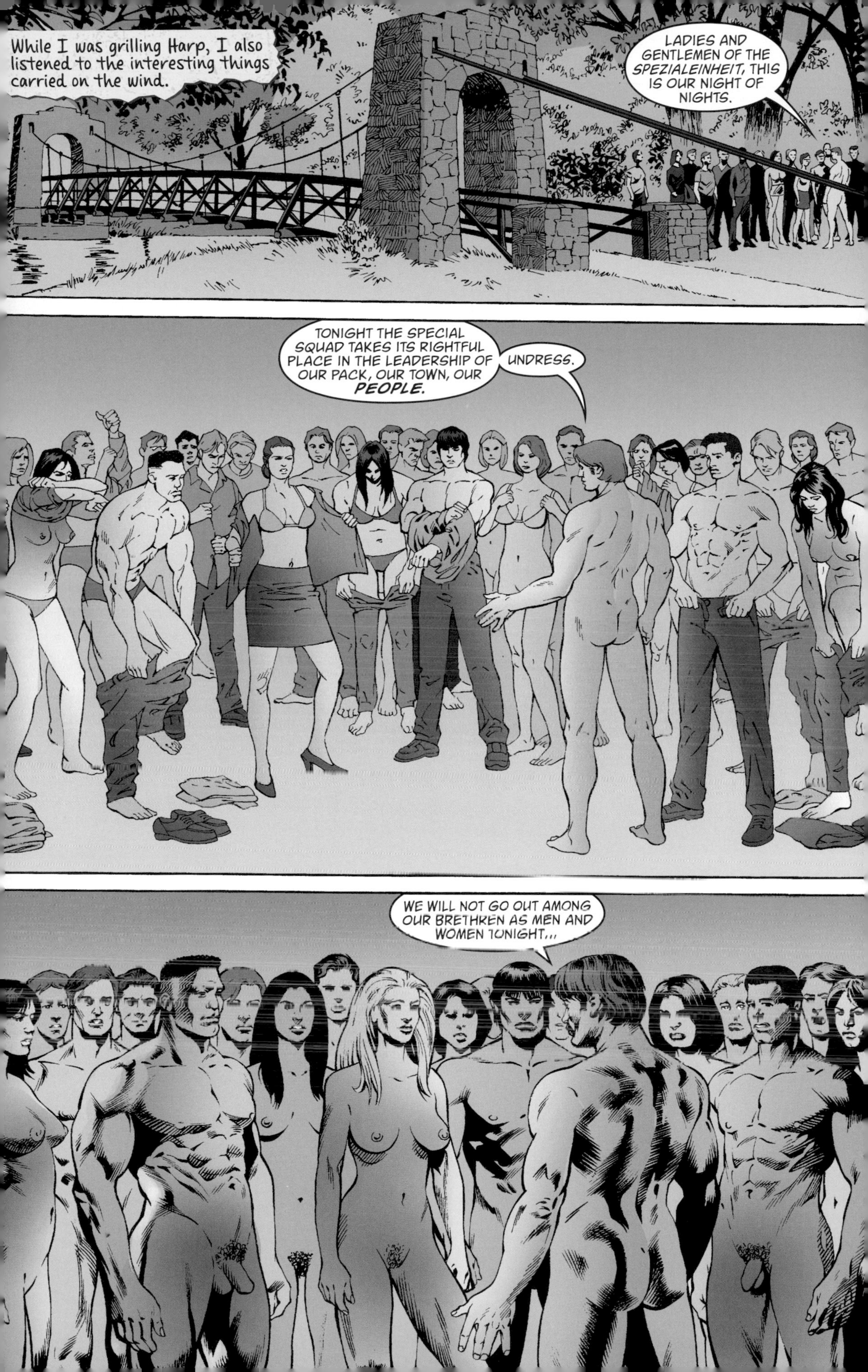
While I was grilling Harp, I also listened to the interesting things carried on the wind.
LADIES AND GENTLEMEN OF THE *SPEZIALEINHEIT*, THIS IS OUR NIGHT OF NIGHTS.
TONIGHT THE SPECIAL SQUAD TAKES ITS RIGHTFUL PLACE IN THE LEADERSHIP OF OUR PACK, OUR TOWN, OUR ***PEOPLE.***
UNDRESS.
WE WILL NOT GO OUT AMONG OUR BRETHREN AS MEN AND WOMEN TONIGHT...

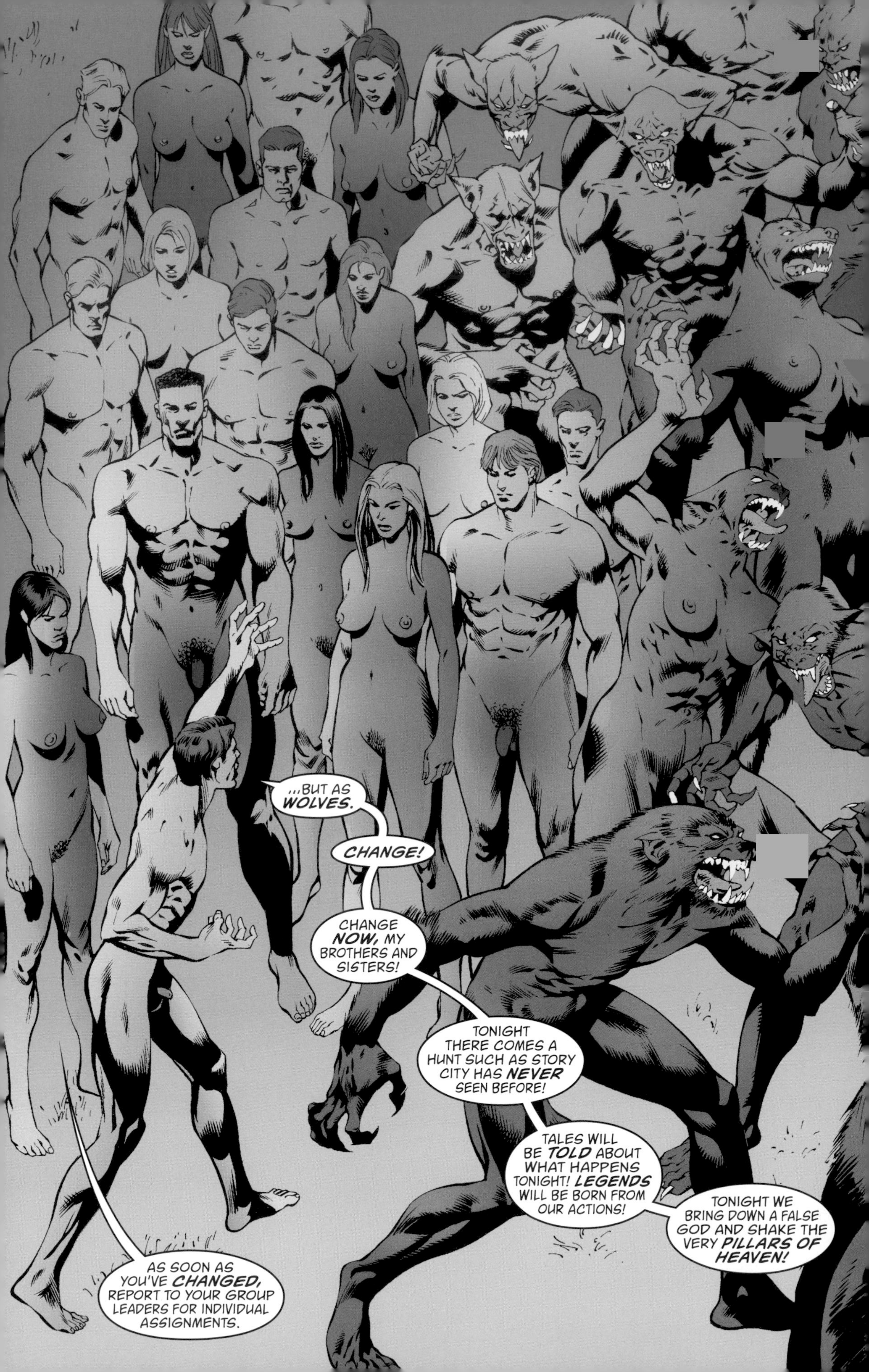
...BUT AS WOLVES.
CHANGE!
CHANGE NOW, MY BROTHERS AND SISTERS!
TONIGHT THERE COMES A HUNT SUCH AS STORY CITY HAS NEVER SEEN BEFORE!
TALES WILL BE TOLD ABOUT WHAT HAPPENS TONIGHT! LEGENDS WILL BE BORN FROM OUR ACTIONS!
TONIGHT WE BRING DOWN A FALSE GOD AND SHAKE THE VERY PILLARS OF HEAVEN!
AS SOON AS YOU'VE CHANGED, REPORT TO YOUR GROUP LEADERS FOR INDIVIDUAL ASSIGNMENTS.

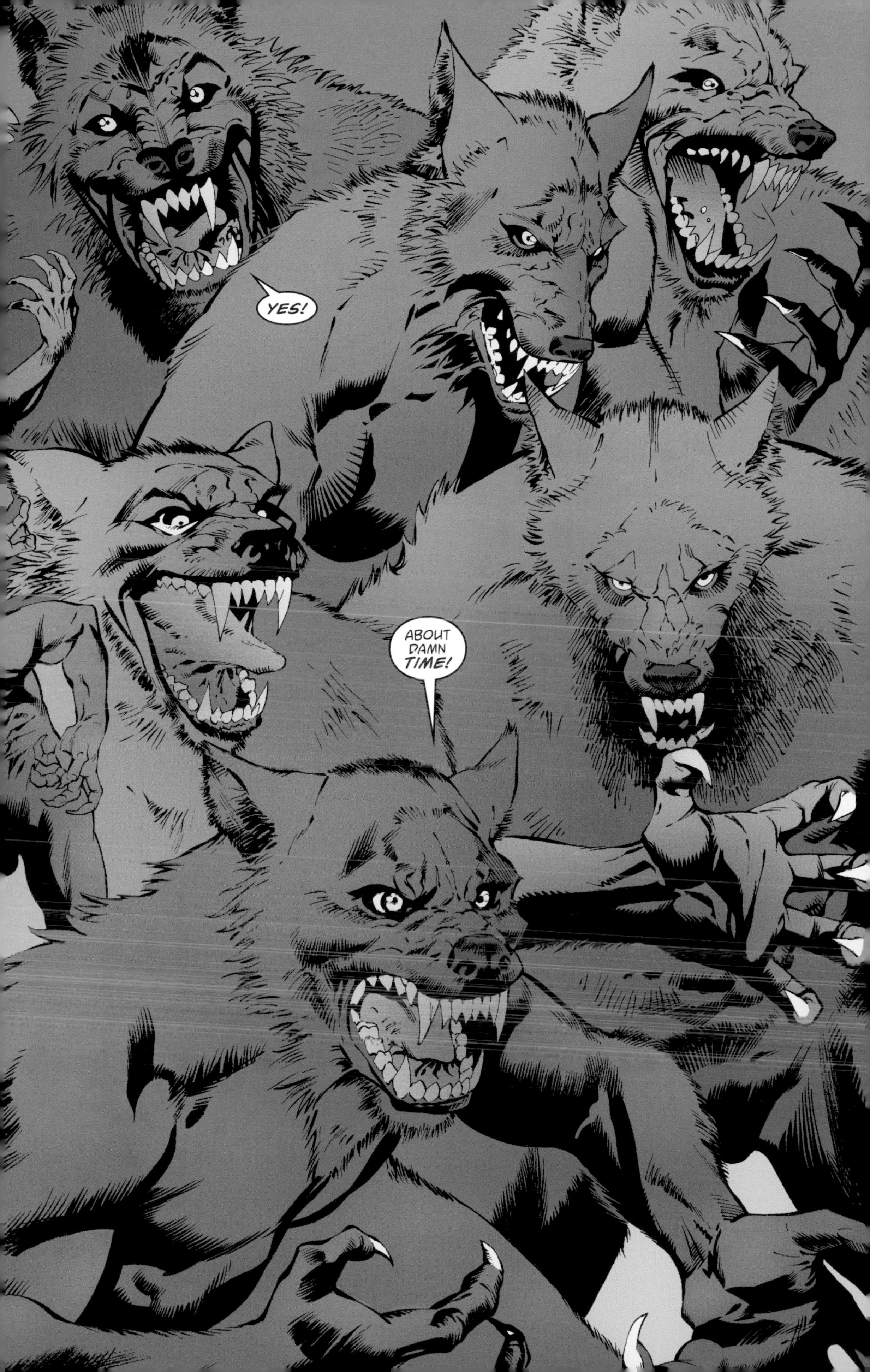
YES!
ABOUT DAMN TIME!

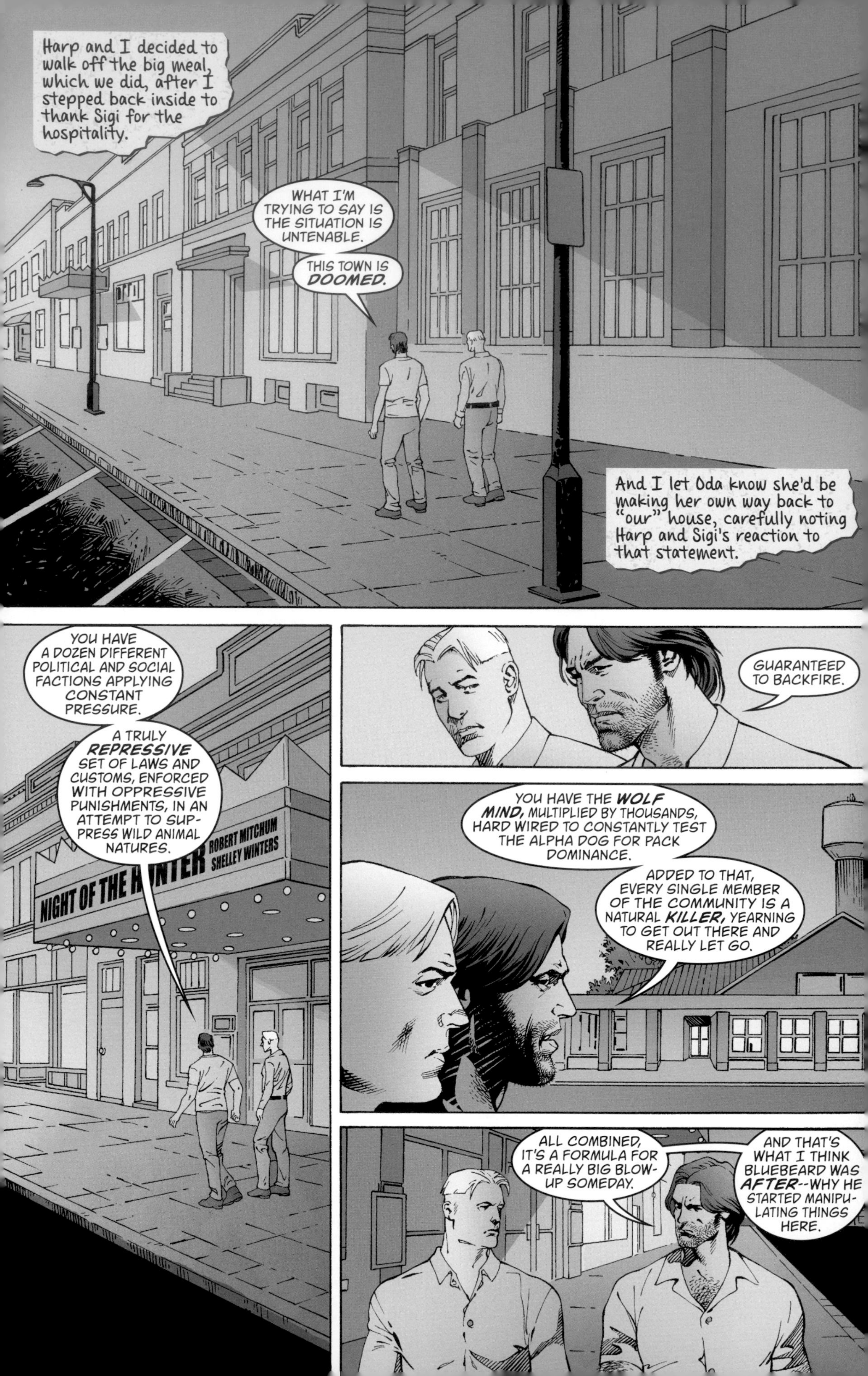
Harp and I decided to walk off the big meal, which we did, after I stepped back inside to thank Sigi for the hospitality.
WHAT I'M TRYING TO SAY IS THE SITUATION IS UNTENABLE.
THIS TOWN IS DOOMED.
And I let Oda know she'd be making her own way back to "our" house, carefully noting Harp and Sigi's reaction to that statement.
YOU HAVE A DOZEN DIFFERENT POLITICAL AND SOCIAL FACTIONS APPLYING CONSTANT PRESSURE.
A TRULY REPRESSIVE SET OF LAWS AND CUSTOMS, ENFORCED WITH OPPRESSIVE PUNISHMENTS, IN AN ATTEMPT TO SUPPRESS WILD ANIMAL NATURES.
ROBERT MITCHUM
SHELLEY WINTERS
NIGHT OF THE HUNTER
GUARANTEED TO BACKFIRE.
YOU HAVE THE WOLF MIND, MULTIPLIED BY THOUSANDS, HARD WIRED TO CONSTANTLY TEST THE ALPHA DOG FOR PACK DOMINANCE.
ADDED TO THAT, EVERY SINGLE MEMBER OF THE COMMUNITY IS A NATURAL KILLER, YEARNING TO GET OUT THERE AND REALLY LET GO.
ALL COMBINED, IT'S A FORMULA FOR A REALLY BIG BLOW-UP SOMEDAY.
AND THAT'S WHAT I THINK BLUEBEARD WAS AFTER--WHY HE STARTED MANIPULATING THINGS HERE.

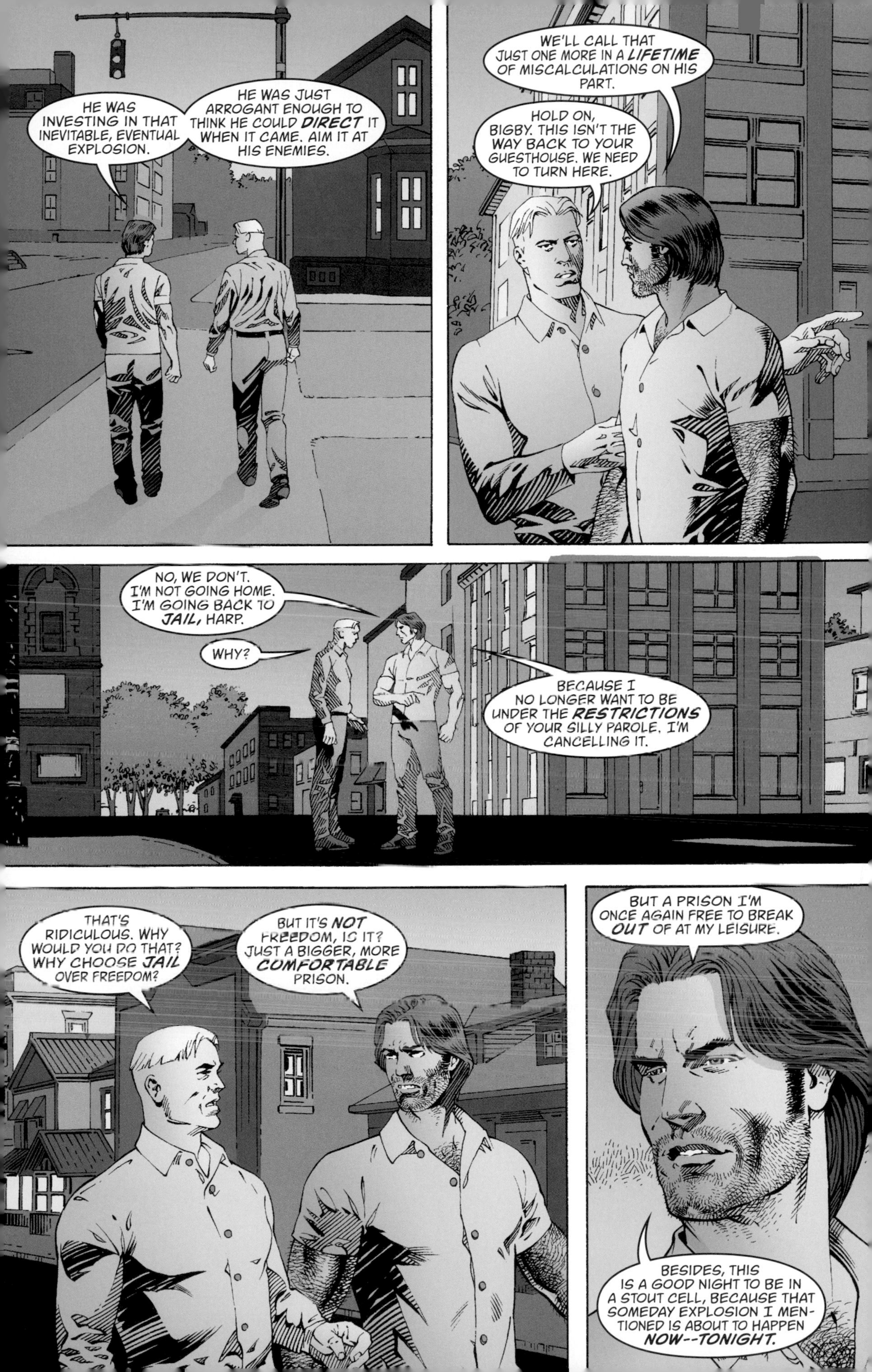
HE WAS INVESTING IN THAT INEVITABLE, EVENTUAL EXPLOSION.
HE WAS JUST ARROGANT ENOUGH TO THINK HE COULD DIRECT IT WHEN IT CAME. AIM IT AT HIS ENEMIES.
WE'LL CALL THAT JUST ONE MORE IN A LIFETIME OF MISCALCULATIONS ON HIS PART.
HOLD ON, BIGBY. THIS ISN'T THE WAY BACK TO YOUR GUESTHOUSE. WE NEED TO TURN HERE.
NO, WE DON'T. I'M NOT GOING HOME. I'M GOING BACK TO JAIL, HARP.
WHY?
BECAUSE I NO LONGER WANT TO BE UNDER THE RESTRICTIONS OF YOUR SILLY PAROLE. I'M CANCELLING IT.
THAT'S RIDICULOUS. WHY WOULD YOU DO THAT? WHY CHOOSE JAIL OVER FREEDOM?
BUT IT'S NOT FREEDOM, IS IT? JUST A BIGGER, MORE COMFORTABLE PRISON.
BUT A PRISON I'M ONCE AGAIN FREE TO BREAK OUT OF AT MY LEISURE.
BESIDES, THIS IS A GOOD NIGHT TO BE IN A STOUT CELL, BECAUSE THAT SOMEDAY EXPLOSION I MENTIONED IS ABOUT TO HAPPEN NOW--TONIGHT.

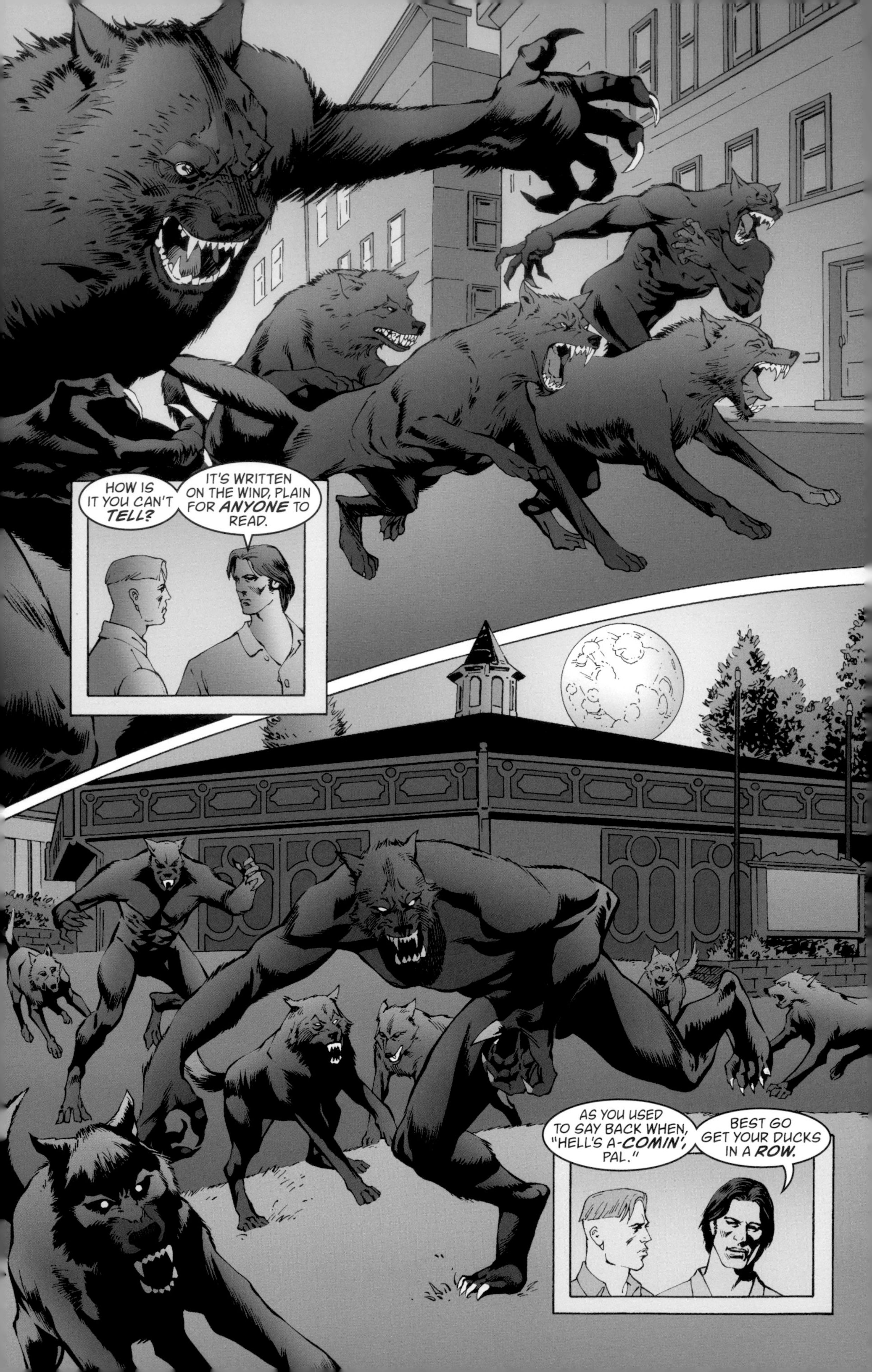
HOW IS IT YOU CAN'T TELL?
IT'S WRITTEN ON THE WIND, PLAIN FOR ANYONE TO READ.
AS YOU USED TO SAY BACK WHEN, "HELL'S A-COMIN', PAL."
BEST GO GET YOUR DUCKS IN A ROW.

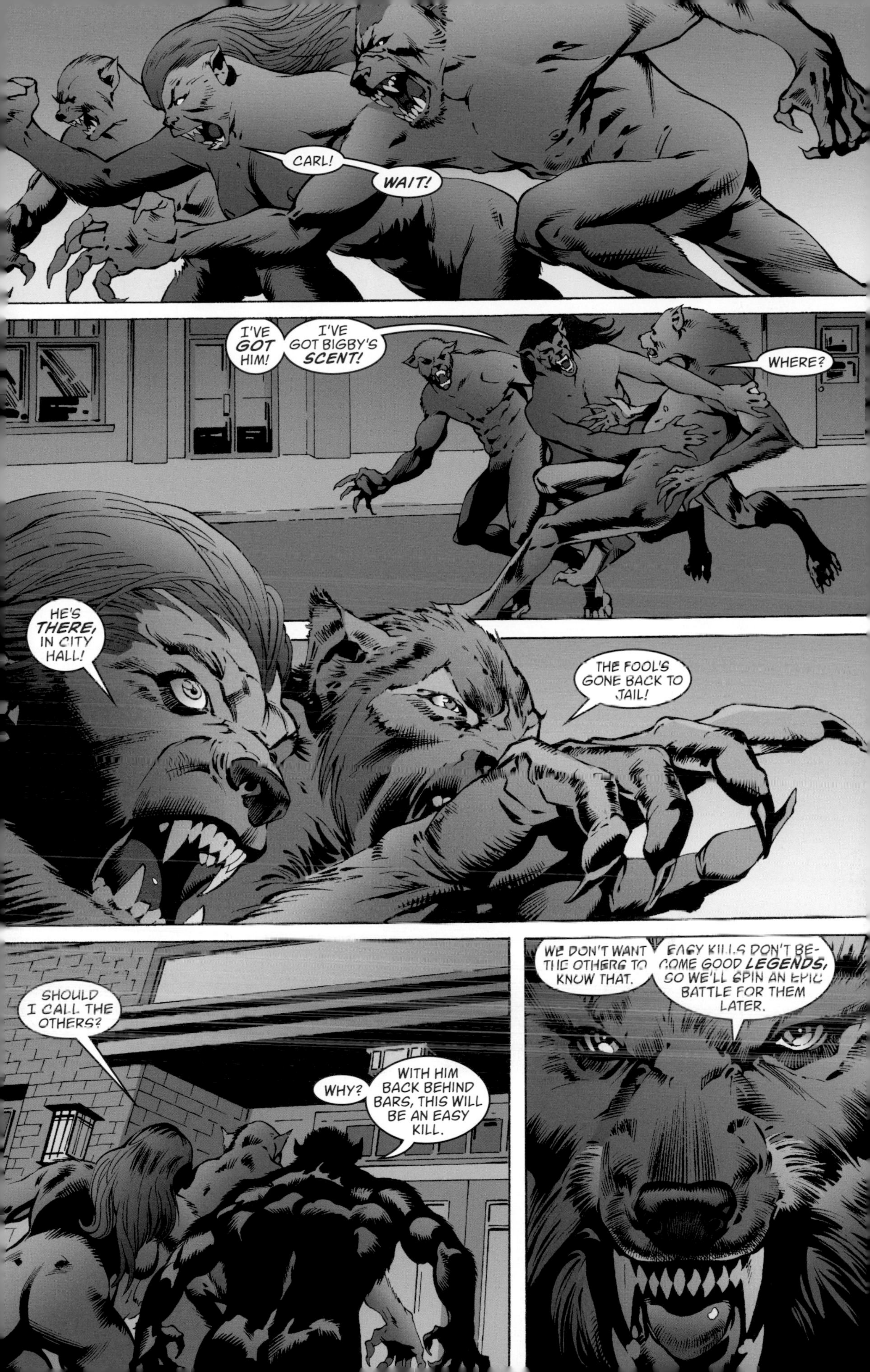
CARL!
WAIT!
I'VE GOT HIM!
I'VE GOT BIGBY'S SCENT!
WHERE?
HE'S THERE, IN CITY HALL!
THE FOOL'S GONE BACK TO JAIL!
SHOULD I CALL THE OTHERS?
WHY?
WITH HIM BACK BEHIND BARS, THIS WILL BE AN EASY KILL.
WE DON'T WANT THE OTHERS TO KNOW THAT.
EASY KILLS DON'T BECOME GOOD LEGENDS, SO WE'LL SPIN AN EPIC BATTLE FOR THEM LATER.

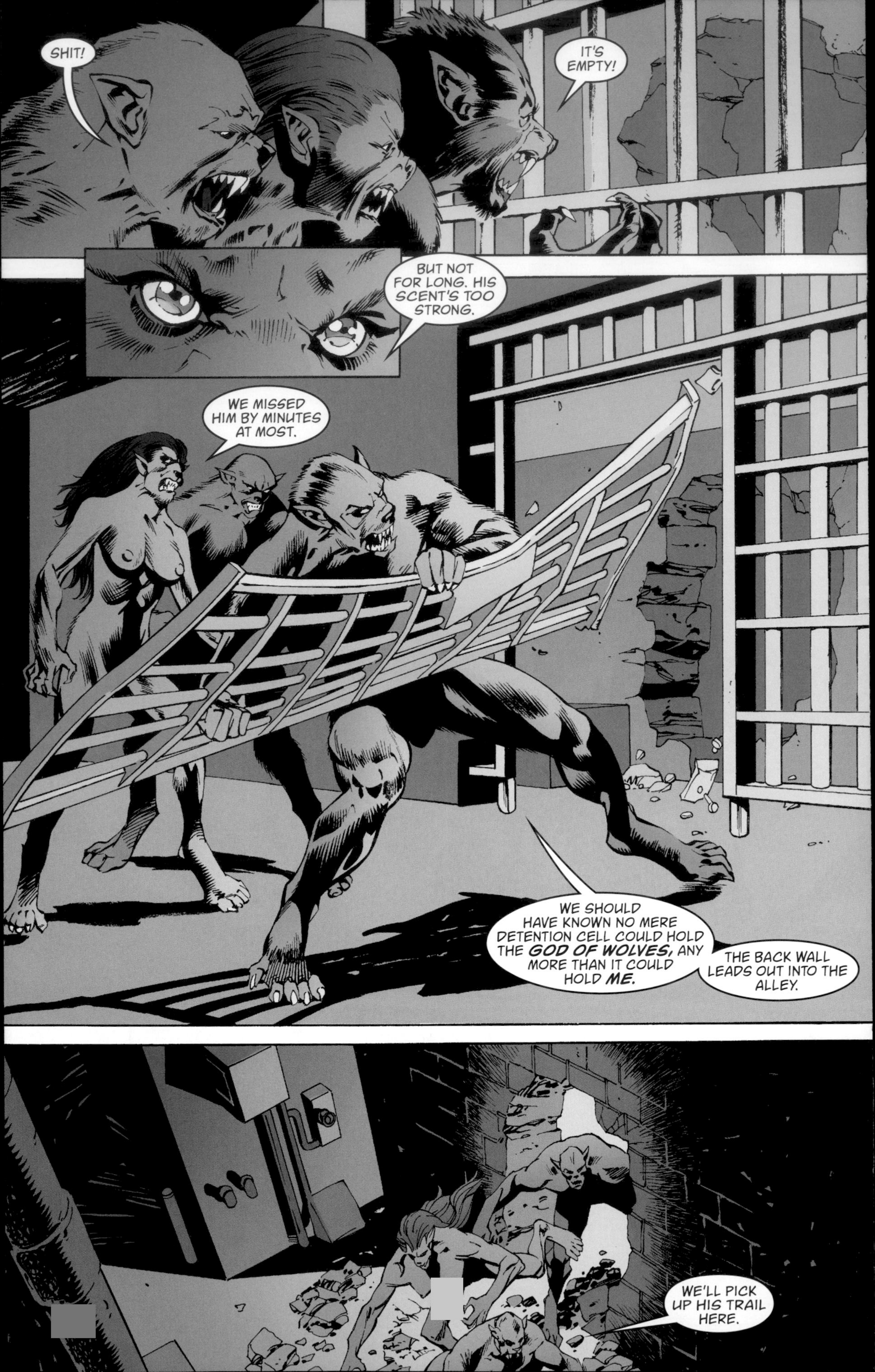
SHIT!
IT'S EMPTY!
BUT NOT FOR LONG. HIS SCENT'S TOO STRONG.
WE MISSED HIM BY MINUTES AT MOST.
WE SHOULD HAVE KNOWN NO MERE DETENTION CELL COULD HOLD THE GOD OF WOLVES, ANY MORE THAN IT COULD HOLD ME.
THE BACK WALL LEADS OUT INTO THE ALLEY.
WE'LL PICK UP HIS TRAIL HERE.

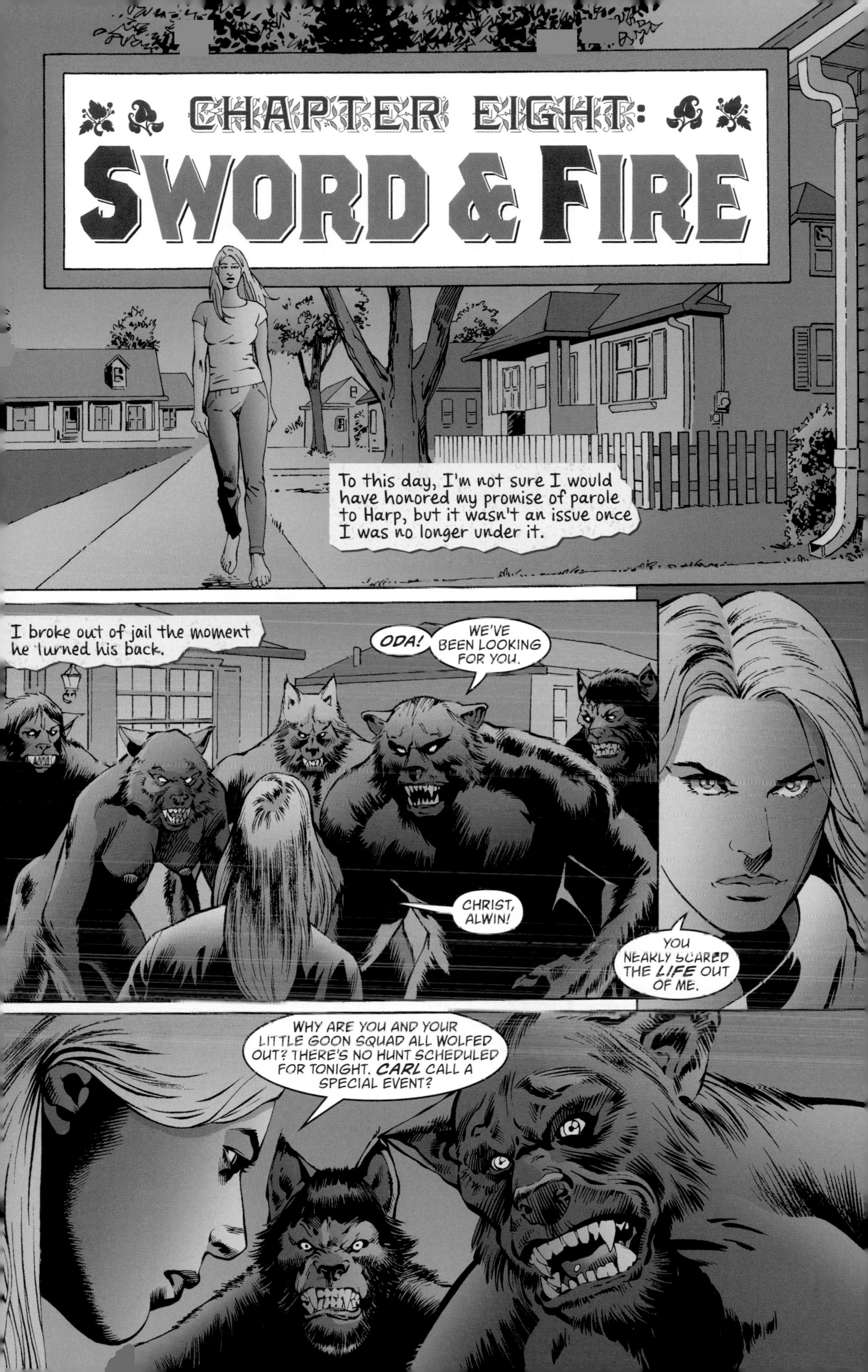
CHAPTER EIGHT:
SWORD & FIRE
To this day, I'm not sure I would have honored my promise of parole to Harp, but it wasn't an issue once I was no longer under it.
I broke out of jail the moment he turned his back.
ODA!
WE'VE BEEN LOOKING FOR YOU.
CHRIST, ALWIN!
YOU NEARLY SCARED THE LIFE OUT OF ME.
WHY ARE YOU AND YOUR LITTLE GOON SQUAD ALL WOLFED OUT? THERE'S NO HUNT SCHEDULED FOR TONIGHT. CARL CALL A SPECIAL EVENT?

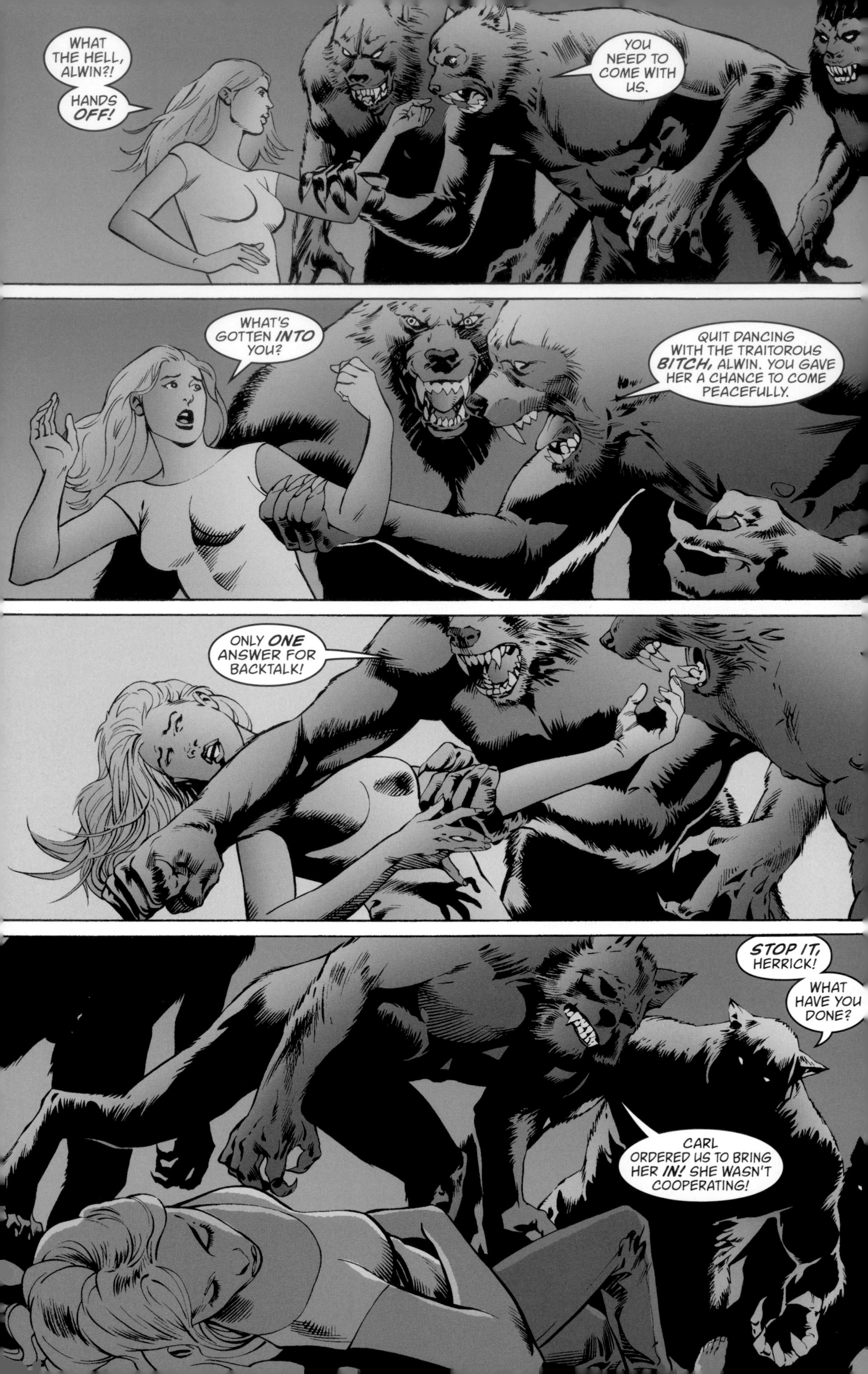
WHAT THE HELL, ALWIN?!
HANDS OFF!
YOU NEED TO COME WITH US.
WHAT'S GOTTEN INTO YOU?
QUIT DANCING WITH THE TRAITOROUS BITCH, ALWIN. YOU GAVE HER A CHANCE TO COME PEACEFULLY.
ONLY ONE ANSWER FOR BACKTALK!
STOP IT, HERRICK!
WHAT HAVE YOU DONE?
CARL ORDERED US TO BRING HER IN! SHE WASN'T COOPERATING!

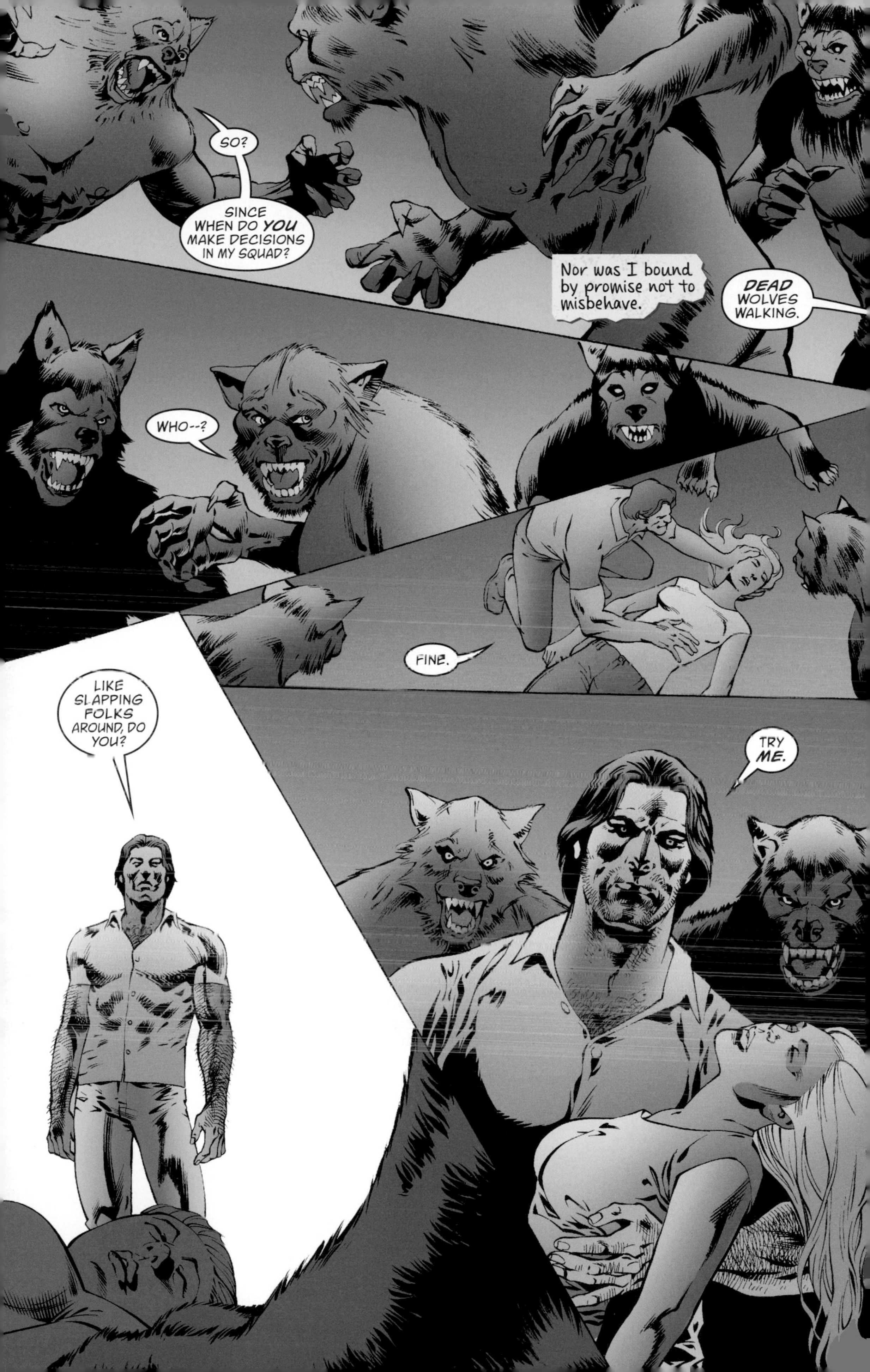
SO?
SINCE WHEN DO YOU MAKE DECISIONS IN MY SQUAD?
Nor was I bound by promise not to misbehave.
DEAD WOLVES WALKING.
WHO--?
FINE.
LIKE SLAPPING FOLKS AROUND, DO YOU?
TRY ME.

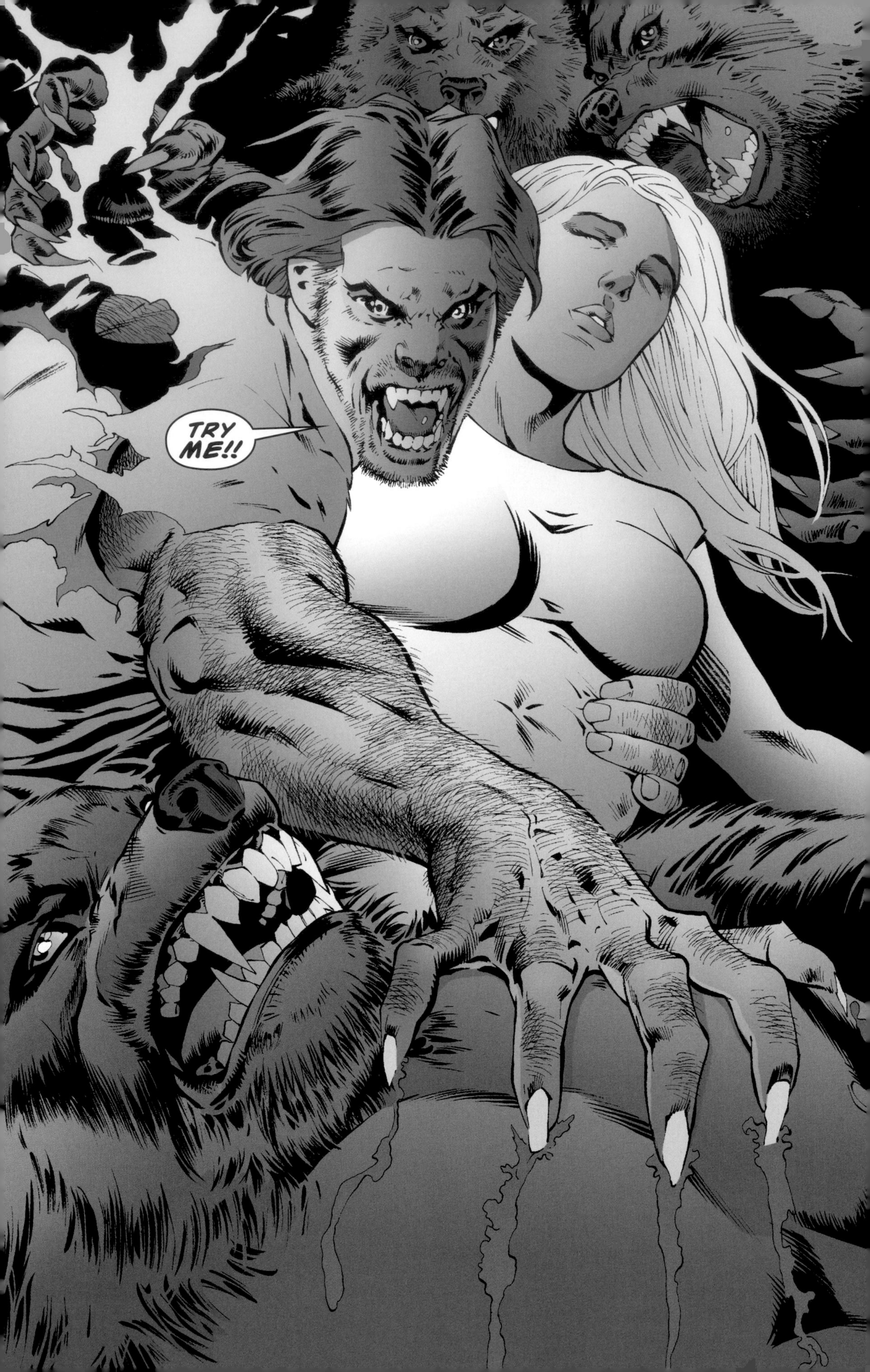
TRY ME!!

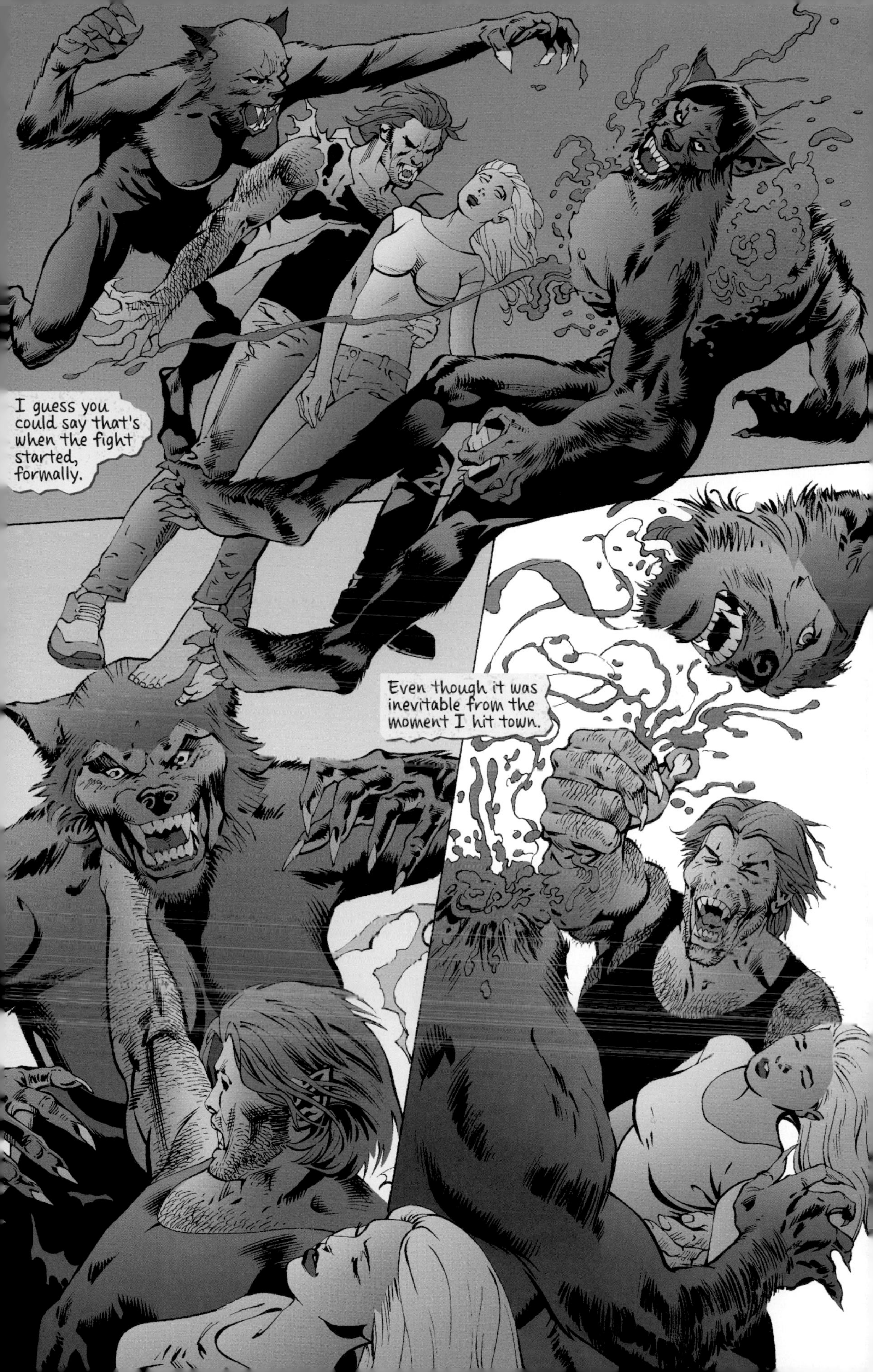
I guess you could say that's when the fight started, formally.
Even though it was inevitable from the moment I hit town.

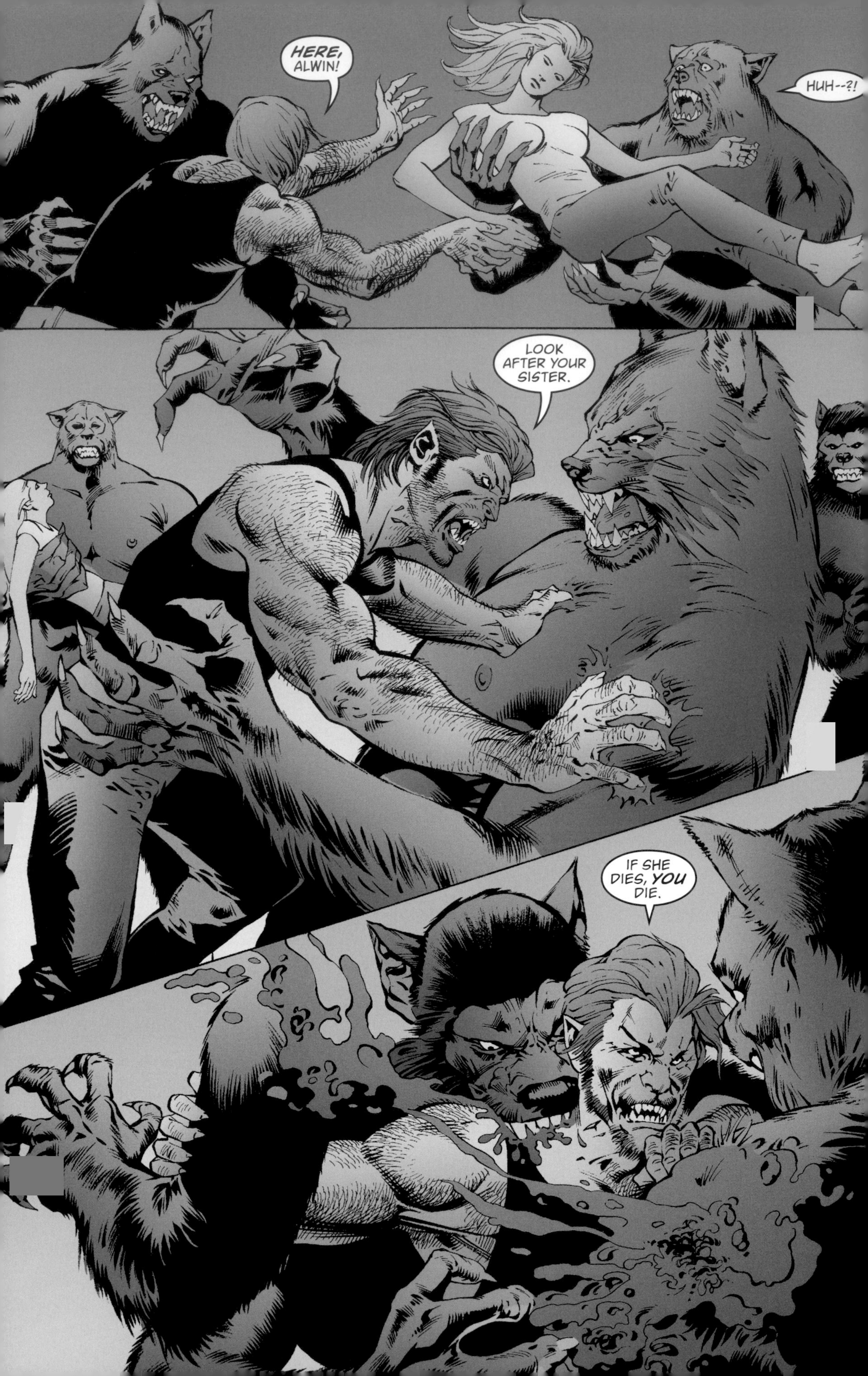
HERE, ALWIN!
HUH--?!
LOOK AFTER YOUR SISTER.
IF SHE DIES, YOU DIE.

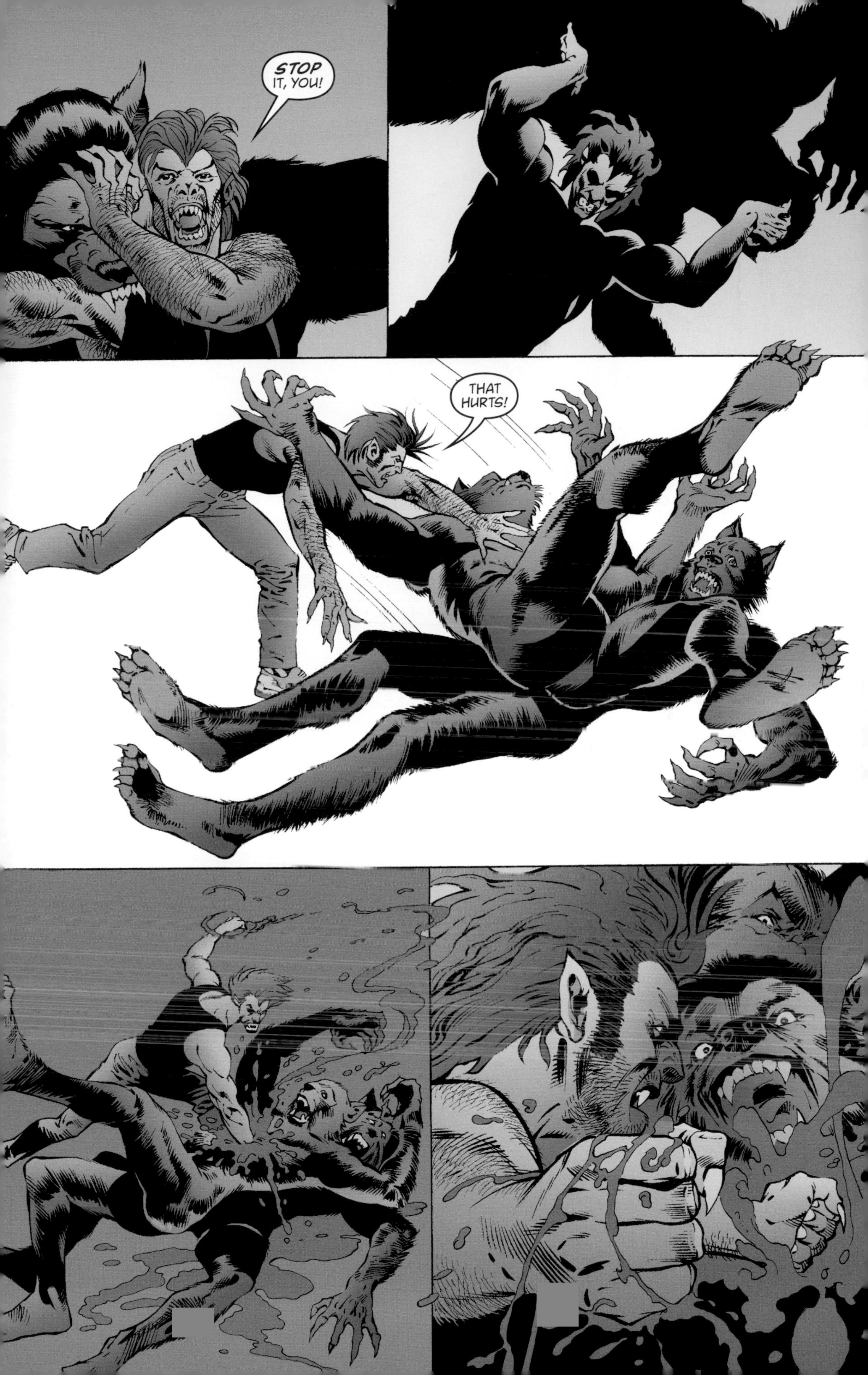
STOP IT, YOU!
THAT HURTS!

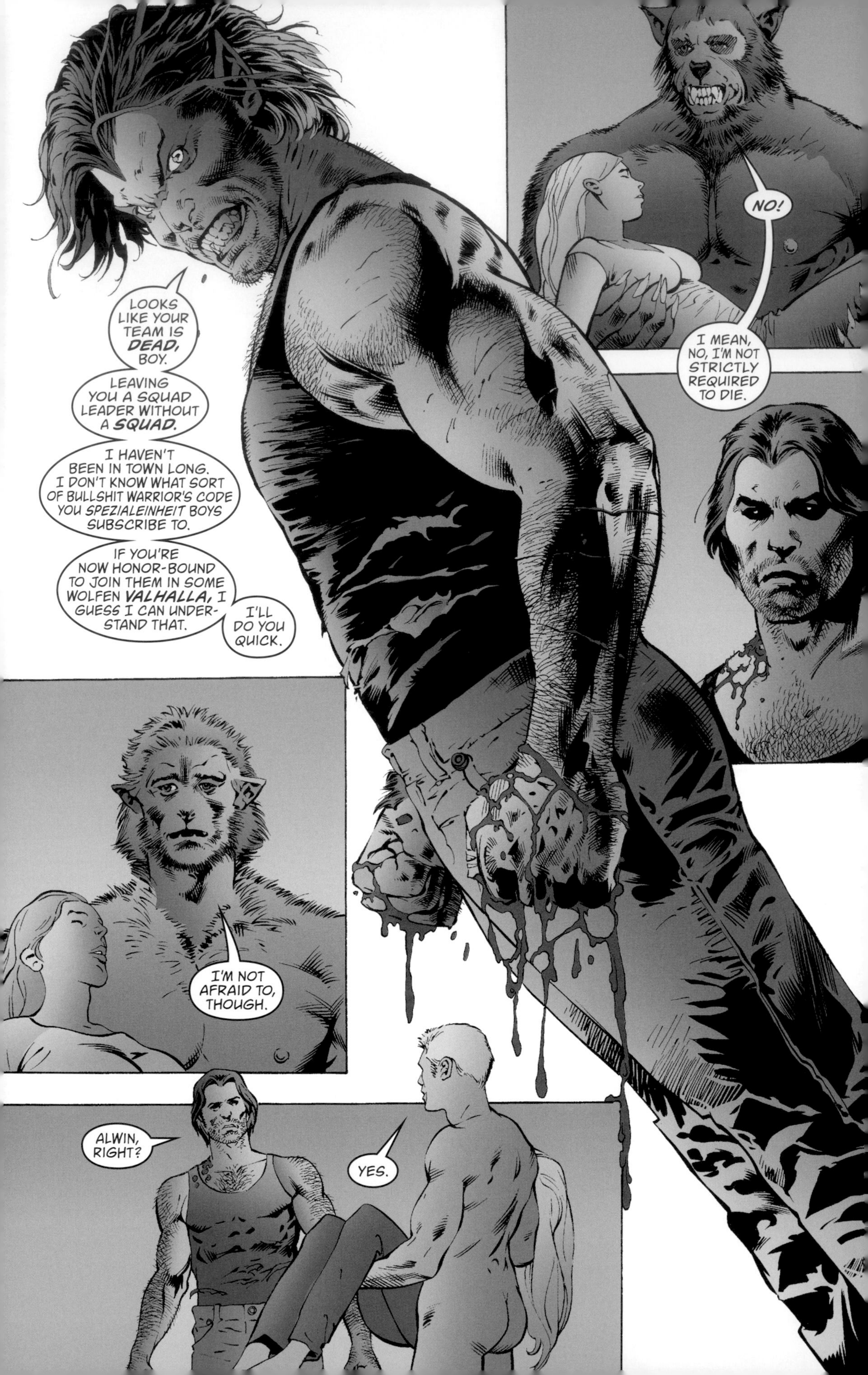

LOOKS LIKE YOUR TEAM IS **DEAD,** BOY.
LEAVING YOU A SQUAD LEADER WITHOUT A **SQUAD.**
I HAVEN'T BEEN IN TOWN LONG. I DON'T KNOW WHAT SORT OF BULLSHIT WARRIOR'S CODE YOU *SPEZIALEINHEIT* BOYS SUBSCRIBE TO.
IF YOU'RE NOW HONOR-BOUND TO JOIN THEM IN SOME WOLFEN **VALHALLA,** I GUESS I CAN UNDERSTAND THAT.
I'LL DO YOU QUICK.
NO!
I MEAN, NO, I'M NOT STRICTLY REQUIRED TO DIE.
I'M NOT AFRAID TO, THOUGH.
ALWIN, RIGHT?
YES.

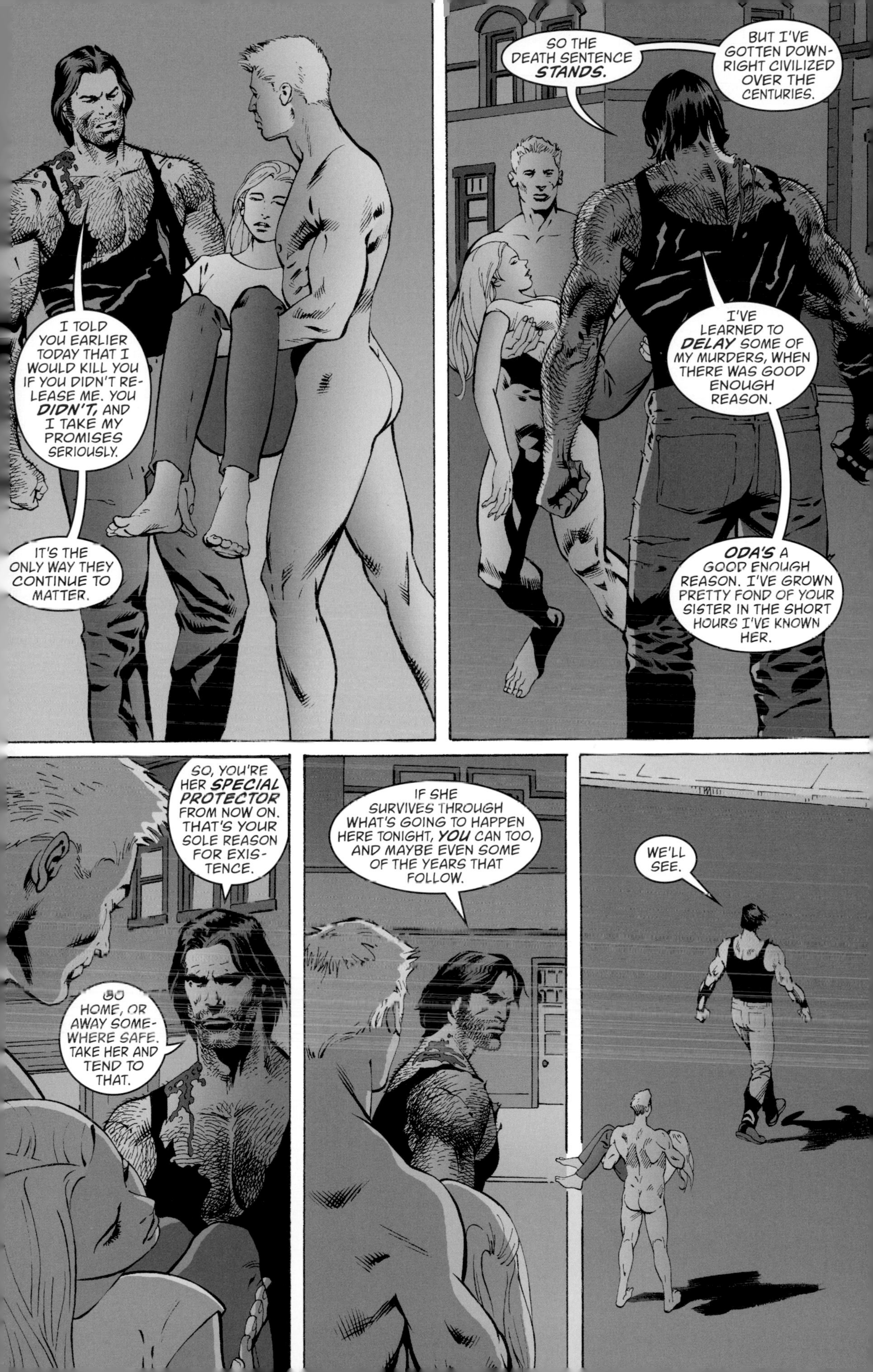

I TOLD YOU EARLIER TODAY THAT I WOULD KILL YOU IF YOU DIDN'T RE-LEASE ME. YOU **DIDN'T,** AND I TAKE MY PROMISES SERIOUSLY.
IT'S THE ONLY WAY THEY CONTINUE TO MATTER.
SO THE DEATH SENTENCE **STANDS.**
BUT I'VE GOTTEN DOWN-RIGHT CIVILIZED OVER THE CENTURIES.
I'VE LEARNED TO **DELAY** SOME OF MY MURDERS, WHEN THERE WAS GOOD ENOUGH REASON.
ODA'S A GOOD ENOUGH REASON. I'VE GROWN PRETTY FOND OF YOUR SISTER IN THE SHORT HOURS I'VE KNOWN HER.
SO, YOU'RE HER **SPECIAL PROTECTOR** FROM NOW ON. THAT'S YOUR SOLE REASON FOR EXIS-TENCE.
GO HOME, OR AWAY SOME-WHERE SAFE. TAKE HER AND TEND TO THAT.
IF SHE SURVIVES THROUGH WHAT'S GOING TO HAPPEN HERE TONIGHT, **YOU** CAN TOO, AND MAYBE EVEN SOME OF THE YEARS THAT FOLLOW.
WE'LL SEE.

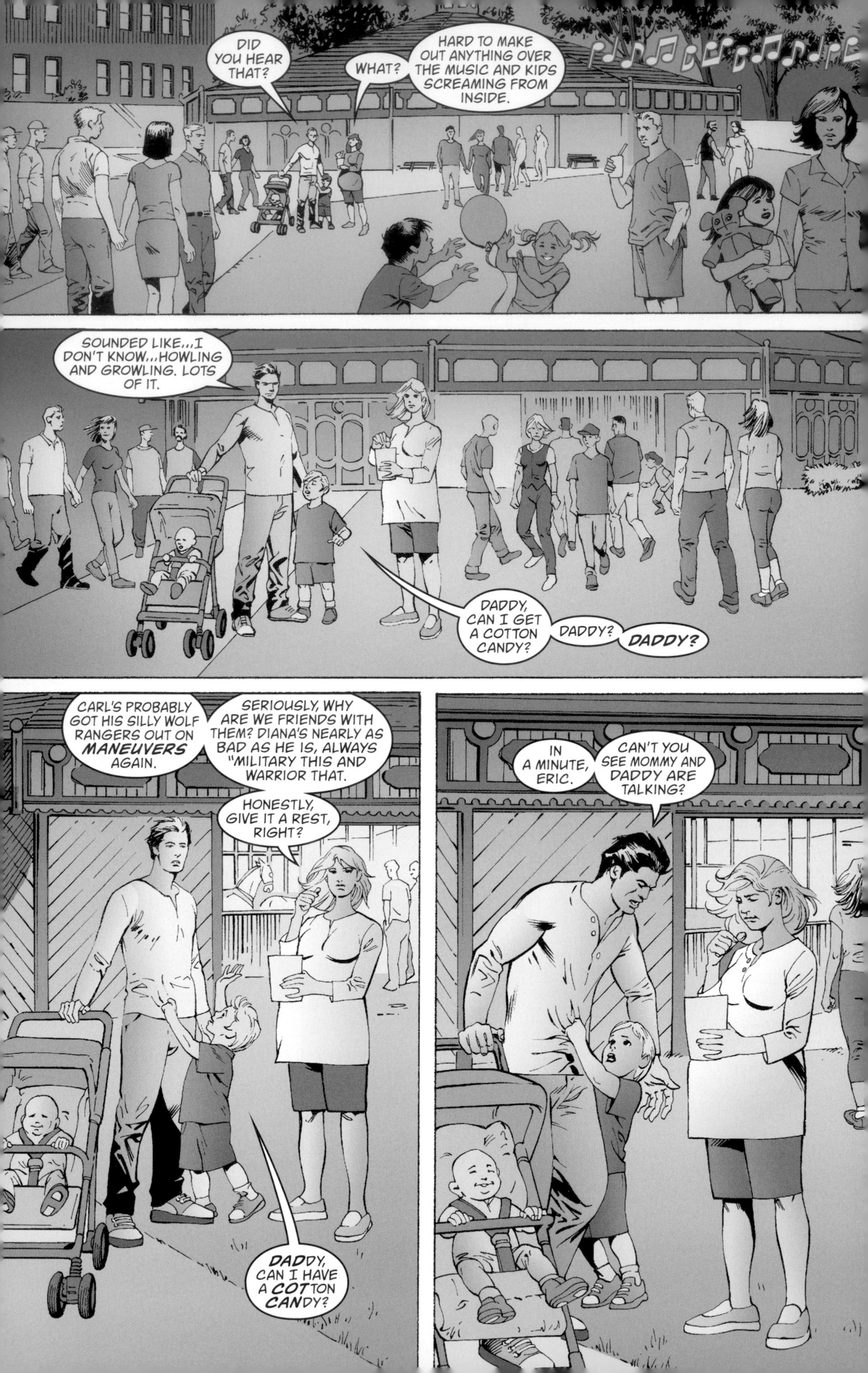

DID YOU HEAR THAT?
WHAT?
HARD TO MAKE OUT ANYTHING OVER THE MUSIC AND KIDS SCREAMING FROM INSIDE.
SOUNDED LIKE...I DON'T KNOW...HOWLING AND GROWLING. LOTS OF IT.
DADDY, CAN I GET A COTTON CANDY?
DADDY?
DADDY?
CARL'S PROBABLY GOT HIS SILLY WOLF RANGERS OUT ON MANEUVERS AGAIN.
SERIOUSLY, WHY ARE WE FRIENDS WITH THEM? DIANA'S NEARLY AS BAD AS HE IS, ALWAYS "MILITARY THIS AND WARRIOR THAT.
HONESTLY, GIVE IT A REST, RIGHT?
DADDY, CAN I HAVE A COTTON CANDY?
IN A MINUTE, ERIC.
CAN'T YOU SEE MOMMY AND DADDY ARE TALKING?

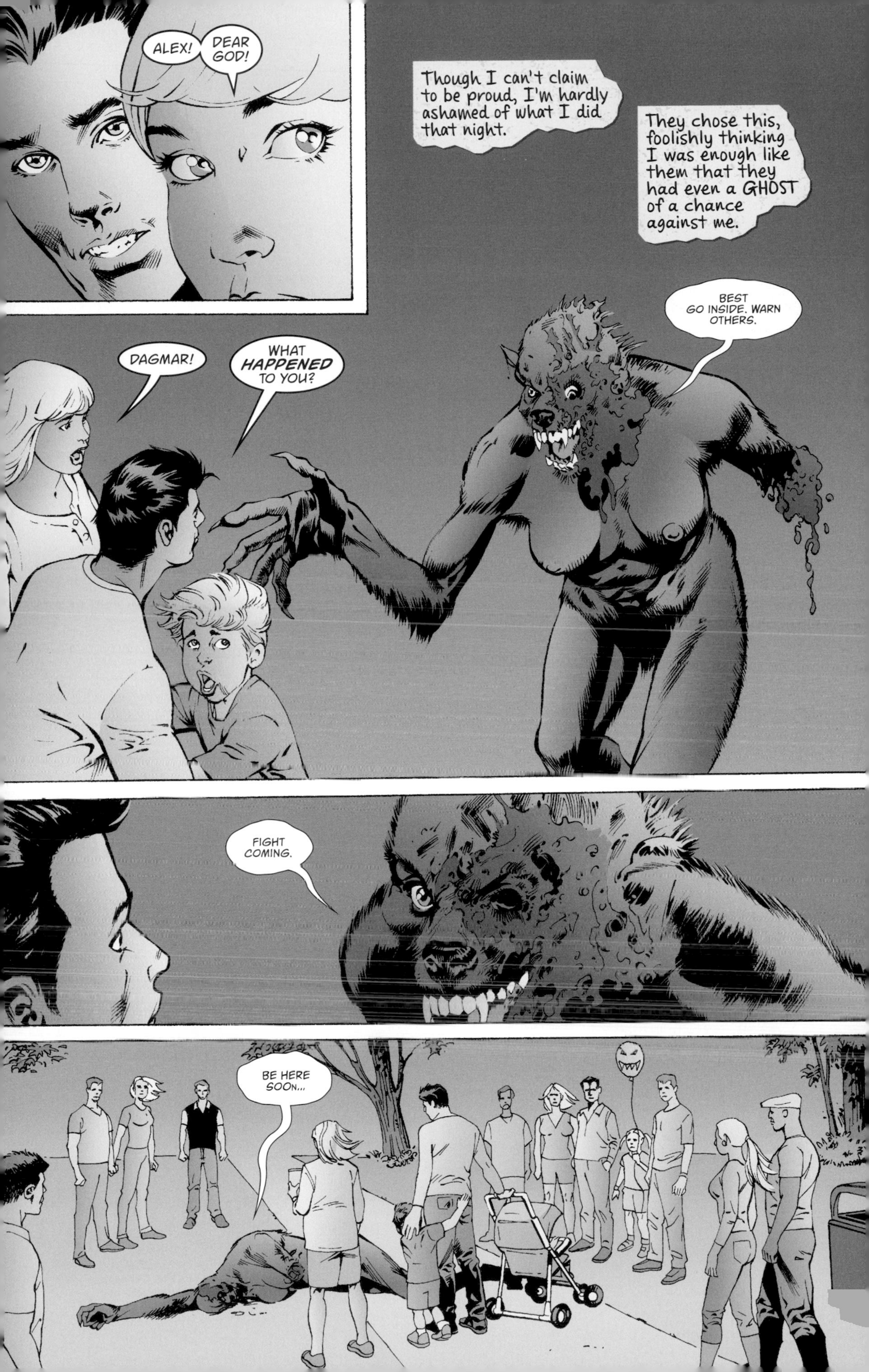
ALEX!
DEAR GOD!
Though I can't claim to be proud, I'm hardly ashamed of what I did that night.
They chose this, foolishly thinking I was enough like them that they had even a GHOST of a chance against me.
DAGMAR!
WHAT *HAPPENED* TO YOU?
BEST GO INSIDE. WARN OTHERS.
FIGHT COMING.
BE HERE SOON...

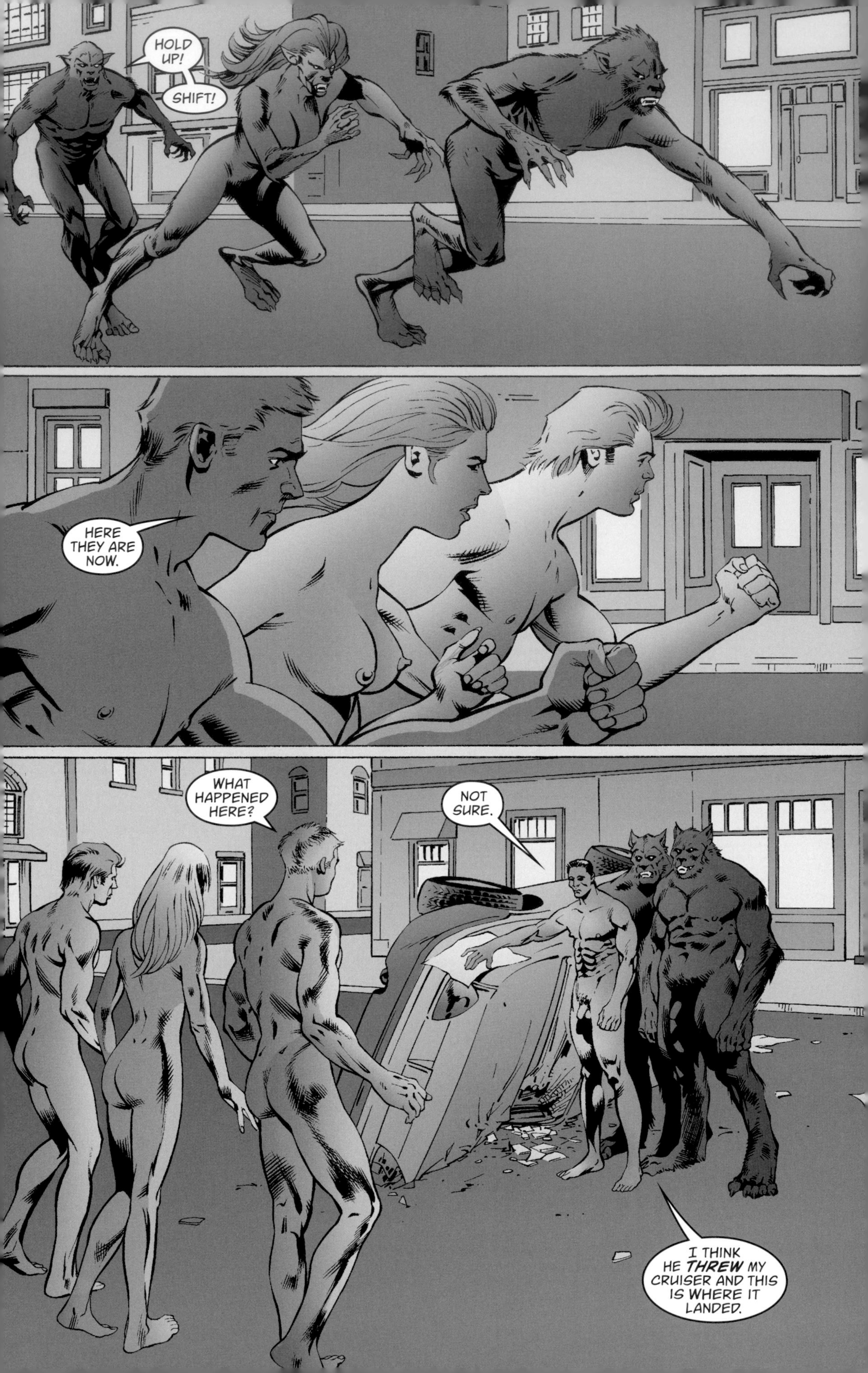
HOLD UP!
SHIFT!
HERE THEY ARE NOW.
WHAT HAPPENED HERE?
NOT SURE.
I THINK HE *THREW* MY CRUISER AND THIS IS WHERE IT LANDED.

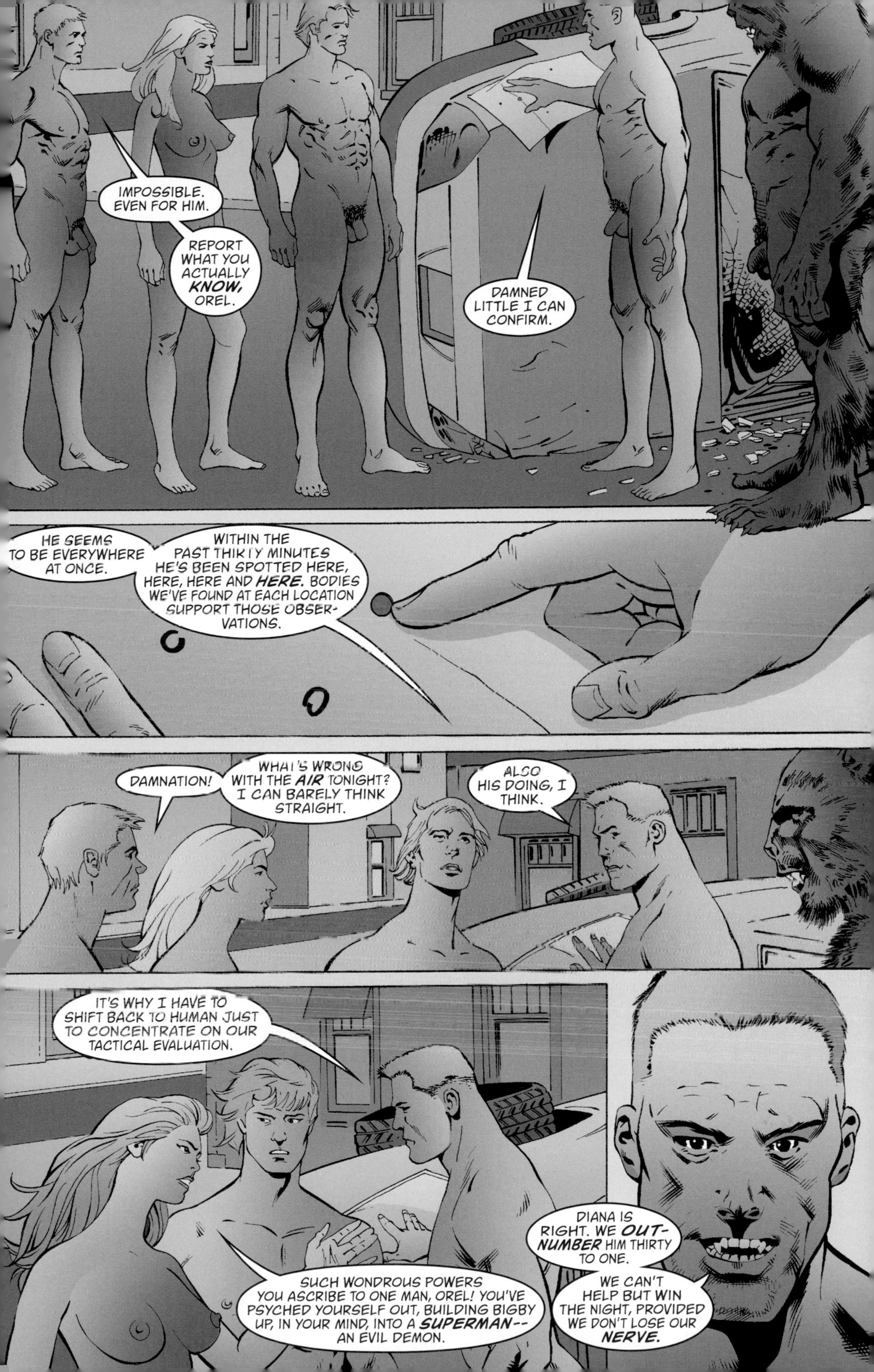
IMPOSSIBLE. EVEN FOR HIM.
REPORT WHAT YOU ACTUALLY **KNOW,** OREL.
DAMNED LITTLE I CAN CONFIRM.
HE SEEMS TO BE EVERYWHERE AT ONCE.
WITHIN THE PAST THIRTY MINUTES HE'S BEEN SPOTTED HERE, HERE, HERE AND **HERE.** BODIES WE'VE FOUND AT EACH LOCATION SUPPORT THOSE OBSER- VATIONS.
DAMNATION!
WHAT'S WRONG WITH THE ***AIR*** TONIGHT? I CAN BARELY THINK STRAIGHT.
ALSO HIS DOING, I THINK.
IT'S WHY I HAVE TO SHIFT BACK TO HUMAN JUST TO CONCENTRATE ON OUR TACTICAL EVALUATION.
SUCH WONDROUS POWERS YOU ASCRIBE TO ONE MAN, OREL! YOU'VE PSYCHED YOURSELF OUT, BUILDING BIGBY UP, IN YOUR MIND, INTO A ***SUPERMAN***-- AN EVIL DEMON.
DIANA IS RIGHT. WE ***OUT- NUMBER*** HIM THIRTY TO ONE.
WE CAN'T HELP BUT WIN THE NIGHT, PROVIDED WE DON'T LOSE OUR ***NERVE.***

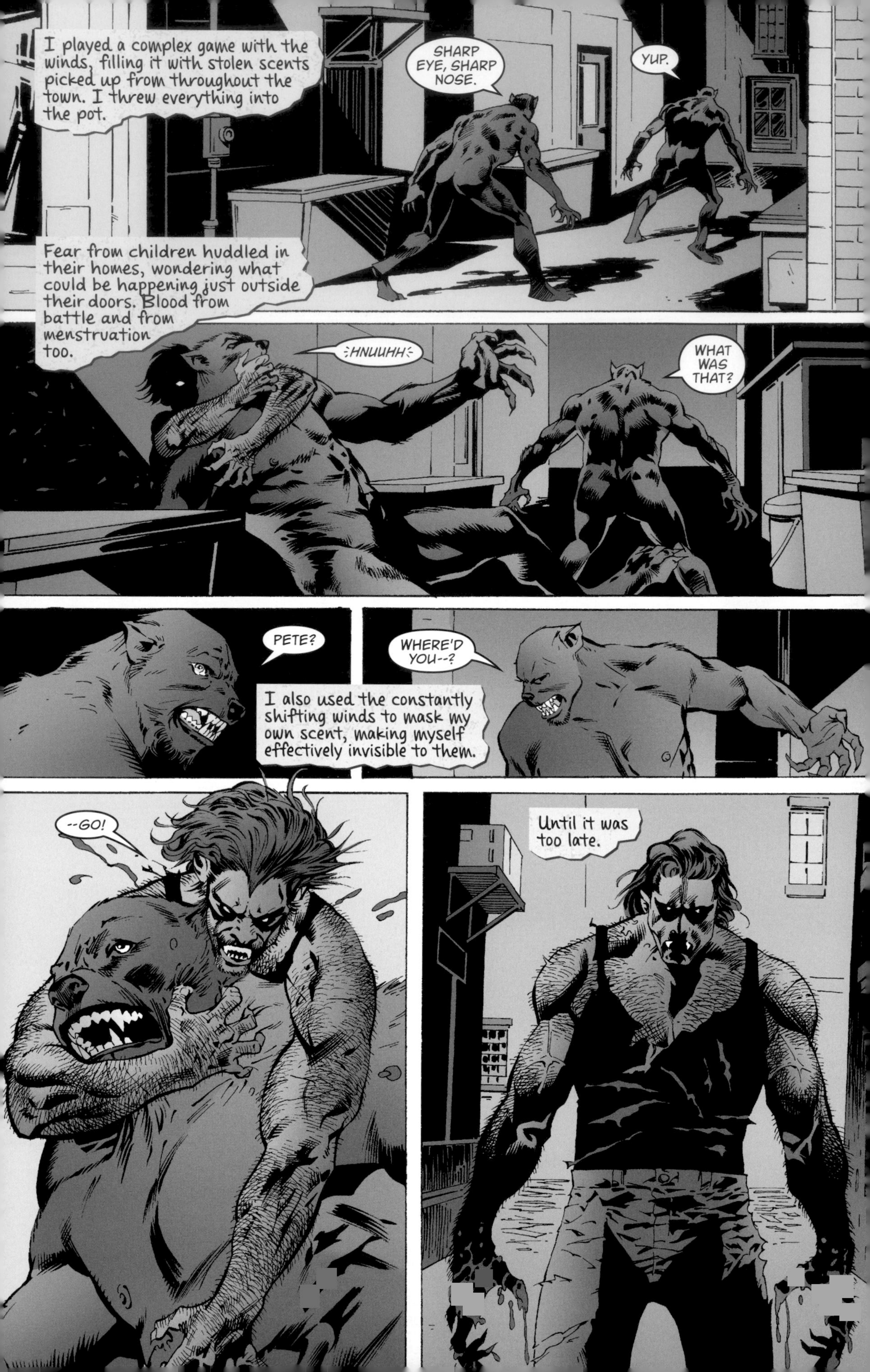
I played a complex game with the winds, filling it with stolen scents picked up from throughout the town. I threw everything into the pot.
SHARP EYE, SHARP NOSE.
YUP.
Fear from children huddled in their homes, wondering what could be happening just outside their doors. Blood from battle and from menstruation too.
HNUUHH
WHAT WAS THAT?
PETE?
WHERE'D YOU--?
I also used the constantly shifting winds to mask my own scent, making myself effectively invisible to them.
--GO!
Until it was too late.

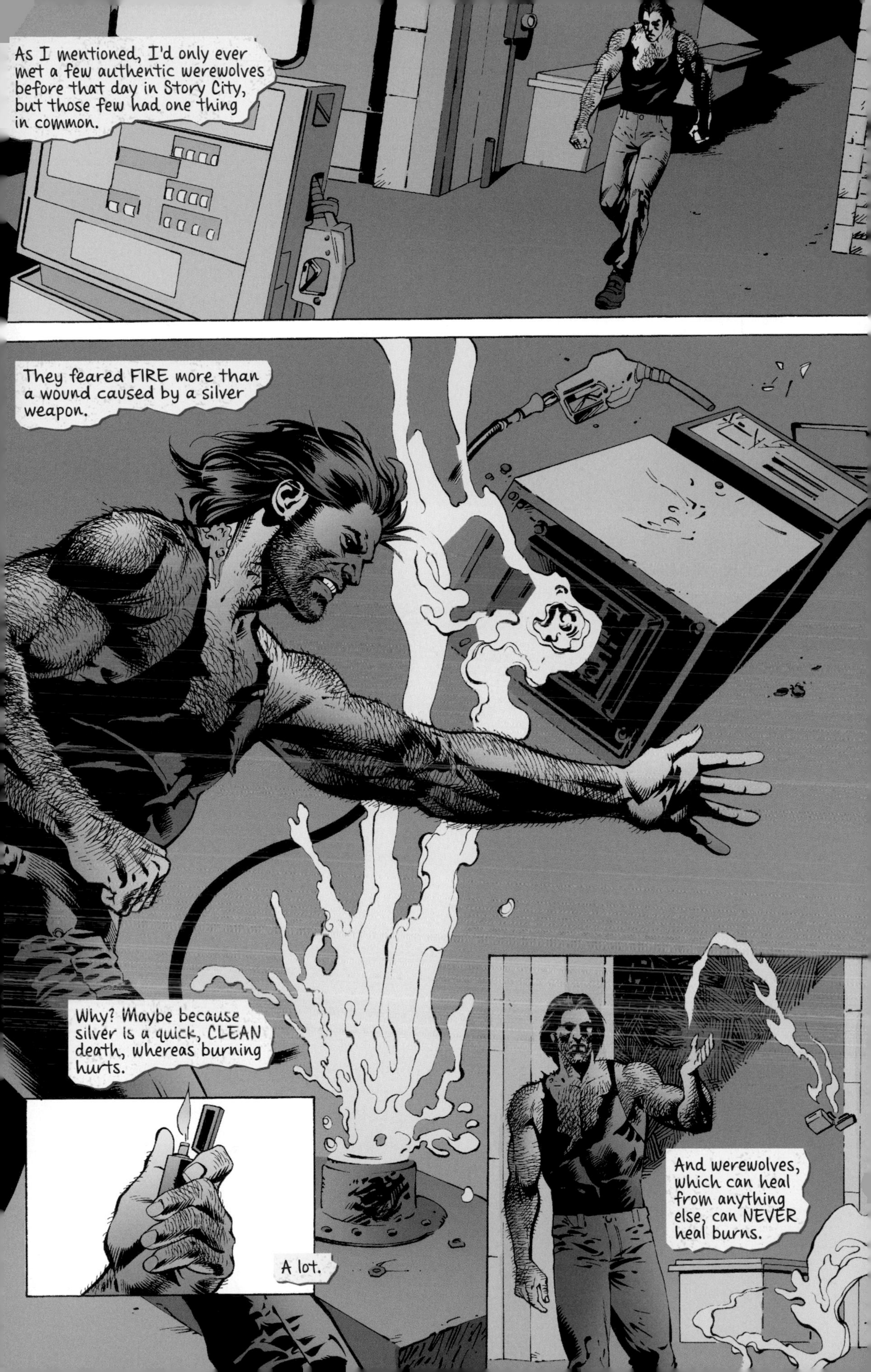
As I mentioned, I'd only ever met a few authentic werewolves before that day in Story City, but those few had one thing in common.
They feared FIRE more than a wound caused by a silver weapon.
Why? Maybe because silver is a quick, CLEAN death, whereas burning hurts.
A lot.
And werewolves, which can heal from anything else, can NEVER heal burns.

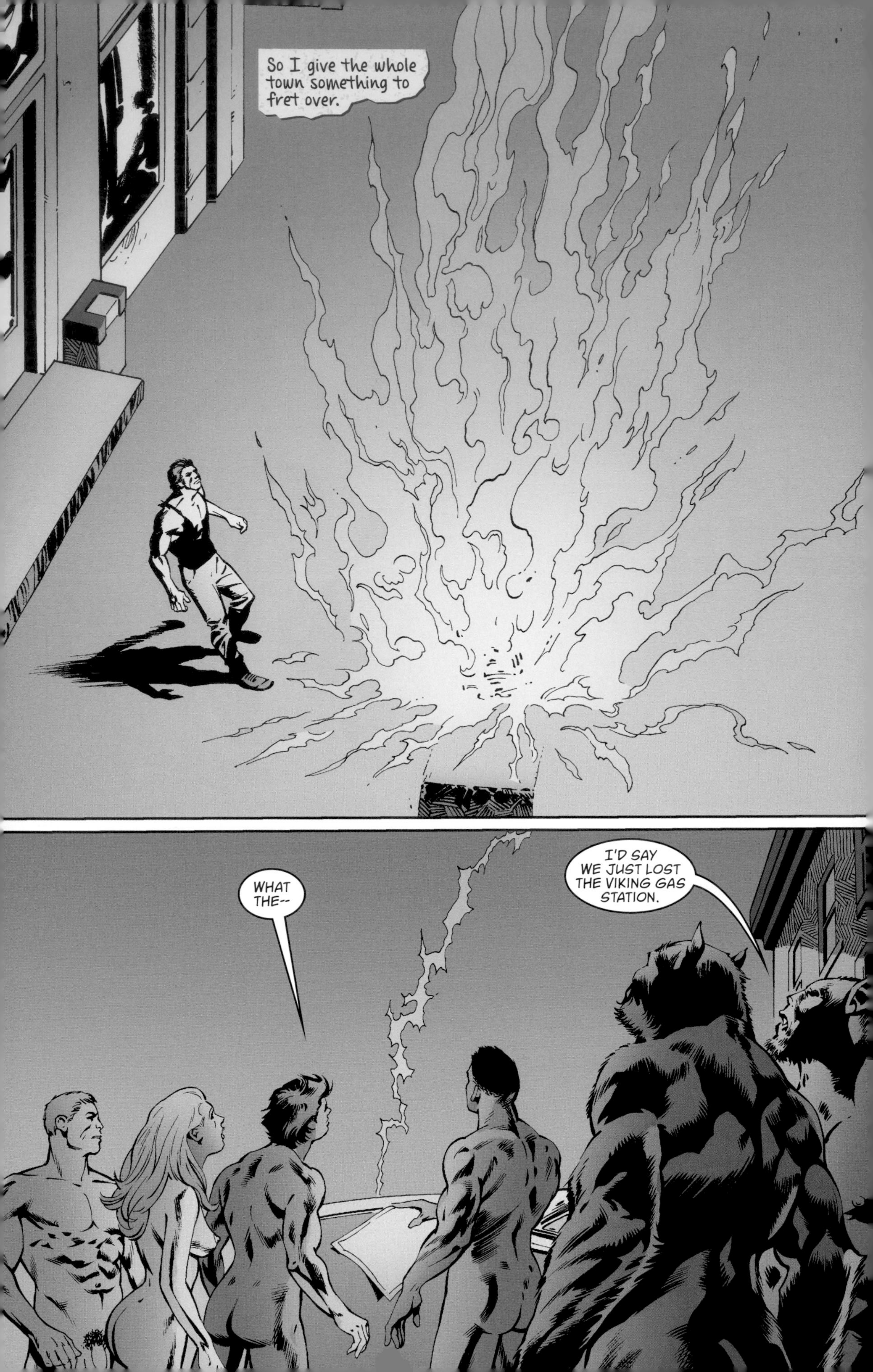
So I give the whole town something to fret over.
WHAT THE--
I'D SAY WE JUST LOST THE VIKING GAS STATION.

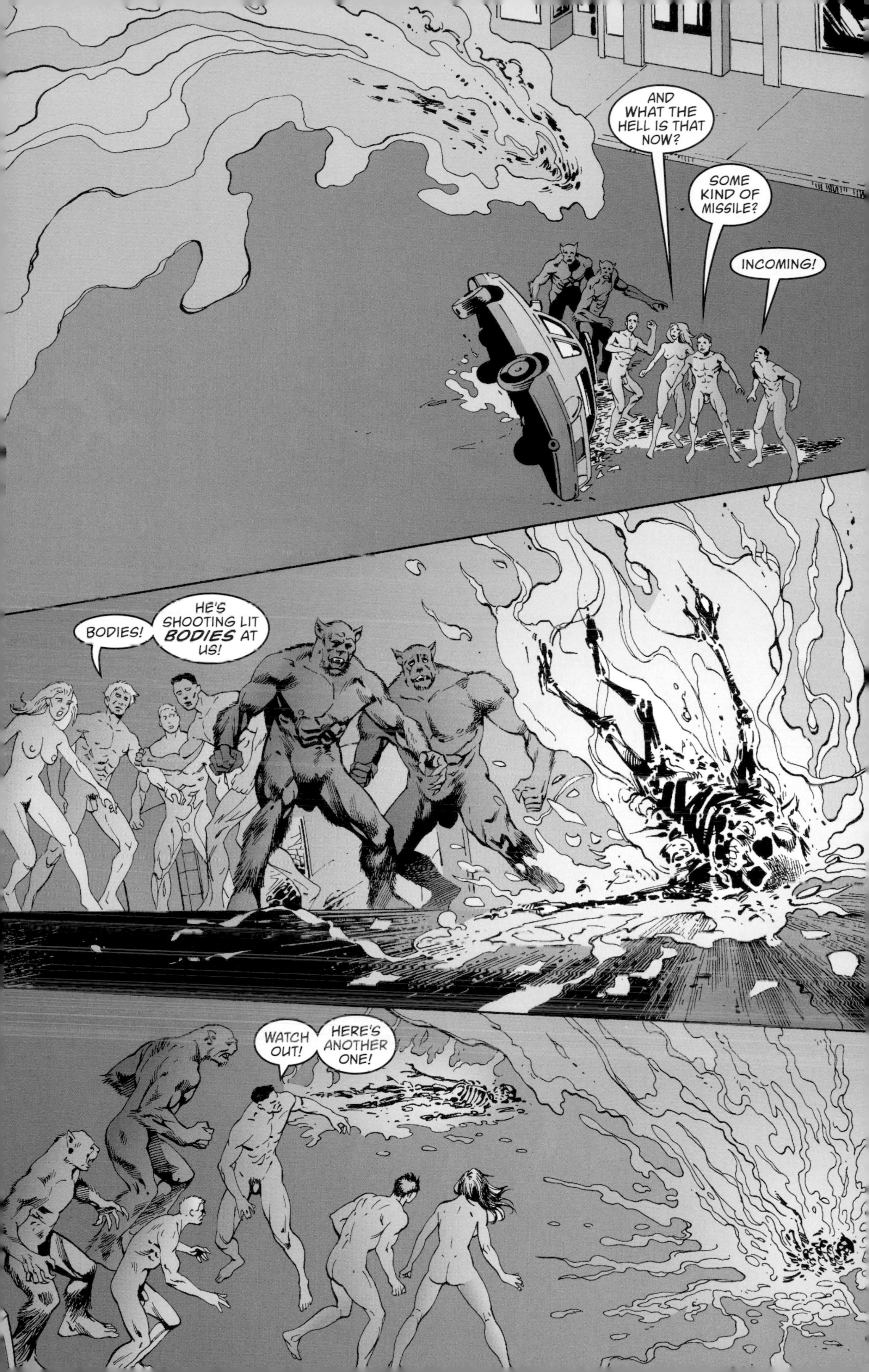
AND WHAT THE HELL IS THAT NOW?
SOME KIND OF MISSILE?
INCOMING!
BODIES!
HE'S SHOOTING LIT BODIES AT US!
WATCH OUT!
HERE'S ANOTHER ONE!

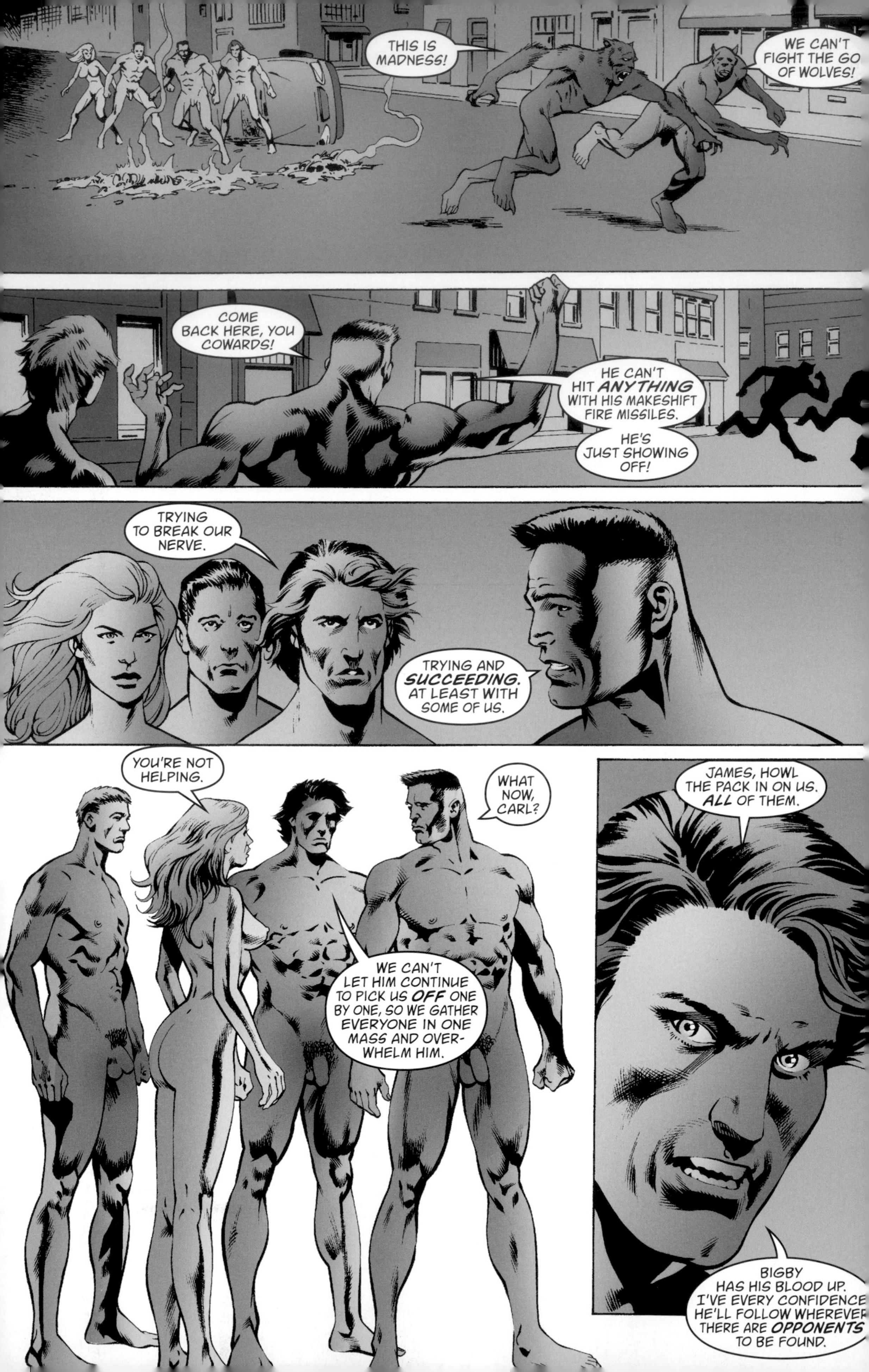

THIS IS MADNESS!
WE CAN'T FIGHT THE GO OF WOLVES!
COME BACK HERE, YOU COWARDS!
HE CAN'T HIT ANYTHING WITH HIS MAKESHIFT FIRE MISSILES.
HE'S JUST SHOWING OFF!
TRYING TO BREAK OUR NERVE.
TRYING AND SUCCEEDING. AT LEAST WITH SOME OF US.
YOU'RE NOT HELPING.
WHAT NOW, CARL?
WE CAN'T LET HIM CONTINUE TO PICK US OFF ONE BY ONE, SO WE GATHER EVERYONE IN ONE MASS AND OVER-WHELM HIM.
JAMES, HOWL THE PACK IN ON US. ALL OF THEM.
BIGBY HAS HIS BLOOD UP. I'VE EVERY CONFIDENCE HE'LL FOLLOW WHEREVER THERE ARE OPPONENTS TO BE FOUND.

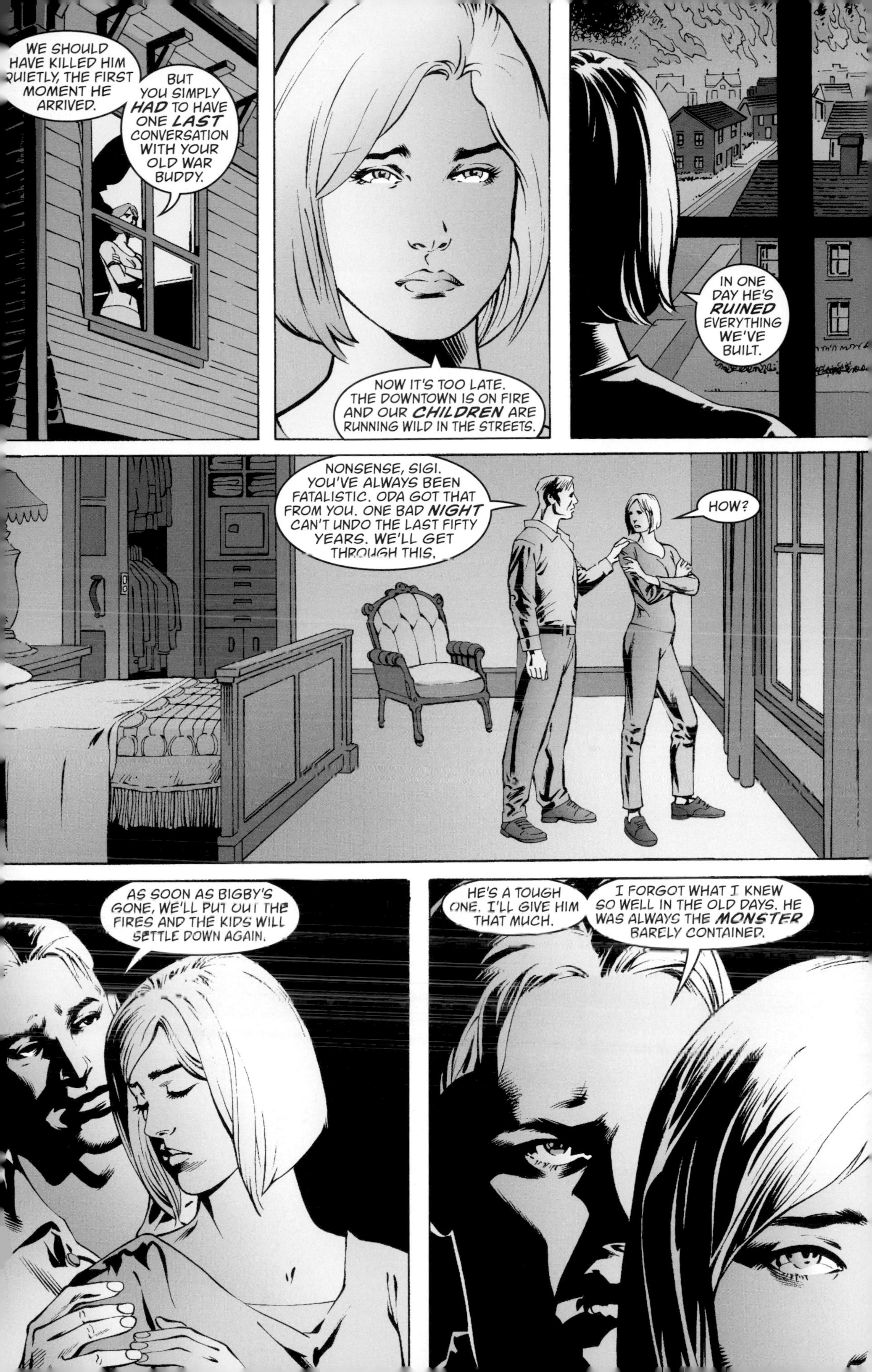
WE SHOULD HAVE KILLED HIM QUIETLY, THE FIRST MOMENT HE ARRIVED.
BUT YOU SIMPLY HAD TO HAVE ONE LAST CONVERSATION WITH YOUR OLD WAR BUDDY.
NOW IT'S TOO LATE. THE DOWNTOWN IS ON FIRE AND OUR CHILDREN ARE RUNNING WILD IN THE STREETS.
IN ONE DAY HE'S RUINED EVERYTHING WE'VE BUILT.
NONSENSE, SIGI. YOU'VE ALWAYS BEEN FATALISTIC. ODA GOT THAT FROM YOU. ONE BAD NIGHT CAN'T UNDO THE LAST FIFTY YEARS. WE'LL GET THROUGH THIS.
HOW?
AS SOON AS BIGBY'S GONE, WE'LL PUT OUT THE FIRES AND THE KIDS WILL SETTLE DOWN AGAIN.
HE'S A TOUGH ONE. I'LL GIVE HIM THAT MUCH.
I FORGOT WHAT I KNEW SO WELL IN THE OLD DAYS. HE WAS ALWAYS THE MONSTER BARELY CONTAINED.

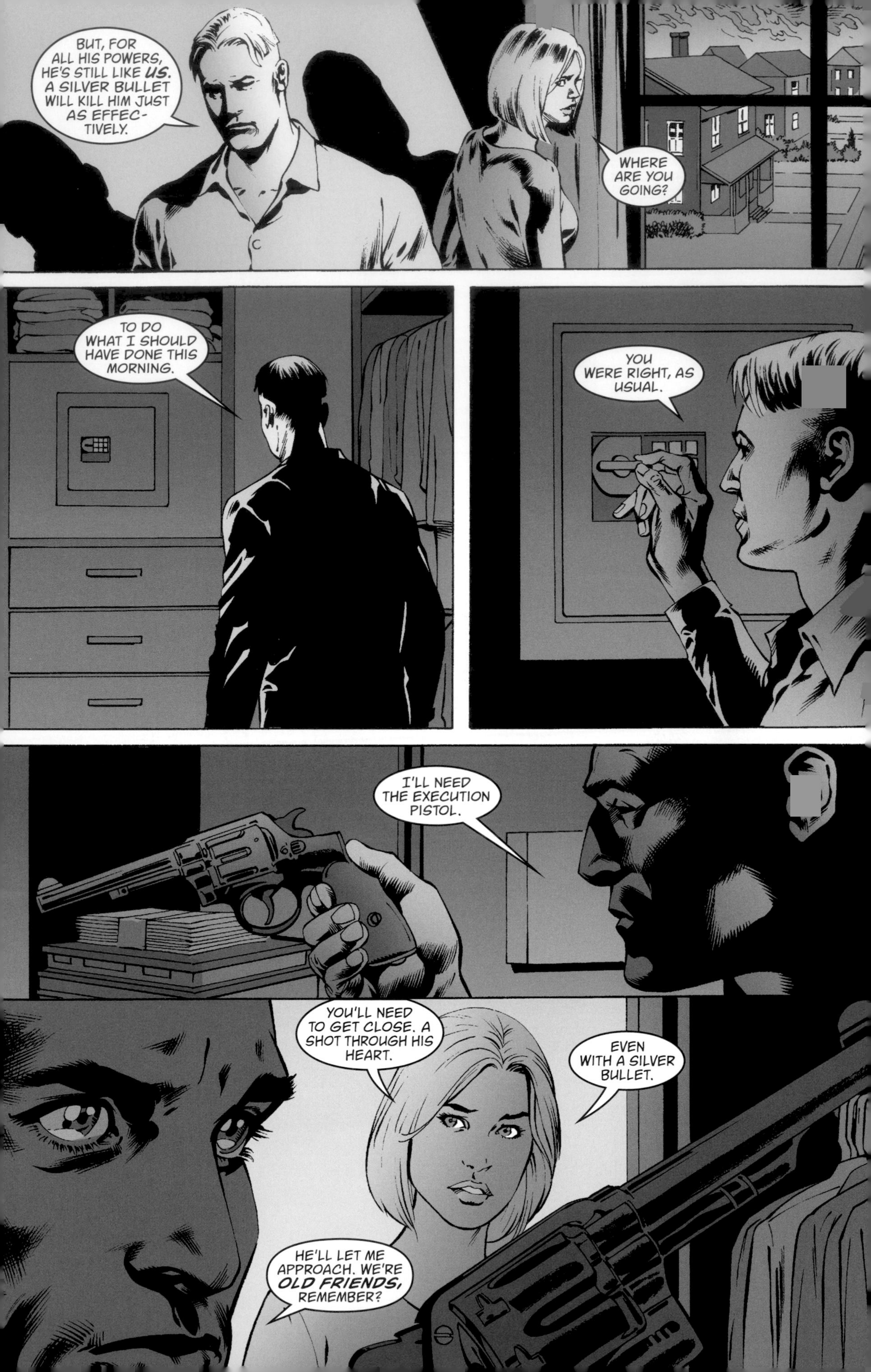
BUT, FOR ALL HIS POWERS, HE'S STILL LIKE US. A SILVER BULLET WILL KILL HIM JUST AS EFFEC-TIVELY.
WHERE ARE YOU GOING?
TO DO WHAT I SHOULD HAVE DONE THIS MORNING.
YOU WERE RIGHT, AS USUAL.
I'LL NEED THE EXECUTION PISTOL.
YOU'LL NEED TO GET CLOSE. A SHOT THROUGH HIS HEART.
EVEN WITH A SILVER BULLET.
HE'LL LET ME APPROACH. WE'RE OLD FRIENDS, REMEMBER?

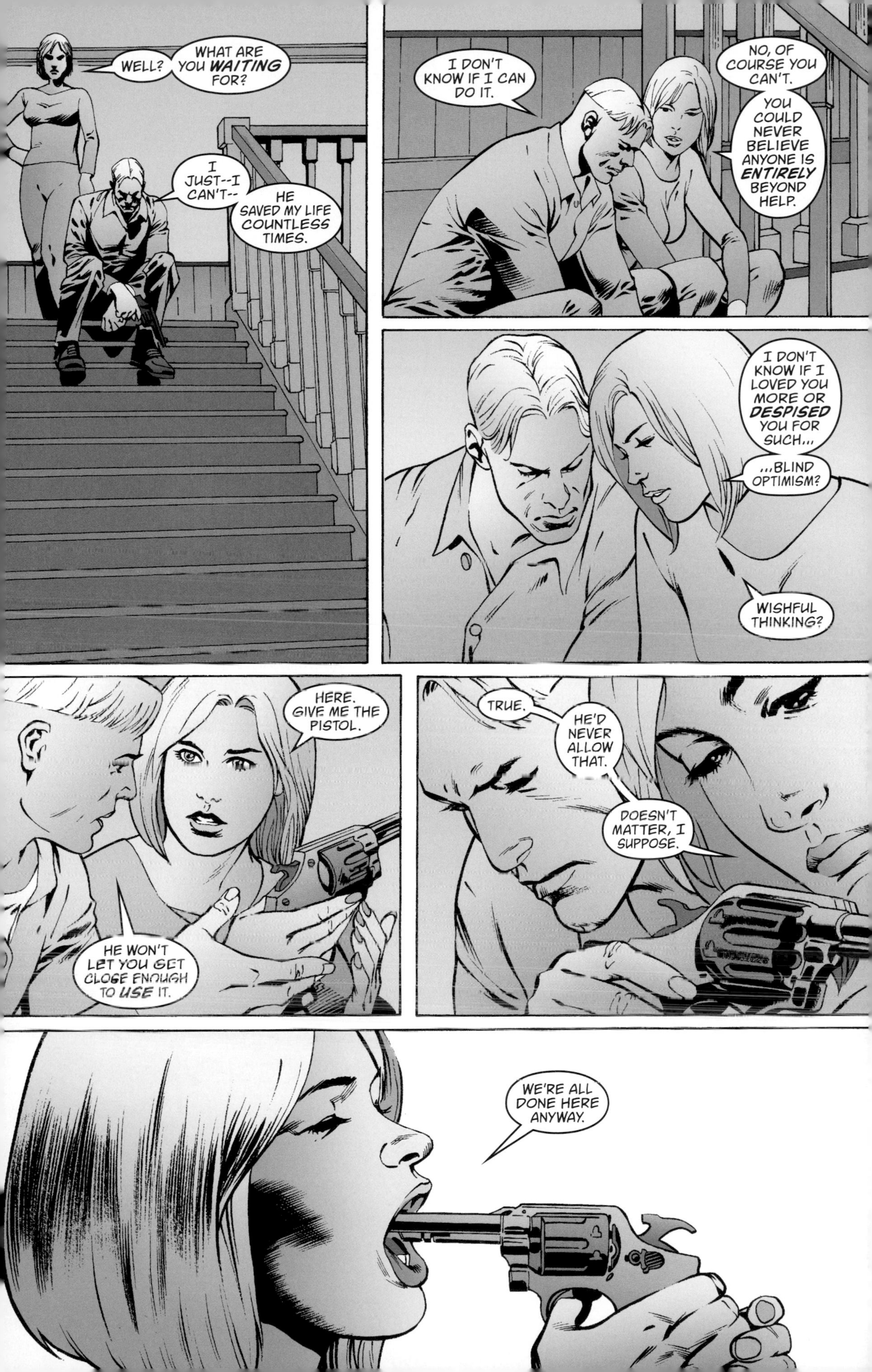

WELL?
WHAT ARE YOU WAITING FOR?
I JUST--I CAN'T--
HE SAVED MY LIFE COUNTLESS TIMES.
I DON'T KNOW IF I CAN DO IT.
NO, OF COURSE YOU CAN'T.
YOU COULD NEVER BELIEVE ANYONE IS ENTIRELY BEYOND HELP.
I DON'T KNOW IF I LOVED YOU MORE OR DESPISED YOU FOR SUCH...
...BLIND OPTIMISM?
WISHFUL THINKING?
HERE. GIVE ME THE PISTOL.
HE WON'T LET YOU GET CLOSE ENOUGH TO USE IT.
TRUE.
HE'D NEVER ALLOW THAT.
DOESN'T MATTER, I SUPPOSE.
WE'RE ALL DONE HERE ANYWAY.

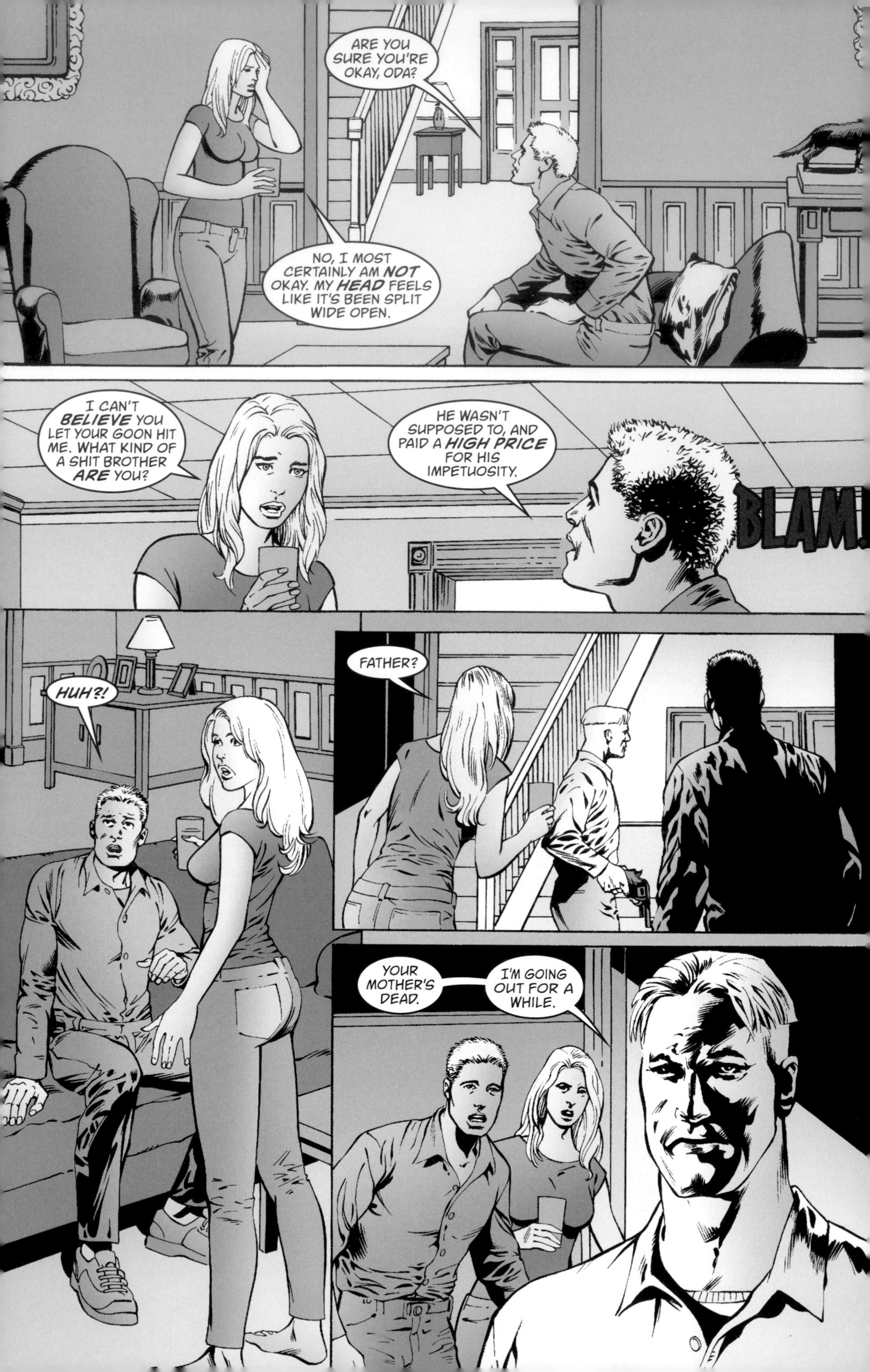
ARE YOU SURE YOU'RE OKAY, ODA?
NO, I MOST CERTAINLY AM NOT OKAY. MY HEAD FEELS LIKE IT'S BEEN SPLIT WIDE OPEN.
I CAN'T BELIEVE YOU LET YOUR GOON HIT ME. WHAT KIND OF A SHIT BROTHER ARE YOU?
HE WASN'T SUPPOSED TO, AND PAID A HIGH PRICE FOR HIS IMPETUOSITY.
BLAM!
HUH?!
FATHER?
YOUR MOTHER'S DEAD.
I'M GOING OUT FOR A WHILE.

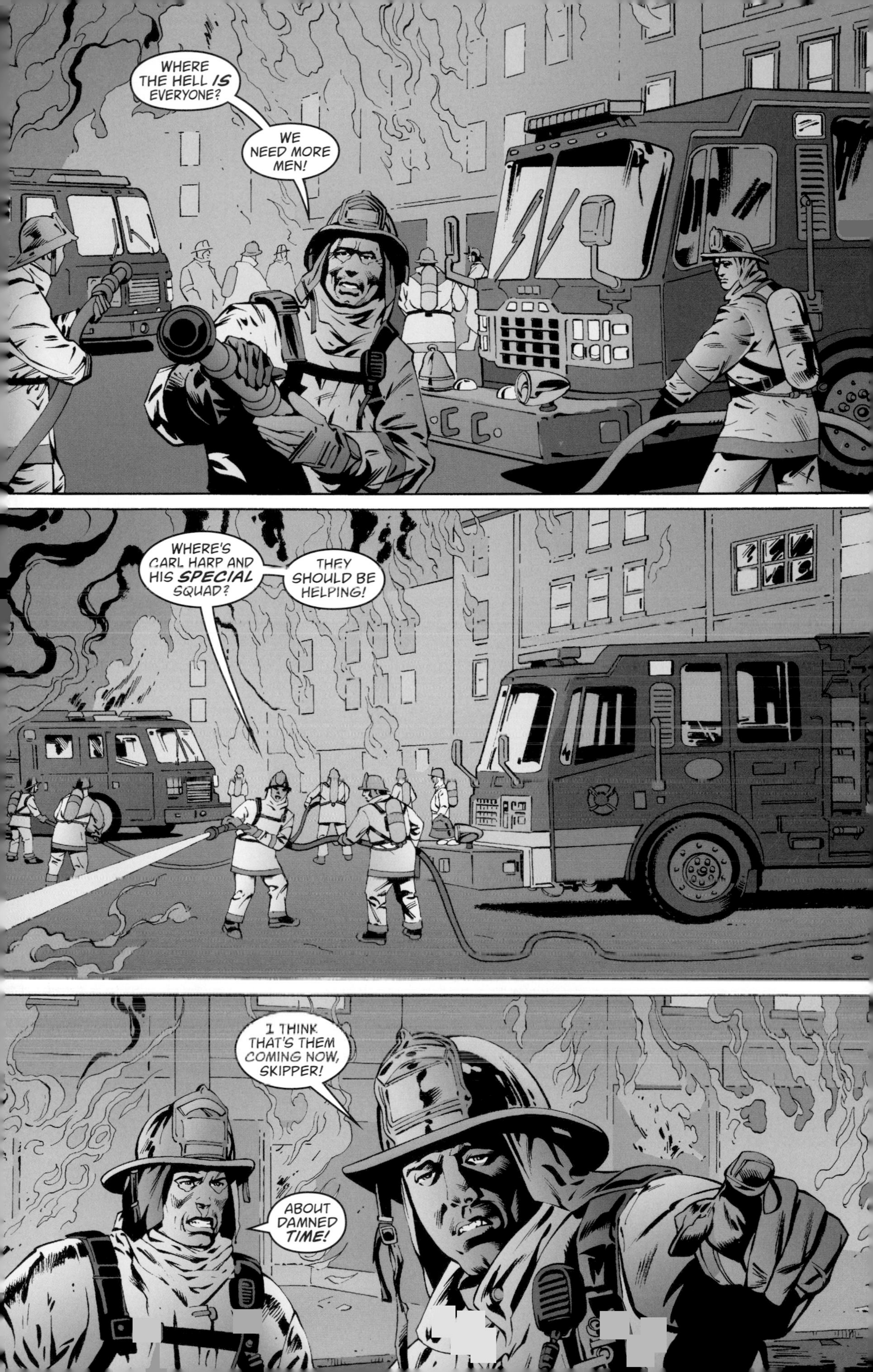
WHERE THE HELL IS EVERYONE?
WE NEED MORE MEN!
WHERE'S CARL HARP AND HIS SPECIAL SQUAD?
THEY SHOULD BE HELPING!
I THINK THAT'S THEM COMING NOW, SKIPPER!
ABOUT DAMNED TIME!

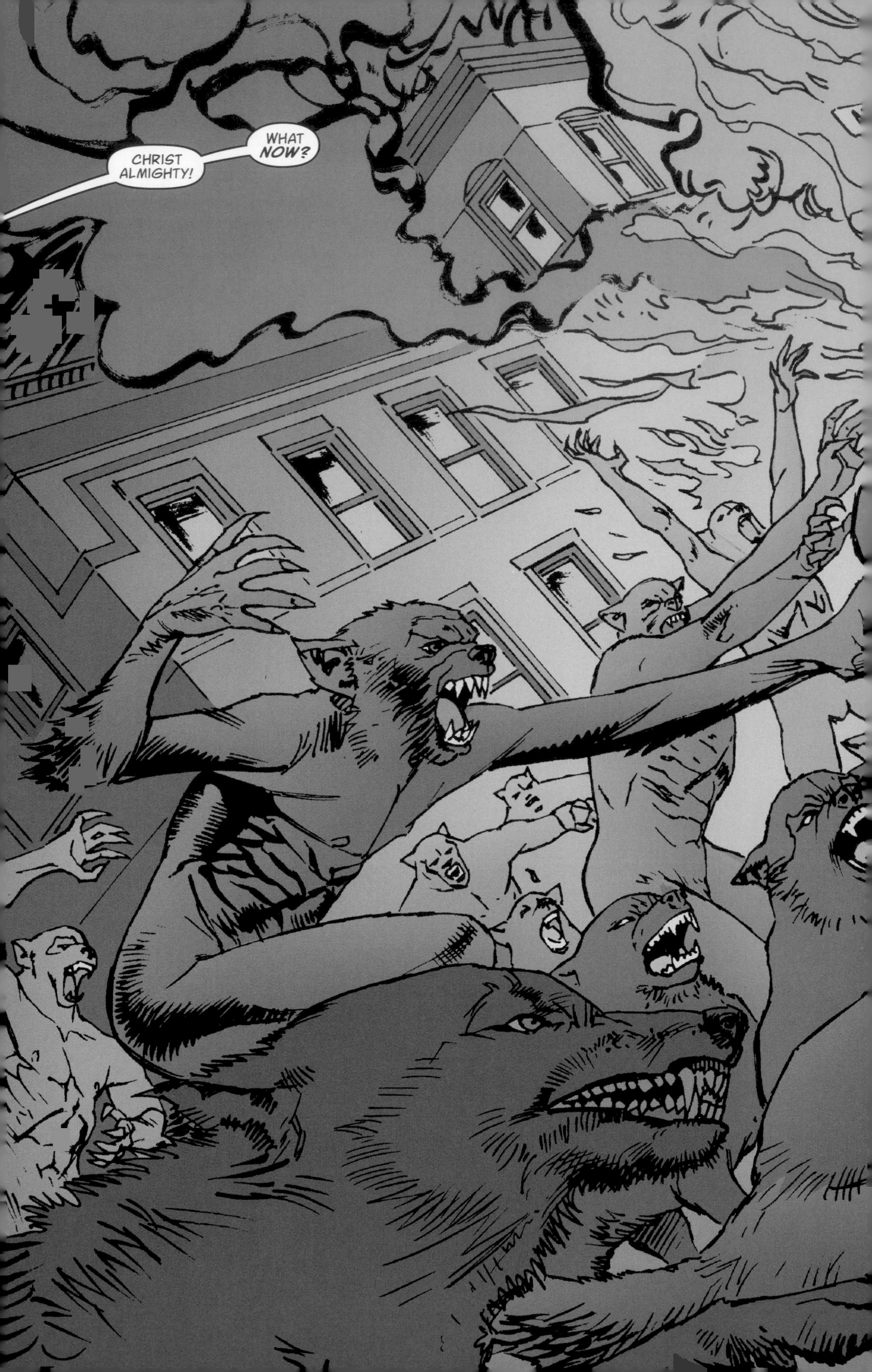
CHRIST ALMIGHTY!
WHAT NOW?

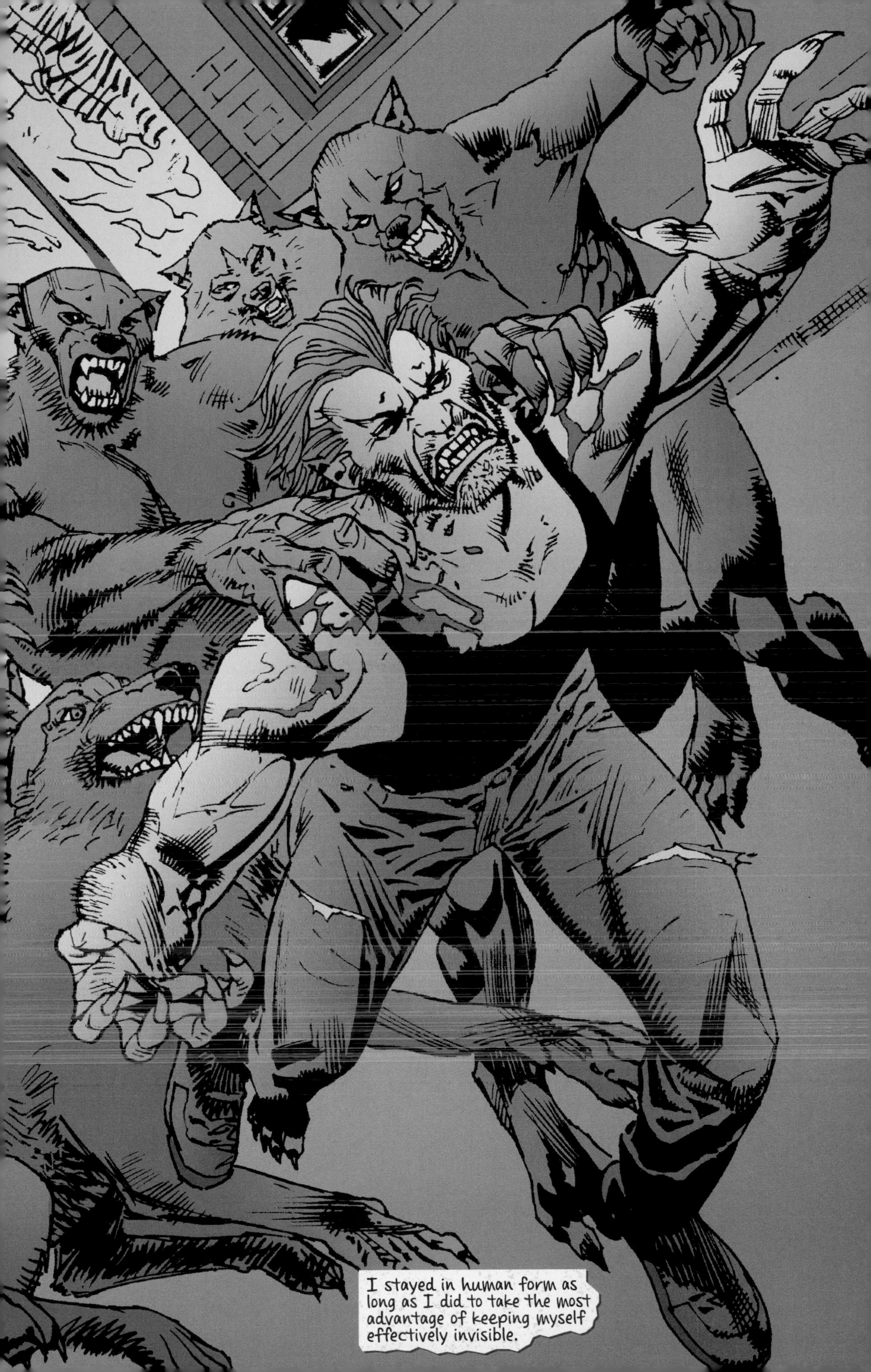
I stayed in human form as long as I did to take the most advantage of keeping myself effectively invisible.

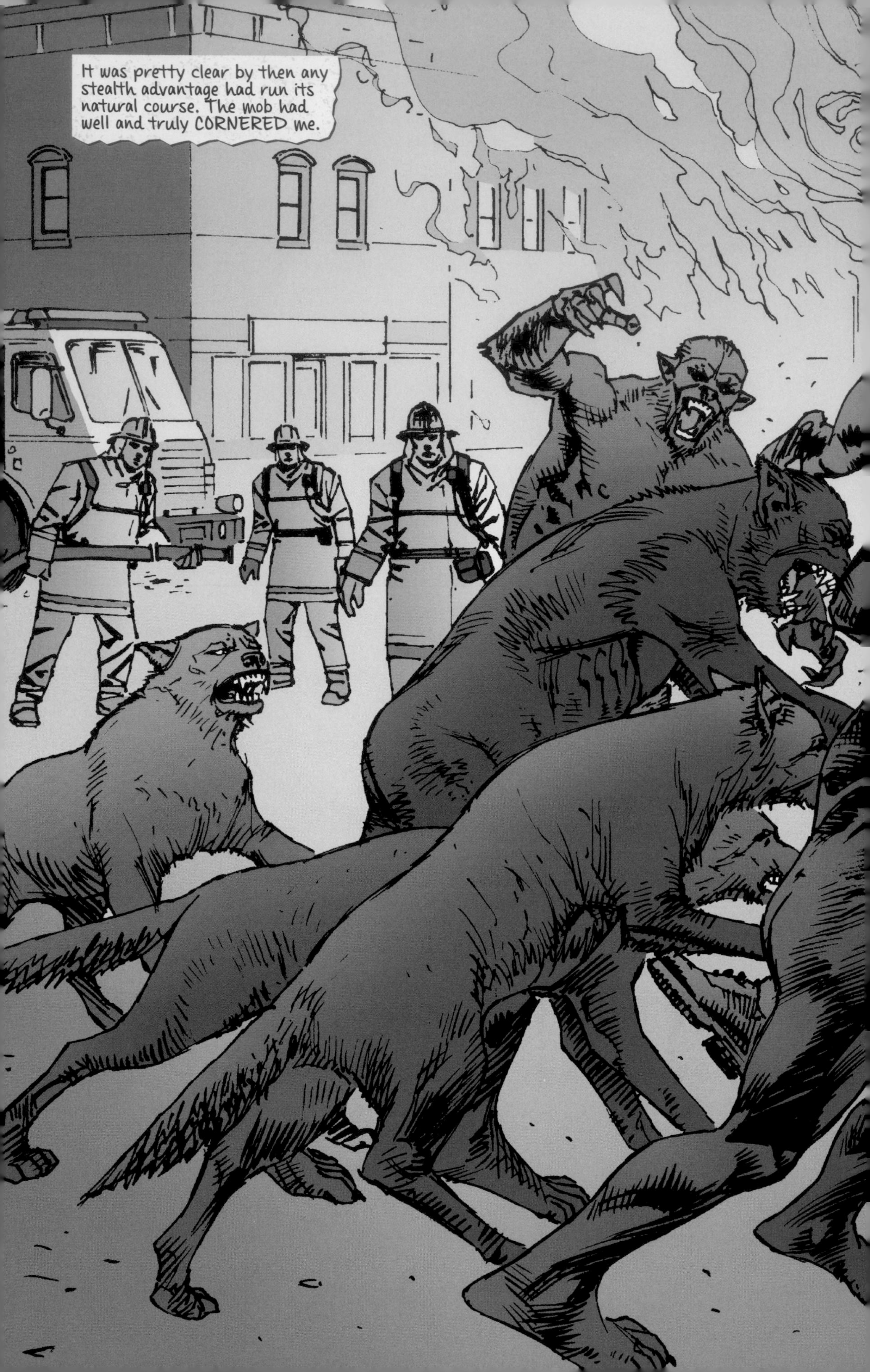
It was pretty clear by then any stealth advantage had run its natural course. The mob had well and truly CORNERED me.

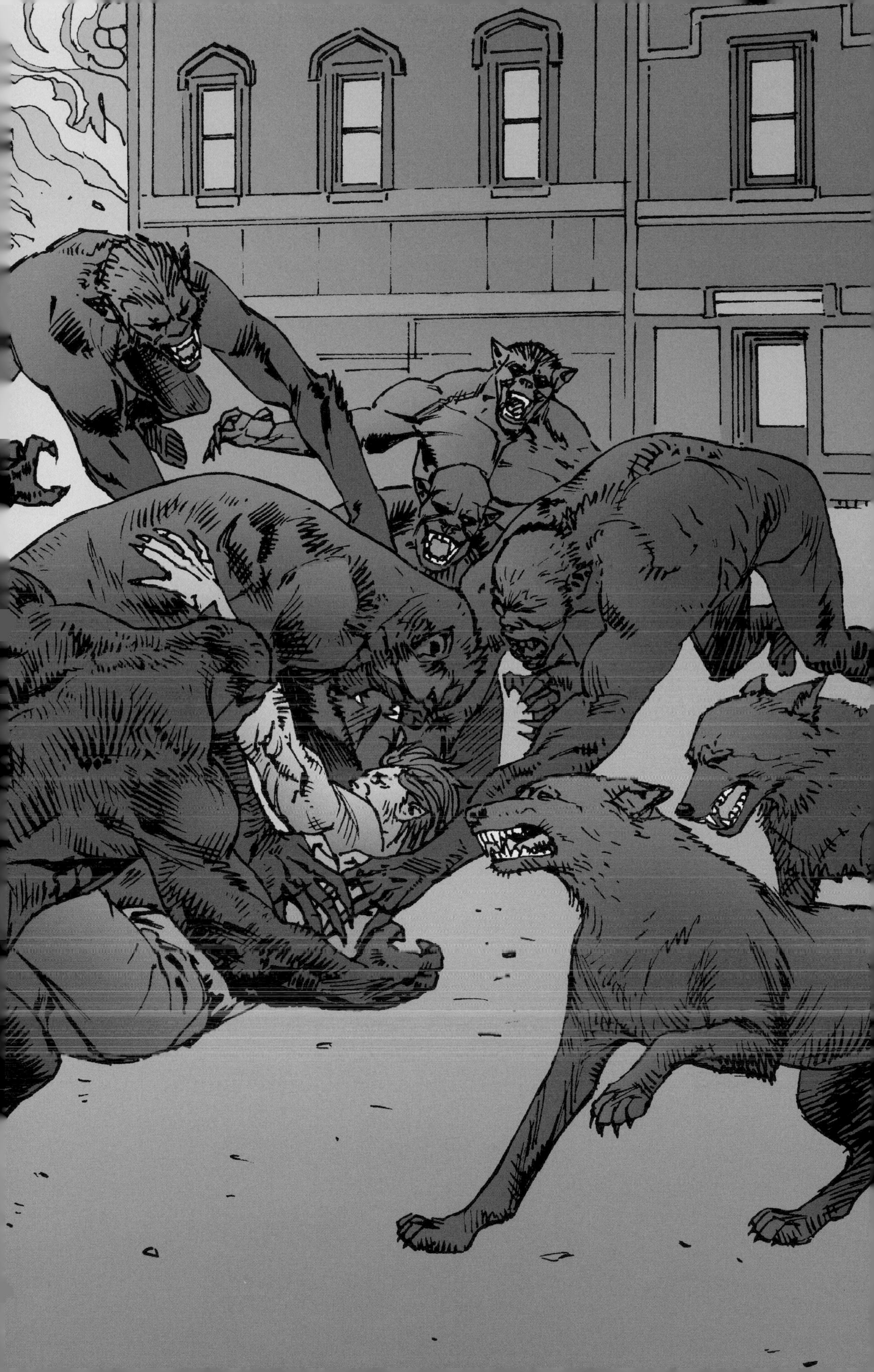

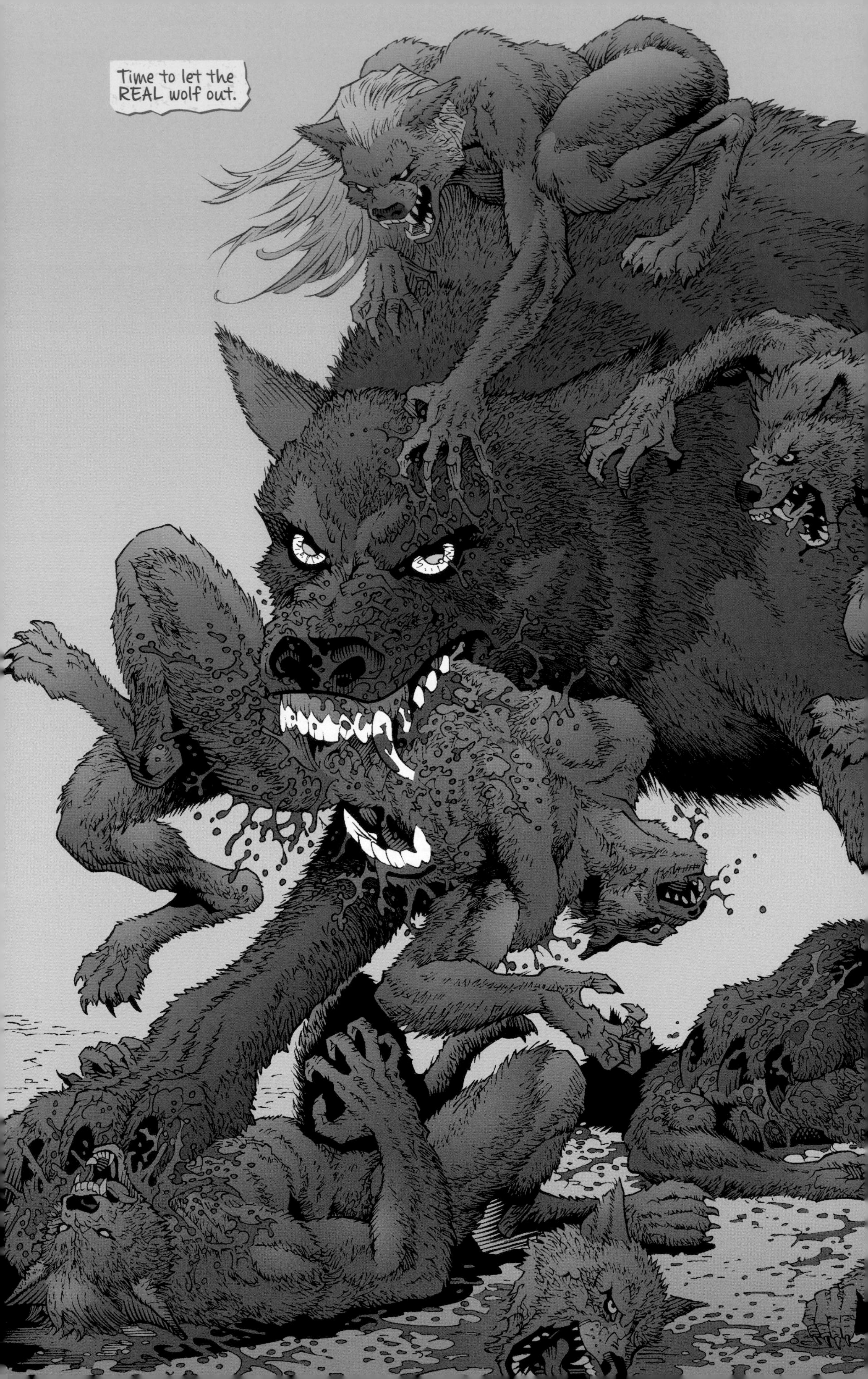
Time to let the REAL wolf out.

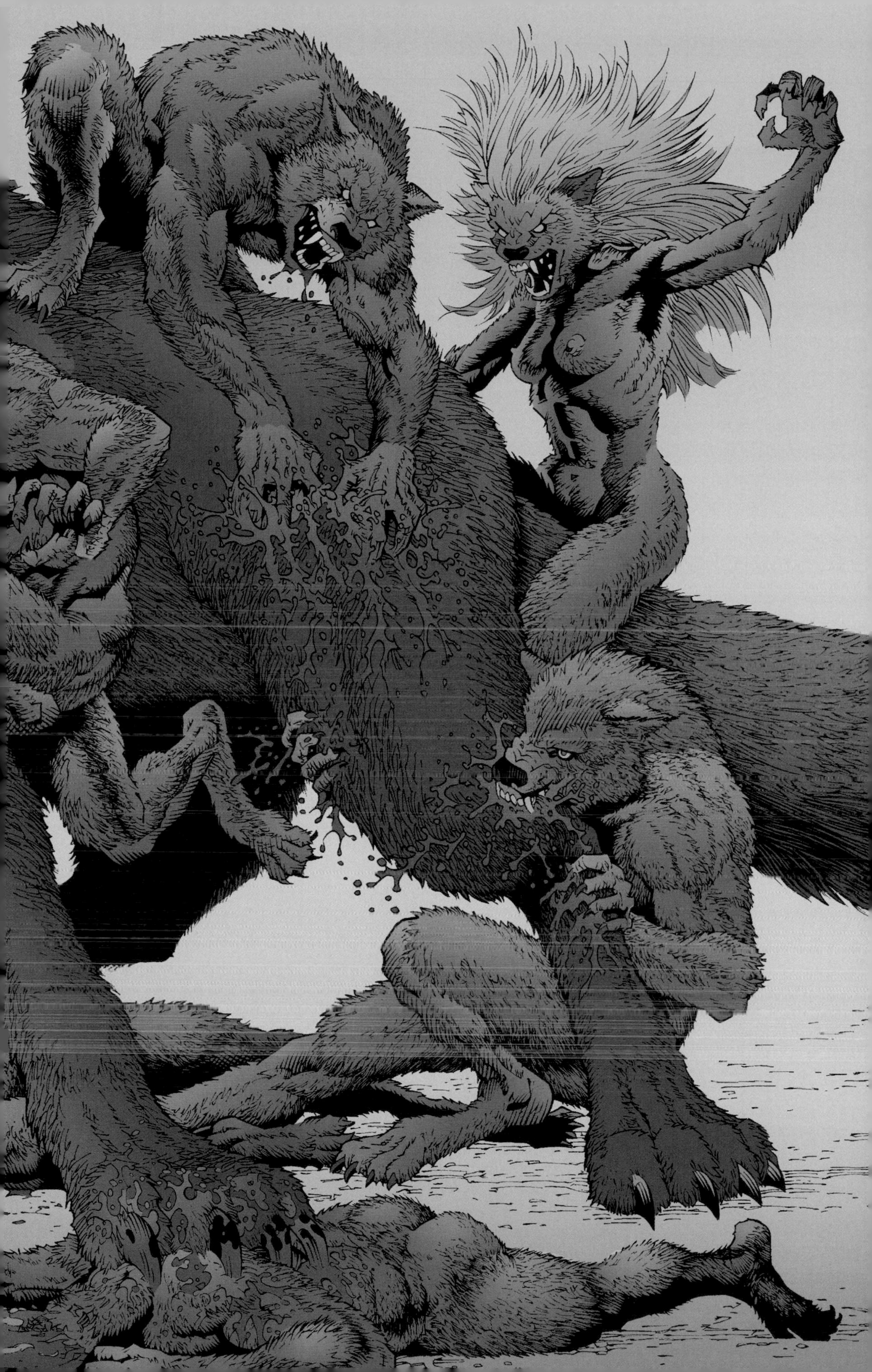

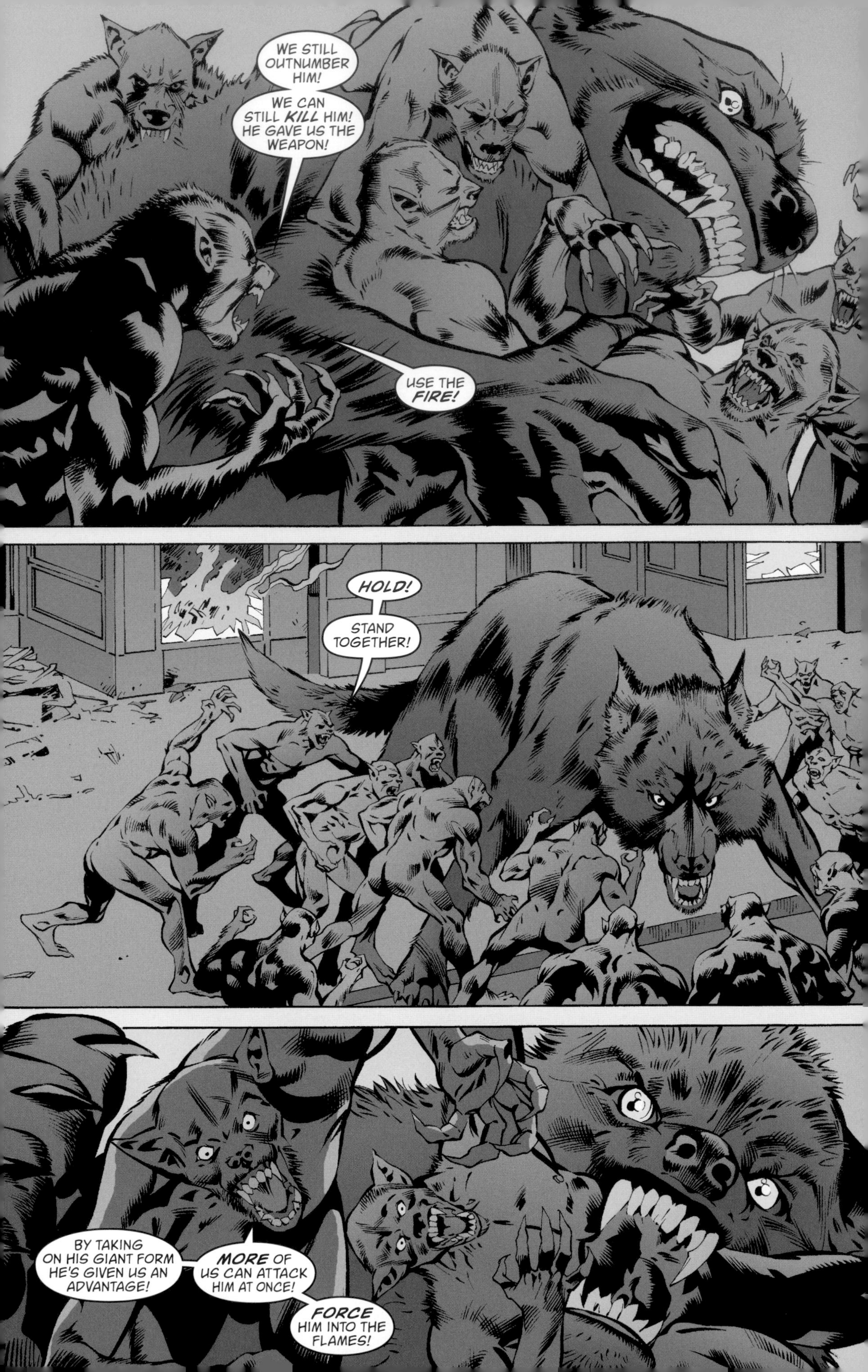
WE STILL OUTNUMBER HIM!
WE CAN STILL KILL HIM! HE GAVE US THE WEAPON!
USE THE FIRE!
HOLD!
STAND TOGETHER!
BY TAKING ON HIS GIANT FORM HE'S GIVEN US AN ADVANTAGE!
MORE OF US CAN ATTACK HIM AT ONCE!
FORCE HIM INTO THE FLAMES!

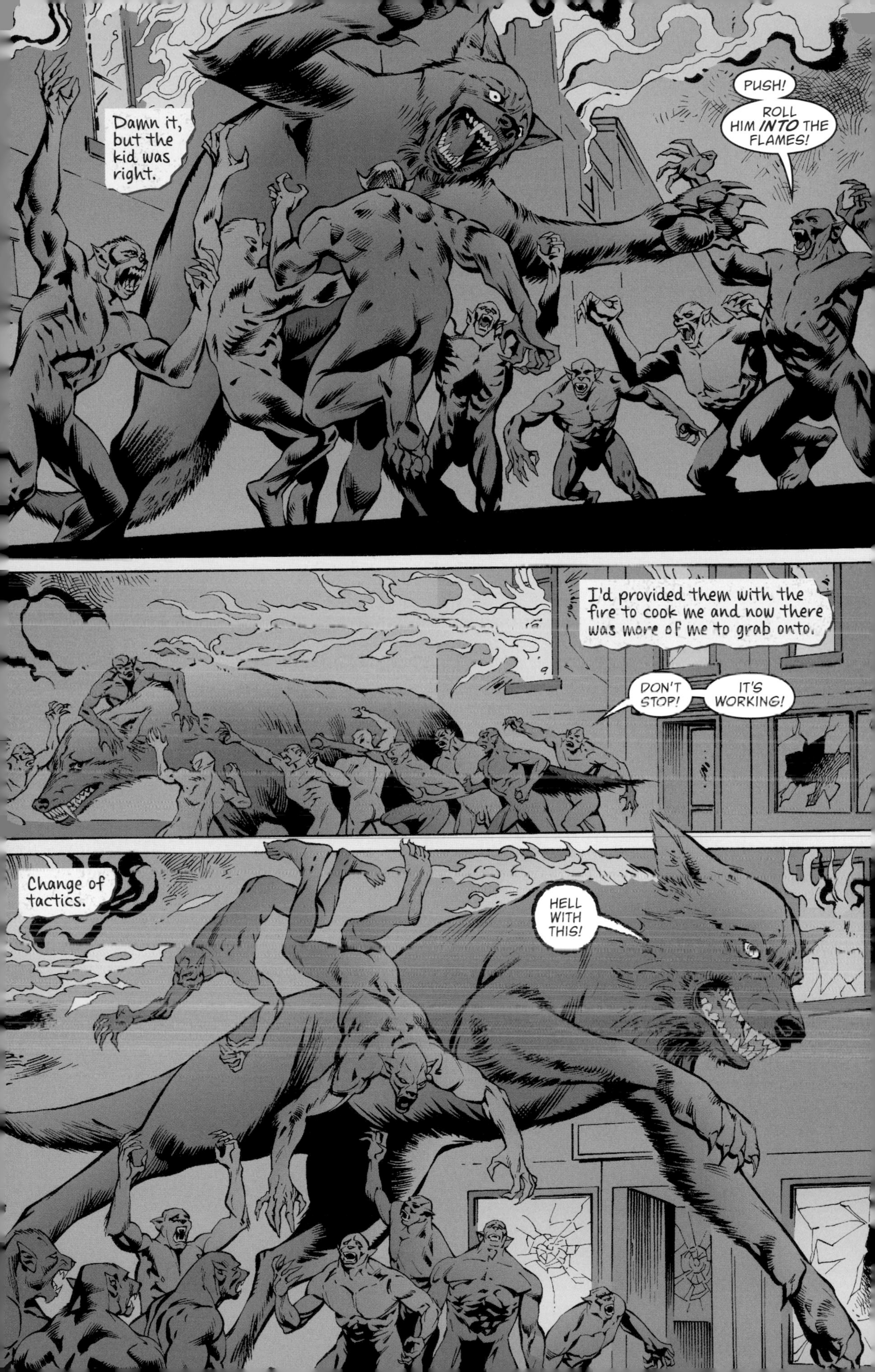
Damn it, but the kid was right.
PUSH!
ROLL HIM INTO THE FLAMES!
I'd provided them with the fire to cook me and now there was more of me to grab onto.
DON'T STOP!
IT'S WORKING!
Change of tactics.
HELL WITH THIS!

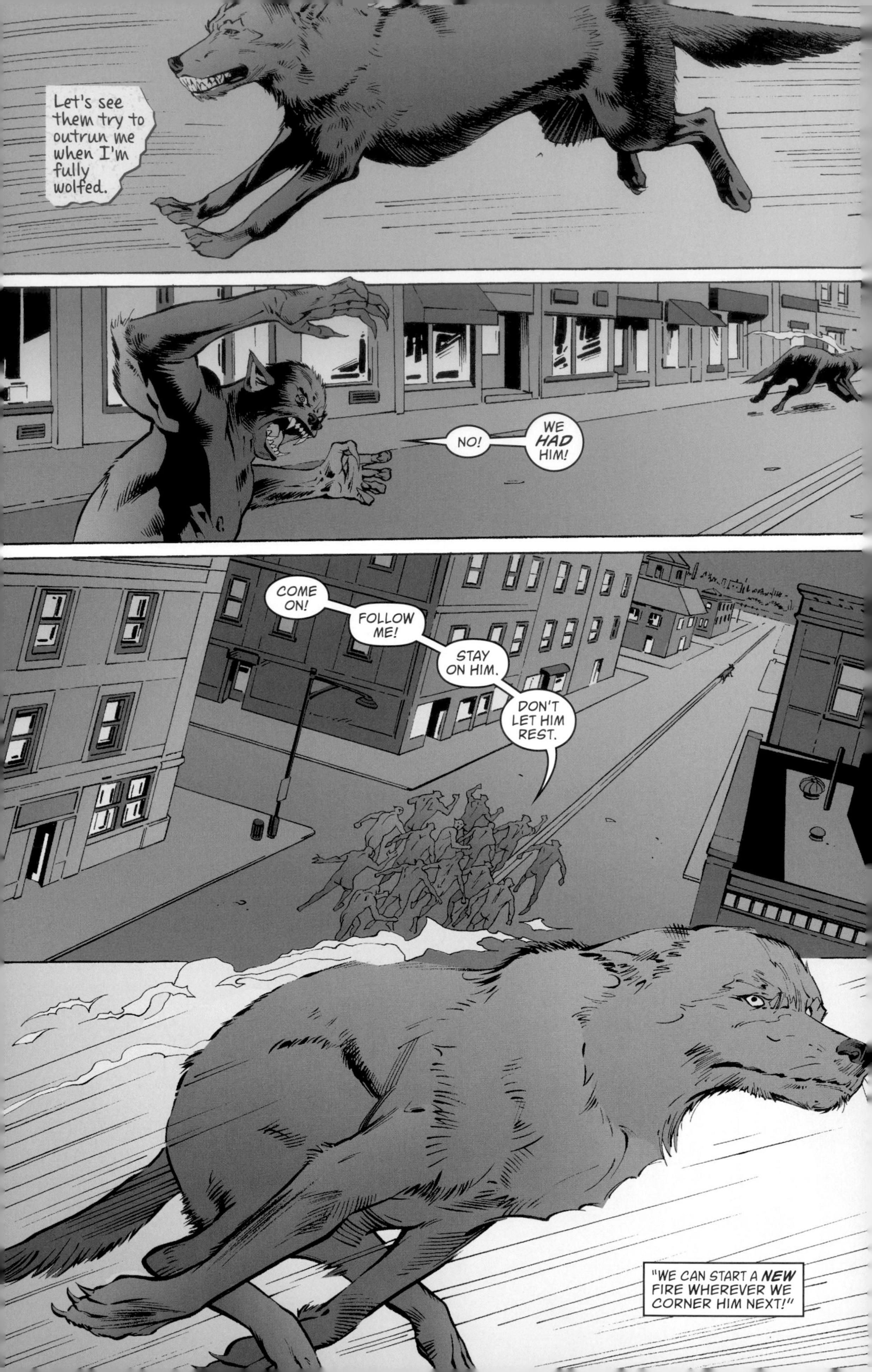
Let's see them try to outrun me when I'm fully wolfed.
NO!
WE HAD HIM!
COME ON!
FOLLOW ME!
STAY ON HIM.
DON'T LET HIM REST.
"WE CAN START A NEW FIRE WHEREVER WE CORNER HIM NEXT!"

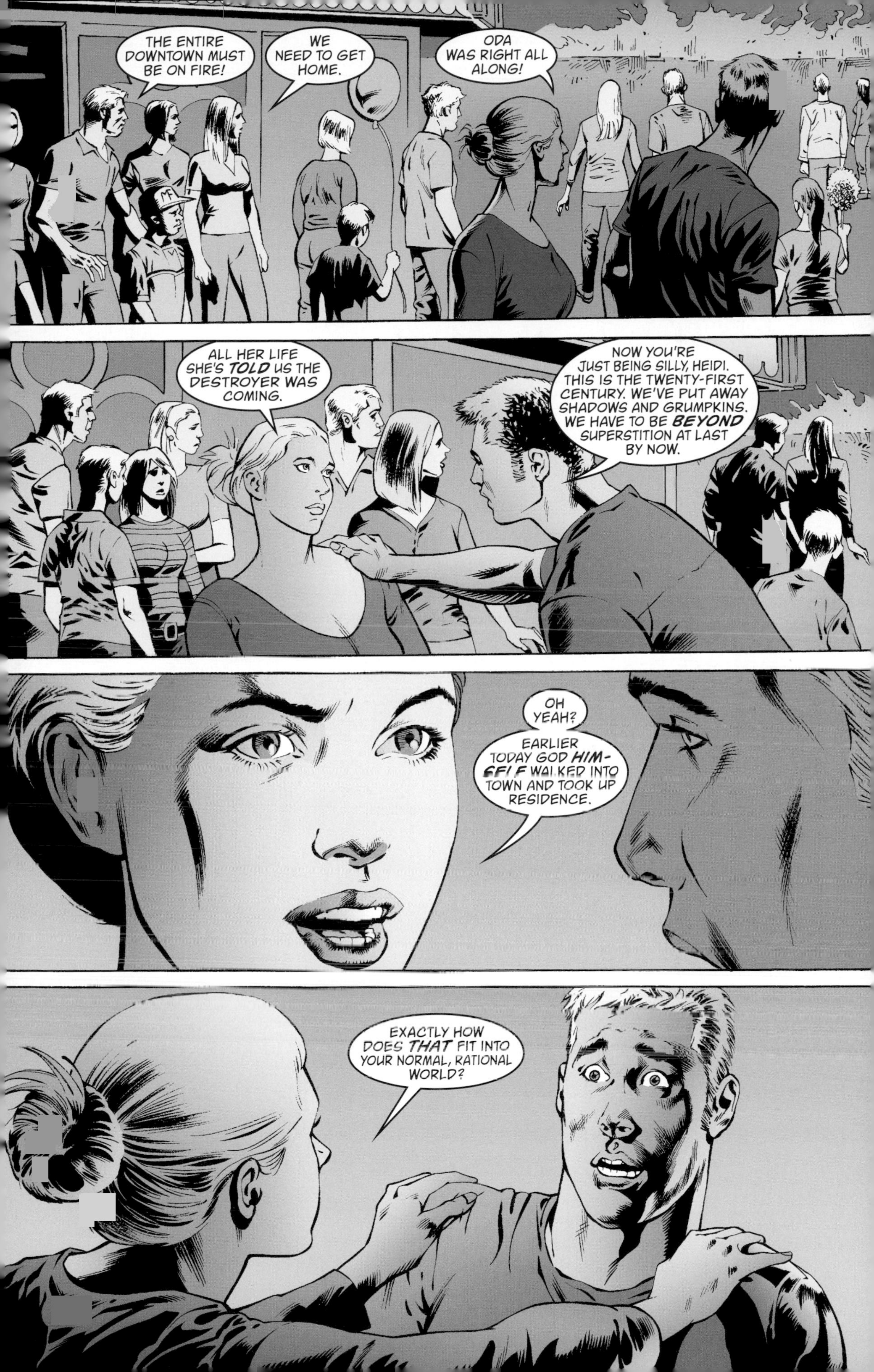
THE ENTIRE DOWNTOWN MUST BE ON FIRE!
WE NEED TO GET HOME.
ODA WAS RIGHT ALL ALONG!
ALL HER LIFE SHE'S TOLD US THE DESTROYER WAS COMING.
NOW YOU'RE JUST BEING SILLY, HEIDI. THIS IS THE TWENTY-FIRST CENTURY. WE'VE PUT AWAY SHADOWS AND GRUMPKINS. WE HAVE TO BE BEYOND SUPERSTITION AT LAST BY NOW.
OH YEAH?
EARLIER TODAY GOD HIM- SELF WALKED INTO TOWN AND TOOK UP RESIDENCE.
EXACTLY HOW DOES THAT FIT INTO YOUR NORMAL, RATIONAL WORLD?

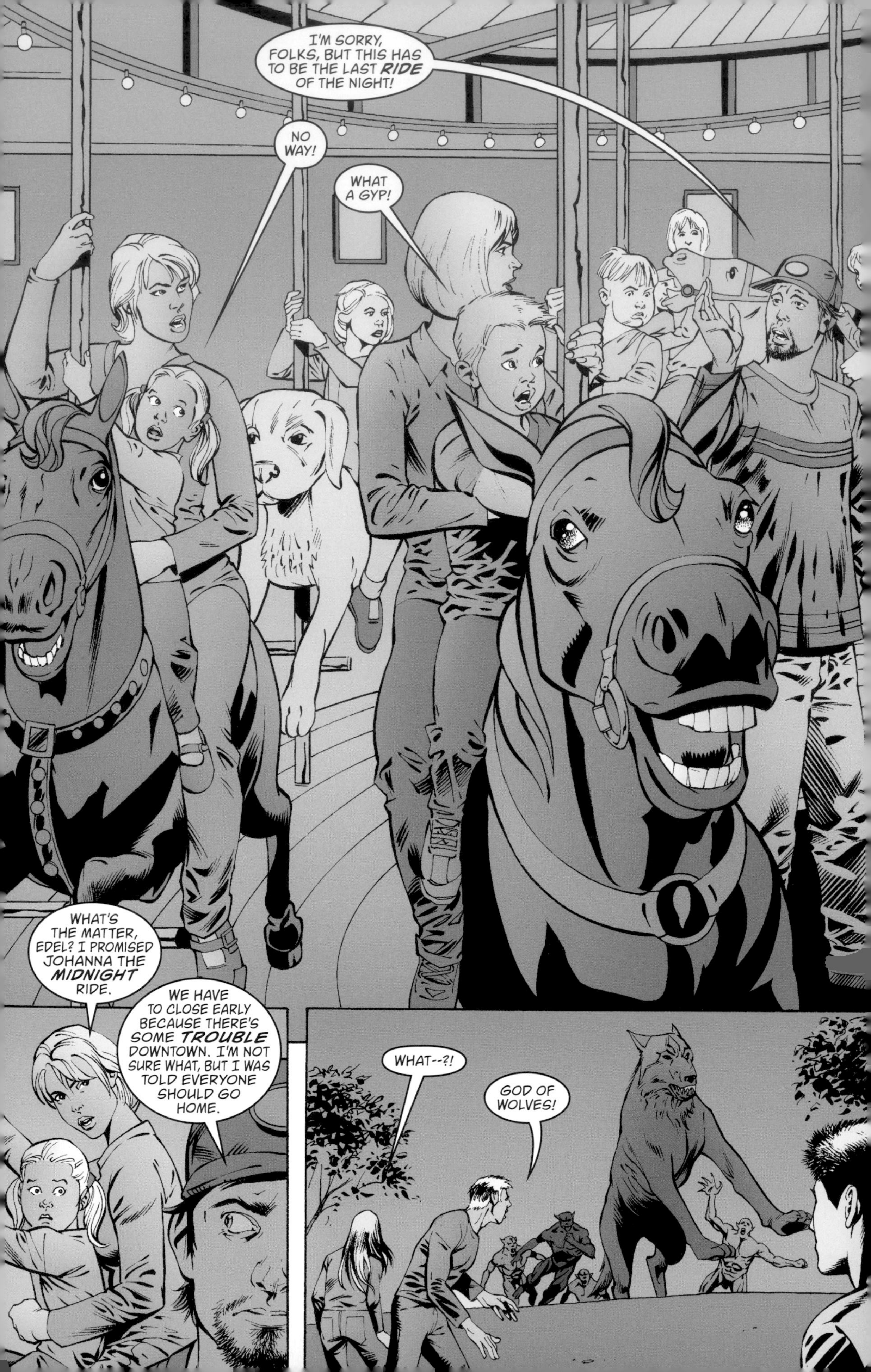
I'M SORRY, FOLKS, BUT THIS HAS TO BE THE LAST RIDE OF THE NIGHT!
NO WAY!
WHAT A GYP!
WHAT'S THE MATTER, EDEL? I PROMISED JOHANNA THE MIDNIGHT RIDE.
WE HAVE TO CLOSE EARLY BECAUSE THERE'S SOME TROUBLE DOWNTOWN. I'M NOT SURE WHAT, BUT I WAS TOLD EVERYONE SHOULD GO HOME.
WHAT--?!
GOD OF WOLVES!

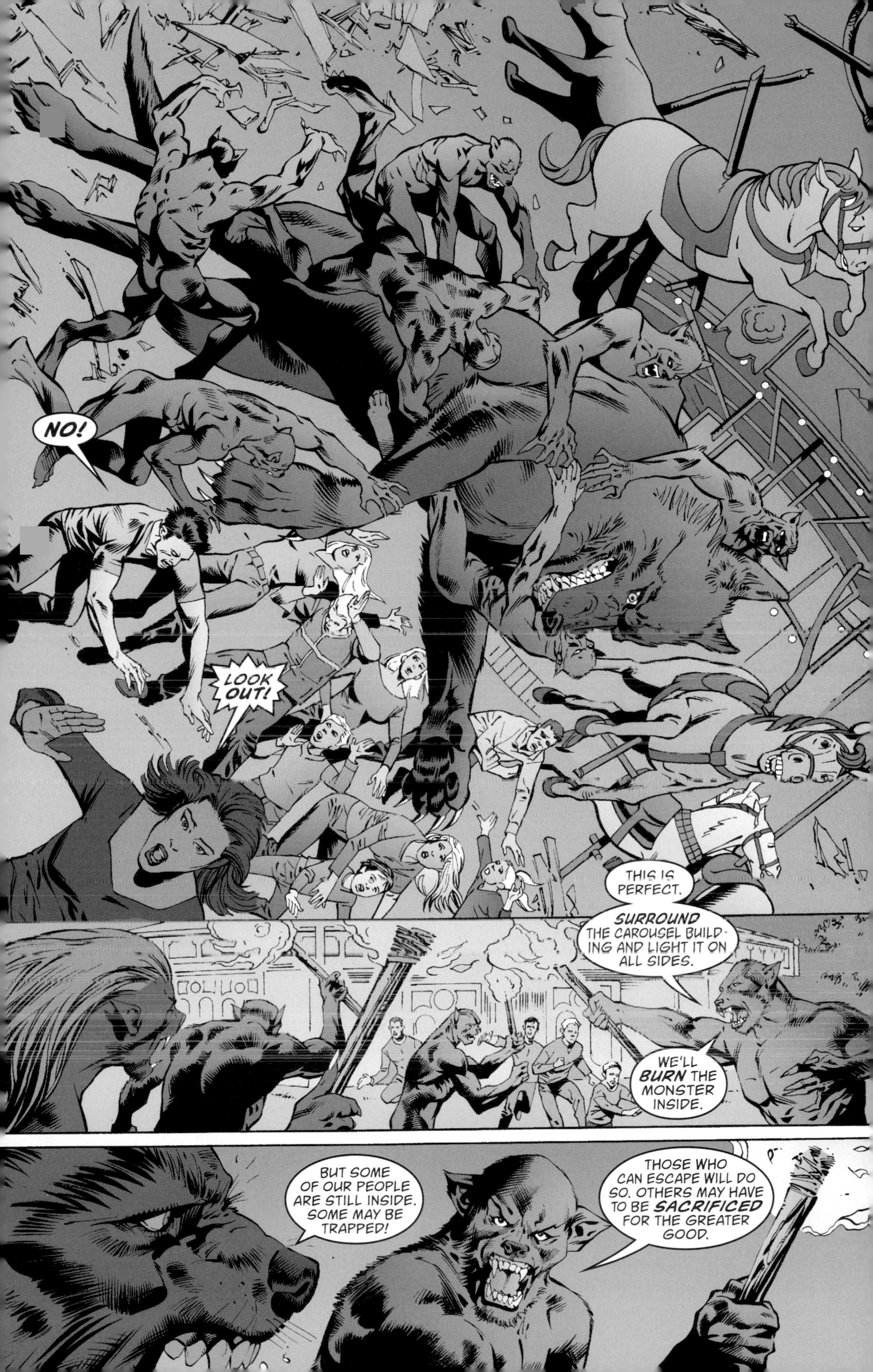
NO!
LOOK OUT!
THIS IS PERFECT.
SURROUND THE CAROUSEL BUILDING AND LIGHT IT ON ALL SIDES.
WE'LL BURN THE MONSTER INSIDE.
BUT SOME OF OUR PEOPLE ARE STILL INSIDE. SOME MAY BE TRAPPED!
THOSE WHO CAN ESCAPE WILL DO SO. OTHERS MAY HAVE TO BE SACRIFICED FOR THE GREATER GOOD.

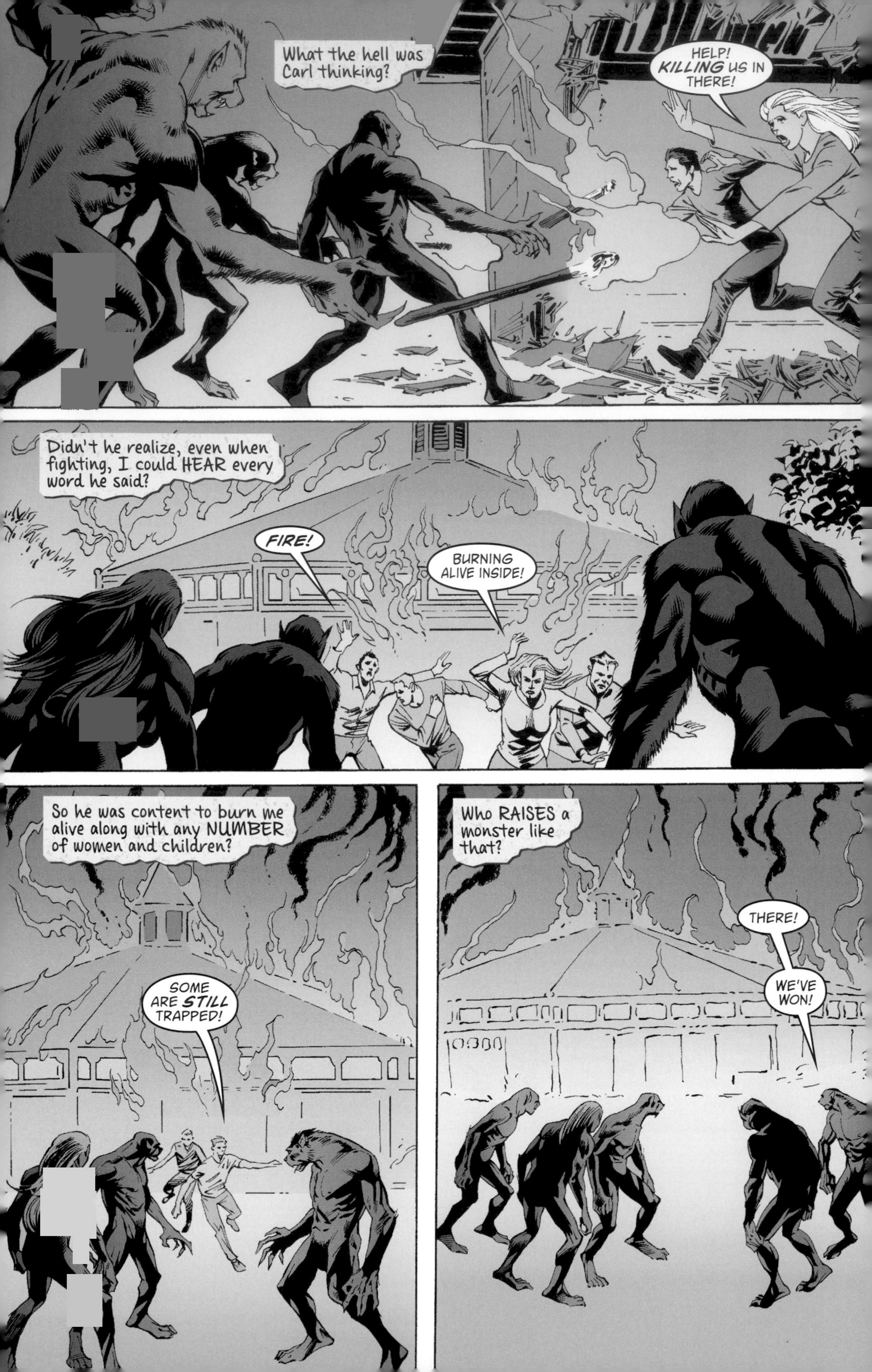
What the hell was Carl thinking?
HELP! KILLING US IN THERE!
Didn't he realize, even when fighting, I could HEAR every word he said?
FIRE!
BURNING ALIVE INSIDE!
So he was content to burn me alive along with any NUMBER of women and children?
SOME ARE STILL TRAPPED!
Who RAISES a monster like that?
THERE!
WE'VE WON!

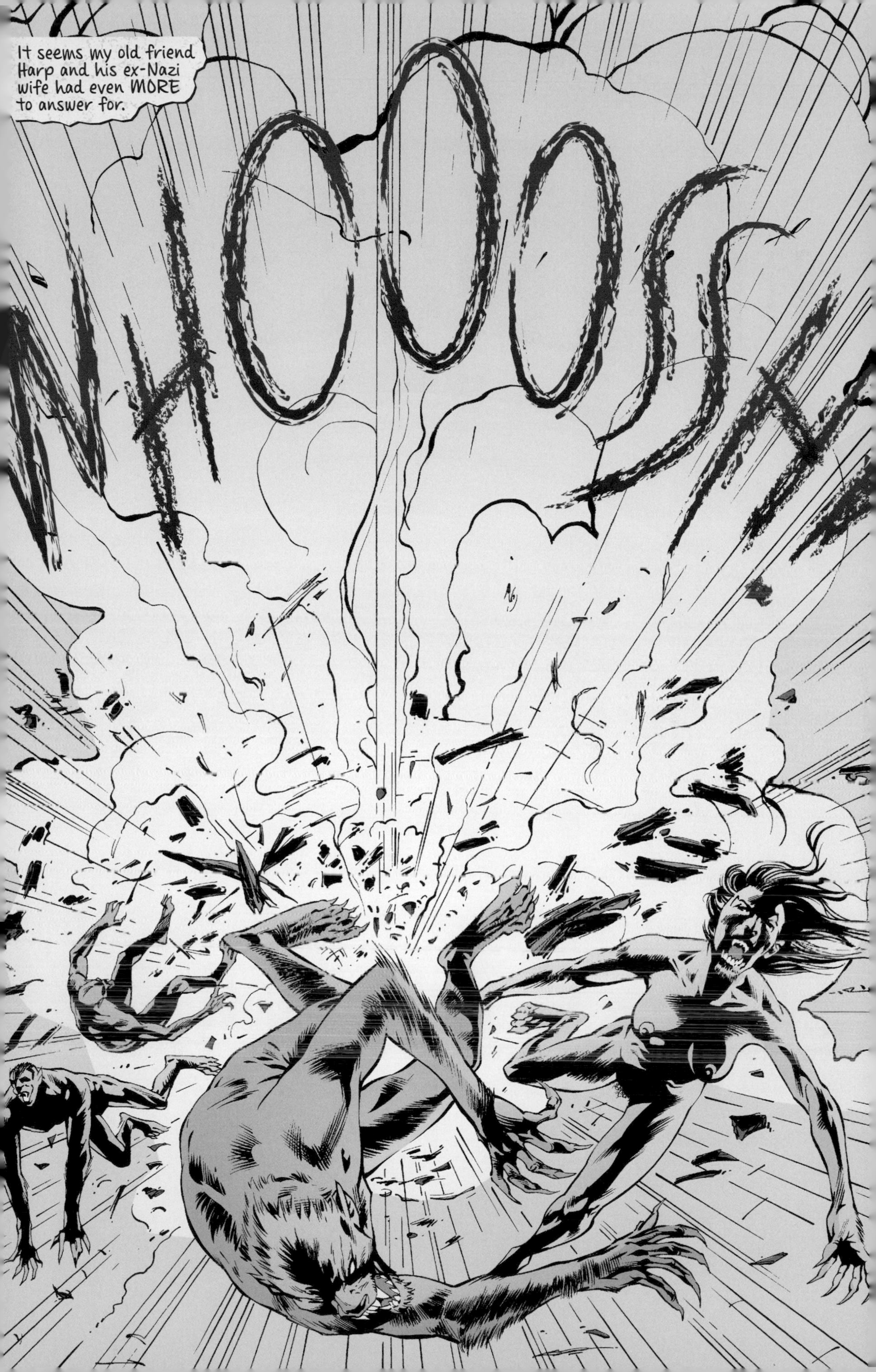
It seems my old friend Harp and his ex-Nazi wife had even MORE to answer for.
WHOOOSH

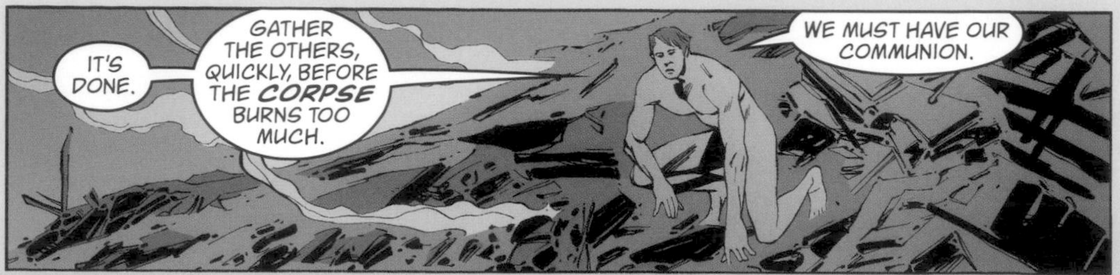
IT'S DONE.
GATHER THE OTHERS, QUICKLY, BEFORE THE CORPSE BURNS TOO MUCH.
WE MUST HAVE OUR COMMUNION.

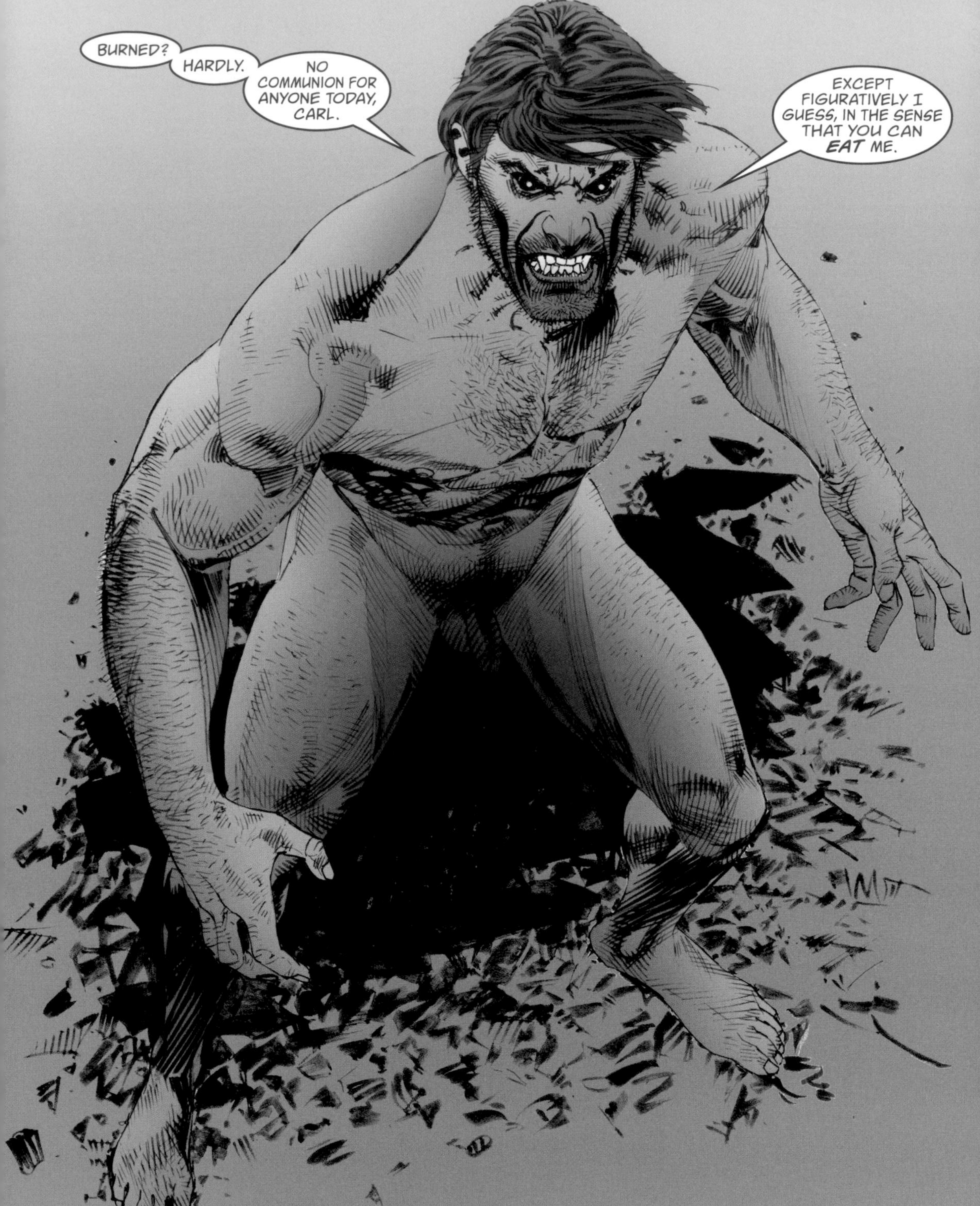
BURNED?
HARDLY.
NO COMMUNION FOR ANYONE TODAY, CARL.
EXCEPT FIGURATIVELY I GUESS, IN THE SENSE THAT YOU CAN EAT ME.

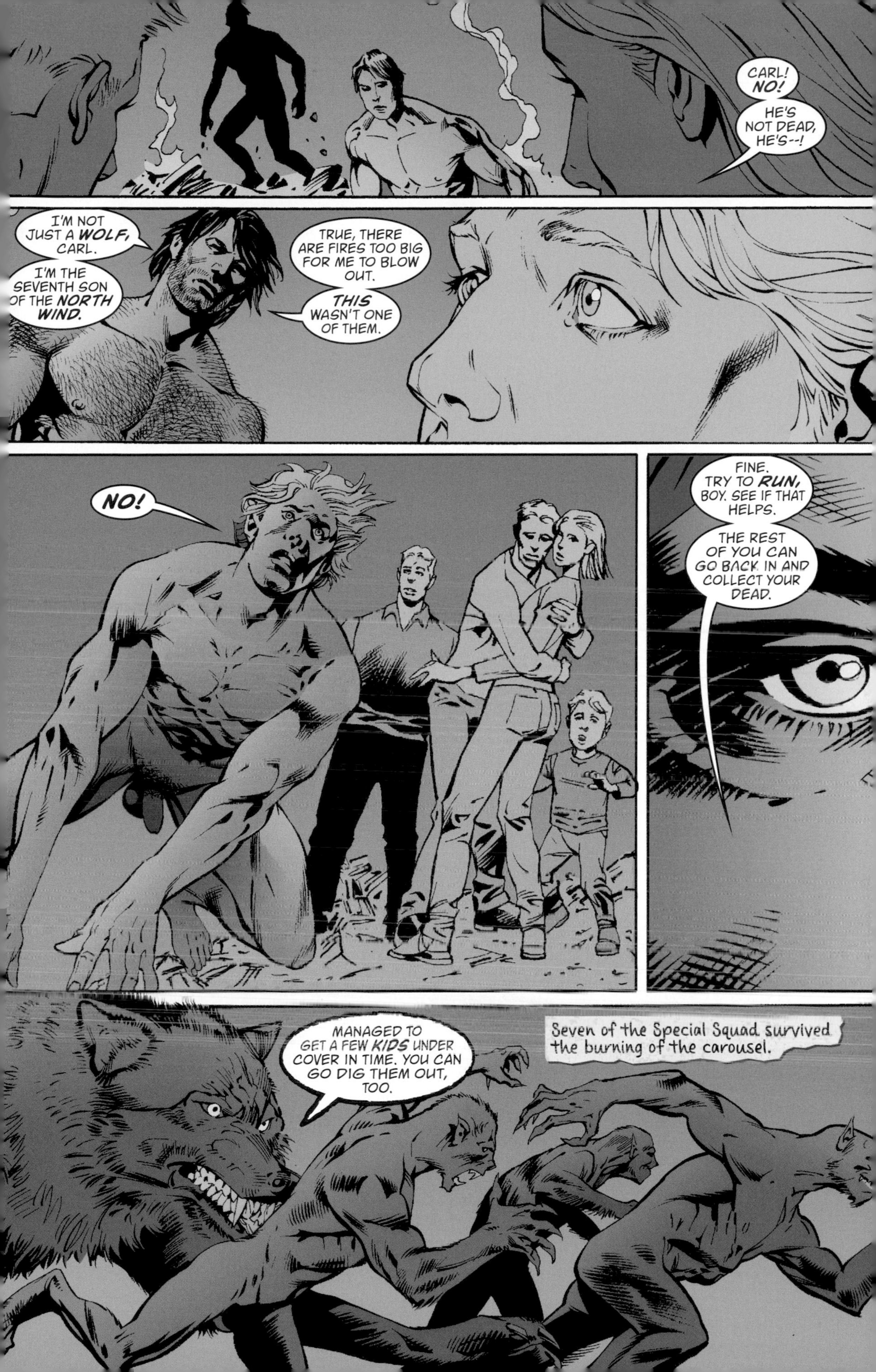
CARL! NO!
HE'S NOT DEAD, HE'S--!
I'M NOT JUST A WOLF, CARL.
I'M THE SEVENTH SON OF THE NORTH WIND.
TRUE, THERE ARE FIRES TOO BIG FOR ME TO BLOW OUT.
THIS WASN'T ONE OF THEM.
NO!
FINE. TRY TO RUN, BOY. SEE IF THAT HELPS.
THE REST OF YOU CAN GO BACK IN AND COLLECT YOUR DEAD.
MANAGED TO GET A FEW KIDS UNDER COVER IN TIME. YOU CAN GO DIG THEM OUT, TOO.
Seven of the Special Squad survived the burning of the carousel.

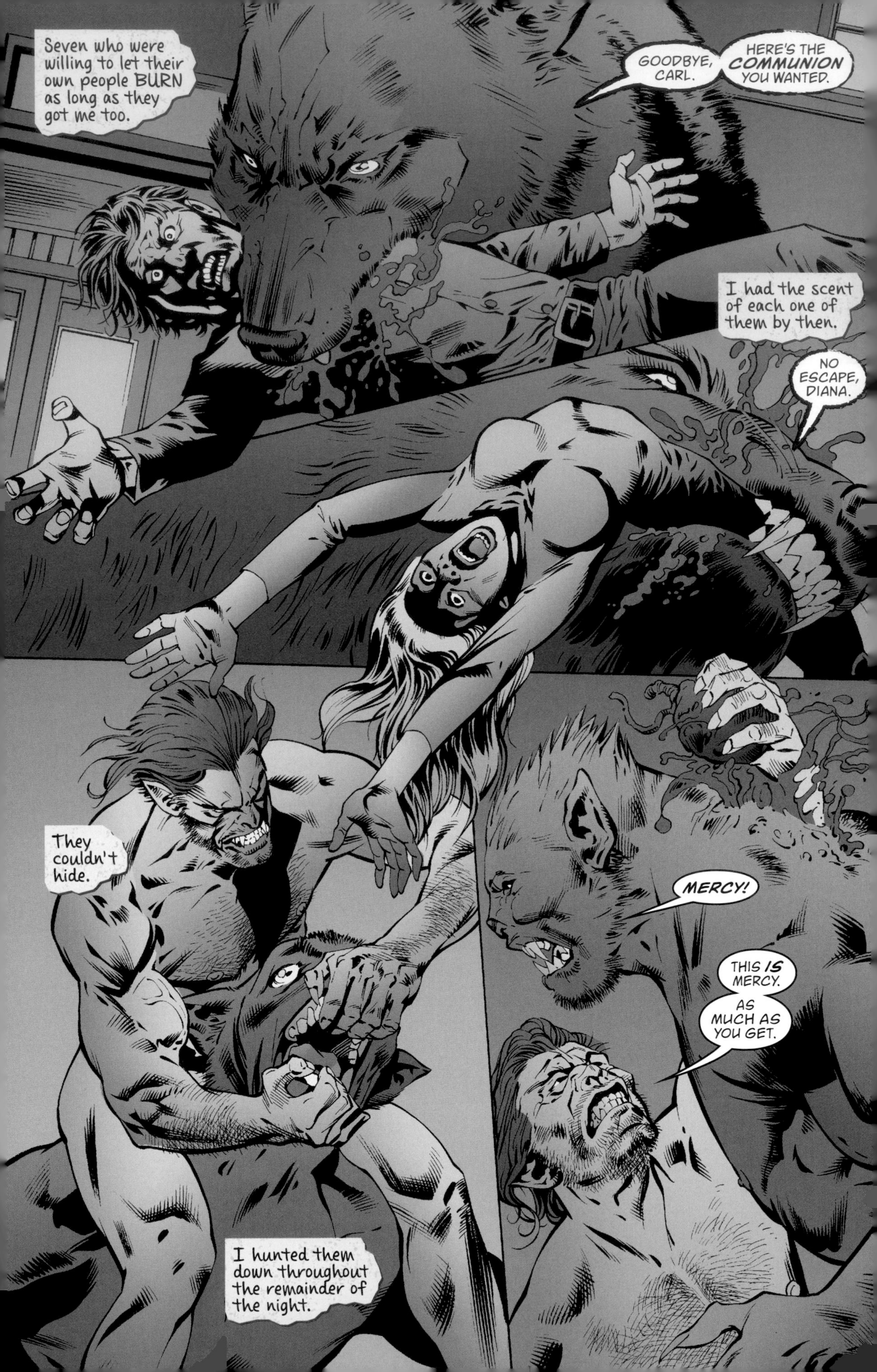
Seven who were willing to let their own people BURN as long as they got me too.
GOODBYE, CARL.
HERE'S THE COMMUNION YOU WANTED.
I had the scent of each one of them by then.
NO ESCAPE, DIANA.
They couldn't hide.
MERCY!
THIS IS MERCY.
AS MUCH AS YOU GET.
I hunted them down throughout the remainder of the night.

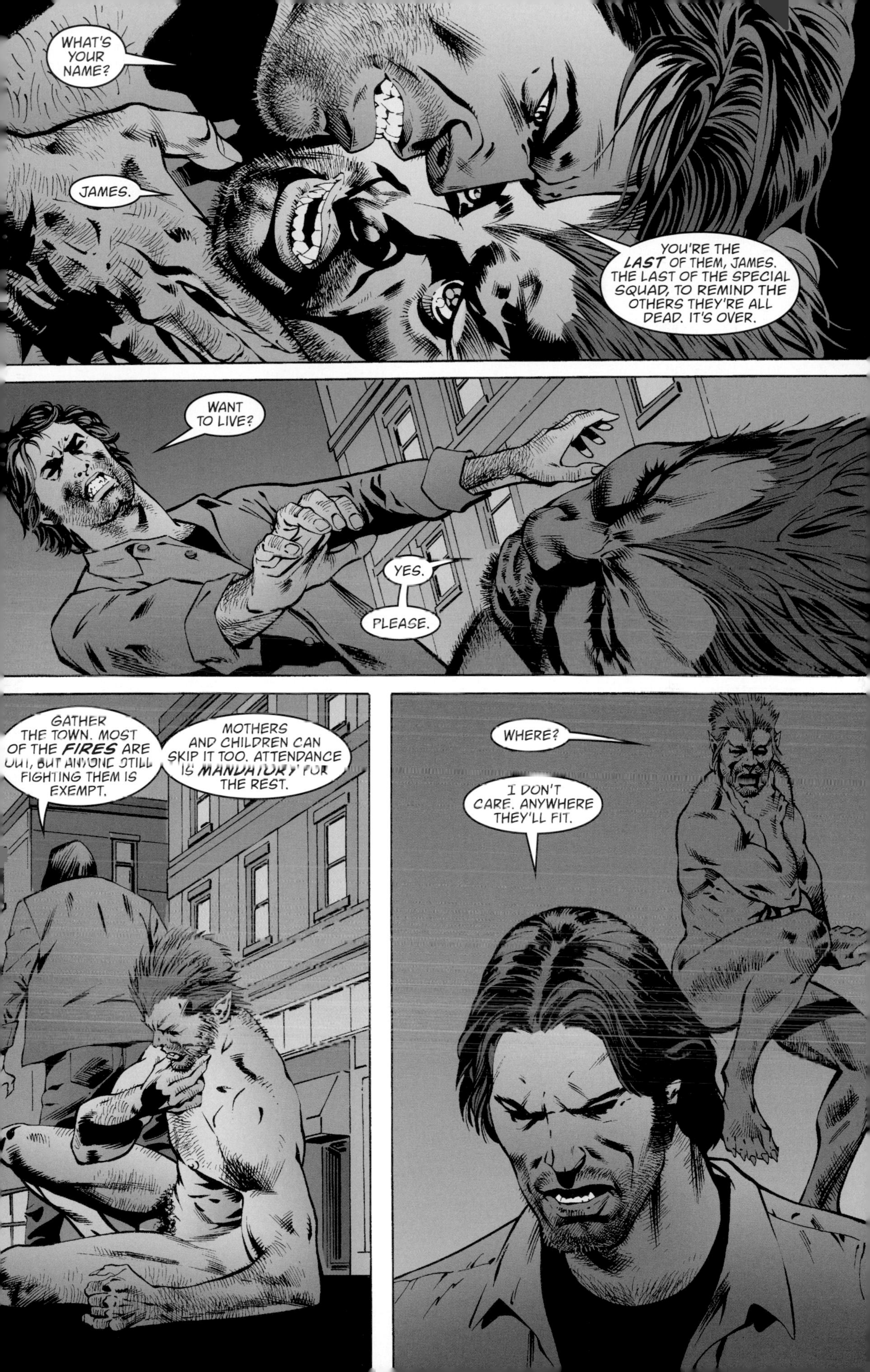
WHAT'S YOUR NAME?
JAMES.
YOU'RE THE LAST OF THEM, JAMES. THE LAST OF THE SPECIAL SQUAD, TO REMIND THE OTHERS THEY'RE ALL DEAD. IT'S OVER.
WANT TO LIVE?
YES.
PLEASE.
GATHER THE TOWN. MOST OF THE FIRES ARE OUT, BUT ANYONE STILL FIGHTING THEM IS EXEMPT.
MOTHERS AND CHILDREN CAN SKIP IT TOO. ATTENDANCE IS MANDATORY FOR THE REST.
WHERE?
I DON'T CARE. ANYWHERE THEY'LL FIT.

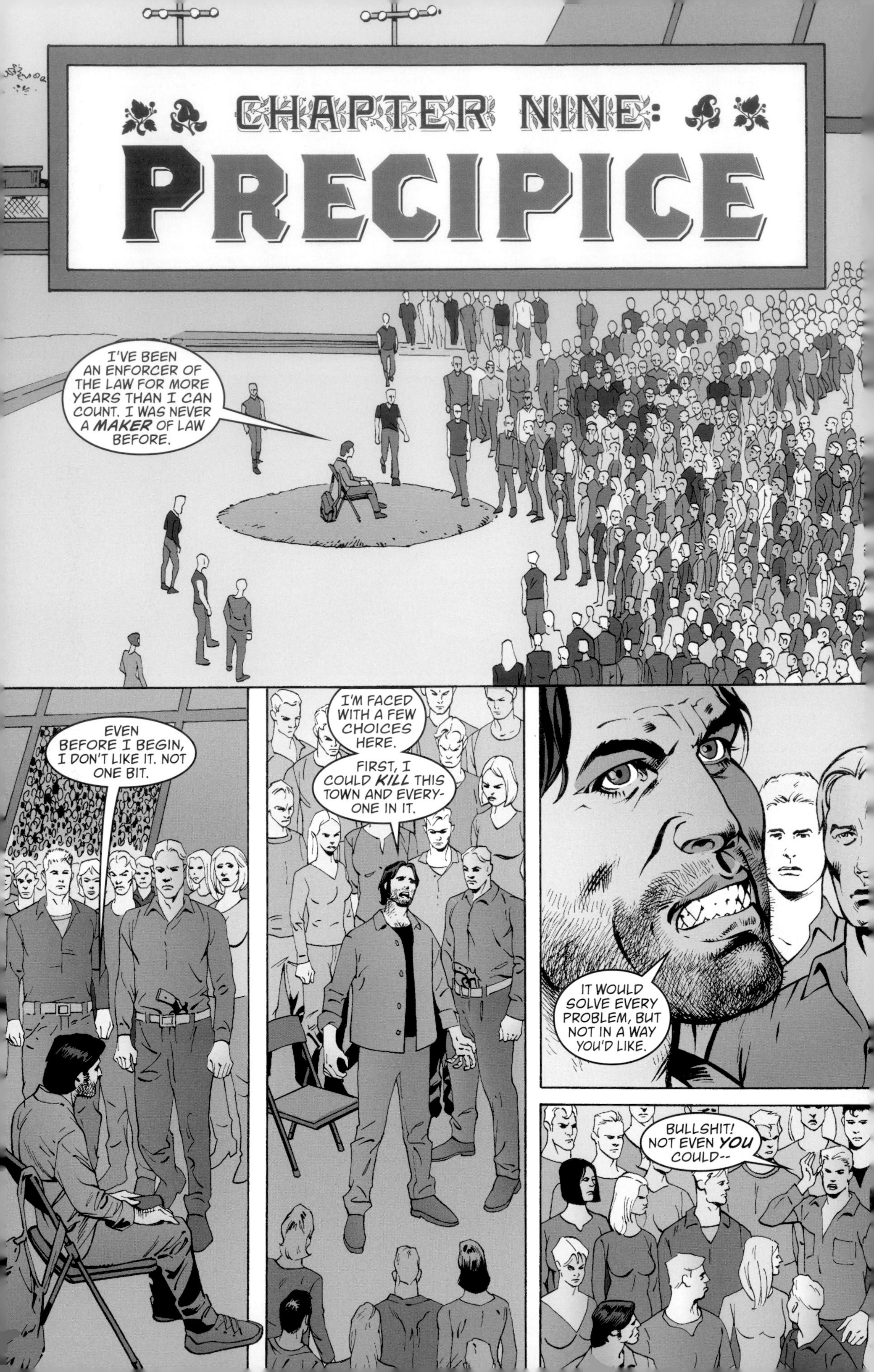
CHAPTER NINE:
PRECIPICE
I'VE BEEN AN ENFORCER OF THE LAW FOR MORE YEARS THAN I CAN COUNT. I WAS NEVER A MAKER OF LAW BEFORE.
EVEN BEFORE I BEGIN, I DON'T LIKE IT. NOT ONE BIT.
I'M FACED WITH A FEW CHOICES HERE.
FIRST, I COULD KILL THIS TOWN AND EVERY-ONE IN IT.
IT WOULD SOLVE EVERY PROBLEM, BUT NOT IN A WAY YOU'D LIKE.
BULLSHIT! NOT EVEN YOU COULD--

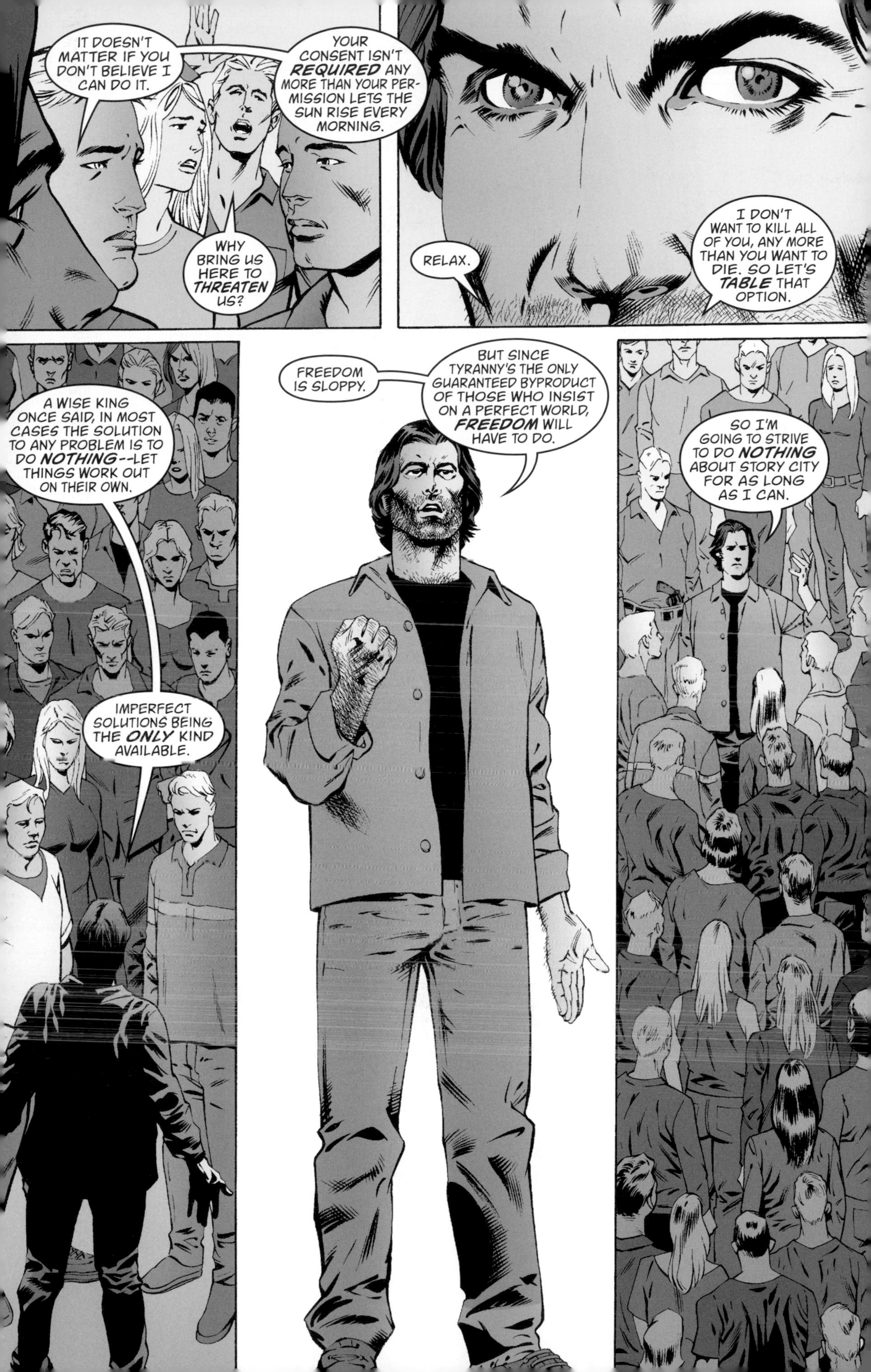
IT DOESN'T MATTER IF YOU DON'T BELIEVE I CAN DO IT.
YOUR CONSENT ISN'T REQUIRED ANY MORE THAN YOUR PERMISSION LETS THE SUN RISE EVERY MORNING.
WHY BRING US HERE TO THREATEN US?
RELAX.
I DON'T WANT TO KILL ALL OF YOU, ANY MORE THAN YOU WANT TO DIE. SO LET'S TABLE THAT OPTION.
A WISE KING ONCE SAID, IN MOST CASES THE SOLUTION TO ANY PROBLEM IS TO DO NOTHING--LET THINGS WORK OUT ON THEIR OWN.
IMPERFECT SOLUTIONS BEING THE ONLY KIND AVAILABLE.
FREEDOM IS SLOPPY.
BUT SINCE TYRANNY'S THE ONLY GUARANTEED BYPRODUCT OF THOSE WHO INSIST ON A PERFECT WORLD, FREEDOM WILL HAVE TO DO.
SO I'M GOING TO STRIVE TO DO NOTHING ABOUT STORY CITY FOR AS LONG AS I CAN.

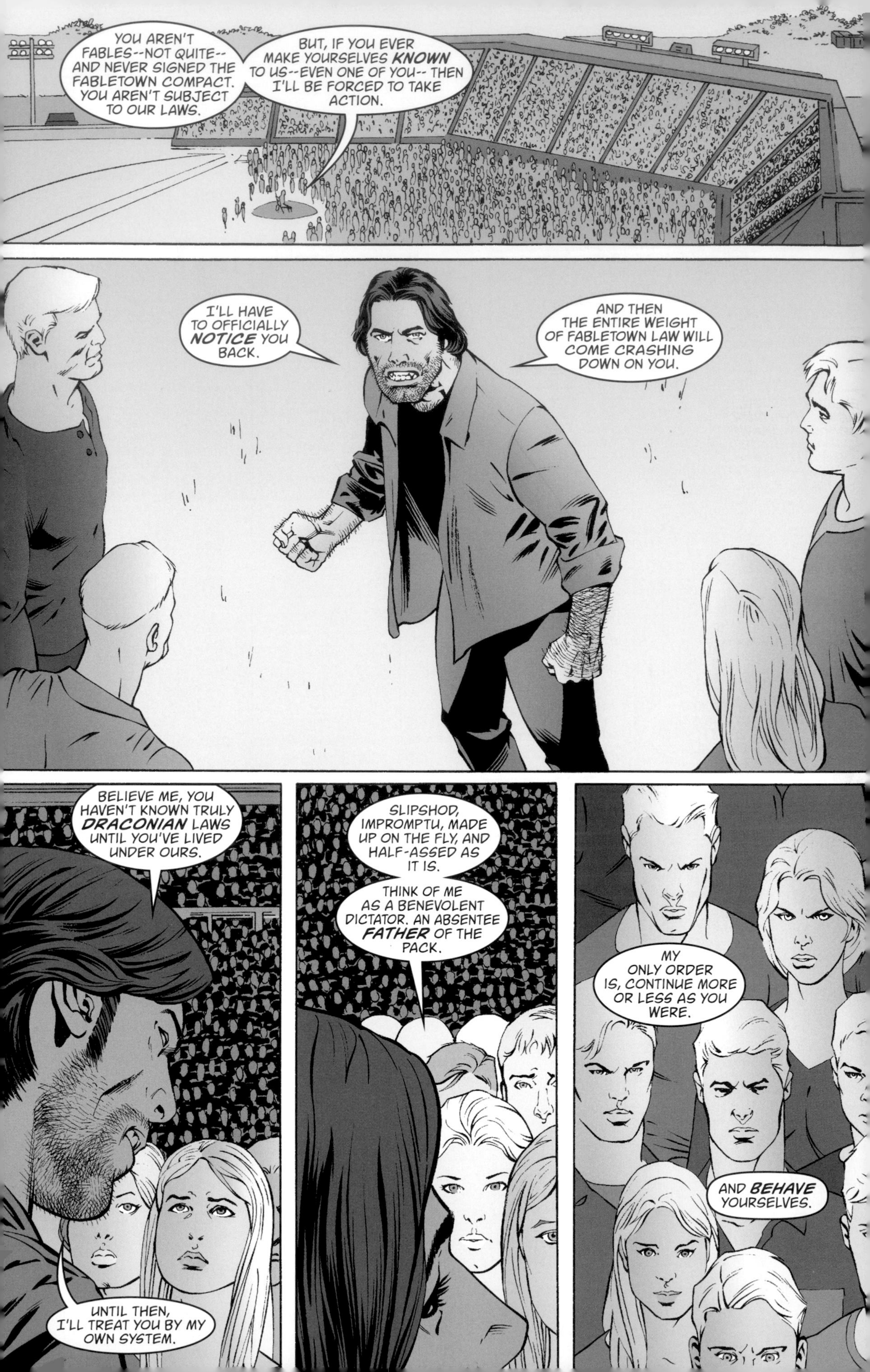
YOU AREN'T FABLES--NOT QUITE--AND NEVER SIGNED THE FABLETOWN COMPACT. YOU AREN'T SUBJECT TO OUR LAWS.
BUT, IF YOU EVER MAKE YOURSELVES KNOWN TO US--EVEN ONE OF YOU-- THEN I'LL BE FORCED TO TAKE ACTION.
I'LL HAVE TO OFFICIALLY NOTICE YOU BACK.
AND THEN THE ENTIRE WEIGHT OF FABLETOWN LAW WILL COME CRASHING DOWN ON YOU.
BELIEVE ME, YOU HAVEN'T KNOWN TRULY DRACONIAN LAWS UNTIL YOU'VE LIVED UNDER OURS.
UNTIL THEN, I'LL TREAT YOU BY MY OWN SYSTEM.
SLIPSHOD, IMPROMPTU, MADE UP ON THE FLY, AND HALF-ASSED AS IT IS.
THINK OF ME AS A BENEVOLENT DICTATOR. AN ABSENTEE FATHER OF THE PACK.
MY ONLY ORDER IS, CONTINUE MORE OR LESS AS YOU WERE.
AND BEHAVE YOURSELVES.

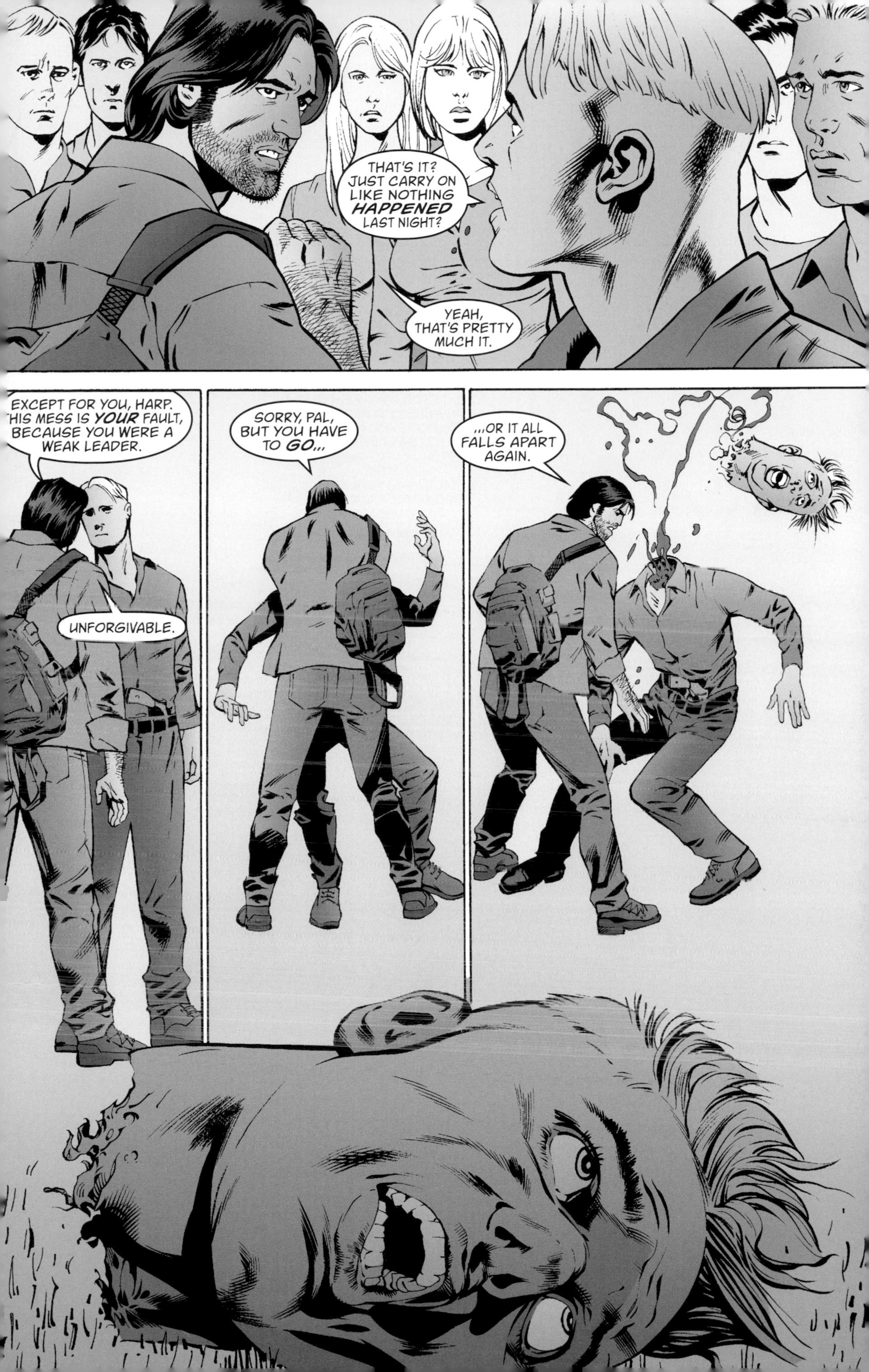
THAT'S IT? JUST CARRY ON LIKE NOTHING HAPPENED LAST NIGHT?
YEAH, THAT'S PRETTY MUCH IT.
EXCEPT FOR YOU, HARP. THIS MESS IS YOUR FAULT, BECAUSE YOU WERE A WEAK LEADER.
UNFORGIVABLE.
SORRY, PAL, BUT YOU HAVE TO GO...
...OR IT ALL FALLS APART AGAIN.

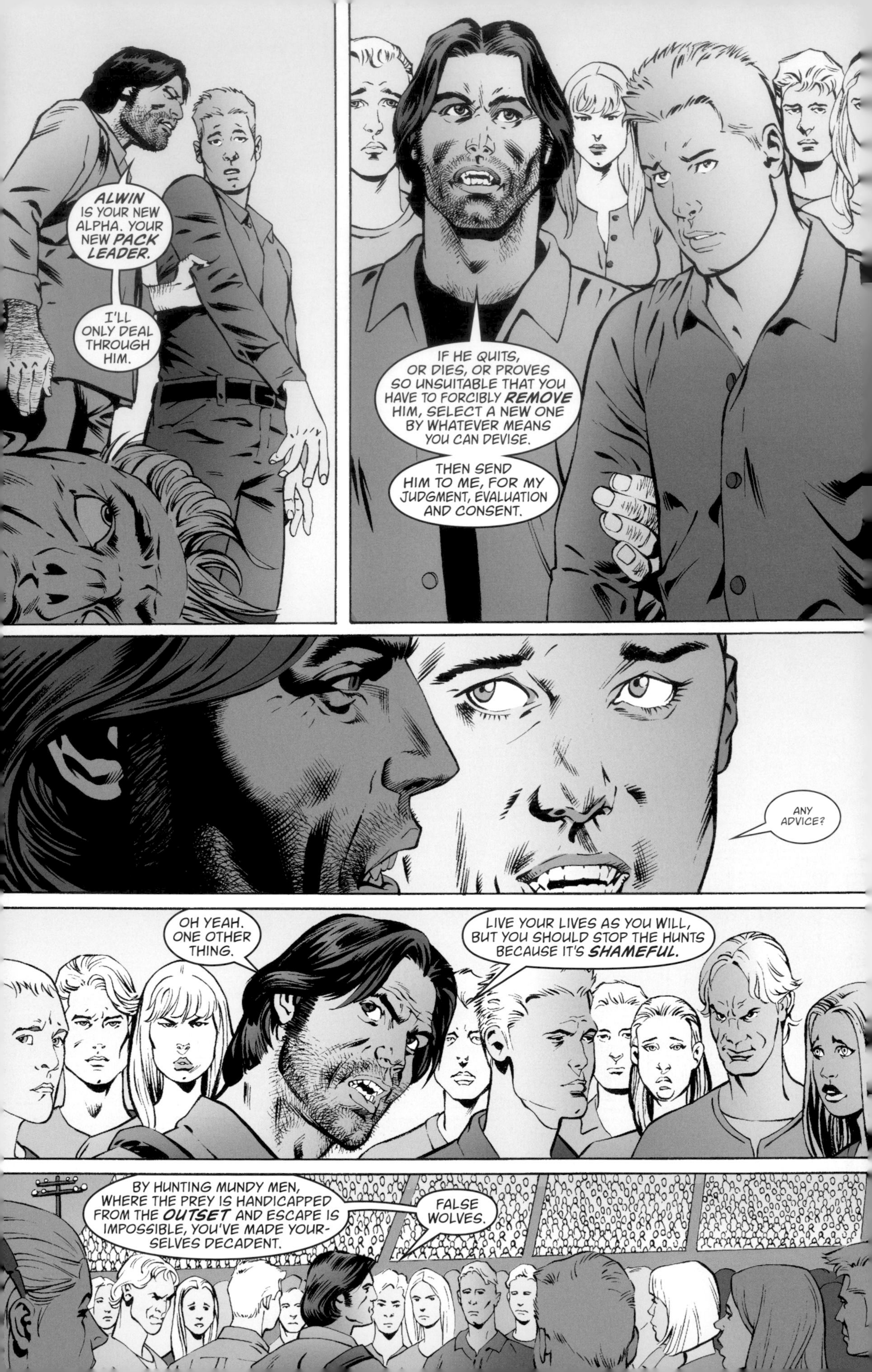
ALWIN IS YOUR NEW ALPHA. YOUR NEW PACK LEADER.
I'LL ONLY DEAL THROUGH HIM.
IF HE QUITS, OR DIES, OR PROVES SO UNSUITABLE THAT YOU HAVE TO FORCIBLY REMOVE HIM, SELECT A NEW ONE BY WHATEVER MEANS YOU CAN DEVISE.
THEN SEND HIM TO ME, FOR MY JUDGMENT, EVALUATION AND CONSENT.
ANY ADVICE?
OH YEAH. ONE OTHER THING.
LIVE YOUR LIVES AS YOU WILL, BUT YOU SHOULD STOP THE HUNTS BECAUSE IT'S SHAMEFUL.
BY HUNTING MUNDY MEN, WHERE THE PREY IS HANDICAPPED FROM THE OUTSET AND ESCAPE IS IMPOSSIBLE, YOU'VE MADE YOURSELVES DECADENT.
FALSE WOLVES.

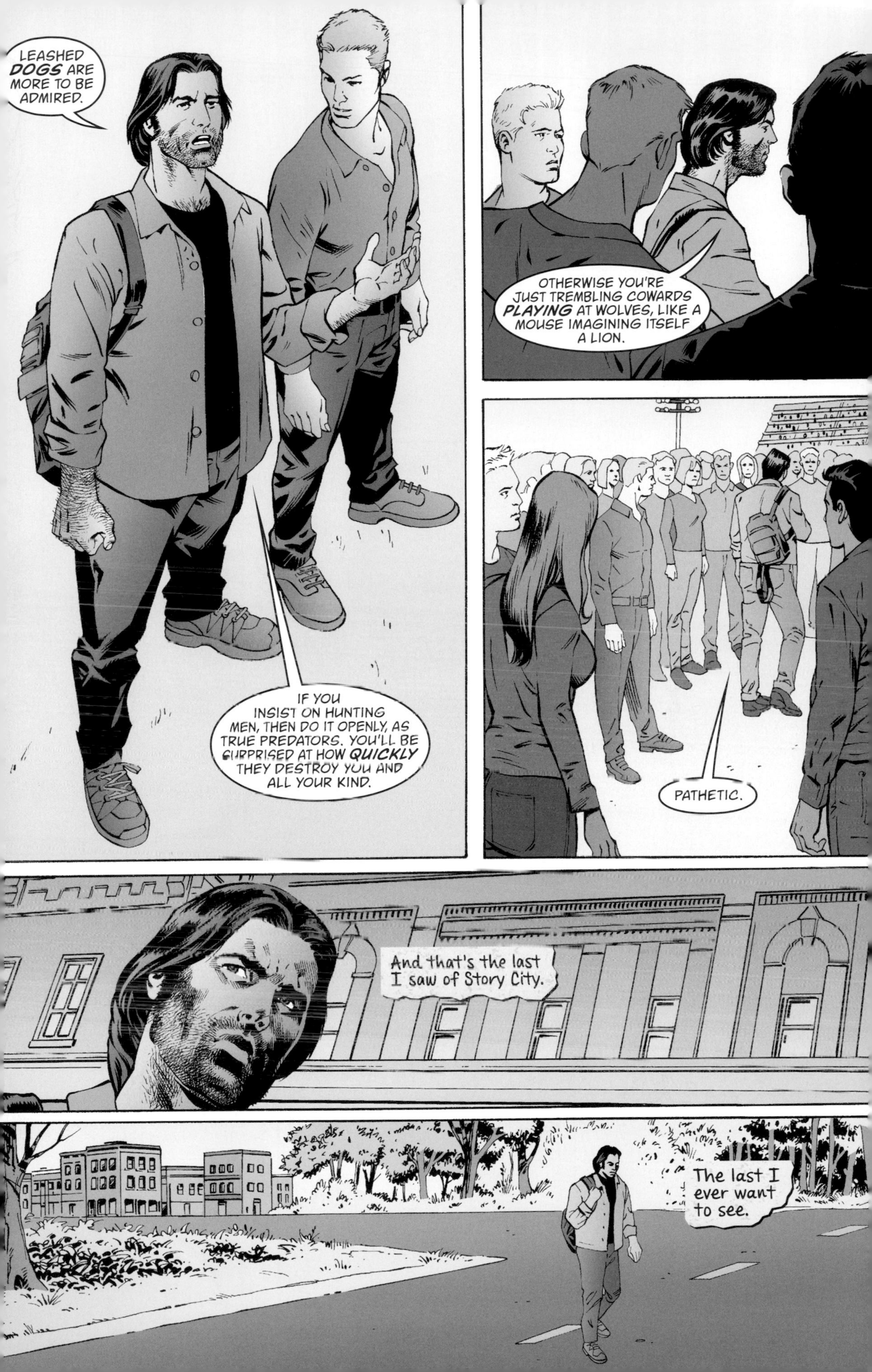
LEASHED DOGS ARE MORE TO BE ADMIRED.
IF YOU INSIST ON HUNTING MEN, THEN DO IT OPENLY, AS TRUE PREDATORS. YOU'LL BE SURPRISED AT HOW QUICKLY THEY DESTROY YOU AND ALL YOUR KIND.
OTHERWISE YOU'RE JUST TREMBLING COWARDS PLAYING AT WOLVES, LIKE A MOUSE IMAGINING ITSELF A LION.
PATHETIC.
And that's the last I saw of Story City.
The last I ever want to see.

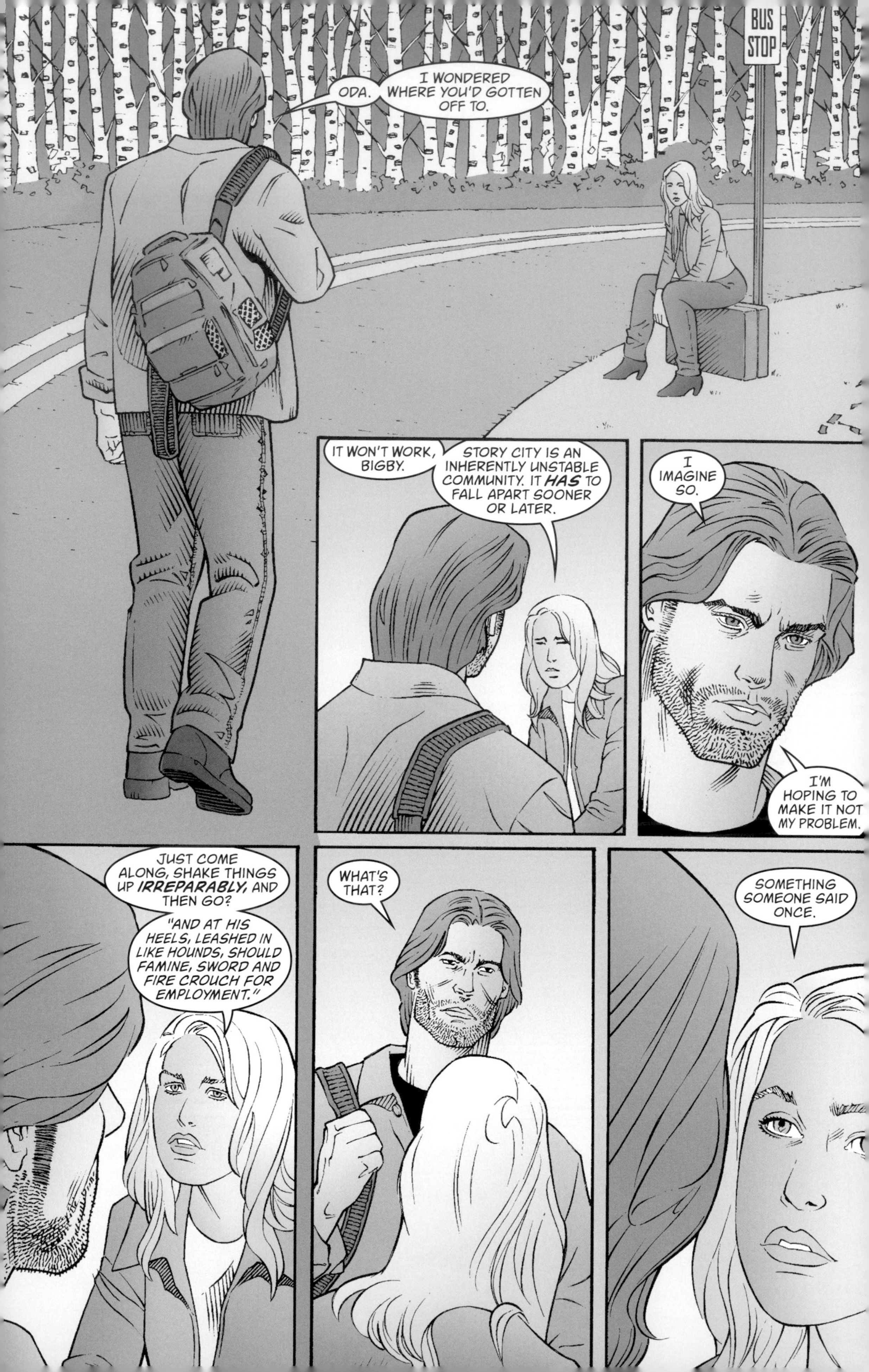
BUS STOP
ODA.
I WONDERED WHERE YOU'D GOTTEN OFF TO.
IT WON'T WORK, BIGBY.
STORY CITY IS AN INHERENTLY UNSTABLE COMMUNITY. IT *HAS* TO FALL APART SOONER OR LATER.
I IMAGINE SO.
I'M HOPING TO MAKE IT NOT MY PROBLEM.
JUST COME ALONG, SHAKE THINGS UP *IRREPARABLY,* AND THEN GO?
"AND AT HIS HEELS, LEASHED IN LIKE HOUNDS, SHOULD FAMINE, SWORD AND FIRE CROUCH FOR EMPLOYMENT."
WHAT'S THAT?
SOMETHING SOMEONE SAID ONCE.

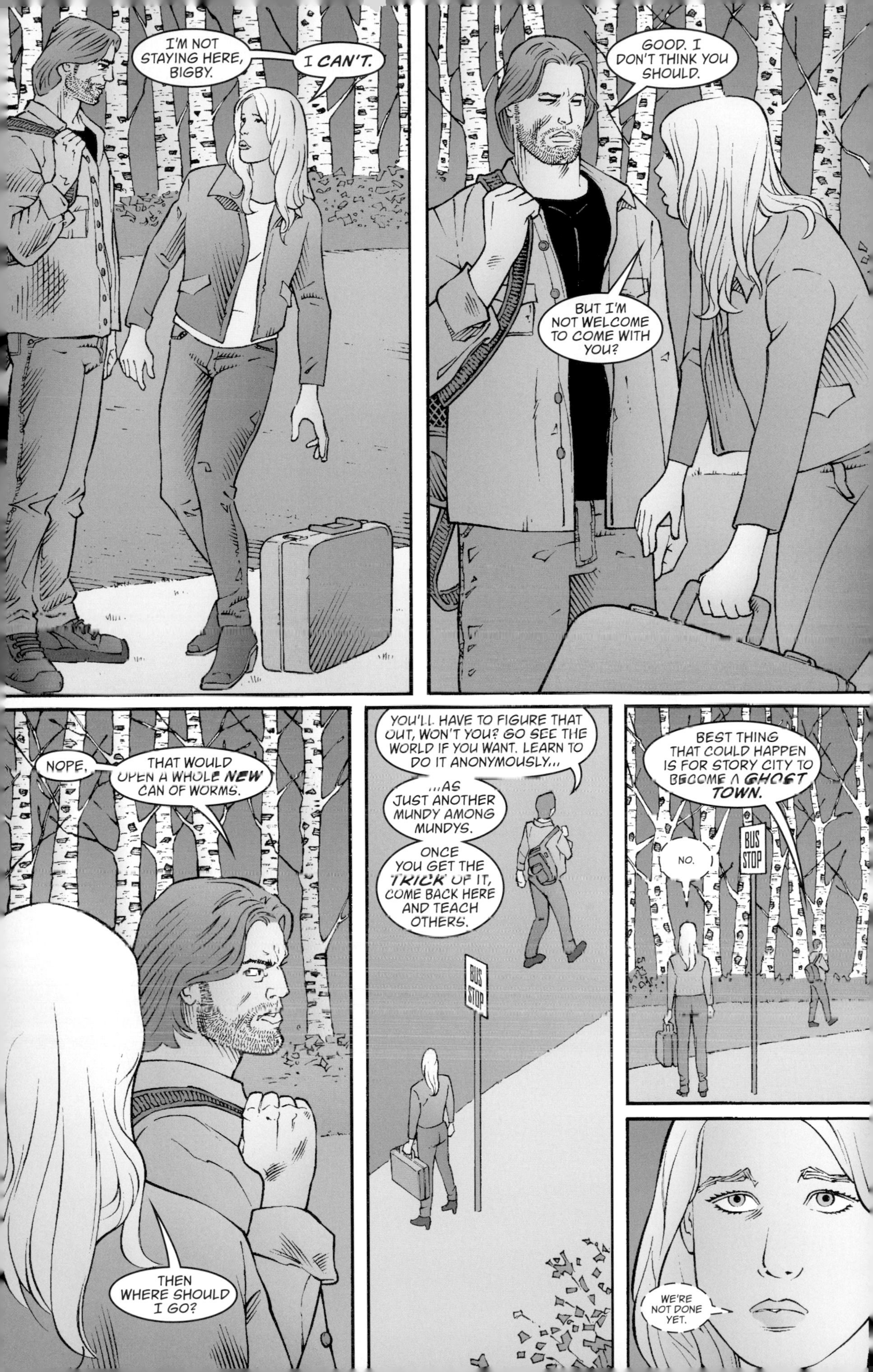
I'M NOT STAYING HERE, BIGBY.
I CAN'T.
GOOD. I DON'T THINK YOU SHOULD.
BUT I'M NOT WELCOME TO COME WITH YOU?
NOPE.
THAT WOULD OPEN A WHOLE NEW CAN OF WORMS.
THEN WHERE SHOULD I GO?
YOU'LL HAVE TO FIGURE THAT OUT, WON'T YOU? GO SEE THE WORLD IF YOU WANT. LEARN TO DO IT ANONYMOUSLY...
...AS JUST ANOTHER MUNDY AMONG MUNDYS.
ONCE YOU GET THE TRICK OF IT, COME BACK HERE AND TEACH OTHERS.
BUS STOP
BEST THING THAT COULD HAPPEN IS FOR STORY CITY TO BECOME A GHOST TOWN.
NO.
BUS STOP
WE'RE NOT DONE YET.

THE
END

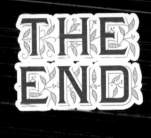

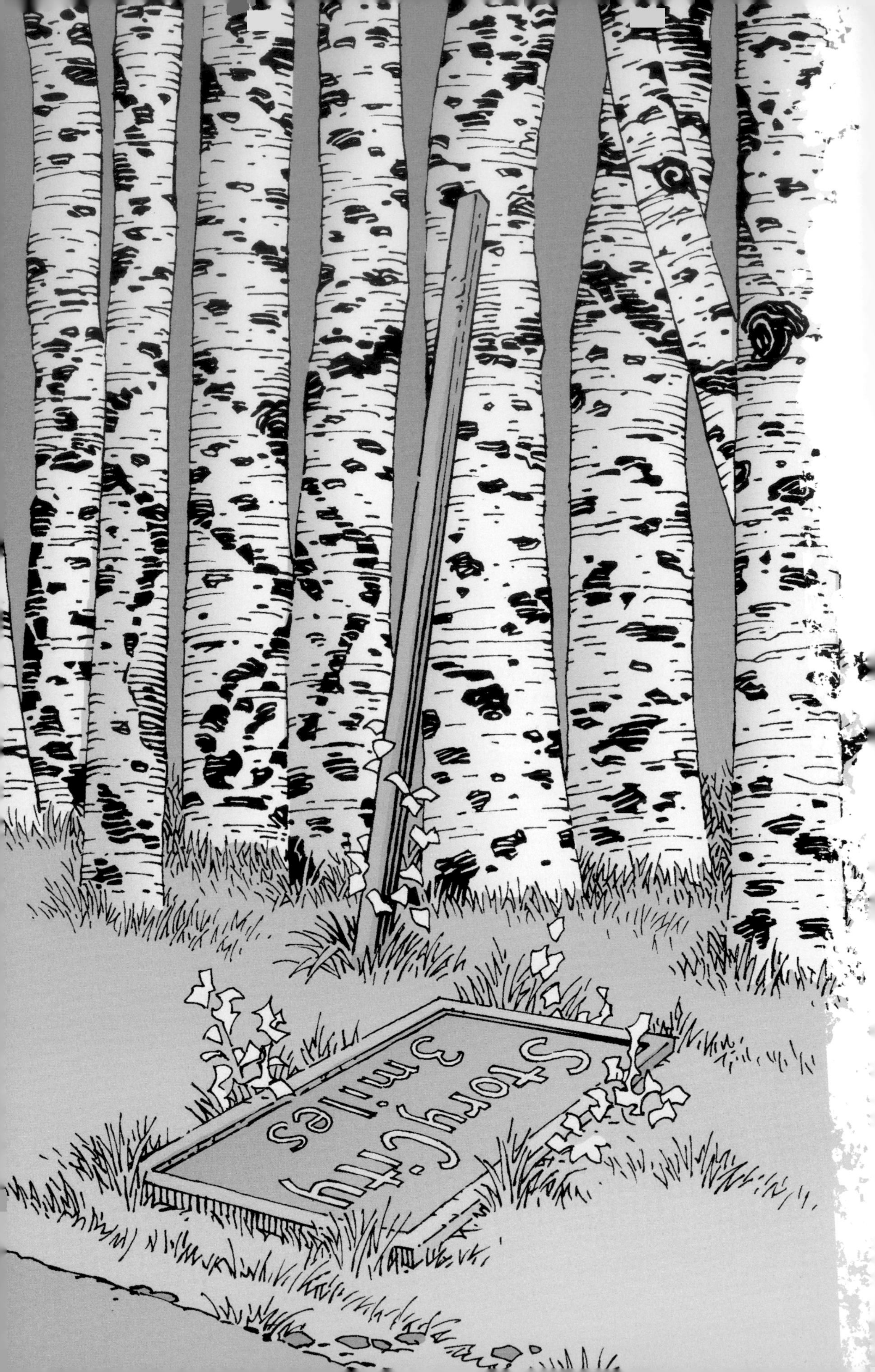
Story City
3 miles

Afterword
In which Bill explains, illuminates and apologizes
By Bill Willingham

A little over three years ago, as these lines are being written, I was driving across country, moving from Las Vegas to Minnesota, when I happened across a road sign pointing out I was a few short miles away from a place I'd never heard of before, called Story City. Like it says in the story you just read, you'll find it on Interstate 35, in Iowa, a wee bit north of Ames.

As it was closing in on lunchtime that afternoon three years back, and considering my chosen profession, how could I not pull over in a place called Story City, despite the good time I'd been making? An aside: at some point in my life I've turned into my father in several key respects, among which is the driving need (pun intended, I suppose) to "make good time" when on the road. I'm not sure how many wonderful roadside attractions I've missed discovering and how many picturesque towns I've missed exploring, all sacrificed on the altar of "making good time," but I have to believe it's not a low number.

In any case, even though I was making good time, I decided I had to stop for lunch at a place called Story City, or forever disabuse myself of the notion that I'm the often whimsical and always-impractical man I like to imagine myself to be.

I stopped in at the Happy Chef Restaurant, on Broad Street, found a nice table, and ordered an open-faced turkey sandwich, a Coke and a story.

"Excuse me?" the waitress said.

I repeated my order.

"A story?" she said. "I don't understand."

"Isn't this Story City?" I said. "So, along with lunch, I'll be wanting my story."

"Oh," she said. Then, after an extended pause, "No one's ever asked that before."

Our enjoyable back and forth banter went on for a spell, until the Happy Chef's manager finally explained that Story City was so named not because it was a near magical place of wonderful stories for the asking, but after the famous Supreme Court Justice Joseph Story, 1779-1845. Of course. I should've thought of that.

It didn't matter though. Story City had transformed itself into a near magical place of wonderful stories for the asking at the moment I decided to visit. The damage was done.

After lunch I drove about the town and found it to be a delightful place, nestled along the Skunk River (not so named due to its smell, as far as I could tell), with its hanging, swaying bridge, historical carousel, and various other small town pleasures. Sometime during that drive I came to the conclusion I'd have to set a FABLES story there. How could I not?

Since at about the same time I had just started noodling with the rudiments of what would eventually become WEREWOLVES OF THE HEARTLAND, and since that story needed to be set somewhere in America's heartland (or else we'd have to adjust the title), it seemed both obvious and ideal to set the tale in Story City.

The rest you've seen for yourself, in the story you just read.

And so now we should get to the apology part of this end note, an apology directed to the residents of the real Story City: I'm sorry we burned a substantial part of your town and wrecked a good deal of the rest of it, including your historic carousel, which has withstood the ravages of years and the many real calamities that have visited our country over the years. We didn't mean anything by it. It just so happens that many FABLES stories get a bit rambunctious and things tend to get broken along the way. It's the inescapable nature of action/adventure comics. Since the real town was left undamaged, and the fictional version promises to be rebuilt and restored, quickly and in good order, I hope you'll forgive the mess we made while we were your guests in the area.

And to the readers of this tale, let me assure you the real Story City is not, to my knowledge, currently overrun with ravenous werewolves, divided into secret cabals of murderous intent. That's one of the made-up elements of the yarn we just spun out for you. The real residents are quite nice, fully human, never transform into any sorts of beasts at all, and won't hunt you in the night, just because you happened to wander by. Trust me on this.

Oh, and one last observation before we go. That waitress was at least partly wrong back then. Although one can't count on a free story served up along with one's turkey sandwich at the Happy Chef café, Story City is in fact a place of storytelling. Having finally embraced the inescapable double meaning of its name, beginning in 2006 the town began hosting their annual Story City Story Festival in September of each year.

It looks like fun. We should go.

Follow the monthly adventures of the multiple Eisner Award-winning FABLES series:

FABLES
Legends in Exile

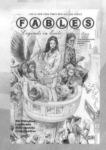

Vol. 1: LEGENDS IN EXILE
The immortal characters of popular fairy tales have been driven from their homelands and now live hidden among us, trying to cope with life in 21st-century Manhattan.

FABLES
ANIMAL FARM

Vol. 2: ANIMAL FARM
Non-human Fable characters have found refuge in upstate New York on The Farm, miles from mankind. But a conspiracy to free them from their perceived imprisonment may lead to a war that could wrest control of the Fables community away from Snow White.

FABLES
STORYBOOK LOVE

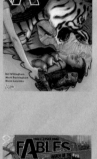

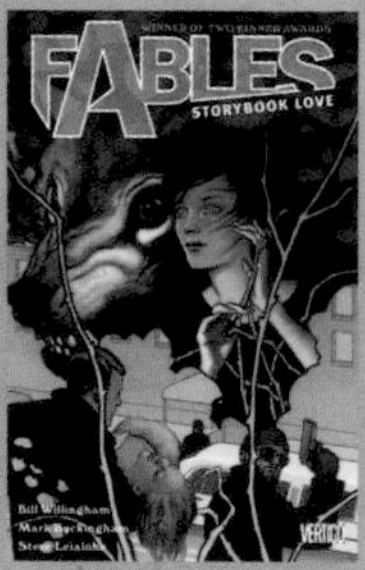

Vol. 3: STORYBOOK LOVE
Love may be blooming between two of the most hard-bitten, no-nonsense Fables around. But are Snow White and Bigby Wolf destined for happiness – or a quick and untimely death?

FABLES
MARCH OF THE WOODEN SOLDIERS

Vol. 4: MARCH OF THE WOODEN SOLDIERS
When Little Red Riding Hood suddenly walks through the gate between this world and the lost Fable Homelands, she's welcomed as a miraculous survivor by nearly everyone – except for her old nemesis, Bigby Wolf, who smells spying and subversion more than survival.

FABLES
THE MEAN SEASONS

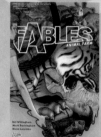

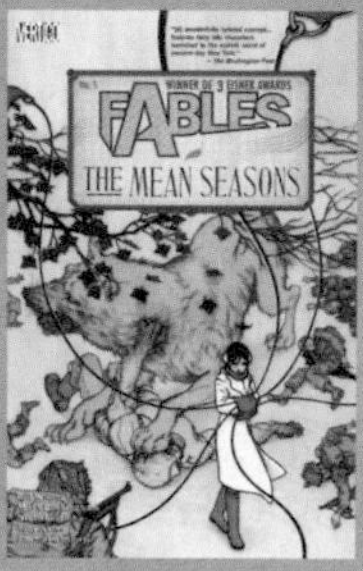

Vol. 5: THE MEAN SEASONS
This trade paperback features two tales of Bigby's exploits during World War II as well as "The Year After," which follows the aftermath of the Adversary's attempt to conquer Fabletown – including the birth of Snow White and Bigby's cubs!

FABLES
HOMELANDS

Vol. 6: HOMELANDS
Boy Blue is on a mission of revenge as he uncovers the Adversary's true identity! Plus, the two-part story of Jack's adventures in Hollywood, and the tale of Mowgli's return to Fabletown.

FABLES
ARABIAN NIGHTS (AND DAYS)

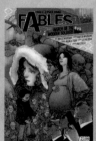

Vol. 7: ARABIAN NIGHTS (AND DAYS)
Opening a new front in the struggle between the Fables and the Adversary, the worlds of the Arabian Fables are invaded – leading to an unprecedented diplomatic mission to Manhattan and a nasty case of culture shock.

FABLES
wolves

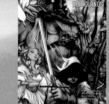

Vol. 8: WOLVES
The community of Fables living undercover in our midst has endured plenty of suffering at the hands of the Adversary. Now it's time to return the favor, but the one Fable who can accomplish this mission has hidden himself away in the wild and will take some convincing if he can even be found.

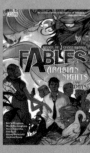

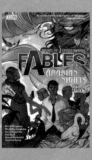

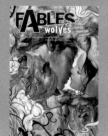

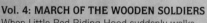

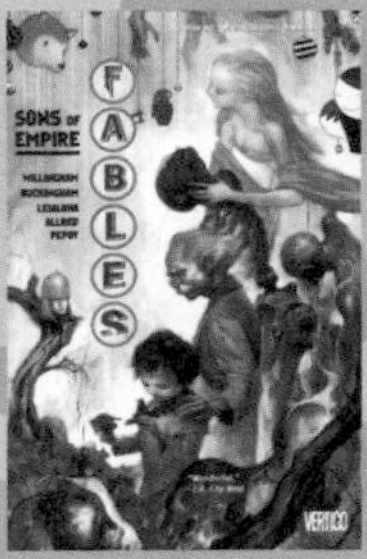
SONS OF EMPIRE
FABLES

Vol. 9: SONS OF EMPIRE
Pinocchio suffers seriously divided loyalties between his father, the evil Adversary, and his fellow Fable refugees in New York City. Plus, Bigby Wolf reluctantly decides it's finally time to square accounts with his long estranged father, the North Wind, and makes a journey with Snow White and their cubs to find him.

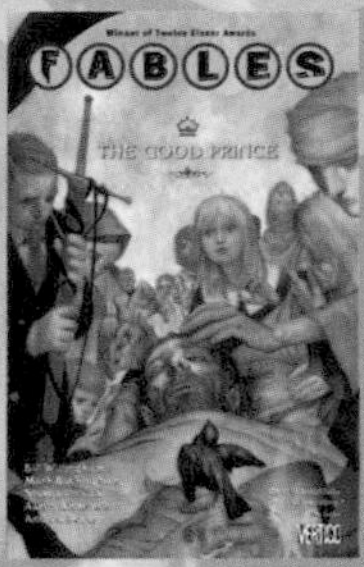
FABLES
THE GOOD PRINCE

Vol. 10: THE GOOD PRINCE
Flycatcher is drawn into the spotlight as he discovers the startling truth about his own past as The Frog Prince. At the same time, he learns that the Adversary plans to destroy his foes once and for all. Can the meek Flycatcher actually stop this deadly foe?

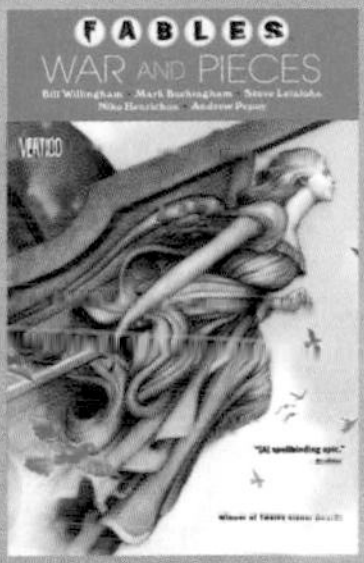
FABLES
WAR AND PIECES
Bill Willingham · Mark Buckingham · Steve Leialoha · Niko Henrichon · Andrew Pepoy

Vol. 11: WAR AND PIECES
The war against Fabletown heats up! Cinderella heads out on a cloak-and-dagger mission to bring a mysterious package back into town. But when the Empire goes after the same prize, there's no telling who will be left standing when the smoke clears.

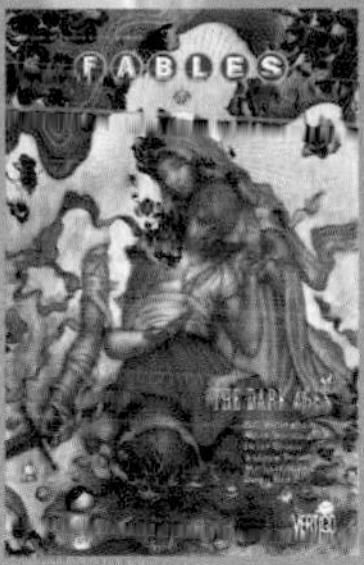
FABLES
THE DARK AGES

Vol. 12: THE DARK AGES
In the post-war chaos of the Adversary's former realm, a terrible force is about to be unleashed – an evil that threatens not just Fabletown but the entire mundane world.

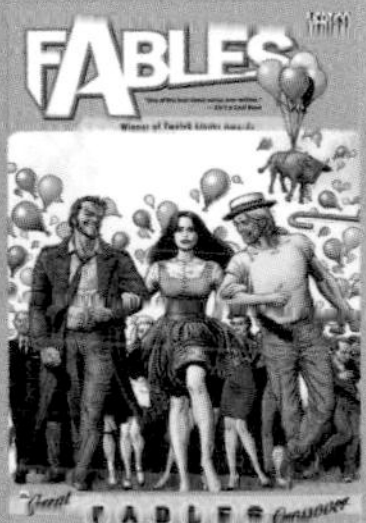
FABLES
The Great FABLES Crossover

Vol. 13: THE GREAT FABLES CROSSOVER
As the free Fables struggle to regroup following the destruction of their New York City stronghold, they are suddenly faced with a wholly new menace – one that threatens not only their adopted world, but all of reality itself!

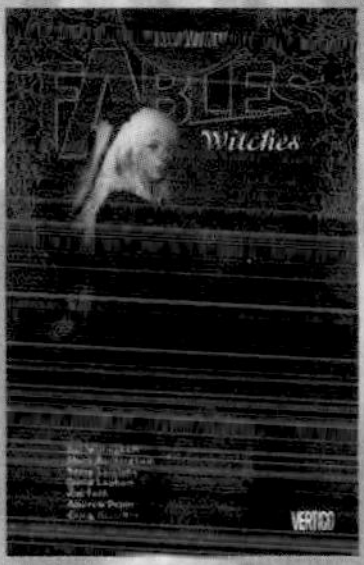
FABLES
Witches

Vol. 14: WITCHES
The exiled Fables are forced to turn to their oldest and most powerful members – the witches and warlocks who once occupied the Woodland's 13th floor – to defeat their latest adversary, Mister Dark. But rivalries within the Fables' sorcerer community threaten to fracture their united front – and leave them open to destruction.

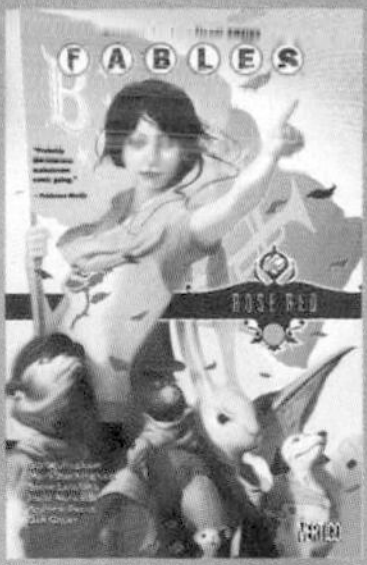
FABLES
ROSE RED

Vol. 15: ROSE RED
As the Free Fables try desperately to shield themselves from the withering power of Mister Dark, Rose Red – the Farm's ostensible leader – is finally jolted out of her deep depression and into action by a timely revelation from her storybook past. This volume also includes a special sketch section from Mark Buckingham.

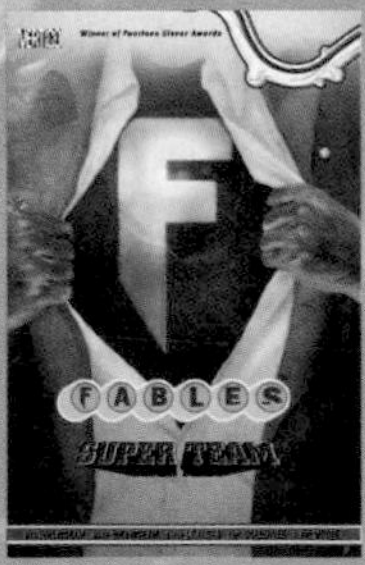
FABLES
SUPER TEAM

Vol. 16: SUPER TEAM
Evil stalks the border of Haven. Fed by fear and driven by darkness, Mister Dark has risen and the day of doom is upon our beloved Fables – unless Ozma and Pinocchio can assemble the F-Men to defeat Mister Dark once and for all. A send-up of – what else but?! – team books to end all others.

Peter & Max
a FABLES novel
"Fast-paced, witty, and fun from start to finish."
— George R.R. Martin
BILL WILLINGHAM
ILLUSTRATIONS BY STEVE LEIALOHA

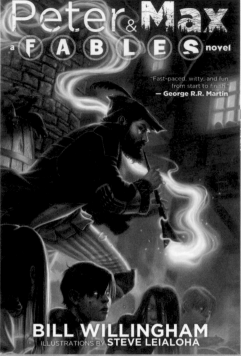

FABLES: PETER & MAX

The first FABLES prose novel

Written by Bill Willingham with illustrations by Steve Leialoha

In the deepest dark of the Black Forest, two brothers will come undone. Peter Piper and his brother Max star in an epic tale of sibling rivalry, magic, music and revenge that spans medieval times to the present day, when their deadly conflict surfaces in the calm of modern-day Fabletown.

NO ONE DESERVES HIS OWN COLLECTION MORE THAN
JACK OF FABLES
THE (NEARLY) GREAT ESCAPE
"Intriguing."
— The Onion
BILL Willingham
MATTHEW Sturges
TONY Akins
ANDREW Pepoy
VERTIGO

JACK OF FABLES

Follow the adventures of Jack of the Tales, the ultimate thief, lout and trickster in this 50-issue, 9-volume series.

From the pages of FABLES
FAIREST
Wide Awake
VERTIGO
BILL WILLINGHAM · PHIL JIMENEZ
ANDY LANNING · MARK FARMER

FAIREST Vol. 1: Wide Awake

Sleeping Beauty and the Snow Queen take center stage as the female Fables, from fatales to fearless leaders, are featured in this companion series to FABLES.

FABLES: DELUXE Editions

Oversized, beautifully designed hardcover volumes of the series featuring introductions by noted professionals

BILL WILLINGHAM
FABLES
THE DELUXE EDITION
BOOK ONE
Lan Medina
Mark Buckingham
Steve Leialoha
Craig Hamilton
VERTIGO

BILL WILLINGHAM
FABLES
THE DELUXE EDITION
BOOK TWO
Mark Buckingham Lan Medina Craig Hamilton
Bryan Talbot Linda Medley Steve Leialoha P. Craig Russell
VERTIGO

BILL WILLINGHAM
FABLES
THE DELUXE EDITION
BOOK THREE
Mark Buckingham Steve Leialoha
Tony Akins Jimmy Palmiotti
VERTIGO

BILL WILLINGHAM
FABLES
THE DELUXE EDITION
BOOK FOUR

BILL WILLINGHAM
FABLES
THE DELUXE EDITION
BOOK FIVE
Mark Buckingham Steve Leialoha
David Hahn Lan Medina
VERTIGO

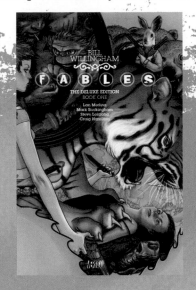

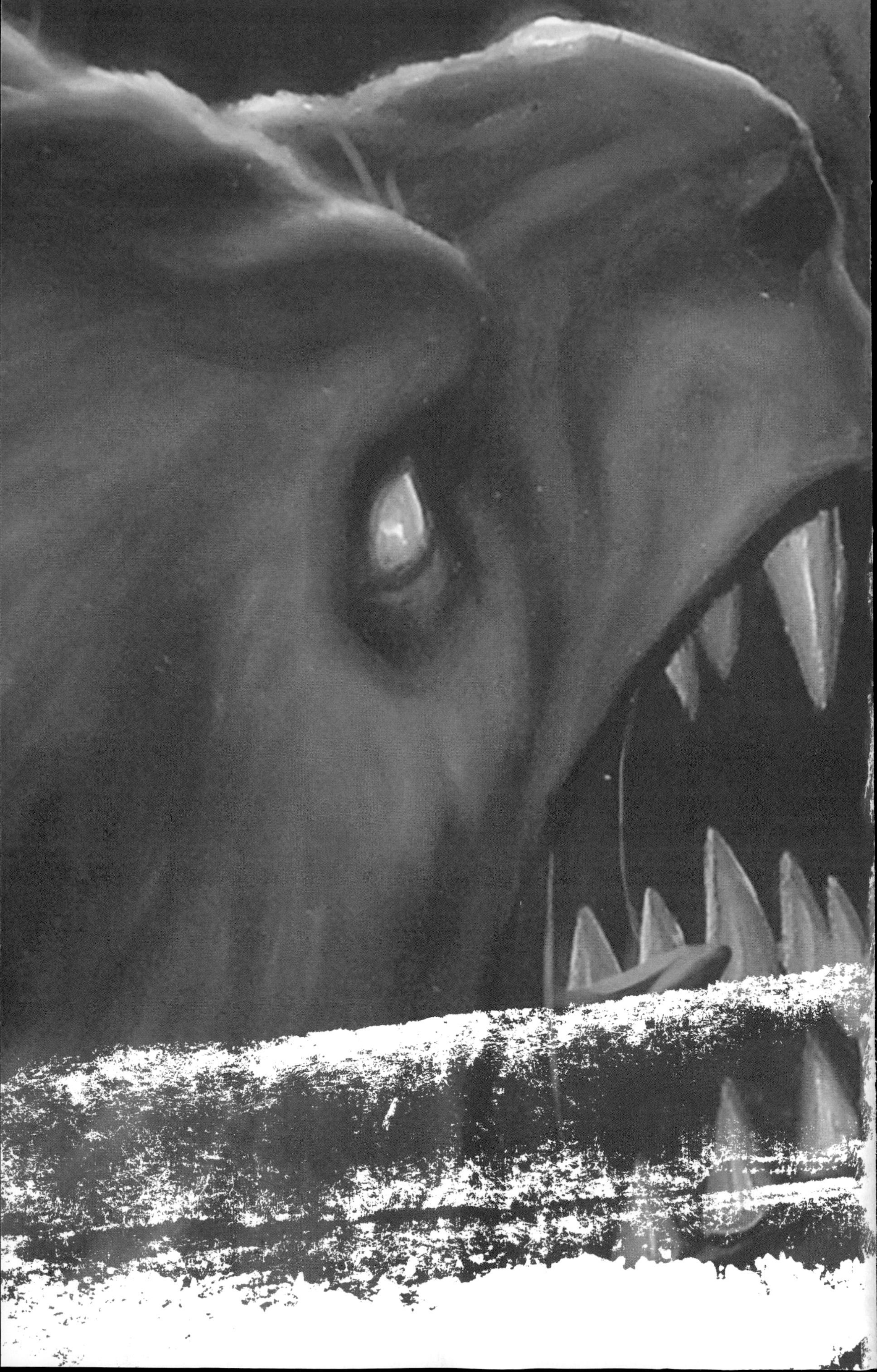